To:
Rick —
WITH DEEP APPRECIATION
AND VERY BEST WISHES!

Ken D. Hunt
1/28/03

Praise for I Shall Not Die!

"I Shall Not Die", the autobiography of Hart N. Hasten is a must read for any Jew whose heart beats to the rhythm of Jewish History. It is a veritable modern-day Passover Haggadah, beginning with the degradation of the holocaust and concluding with the praise of an individual whose life has been devoted to the future of the Jewish people in Indianapolis, in the United States in general and especially in the State of Israel. The book is peopled with unforgettable personalities, from the shteitle elder, Avraham Yechiel Michel Halpern to Arik Sharon. It is a paean of praise to the will to live – not merely to survive, but to live as a complete Jew committed to his roots and dedicated to his future. Rav Kook teaches that there are some hearts that are made of stone and some stones – the stones of the Kotel – which are also hearts. Hart Hasten has captured the heart and the soul of Jewish History in his very moving autobiography, "I Shall Not Die".

Rabbi Shlomo Riskin

This moving autobiography… reveals a remarkable man – amidst an equally remarkable family – of indomitable courage, extraordinary willpower and tremendous dignity.

The book documents the transformation in America of a penniless young Holocaust survivor into a proud American patriot and a highly respected businessman, civic leader and philanthropist

Yehuda Blum
FORMER ISRAELI AMBASSADOR
to the United Nations

I heartily recommend this book as a history of the Jewish people post-Holocaust. [Hasten's] life is an inspiration to both Jew and Gentile.

Mandell I. Ganchrow, MD
EXECUTIVE VICE PRESIDENT
Religious Zionists of America

…continued on next page

The resilience, initiative and commitment of one person reflects the distinctive genius of the Jewish people: the capacity to transform the ashes of annihilation into the glow of redemption, culminating in the establishment of the Jewish State and the revitalization of the Jewish heritage in America.

Rabbi Richard G. Hirsch
HONORARY LIFE PRESIDENT
World Union for Progressive Judaism

Hart and Simona Hasten's personal friendship with the Begin family (described in a major chapter in this fascinating, well-written autobiography) is a cameo that adds color to the multi-faceted Begin story. Hasten looks back on his 70 years of struggle and success, of belief and faith and he passes the saga on as a legacy to his children and grandchildren.

Harry Hurwitz
Head of the Menachem Begin Heritage Center

This is the fascinating story about the victory of the proud Jew with the courageous character and the triumph of faith in the destiny of the Jewish people.

Yechiel Kadishai

Hart Hasten's moving autobiography is an individual story, which exemplifies the phoenix-like resurrection of the Jewish people from the ashes of the *Shoah* (Holocaust).

Isi Leibler
SENIOR VICE PRESIDENT
World Jewish Congress

A poignant book – Hart Hasten vowed that the most significant part of his life should not only be the horrible memories that Hitler forced upon him, but the memories he himself forged as a committed Jewish leader who was determined to make a difference, each and every day of his life.

Rabbi Marvin Hier
DEAN AND FOUNDER,
Simon Wiesenthal Center

I SHALL NOT DIE!

a personal memoir by
Hart N. Hasten

gefen
publishing house בית הוצאה לאור
JERUSALEM ♦ NEW YORK

Typesetting: Raphaël Freeman, Jerusalem Typesetting
Cover Design: S. Kim Glassman, Jerusalem

1   3   5   7   9   8   6   4   2

Gefen Publishing House
POB 36004, Jerusalem 91360, Israel
972-2-538-0247 • orders@gefenpublishing.com

Gefen Books
12 New Street Hewlett, NY 11557, USA
516-295-2805 • gefenny@gefenpublishing.com

www.israelbooks.com

Printed in Israel   *Send for our free catalogue*

ISBN 965-229-302-4 (alk. paper)

Library of Congress Cataloging-in-Publication Data:
Hasten, Hart N.
I Shall Not Die!: an autobiography of Hart N. Hasten
p. cm.

1. Hasten, Hart N. 2. Jews – United States – Biography.
3. Jews – United States – Politics and government – 20th century.
4. Refugees, Jewish – United States – Biography.
5. Jewish businesspeople – United States – Biography.
6. World War, 1939–1945 – Jews – Soviet Union – Biography.
7. Refugees, Jewish – Soviet Union – Biography. 8. United States – Biography. I. Title.

E184.37.H37 2002 • CIP NO: 2002028602

To my father, my Tatu,
whose intense love and compassion for me
I felt with my whole being

"As compassionate as a father to his children…"
PSALMS, 103:13

כרחם אב על בנים...

תהילים ק"ג:יג

and

To my mother, my Mameh,
who, with every breath and her entire soul,
praised Hashem thoughout her life

"Let the entire soul praise Hashem."
PSALMS, 150:6

כל הנשמה תהלל יה.

תהילים ק"נ:ו

Contents

Special Thanks and Acknowledgements

My deepest appreciation is extended to Peter Weisz whose assistance in all aspects of the production of this book was truly invaluable.

Special thanks are extended, as well, to...

My wife, Simona, for sharing her memories and extending her patience; My brother, Mark, for his suggestions and support; Alvin Rosenfeld for his editorial guidance; Jerry Rubin, for his review and remembrance; Elie Wiesel, for his inspirational assistance; Gisela Weisz, for her outspoken opinions; Yechiel and Bambi Kadishai, for their encouragement and for remembering the little details; Conrad Uitts, for his interest and integrity; Martha Havely for her dedicated efficiency; Alla Weisz, for help with Russian and Hungarian; Ilan Greenfield, at Gefen Publishing, for turning a manuscript into a miracle; Smadar Belilty, at Gefen Publishing, for her patience and hard work; Esther Herskovics, at Gefen Publishing, for her editing excellence; Stephanie A. Holt, Online Freelance Editor, for more editing excellence; Simon Wiesenthal for helping me come full circle.

For their valuable research assistance...

Joel Ives, Fair Lawn, New Jersey; Joyce Field, JewishGen Vice President, Research, West Lafayette, Indiana; Suzan Wynne (*Finding Your Jewish Roots in Galicia*, Avotaynu Publishing) for directing me to *LeToledot ha-Kehillot bePolin*, Yad Vashem; Naomi Fatouros, Bloomington, Indiana; Zvi Bernhardt at Information Services of Yad Vashem, Israel, for directing me to the *Pinkas Kehillot* book; Rachel Reisman, Technical Coordinator, JewishGen's Yad Vashem Project; Beth Hatefutsoth Museum of the Jewish Diaspora, Tel Aviv, Israel; Shelley K. Pollero, Coordinator, Gesher Galicia, Severna Park, Maryland; Melody Katz, Research Coordinator, Gesher Galicia; Leon Gold, President, Gesher Galicia, Santa Barbara, California; Mark Halpern, AGAD

Archive Coordinator; Bella Baram, Assistant Librarian, The Simon Wiesenthal Center Documentation Center, Los Angeles, California; Efraim Zuroff, The Simon Wiesenthal Center, Jerusalem, Israel; Vanessa M. Johnson, Corporate Manager, Human Resources, The Bemis Company, Inc., Minneapolis, Minnesota, for scouring the archives and locating my old employment records; Anita Heppner Plotinsky, *The Hebrew Academy of Indianapolis, 1971–1986*

...and, of course, my greatest thanks to Hashem.

Foreword

I have known Hart Hasten for many years, but not until I read his autobiography did I truly understand how he has come to be the unusually strong and resolute person he is. The book's title – *I Shall Not Die!* – evokes the man's passion for life and determination to prevail against all odds, but the sources of his drive were never before so fully apparent. Now, with this very personal telling of his story, Hart discloses the people, places, events, and ideas that have given shape and purpose to his life.

Born in the small eastern Galician town of Bohorodczany, Hart – or Hetche, as he was called at the time – managed to escape the fate of most of Polish Jewry thanks largely to his father, who had the foresight to flee the invading Nazi forces in the nick of time. Living for several years in impoverished conditions in Kazakhstan and Austrian DP camps, the Hastens had to contend with circumstances that most Americans would find unimaginable. Hunger, sickness and other assorted threats to life were part of the daily round and posed constant challenges to their safety and well-being. Yet through it all, the Hastens kept together, retained their dignity, and remained faithful to the traditions of Judaism that helped to preserve them as a loyal and devoted family. Indeed, part of the core of Hart Hasten's personal philosophy – that "before physical survival can occur, spiritual survival must first be achieved" – was formed during the war years and in their immediate aftermath under conditions of extreme duress.

Deprived of the normal school experiences of most youngsters in the West, Hart learned to deal with life's necessities while on the run in the East. In places like Alga, in Soviet Central Asia, Lvov and Wloclawek, in post-war Poland, and the Ranshofen and Ebelsberg DP camps, in Austria, Hart received a kind of education that would open his eyes to some of the harsher sides of human experience and teach him how to contend with adversity. At the same time, he learned some invaluable lessons in human solidarity. These, too, were formative and would mold his view of life forever after.

The DP camps were a testing ground for personal fortitude and also a fertile ground for political education. In particular, various Zionist groups sought to influence the thinking of the young Jews gathered in these places and win their allegiances. Instinctively drawn to the teachings of Ze'ev Jabotinsky, Hart was won over by the Revisionists and in later years would become an enthusiastic supporter and close personal friend of Menachem Begin. Within the spectrum of Zionist ideology, this orientation put him decidedly on the right, a position that has not made him popular in more liberal circles but one that he has maintained nevertheless without reservation or compromise over several decades. His political views are grounded in the conviction that only through strength – physical, spiritual, and communal – can the Jewish people preserve itself and have a chance for a viable future. Not everyone will agree, but no reader of this autobiography should have any trouble figuring out how the author came to develop his political philosophy, for it stems directly from his wartime experiences and his understanding of what is needed for Jewish national survival.

Readers will also come to understand and, if they are at all like me, be somewhat awed by Hart's transformation from a sometimes destitute and almost always hungry Jewish DP to a highly successful American entrepreneur and Jewish philanthropist. When the Hastens arrived in the United States on April 10, 1951, the family was virtually penniless. Today, Hart, his brother Mark, and their many children are well-established, prosperous people. The story of their achievement is, in part, a tribute to American society and its ethos of openness to the talents of new immigrants, but it is surely also a tribute to the intelligence, perseverance, hard work, and enterprise of Hart Hasten himself.

It is no small thing, after all, to move from the position of being an untrained and largely uneducated newcomer to be the owner and chief executive of several major business enterprises. How Hart has accomplished all of that and, at the same time, managed to marry, raise a family and contribute to a range of significant communal, educational, religious, and Zionist projects is at the heart of this highly informative and often moving narrative. Readers of *I Shall Not Die!* will encounter a story of personal courage as well as family and communal fidelity that is rooted in a chapter of recent Jewish history that we dare not forget. For making his experiences of this history so vivid, we are all in Hart Hasten's debt.

Alvin H. Rosenfeld, Director
Jewish Studies Program
Indiana University

Preface

My earliest conscious memory is of Lonka. He is four years old and so am I. Lonka is my first cousin. The year is 1935. We are playing. I adore him and he adores me as well. We are inseparable. People often mistake us for twin brothers. I call him "Lala" which in the Polish language means "doll." He calls me Lala as well. We are playing…laughing, running and playing.

Lonka's mother, Dina, was my mother's sister, and they were both the daughters of a respected Jewish elder in our *shtetl* (small town) by the name of Avraham Yechiel Michel Halpern. But to Lonka, and his other beloved grandchildren, he was simply Zayde. A broad man whose posture and bearing were as straight as Torah spindles, my Zayde, with his glowing eyes and flowing white beard, served as judge and sage to the Jews of this Carpathian *shtetl* in what was once Eastern Galicia. He was the foundation stone and patriarch of our family as well. And among all of his grandchildren, little Lonka and I were the apples of his eye.

My Zayde would proudly escort us to *cheder* (religious school) through the dusty morning, with each of us tugging on one of his enormous hands. And every Friday afternoon, as we prepared for the arrival of the Sabbath bride, it was Zayde who ushered us to the *Mikvah* for the weekly ritual bath. Then, bedecked in his best white shirt and fur hat, Zayde would stroll with us to "shul" for Shabbat services.

The love my grandfather felt for me, and for all of his grandchildren, was palpably embodied in his mighty hands. As they enveloped and embraced me, his hands were my shields against all of the childhood dangers, both real and imagined, that I faced daily. My "Bubbie," his wife, fell ill and died in 1936, leaving Zayde a widower with time to dote over his growing brood of grandchildren.

As my story unfolds, you will discover how fortunate I was to have been evacuated by my father from our town of Bohorodczany mere days before the occupying armies arrived in July, 1941. My parents, brother and I were among the very few Jews who got away just in time. My Zayde and little Lonka, sadly, were not. It was some years later, and from three independent sources, that I learned of their fate.

As the Germans went about the business of rounding up, categorizing, isolating and eventually devouring the Jewish population of each community they conquered, they began by first creating an efficient infrastructure from within the Jewish community to facilitate the task of destroying it. The program called for the establishment of a Council of Jewish Elders, or *Judenrat*, to serve as a liaison between the Jews and the new masters of their fate. The Judenrat would be charged with managing the newly established ghetto, and its members would be responsible with their lives for implementing German directives to the letter.

After a few well-placed questions, the Germans quickly learned who constituted the Jewish communal leadership in our town. They immediately ordered my Zayde to serve as the head of the new council, but he defiantly refused. He would not collaborate with the destroyers of our people.

Upon hearing news of his refusal, the German commandant ordered all the Jews to assemble in the square, under penalty of death. Zayde, of course, was there clutching the hand of his grandson Lonka, who was now ten years old. Lonka stood proudly alone beside his tall grandfather. Had I been there I would have been at Zayde's side as well. I am sure of it.

The ss commandant, in his shiny black boots, strutted through the square and announced, "I intend to send a clear message to the stiff-necked Jews of this town." He ordered my Zayde to step forward. Zayde did so, still holding onto Lonka's hand.

"This Jew was ordered to do his duty by serving on the Judenrat…but he refused! Observe what happens when a Jew disobeys a German order."

The commandant quickly removed his pistol and shot Zayde through the temple. As Zayde's body fell dead to the ground before him, Lonka screamed in horror, and the commandant fired again, publicly ending my cousin's short, sweet life.

Had I been there, had my father not had the blessed foresight to pull our family from the path of the Nazi onslaught at the last moment, I would have surely met the same fate. I would undoubtedly have fallen alongside my grandfather and cousin that day. I am sure of it.

Contemplating twists of fate such as this can send the mind reeling. If Lonka had escaped and I had stayed behind instead, would he be sitting here right now in this chair writing these words? At times, I am washed by a wave of guilt and wish that it had been I, rather than little Lonkella, who had perished so cruelly.

These are avenues down which I have not often ventured. Yet, it is thoughts of Lonka, of my Zayde, and of the world I left behind that come into sharper focus with each passing day. Sometimes the memories arrive in a trickle, but more often, in a torrent. And always bittersweet. I have carried a mental photograph of the shootings of Zayde and my beloved Lonka with me my entire life. And as I write these words today, at the age of seventy, exactly my Zayde's age at the time of his murder, I have come to understand how this image has shaped the very core of my identity. It is the compelling desire to record these memories that has prompted me to write this book.

Writing one's life story is certainly no act of humility. But neither is it out of arrogance that I seek to provide a testimony of my days. Looking back at the events of my life I am able to discern the handiwork of a greater power. I am convinced that the Almighty is more powerful than the Nazis, the Soviets, the PLO and all of the enemies that have risen up against the Jewish people throughout history. And like the Jewish people, I have been brought close to destruction many times, only to be saved by the outstretched hand of G-d. It is in this context that I selected the title of this book, which is taken from the 118th Psalm:

"I shall not die! But I shall live and relate the deeds of G-d.
G-d has chastened me exceedingly, but He did not let me die.
Open for me the gates of righteousness, I will enter and thank G-d."

Psalms 118:17–19

Hence, the reader should not regard this book's title as a furtherance of my own notions of immortality. To paraphrase the Psalmist, the title expresses the fact that I did not die, but was allowed to live in order to relate what the Almighty has done. This book is not only my testimony, but also my proclamation and my expression of gratitude to my G-d who has *"chastened me exceedingly,"* but has, to this day, permitted me to live in order to recount His deeds.

Chapter One

Bohorodczany

SOMETIMES, just a scent will take me back. Sauerkraut. Briny pickled green tomatoes. Even horse manure. Suddenly a door is unlocked by a forgotten, yet pungently familiar, odor – and for a brief, sweet moment, my other senses fall into step.

More and more, that doorway of sensation leads to a summer's night in 1941 in the Jewish quarter of Bohorodczany *(boh'-horod-chohn'-eh)*. I am ten and my brother, Munjee, is fifteen as we sit around the kitchen table and listen to my father plead with my mother once again. This particular kitchen drama was somehow different from their typical exchanges about money, family and *de kinder*. This time, our parents were discussing the macro-events that had finally come to roost directly on our heads. Politics. Hitler. Stalin. Evacuation. We had heard these words regularly in the *reidlach*, a circle of serious, standing men, who convened daily in parks and on street corners of our town to exchange the news and opinions of the day. In addition to attending these open-air Op Ed pages, Jewish men, like my father, pored over the newspaper each day as if it were the Talmud, trying to understand where our shtetl stood in a world increasingly turned upside down.

And, of course, we had heard all these words on the radio. Hitler's strident harangues blaring out in German against *die Juden* (the Jews) were a part of our regular diet. But to a young boy, in the comfortable security of his family, these words were for the street, for the newspaper, and for the radio. What were they doing here in our home?

The ethnically Polish town of Bohorodczany was tucked into the eastern slopes of the Carpathian Mountains in what was known as Eastern Galicia under the Austro-Hungarian regime. The town sat then, as it does today, in a sheltered valley on the Carpathian Highway between Stanislawow and Nadworna. Stanislawow was home to the ghetto to which all 1,200 of Bohorodczany's remaining Jews were shipped by the Nazis prior to extermination in June of 1942. Demographics had not changed drastically since the census of 1880, which revealed that there were 2,009 Jews among the town's 4,597 residents. By 1939 roughly half of Bohorodczany's population of 5,000 was Jewish. In Yiddish, our town was called by its colloquial name, Brotchin *(broht'chen)*.

After World War I and the Russo-Polish War (1920–21), the province returned to Polish administration. Bohorodczany's main industry in the 19th century was shoemaking and leatherwork, and the latter was my father's first trade.

Bernard Hasten moved to Brotchin from Chodorov in the early 1920s after having been betrothed to one of the daughters of a well-to-do sawmill operator from the town's old quarter *(Stareye Bohorodczany)*. The couple had two children. My brother Mordechai was nicknamed Munjee. As a name for their second son, my parents selected Naftali Hertz, and soon I was known as Hetche.

My early schooling was carried out at the *cheder*, where I was an exceptional student and was often held up as a paragon to the other children. I was something of a prodigy when it came to reciting by rote the ancient Hebrew liturgies. My father would often place me in the middle of a *reidle* to show me off, and then insist that the other men listen as his five-year-old "genius" would not only chant the entire *Shir Ha-Shirim* (Song of Songs) using an obscure melody, but the little genius would also translate the text from Hebrew to Yiddish, all the while offering interpretation and commentary.

While corporal punishment was the rule in our classroom, thanks to my somewhat exalted status, I never once felt the sting of the whip. Despite this sparing of the rod, I am still able to retain, to this day, the liturgical melodies learned at that tender age.

With my father occupied with his wholesale hides and leather trade and my mother also busy helping with *parnosa* (making a living), my upbringing was often left in the strong and calloused hands of my Zayde. Those hands. Those big and meaty hands. The skin, having been toughened for years in the family sawmill, felt like the leather hides that my father traded. But nowadays Zayde's weathered hands were kept busy sorting the many hand-written slips of paper he went through regularly after every Sabbath as he went about organizing his various business interests. I know that I never felt as safe as when one of those warm and mighty hands was clutching onto one of mine.

Zayde would constantly quiz me about my studies, and he would help me to understand the subtleties and subtexts of the Torah. He was as learned as any rabbi, but he was not a fundamentalist. He was a simple, pious and essentially pragmatic man.

My mother would tell us how this pragmatism sometimes created problems. When my Zayde was engaged to be married, his bride's family observed that he did not remain standing for as long as they deemed customary during the *Shemoneh Esrei* portion of the daily afternoon *Mincha* prayers. His attitude was "stand up, say the prayer, and sit down." But to his new in-laws, who preferred to outdo each other when it came to demonstrable ritual, this lapse in religious protocol called his level of observance into question. Evidently, the family overcame their concerns, since the wedding took place as planned.

Zayde dressed according to the general fashion and wore a normal felt hat outdoors, which he replaced with a *yarmulke* (skullcap) when indoors. On the Sabbath, he would don a *shtreimel* (circular fur hat), as did the other Chassidic men of our town.

Brotchin's observant community was dominated by two competing *Chassidic* sects: the followers of the Vizsnitzer Rebbe and those who adhered to the teachings of the Strettiner Rebbe. While my grandfather was aligned with the minority Strettiners, my father eschewed both houses. Dad was considered a *misnahgged*, or "contrarian." *Misnahggeds* took pride in their independence, and while every bit as scrupulously observant of Jewish law as the *Chassids*, they owed no allegiance to any particular religious leader.

These struggles between the two religious sects would soon dissolve into irrelevance as forces beyond our *shtetl*, and beyond our imagination, began to assemble against us. These forces would soon destroy our cherished way of life and hasten our world's descent into the nightmare of destruction.

On September 1, 1939, Germany invaded Poland in a campaign that lasted all of four weeks and marked the beginning of the Second World War. Far from encountering Soviet resistance, the Germans were actually aided by the simultaneous Soviet conquest of Eastern Poland. Hitler and Stalin had carved Poland in two like a juicy pullet, putting the western provinces (west of the Bug and part of the San rivers) under German administration. The areas of Western and Northern Poland, including the second largest Polish city of Lodz, were annexed directly into the Reich, while the areas of Southern-Central Poland, including Warsaw, Cracow and Lublin, became a separate administrative entity known as the General Government.

Areas east of the dividing line, including the towns of Bialystok and Lvov, as well as our town of Bohorodczany, fell under Soviet occupation. Our provinces served as Stalin's spoils for agreeing not to oppose Hitler's aggression. In half a heartbeat, our homeland of Poland was no more and, like the other 1.3 million Jews who found themselves living in what had now become the Ukraine, our family had to adjust to life under the domination of the Red Army.

Our lives changed dramatically as the primitive Soviet soldiers stripped our shops and squares of anything of value. I can recall soldiers stuffing sausages into their boots to free their hands for further plundering. They were starved for any sort of material goods and would rabidly seize our many consumer treasures that were completely unavailable to them back home. Of course, to admit to this apparent deficiency in the Soviet economic system was considered bourgeois treachery. This made for some rather strange verbal exchanges.

A Red Army sergeant would instruct: "Give me those handbags. Of course, we have much better handbags back home and plenty of them, but I want some to show my wife the difference."

"Do you have this type of watch in Russia?" a shopkeeper would ask. "Oh, yes, indeed. We have wonderful watches, shoes, cars, jewelry…everything we could possibly want in Russia. We have it all."

Upon hearing this, the shopkeeper would remark to his partner in Polish: "*Ya vountp'yeh*," meaning "I doubt it." The Russian sergeant, upon hearing this (but not understanding the Polish words) would reflexively spout back: "*Vountp'yeh*? Of course, we also have plenty of *Vountp'yeh* in Russia! Not only that. Our *Vountp'yeh* is much better than your stinking Polish *Vountp'yeh!*"

In addition to ravaging our property, the Russians also eradicated our political and economic freedoms. Anyone suspected of bourgeois tendencies was arrested and packed off to the Siberian gulag. Churches were boarded up and covered with posters of Stalin. Although I was too young to fully understand what was going on, I could tell that things were changing. Men no longer wore neckties. Women got rid of their hats and put on headscarves. And the streets always stank of garbage. But as bad as conditions became, we received only glimpses of what was happening to the Jews in German-occupied Poland.

About 250,000 Jews had escaped from the areas overrun by the Nazis to our Soviet-occupied zone. Until the winter of 1939–40, the new German-Soviet border was somewhat porous. Some of these Jewish refugees made their way to our community, and they brought with them horrible stories of Nazi atrocities.

We, and the rest of Soviet-occupied Poland, lived under Stalin's yoke for only eighteen months. Hitler's thirst for conquest was not quenched for long, and on June 22, 1941, in brazen violation of the Molotov-Von Ribbentrop Non-Aggression Pact, Germany invaded the Soviet Union on multiple fronts, including the Polish frontier. As German Panzer divisions, followed by mobile extermination squads known as *Einsatzgruppen*, poured into Eastern Poland, Jews found themselves caught in the claws of a terrible vise.

From the west came the marauding armies of the master race; to the

east stood the implacable face of Russian anti-Semitism. Amazing as it may
seem, many Jews actually welcomed the Germans as they poured across the
border, since Germany was viewed by many as a more developed and civilized nation than brutish Russia, with its long history of persecution and
pogroms. The Germans represented *Kultur* and mannered civility, while the
Russians were viewed as primitive and steeped in a heritage of anti-Jewish
hatred. Furthermore, German was the language of the educated and the elite.
In fact, we took some pride in our use of "Germanic" (rather than Polish)
Yiddish in our home. Part of this Deutsch-leaning attitude stemmed from
the fact that there were many in our town who fondly recalled the German
liberators from the last war and still remembered how German and Jewish
soldiers (such as my own father) served side-by-side in the Kaiser's army.

But in this war, things were far different. ss leader Rudolph Heydrich
was under direct orders from Himmler to eradicate the "source of Jewish
Bolshevism in the East." He dispatched hand-picked and specially-trained
troops that were organized into the *Einsatzgruppen* or mobile killing squads.
These squads were charged with the task of identifying and destroying all
Jewish elements they encountered in the newly conquered territories. Mass
communication was so poor and so well-manipulated by the Nazis that most
Jews could never imagine the truth: that so-called "civilized Germans" could
act more viciously barbaric than any of history's many previous Jew-killers.

The night I remember so well occurred six days after the German invasion. Their advances had not yet reached out *shtetl*, but we knew they would
be upon us any day. Although we were ignorant of it at the time, the pattern
of German conquest was already quite well defined. As the military forces
pushed deeper eastward, they overcame any meager resistance and placed
each town and village under military law. The first command always dealt
with the Jews. They were ordered to register and otherwise make themselves
known to the authorities. Within a few days, a detachment of *Einsatzgruppen*
would arrive and begin rendering each village *judenrein*...cleansed of Jews.

Like almost all Jews in our community, my brother, my mother and I were
oblivious to the extent of the danger. But this was not the case with my father.
Unlike his neighbors, my father came to recognize the impending danger and
took appropriate action. But how did only he and a handful of others from
among the several thousand Jews of Bohorodczany, come to understand the
scope of the Nazi threat? And how did he alone find the initiative to flee?

Like the stray grains of sugar falling on the floor as the bag is being emp-
tied, a few Jews here and there managed to get away from the encroaching
inferno. It was from these Jews, driven eastward ahead of the onslaught, who

corroborated the stories told by the refugees from German-occupied Poland the year before, that my father learned the true nature of what was happening and what we might soon expect once the Germans reached our town.

Darwin pointed out that it is not the strongest nor the most intelligent of the species that manage to survive; rather, it is the ones most able to adapt to changing conditions. This was perhaps my father's greatest talent. When the Soviets took charge, he was able to adjust quickly to their world-view. The Communist ideology was such that owning your own business was taboo. My father understood this fully and abandoned all his business interests as soon as the Soviets took over in 1939. He was recognized as a skilled and sensible man who, thanks to his fluent Ukrainian, was accepted by the Soviet authorities to serve on the local volunteer gendarmerie and, as such, would patrol the streets of our *shtetl*. Only two other Jews, one of whom was the son of our neighbor, Moishe Friedman, the local tailor, served on the police force. Through this experience, both my father and Wolfe Friedman gained a clear picture of what the German invasion would soon bring with it. It was this knowledge that saved us from the inferno.

Jews fleeing the onslaught with no money and no papers were being picked up by the local police as they made their way through Bohorodczany. These pathetic refugees related tales of incredible horror. They told of entire Jewish villages being wiped out and of synagogues filled with hundreds of Jews and then set ablaze while machine guns blasted anyone trying to flee. More often than not, these stories were simply regarded as so much war hysteria when mentioned in the newspapers. But hearing of these horrors from the lips of a fellow Jew, speaking in Yiddish, gave them complete credibility.

After several days of listening to such accounts, my father came to a fateful decision. We must leave Bohorodczany, and we must do it immediately, before the first German troops arrived. He was at risk as a Jew in the hands of the Ukrainians; also, as a policeman, he would be rendered a prime target for the Nazis as a suspected Bolshevik collaborator. He recognized that once the town's Soviet rule was lifted, the local Ukrainians would be encouraged to show their solidarity with their new Nazi masters by helping them hunt down and round up the town's Jews.

I have always believed that if only more Jews could have been warned – by credible sources – of what awaited them at the hands of the Nazis, millions could have saved themselves. The Nazis deluded their victims into rejecting the unthinkable when, in fact, the truth should have been believed, and would have been believed had a warning originated from, say, the US State Department. The silence of established sources of credible information was perhaps the Nazis' greatest weapon in their war against the Jews. What convinced my father to pack up his family and to flee was the fact that he, and he alone, had access to such credible information.

It is to his enduring credit that my father did something that few Jews caught in the clutches of the Holocaust were able or willing to do: he gave up hope. He gave up the false hope that he could somehow manage to get by under the Nazi anti-Semites as he had done all his life with the Poles and the Ukrainians. He refused to engage in wishful thinking and self-deluding notions of German civility. He saw the situation clearly for what it was: entirely hopeless. But just as I don't pass judgment on those religious Jewish victims who believed that the Messiah would rescue them from the gas chambers at the last moment, I don't presume to judge the hundreds of innocent Jews in my hometown who clung to their last hope of survival as the death squads roared in. I am only grateful that my father was not among them.

Despite the fact that my father had served side by side with German and Austrian troops in the previous war, he harbored no false illusions about their nature. He believed the danger to be real, and he made the decision to leave without a moment's hesitation. My father made all the necessary preparations and secured food, a team of horses, and an open wagon for the journey. But he still faced a major obstacle: my mother.

My mother, Hannah, was rooted in the soil of Bohorodczany so deeply that people regularly consulted her about the *shtetl's* history. But despite this, she was far from provincial. She was highly literate and had mastered Talmudic texts, often quoting from them, particularly the *Pirkei Avot* (Ethics of our Fathers) and the *Tze'enah Urenah*. She could converse easily in German, Ukrainian, Polish, Russian and Yiddish.

In the years that followed, while my father was the keeper of our family's physical survival, it was left to my mother to look out for our spiritual well-being. She would constantly push and promote our Jewish education, and she would indoctrinate my brother and me with the importance of *Yiddishkeit*.

On June 28, the showdown took place. As Munjee and I sat wide-eyed, my father unveiled the ultimatum.

"We cannot stay," he announced adamantly. "I've bought a team of horses and a carriage and we leave Bohorodczany for the Russian border tonight."

"But, Berish, look around you. Do you see anyone else leaving? Sure, everyone's frightened, but we're tough. We got by with the Poles, with the Russians, with the Ukrainians; we'll manage with these Germans, too."

"Not this time, Hannah."

He had not shared the nightmarish stories of atrocities with his wife, and now he wished that he had. He knew there was only one way to convince her.

"I simply cannot stay," he announced, standing up swiftly. "I am going… with you and the boys, or without you!"

My mother did not act stunned, but Munjee and I looked at each other and I felt the pit of my stomach fall out. What now? I thought. My parents are going to split up. What happens to us? Do I go with my father to G-d knows where? Do I stay and try to protect my mother alone against the Nazi hordes?

In my heart, I knew my father was right. He was always right. He was never hysterical or extreme in any way. He was a solid, methodical and reliable man. If he said this was the end of our way of life, then it must be so. But I knew, just as strongly, that I could never leave my mother alone. How often had she remarked that she would walk into the flames for me? Even as a child, I understood that my life would be worthless if I left my mother behind to face the dangerous and uncertain times ahead without me by her side.

These thoughts coursed through my young mind as I stood in the doorway gazing at a particularly beautiful sunset. Our large home faced west, and I would often admire the setting sun from our front door. On this night, this most important night of my short life, as I imagined our family being dispersed to the four winds, I stared out and realized that this would be the very last time I would view the sunset from my own front door in my own hometown. Soon the sun disappeared entirely and we found ourselves in a deep and enduring darkness – a darkness known today as the Holocaust.

After searching her soul and conferring with Zayde, her sister Dina and her brother, Psachya – my mother finally relented. "I cannot visualize myself staying here alone without my husband," she concluded. "Should I stay here with the children…a woman alone with no husband? Unthinkable!" She reluctantly agreed to uproot herself in the name of preserving our family. It was this decision that saved her life – a life that stretched to age 102 – as well as my life and that of my brother.

As we began the heart-wrenching process of deciding which of our treasured possessions we could take with us, our visibly distressed neighbor, Moishe Friedman, the tailor, paid us a furtive visit. He sat down at the kitchen table with my father.

"I hear you got a wagon and horses. Right?" he said softly, after looking over both shoulders.

"Yeah, Moishe, that's right. We leave tonight," explained Dad. "We're not going to wait for the Germans to march in here and cut our throats."

"Where you gonna go?" asked Moishe.

"What's the difference, just so it's out of their way," said Dad. "We head east towards the Russian border."

"Look, Berish, I know what's what. Wolfe told me about what he's been hearing from the Jews that the police have been picking up. The stories are unbelievable."

The tailor shook his head and clenched his eyes as he recalled the tales of atrocities relayed to him by his twenty-four year old son. When he spoke again, there was a note of pleading in the timbre of his voice.

"My boy, Wolfe, is in the same boat as you. The Germans will round up anyone who worked under the Soviets. And if they find out that they're Jews, they'll be very hard on them. My wife and the girls, we'll be able to get by, but the boys…they must get out of here, too. Just like you."

My dad rubbed the back of his neck as he contemplated adding provisions for four more to our supplies.

Friedman's voice was now a solemn whisper. "I'm begging you. If they stay here, they'll be in big danger."

My father said nothing and looked around the room as he pondered this. The tailor took my dad's silence as an affirmation.

He stood up quickly and said: "They'll be a big help to you on the road, Berish. They're all older than your two and they're hard workers, you know that."

After a few moments of pondering, my father agreed and the Friedman brothers joined our family foursome as we boarded the wagon and rolled out of town on that last night of my childhood.

Against every instinct in her body, my mother, still torn, jumped on the wagon at the last minute and pulled her two boys up with her. Our little group of eight, stealing off into the night, headed to G-d knows where, were among a very small handful of Jews from Bohorodczany's pre-war population of 2,500 to survive the war.

Why was there no mass exodus? Why didn't many more flee just as we did in the face of the Nazi juggernaut? What guided my father's steps and caused him to recognize the danger? These are standard survivor's questions that really distill down to a single question: Why was I permitted to live, while others were marked to die?

Eventually, I found the answers to these questions. And eventually, the sun rose again. But not before we were forced to endure many long years of darkness.

Chapter Two

The Road of Rescue

My memories of those weeks aboard the wagon are populated with lines of bedraggled Russian soldiers retreating from the front and streams of pitiful refugees clogging the endless, dirt roads. We traversed through scores of hamlets and villages. I recall passing through Buczacz – the hometown of famed author and Nobel Prize winner Shmuel Yosef Agnon and the birthplace of famed Nazi hunter, Simon Wiesenthal. As we moved slowly through the town, I recall glancing at the windows of government office buildings to spy Russian bureaucrats burning all of their documents to keep them from falling into Nazi hands.

It was on this road that we became acquainted with a fellow traveler known as Hunger, who would stay with us for years to come. And it was aboard the wagon that I tasted non-kosher food for the first time. My father handed me a piece of salami that he managed to "organize" somehow.

"But, Tatu (the name I called my father)," I cried, "it's *traif* (not kosher)!"

He looked me sternly in the eye and said two words: "Eat it!" I quickly did. I was completely surprised that it tasted good. I had been raised to believe that only kosher food was acceptable, and that anything else was not fit to eat. But *traif* tasted good! This was indeed a great revelation. Years later, my father explained the principle of Jewish law known as *Pikuach Nefesh*, which permits an individual to forego religious observance in cases where one's health or safety is at stake. My father observed my gaunt, undernourished body and decided to invoke this principle, temporarily setting aside Jewish dietary restrictions in favor of the well-being of his two sons.

My mother, however, could not be persuaded to abandon the eating habits of a lifetime simply because she might be facing starvation. Mama would not touch a piece of meat under any circumstances. She wouldn't go near it. She became a complete vegetarian and never once let non-kosher food pass through her lips.

We would often hear shooting and cannon-fire in the near distance, since the front was never far away. Of course, exactly how distant was never clear. Whenever we would ask how far we were from the front, we were invariably told "twenty kilometers." For weeks on end, my father would awake and ask, "Where's the front?" "Twenty kilometers." No matter how fast or how slowly we moved, we always managed to stay exactly twenty kilometers ahead of the fighting.

Fleeing through a war zone held its share of peril for our group. We would often see the wounded being rushed behind the lines. And on a day that will remain with me forever, we found ourselves exposed to a Nazi air attack.

We entered the town of Zhitomir on a sunny afternoon. As we approached the small railway station, we suddenly noticed a swarm of German bombers descending towards the tracks. My father acted quickly. Spotting a nearby field of tall grass, he ordered all of us to jump quickly from the wagon and lie down in the field. "Whatever you do, do not raise your head!" he shouted as the first burst of aircraft fire rained down on the station. Of course, I wanted to see the action and popped up to view a bomber unloading its payload on the depot as explosions ripped the air around me. "Get your head down, Hetche, before they shoot it off!" screamed my father. To my young eyes, this was all an amazing adventure to be fully experienced. I was simply too young to understand the dangers we were facing.

The Friedman brothers were older than Munjee and I, and soon we were very glad that my father had agreed to bring them along. Many a night they pushed the wagon out of muddy ruts along the road. And they soon became full-fledged members of our own family. Years later, I was told by one of the brothers: "Your mother was like an angel from G-d. When she divided the bread for all of us, she made sure that everyone got the same size piece. She didn't give more to her own children, although she easily could have. She was a true *Tzadaykes* (righteous woman)."

The handling of what little bread we could find was, of course, of prime importance. Naturally, the bread could only be shared when my father was able to lay his hands on a loaf here and there. I do not recall a single night over the next four years that I did not go to sleep hungry. I always yearned for just one more piece of bread.

I would constantly ask my father, "Tatu, are we ever going to have enough to eat?"

"Oh, yes, my son. Yes, soon. Very soon we will have enough bread. Just a little longer, my son."

My father always appeared fearless and confident to us. Many times, he must have quietly questioned the wisdom of our course: running into the arms of the Russians who were notorious for their hatred and mistreatment of Jews. But my father never let us see any doubt or equivocation. He spoke the language of the Russians and never appeared intimidated in their presence. When we needed fresh horses or feed, he would march into a *Kolchoz* (collective farm) and commandeer whatever he needed through bluster and *chutzpah* (nerve).

I recall how he would walk up to a *"Natchalnik,"* one of the farm managers, and say, "Listen, I need a horse. You've got to trade me something because my horse cannot go on and we have to keep moving. The Germans are only 20 kilometers away!" Dad would often appeal persuasively to the *Natchalnik*'s socialist sensibilities to get what he wanted: "Now listen, *tovarish*, I'm as equal as you are. If I need something and you have the ability to give me what I need, you are obliged, as a true socialist, to give it to me. This is basic Marxist-Leninism." As I recollect, this approach worked well if we were in return able to provide for some of the *Natchalnik*'s needs for good shoes or jewelry.

Many times, we would travel through the night. But when we felt the horses needed rest, we would pitch camp and sometimes wind up sleeping in a farmer's haystack. The strong smell of the hay has stayed with me to this day, and it brings with it a torrent of youthful memories. You see, I first discovered sex in one of those haystacks. Not as a participant, but rather as a witness.

Occasionally, when we stopped for the night, we were offered a semblance of shelter by being allowed to park in the yard of a *Kolchoz*. Young couples of the collective, seeking a private spot after a night of drinking, would occasionally find a "roll in the hay" quite appealing. They were too involved in their passions to pay much notice to the wide-eyed little boy in the dark. Such was the method of my sex education. It seemed to be effective, because when my time came to be more than a spectator, nothing was a mystery to me.

The wagon itself was an open affair with no covering to protect us from the sun or rain. I can still see us riding, soaked to the skin, for miles on end in the driving rain. "If the horses can stand it, so can we," Dad would pronounce whenever any of us would voice a complaint.

The most egregious aspect of our travel was the fact that we had no specific destination. Just keep moving – that was our sole directive. Stay ahead of the advancing Germans and don't look back. The towns we passed through blur into each other in my memory: Stanislawow, Buczacz, Tarnopol, Zhitomir, Kiev, Kremenchuk, Dniepropetrovsk and Kharkov. Only Kiev stands out because of its smooth paved roads. Everywhere else along the bumpy journey, we traveled on mud or upon the occasional gravel road.

Finally, after nearly five weeks on the open highway, we arrived at Voronezh. There, we discovered the first functioning train station that had not, as yet, been bombed out or abandoned. Making a deal with the stationmaster, my father quickly exchanged the horse and wagon for passage aboard the caboose of the next eastbound train. We grabbed whatever we could carry, fought our way through the melee, and scrambled aboard our "private coach."

The station was complete chaos; a real *balagan*. People were jumping on whatever train they could board, as long as it was heading away from the fighting. Destinations did not matter. Even tickets didn't matter. Just the overpowering animal instinct to seek safety and refuge. This is what drove us day after day.

Once aboard, we crossed the vast Russian frontier. We passed through the desolate Saratovskaya *oblast* (district) and steamed quickly through towns like Balashov, Penza and Syzran. After several days, we arrived in Kuybyshev, where we changed trains and headed south through Orenburg, and then on into the Soviet state of Kazakhstan. Our first glimpse of life in Kazakhstan was in the town of Aktyubinsk, the capital city of the *oblast*. While seriously impoverished, Aktyubinsk appeared totally untouched by the war. In the district known as Klutchevoy Rayon, we disembarked for the last time at a place called Stantzia Alga, or Alga Station. My father had learned aboard the train that he might find work in Alga, and this was enough for him to select this forsaken place as our stopping point.

I recall staring wide-eyed at the odd-shaped buildings once we got away from the train station. This strange, primitive world was to be our new home until further notice. There were no streetcars, no cafés and no amusement parks – but there were also no bombers, no soldiers, and a relative feeling of calm and normalcy, since we were finally hundreds of kilometers from the front.

My father did, in fact, find work quickly, as did my brother. Dad was hired as a guard at a local labor camp. He was issued a ratty uniform and an ancient rifle, and he drew a regular salary. The labor camp was populated with common criminals, counter-revolutionary political prisoners, and some Jews.

Dad was able to befriend a local physician, Dr. Krylov, with whom he collaborated in hustling the Jewish prisoners out of the camp from time to time. Dr. Krylov would be called in to examine a prisoner who was complaining of some feigned illness and promptly declare his condition to be contagious. Once these Jews were ejected from the camp, they had no place to go. Often my father would smuggle them into our little home in the dead of night. I recall being awakened in the middle of the night only to greet some recent prison escapees that my father had invited in. They would be sitting by the fire delousing themselves by pulling the vermin from their clothing. They would then crack the carapace of each louse between their thumbnails with a little crunch and flip the remains into the fire. What little food we had, we were required to share with these poor souls until they were able to smuggle themselves out of town. In this way, my father was able to rescue a good number of Jews from being swallowed up into the *gulag* (Soviet prison system).

My father carried out his rescue work not only because he was a humanitarian, but also because of his understanding and observance of one of Judaism's most sacred obligations: the commandment of *Pidyun Shevuyim* (the ransoming of captives). This principle is given, under Jewish law, a higher priority than even the obligation to feed the poor. He and my mother were both familiar with the Jewish teaching that, if a synagogue is faced with the dilemma of selling its holiest possession, its Torah scroll, in order to raise the ransom money needed to free one of its members, it is obligated to do so. While my father did not have the funds to buy these Jewish prisoners' freedom, he felt a kinship to them and bravely paid the price by risking his own freedom to secure their escape.

Munjee also soon found a job and went to work every day at a nearby chemical plant, assisting in the Russian war effort. My mother not only busied herself in setting up a kosher home at the edge of the universe, but she also found employment in the homes of several neighboring farm families, tending to their all-important private gardens.

The great workers' paradise that was the USSR was unable to produce enough food to keep its population from famine, even during peacetime. During the war, the meager gleanings of the collective farms were further reduced, since most male farm workers were forced into the Red Army. The Soviet model permitted individual families to provide for their own nutrition by cultivating small plots of earth immediately surrounding their homes. Growing more than you could consume and selling or bartering the remainder was not legally permitted. However, the practice was universally condoned, since it became obvious that without these private garden plots, the Soviet population would soon face starvation.

My mother labored outdoors throughout the spring and summer, leaving each morning with her trusty spade over her shoulder, and then returning after sunset with her calloused hands raw and bloody. But she brought home with her cucumbers, potatoes, cabbages and sweet corn. And in this way she kept her own family from starvation.

Conditions in Alga were unbelievably primitive. Houses were made of "bricks" that were formed and drawn from mud pits filled with straw and stamped by foot in much the same way as the Egyptians made bricks centuries before. The mud walls of the house were smoothed by hand. There were usually only two rooms, a fireplace, and sometimes a window. The roof was mud as well, and had to be rebuilt after each rainfall.

We lacked the most basic sanitary facilities. We were required to walk two kilometers each day to fetch fresh water. A toilet was a hole in the ground in the summer and a snow igloo in the winter. I'll always recall with disgust my first attempt at using an outdoor cesspool to relieve my bowels. As I squatted in the mud with my pants around my knees, I was joined by our landlord's wife. She hiked up her skirt, hunkered down next to me and relieved herself just like an animal. This was too much for my cultured sensibilities. I pulled up my trousers and ran off distraught. Eventually, as my modesty crumbled and as my bodily needs could not be ignored, I reluctantly learned to use the cesspool with daily regularity.

Despite all of this, we were together. We were alive, and we were able to stop running for a moment and catch our breath. Most importantly, we were able to feel semi-protected from the dangers we had escaped. Unforeseen new perils, however, lay just ahead.

Chapter Three
Alga

WHILE RELIGIOUS practice was forbidden under the Soviet regime, the town of Alga was, nevertheless, a spicy blend of Moslem and Eastern Orthodox cultures. Our family became a part of Alga's tiny band of less than twenty-five "closet" Jews. There was no synagogue, and weekly Sabbath observance was impossible. Nevertheless, some level of Jewish communal life still managed to seep through the twin barriers of local anti-Semitism and official atheist dogma. For example, we had a *shochet* (kosher ritual slaughterer) who claimed to slaughter the rare chicken that came our way in accordance with Jewish law. My mother, however, questioned this man's credentials as a *shochet*, since she once observed him emerging from a non-kosher eatery. Therefore she would not consume any meat that he produced. I do recall that a *minyan* (quorum) was assembled every year on the High Holidays at someone's home, and that secret prayer services were conducted, using my mother's prayer book, after all the windows were covered over with bed sheets.

Knowing exactly when to celebrate the Jewish holidays, such as Yom Kippur, was no easy task for our little group. My mother took it upon herself to maintain the *luach* or Jewish calendar. This is a lunar calendar that predates the solar calendar developed by the Romans. Since it follows the cycles of the moon, rather than the yearly cycle of the sun, a Jewish holiday may fall on a different secular date each year. My mother was somehow able to produce and refer to her little calendar year after year, whenever any Jew needed to know the correct date of a holiday or the date of a *yahrtzeit* (annual memorial of a deceased family member).

The town of Alga had several elementary schools and a few "basic" schools that just taught reading and writing. But even though I was of school age, I did not attend. My father prohibited me from doing so. He absolutely forbade it. My father correctly understood that sending me to a Stalinist school would indoctrinate my young mind into the Soviet mold. When I would ask him about school, he would reply: "I do not want them to turn you into a Communist, Hetche. You study here at home with Mama and it will be okay."

Mama did what she could, but she had her calloused hands full working in the neighbors' vegetable gardens and keeping our little family together. My father's reasoning did not make sense to me at the time. In fact, it angered me. I loved my father, but I also loved learning, reading, the arts and music. I never quite forgave him for depriving me of my childhood education, although I fully agree with his motives.

This was a time and a place that innocent parents were routinely denounced as "profiteers and speculators" by their own children for merely attempting to raise a little money to feed their families. My father did not wish to turn me into a spy for the state who would report to his teachers that his father had spouted some counter-revolutionary remarks against the glorious Soviet worker's paradise last night over dinner. By keeping me out of school, he was protecting himself and our family from this sort of dangerous exposure.

In his enduring wisdom, he resisted all efforts for our family to become "Russofied." We kept our Polish documents and our Polish national identity. This policy caused him a good deal of grief. He was often called in by the local NKVD authorities and questioned. They quite simply wanted him to become a Russian.

"You live here, you work here…why aren't you a Russian citizen?" they would demand.

"Because I'm a Pole. After the war, we will return to our home in Poland," he would insist.

He would take this stand despite the fact that Poland as a nation was no more, and despite the enormous pressure placed upon him to recant. The Friedman brothers, on the other hand, were forced to forfeit their Polish passports and elected to become Russian citizens. This decision fixed their course for the remainder of their lives. While we were permitted to return home after the war, the Friedmans were required to stay put in their new Soviet homeland.

So, with no school available, and finding myself all alone for most of the day, I began to teach myself. I learned the Russian language and I could soon speak, read and write fluently. I obtained access to a library of Russian books and particularly enjoyed Shakespeare. I read his complete works in Russian, and to this day, my first mental image of the melancholy Dane is of a young Hamlet speaking in Russian. I soon went on to devour the vast range of Russian literature, including *War and Peace*, *Anna Karenina*, and many of the classics. I could not get enough. The more I felt deprived of my regular school routine, the more I ran to embrace the world of great literature.

My childhood years in Alga were bereft of any social activity, any sports, or any normal childhood experiences. For four years, I did not enjoy a single friendship. It was during these years that I should have celebrated my Bar Mitzvah, but this too was abandoned. I indeed did become a man at this stage of my life, but was not able to celebrate this Jewish rite of passage due to war and circumstance.

But the day also left time for work and I became a self-employed tin-smith. This was a trade I had picked up back in Bohorodczany. In what now seemed like the "good old days," our family had owned a building that covered a city block. Our home was an apartment in the back of the building. Our extended family lived in several other apartments, and the rest of the space in the front was rented out to commercial tenants. One shopkeeper on our old block was a tinsmith, and I loved to observe him at his craft and help him after school as he fashioned all sorts of tin household goods.

Once in Alga, mother trained me in the finer points of tinsmithing until I became skilled at making, without the use of solder, tin pails that did not leak. Whenever I could "organize" some scrap of tin from here or there, usually from a rundown rooftop, I would quickly fashion it into tin cups, and then head to the marketplace and barter them for food.

I would most often trade my cups for milled flour, although even this most elementary bit of commerce was frowned upon by the Soviet authorities, who considered any form of enterprise as *spekulatzia* and clearly counter-revolutionary. I had to be very careful to avoid being apprehended for this criminal activity. In fact, some years later, in Lvov, I was caught and charged with profiteering.

The flour I obtained in this way would most frequently wind up mixed with hot water to make a light gruel known as *zatyerucha*, which was more or less the national food of Kazakhstan. Food, and the search for it, was a never-ending obsession in Alga. It seems incredible today, but one of my fondest memories of this period is of the day that my father, after having bartered at Stantzia Alga with a traveler from Tashkent, came home with that rarest of prizes: a small fresh apple. None of us had seen an apple for years. I recall how he sliced it into sections, reserving the largest piece for me, his growing boy. We savored the taste of that sweet apple with such joy and passion. We even devoured the stem and seeds until all that was left was its memory. We would have consumed its shadow, too, if that were possible.

A summertime staple of my years in Alga was seeking out *kizyak*. *Kizyak* were the dried cow manure droppings we would collect during the summer months and store for winter fuel. We owed our survival to this "cow pie" natural resource. Without the methane contained in these nuggets, our only other sources of heat were the dry tumbleweeds that rolled lazily across the Kazahki steppes and the few remaining coal chunks pulled from ashes left behind by the steam locomotives. I would run to Stantzia Alga to meet the train each day and wait for the brakeman to dump the locomotive's ashcan in the dirt. I would then rummage through the ash, looking for remnant pieces of coke while trying to avoid burning my hands. Once collected, this partially used coal would be combined with the tumbleweeds and the *kizyak* to serve as our winter fireplace fodder. Even today, although our home has a very lovely fireplace, I never use it. Building a fire in a fireplace brings back too many wistful memories of a sickly little boy trying to keep warm in front of a failing fire of excrement and sagebrush.

Handling cow droppings could not have contributed to my general health. Another source of exposure was in the queues. Standing in line was a way of life in all the Soviet states, and I became highly adept at it, often standing in three to four lines at the same time. This practice involved a protocol. Rising at 4 AM, I would rush to find the first queue. It didn't matter what was being "given" at the head of the line. Whatever it was, I could be sure that we needed it. I would approach the person at the end of the line and ask, "Are you the last in line?" If he answered yes, I would state, "I'm behind you," and join in until another person would fall in behind me. I would then inform both the person in front and in back of me: "I am here. This is my place." This statement would insure that if I left, I had a right to return to my spot later. They would nod, and I'd be off to do the same routine all over again in another queue. Bouncing back and forth between the queues usually netted me a full "possibility bag," a net mesh sack I carried with me at all times, just in case I could snare something of value on the street.

Of course, high demand consumer goods, such as food staples, required ration cards. Hence I soon mastered the craft of ration card forgery. Using only a razor, a newspaper, my own saliva and my thumb, I could easily alter a 400 g allotment into a 600 g portion. Careful not to raise the amount by too much and thereby risk suspicion, I soon became a true expert in this scoundrel's art. Smoothly scraping the printed digit off the ration card with the razor came first. Next, I would locate the desired digit in the right size and typeface in the daily newspaper. Applying some spit to the paper, I would press the flat of my thumb against the page and pull off quickly, lifting the character as the ink adhered to my flesh. I would then stamp my thumb down onto the coupon, precisely imprinting it with the new digit. This practice, which helped to keep the wolf a bit further from our door, became part of an overall way of life that relied upon deceit, bribery and petty larceny to sustain the most basic level of survival.

Vermin infestation was also a way of life in Alga. Delousing our bodies was a necessary part of our daily personal hygiene. Of course, we carried out this task differently from the local Kazakhs. Each morning as I went outside to relieve myself, I recall watching our neighbors, having just awakened after sleeping outdoors, picking the lice from their bodies, crushing them with their teeth, and then swallowing the remains as a breakfast snack. At first, I was horrified and sickened, but I soon became accustomed to this practice and much worse.

It was at this point that our constant escort, Hunger, was joined by another unwelcome companion: Disease. The three males in our family were continually ill in some way or another. Only my mother remained healthy throughout our years in Alga. Was it because she adhered strictly to the kosher laws and ate only bread, potatoes and vegetables? I don't actually know, but I do not remember her being ill a single day during our sojourn in Alga.

My father suffered from ongoing pulmonary problems that resulted in incessant coughing. He was always seeking out sulfa drugs to combat the frequent bouts of pneumonia he was struck with. My brother and I would come down with a seasonal variety of malaria that caused us to break out in devastating shivering sweats.

Many Jews in our little outpost succumbed to disease. Considering the constant exposure to lice and other vermin, combined with the lack of proper warmth during the winter months, it is amazing that any of us survived. There were a few times when it appeared we would not.

At the age of eleven, I became deathly sick. My stomach was in severe contortions. I ran a high fever, and I saw evidence of internal hemorrhaging. My father's friend, Dr. Krylov, was quickly summoned. He gave me a thorough examination and diagnosed my symptoms as typhus. My parents were advised to keep me quarantined in bed for at least one week in order to prevent an epidemic.

A few months before, Munjee had also come down with typhus and was taken to the local hospital. My mother observed the deplorable conditions and the lack of heat there and was horrified. She ran home and packed up a warm *perreneh* (comforter) and used it to cover Munjee during his recovery. She would tell how she watched several patients around her lose their toes because of the extreme cold. Based on this experience, she refused to permit my transfer to the hospital, which she considered a deathtrap, and instead insisted that I be treated at home.

I was delirious and unable to eat or drink anything. I became increasingly dehydrated and weaker each day. I don't know if I was given any medication, but after the week was over, I began to feel a little better. Still, I was thin as a needle. As I regained my health, my appetite returned in a big way. However, I was warned repeatedly that I must not eat. Eating at this stage would cause complications, according to Dr. Krylov. And how right he was.

Despite all the warnings, I stole out of bed and snuck into the kitchen that night. I found some boiled potatoes that I ravenously devoured. Soon after, I had a complete relapse and was diagnosed with second stage Typhus II. After examining me, Dr. Krylov took my parents aside and gave them the bad news. Unbeknownst to them, I overheard the doctor's dour words: "You'd best say good-bye to your son. He's not going to make it." My parents, obviously devastated, kept up a strong front. They never let on that I was finished. I did not tell them that I had heard the doctor deliver the news, and I tried to act tough in order not to betray my true emotions.

Throughout the constant sweats and the bloody stools, I began to feel that my life was ebbing away. As I drifted in and out of consciousness, I became convinced that I was dying from typhus. But I also came to a realization. If I could only exert sufficient willpower, I could avoid my fate. I desperately fought succumbing to the power of the disease. I turned the struggle into a battle of wills between me and Typhus. "I shall not die! You will not defeat me!" I repeated to myself over and over, all night long.

I recall my poor mother's tear-stained face hovering over me, like a beacon in the fog. As she watched me slipping away, she looked as though her heart was being ripped from her chest. I hated to see her crying, and even more, I hated to think that I was the cause of her suffering. In her tears, I found my strength. Too weak to speak, or even move, I fought back the enveloping darkness with every fiber of my body and spirit.

My parents kept an all night vigil that I'm sure they felt would conclude with a morning burial. But I did not die. In fact, by morning, I was still breathing, and the strength slowly began to return to my wasted and withered body. After a few days, I was overcome with a ravenous hunger and soon felt well enough to get out of bed unassisted. Within a few weeks I was back out on the street selling my tin cups.

Was I somehow being protected? At the air raid at the train station, a bomb ten meters closer would have killed us all. A well-respected doctor had predicted my demise, yet here I was, breathing the air on the earth, not buried in it. How could I explain these near misses, these brushes with death? I didn't understand these things, but I was beginning to think about them more and more as we went about the business of survival in wartime Kazakhstan.

Years later, as I replayed the painful memories of that night in my mind, I concluded that before physical survival can occur, spiritual survival must first be achieved. Extrapolating to the larger case of the Jewish people, our history is sadly filled with similar "near-death" experiences. Throughout recorded history, Jews have gazed into the abyss of extinction repeatedly. As a people, we have survived, despite all those who would destroy us, because we have managed to find the will to live on, no matter what. The Jewish people have found the spiritual strength to declare: "I shall not die!" It is only from this spiritual foundation that we may hope to insure the physical survival of our people.

It was soon after my miraculous recovery, in 1942, that Munjee was called up to join the military. He never returned to Alga after that, and we were only to see each other again after the war in Warsaw. I missed him terribly and yearned for his return. While we did receive an occasional letter, like many wartime families, we lived with the daily dread and uncertainty of not knowing if Munjee was dead or alive. We prayed daily for his safety and talked about him constantly. In this way we kept him close to us.

Because of his age, his poor health, and the fact that he was serving in a quasi-military capacity, my father was not called up into the Army. He was able to stay with us and his presence was a lifesaver on more than one occasion.

The closest brush with destruction our family encountered was during the winter of 1943. We had gone to bed as usual, leaving the fire burning for warmth. I woke up a few hours later because I had trouble breathing. I stumbled out of bed and woke my parents. We were all gasping for air as acrid smoke filled our nostrils and stung our eyes. My father quickly assessed the situation. "Out," he shouted. "Outside! Now!" We heeded and ran out into the cold night air.

My father immediately looked up and observed that no smoke was coming from our chimney. In a flash he was on the roof with a branch in his hand, pulling smoking rags out of the flue. His face was as black as the night when he came down and explained that some bastard had stuffed rags into our chimney. The idea was to block the exhaust, in an attempt to murder us all in our sleep.

"Who would do such a thing, Tatu?" I cried.

"I know who, but I'll never be able to prove it. It was our landlord. He collects our rent every month and, now that times are hard, he kills us to steal our belongings. It would look like an accident. And after we're dead and buried, all of our valuables stay with him since he owns the house."

Nothing was ever said to the police nor to the suspected landlord. We continued going about our normal routine, although we did start checking the chimney several times every night from then on. I could not believe that someone would coldly murder three people in order to steal some silver and jewelry. But these were desperate times and we were dealing with desperate and dangerous people at every turn.

This fact was evident as we attempted to deal with the pervasive anti-Semitism that surrounded us. Despite official proclamations about a classless society, many party officials would bristle when an ordinary citizen, especially a Jew, would address them as *tovarish* (comrade). "*Tovarish*! What sort of *tovarish* am I to you, Jew?" was their most common response.

Bloody noses, along with taunts of "*Zhid*" (dirty Jew) from the neighborhood children, were part of my steady diet. Often we were singled out and labeled "*Abrashah*," a diminutive version of Abraham that branded us as outsiders. Many Jews were targeted because they had difficulty pronouncing the Russian rolling "R" sound, substituting a more guttural version. Jewish boys would be pounced on by bullying gangs and forced to recite a Russian poem about Mt. Ararat, heavily-laden with R's. If their speech betrayed them, they would be beaten with shouts of "*Zhiduha*" and "*Abrashah*." Fortunately, everyone in our family was able to master the Russian dialect perfectly and managed to escape this particular threat.

While we were at a relatively comfortable distance from the fighting, we lived with the fear that Germany would conquer Russia and soon look our way. Learning the truth about what was happening in Europe and the Pacific was next to impossible. The newspapers and radio were filled with constant propaganda. We came to understand that if the radio reported that the Red Army was engaged in a "heroic strategic realignment," it meant they had lost a battle. Of course, reading between the lines could not have given us an inkling of what fate was being meted out to the fellow Jews we left behind. Such things as gas chambers and extermination centers were beyond the limits of our imagination. Like most of the world, we learned of the Nazi death machinery only after the war.

I faced death yet again during one of my regular runs to the water pump located two kilometers down the road from our home. It was my job to carry two empty pails to the pump each day and bring them back filled with water. This task was particularly daunting in the Kazakhstan winters, when temperatures often reached minus twenty-five degrees Celsius. Snow up to my head would cover the roads and we could only pass through via tunnels dug by hand through the tightly packed drifts.

On one such day I was returning with my full buckets, which had turned mostly to ice, when I spotted a huge snarling dog directly in my path. I knew the dog belonged to a neighbor who seldom fed him. As a result, the dog was known to be mean and vicious. I guessed that he had not been able to forage for any food on his own, due to the snow and cold, and had been driven to savagery by hunger. The beast would not let me pass. I cried for help, but my voice was muffled by the huge walls of snow on either side. No one could hear me. My hands became numb, so I put down the buckets. The wind began to whip wildly, which only made the dog more aggressive as he lunged towards me with his front paws, knocking me to the cold ground. I realized that I could not make it back to any shelter before freezing. I determined that I would either have to get past the dog or freeze to death only a few meters from my home.

I scrambled to my feet and summoned up my courage. My father had taught me that the best defense is a good offense. So, I ran toward the animal and delivered a sharp kick directly to its head. The dog yelped and got out of my way, and I ran like the devil back inside my home. My father and I came back later and recovered the buckets that were rock-solid with ice.

This incident did a great deal to enhance my self-respect. It also helped me overcome my fear of dogs. To this day I have never feared them. I began to understand that many problems boil down to a question of will. I had made up my mind to get past that dog, just as I had made up my mind to conquer Typhus, and that was the crucial step that made success possible. There would be many times in the future when I would rely upon pure will to accomplish my objectives. A little luck, a little courage and some brains are all important, but every accomplishment begins with the determination to get the job done. This was the painful and important lesson I learned on that bitter cold day long ago.

Chapter Four

The Rocky Road Back

By the time I reached age fourteen, we knew Hitler was finished and that we had been spared. The fighting had never reached our doorstep. It was just a matter of time before we could think about returning home and reuniting with Zayde and the rest of our large family.

May 8, 1945, VE Day, was marked with jubilation never before witnessed in sleepy Alga. Kazatzka-dancing soldiers with their little accordions adorned every city block – dancing, swigging vodka…dancing the survivor's dance. "War is over and we are here!" Arm in arm and into the night we danced, and we danced even more till we could only gasp: "We are here! Hitler is dead. And we are still here!" But as we were celebrating, my father was again making preparations. "We've got to get out of here, Hetche," he explained. "We've got to go find Munjee and get back to Poland."

This was no easy task. With peacetime, borders once fluid were now becoming fixed. Under Soviet law, a permit was even required just to move across the street. Leaving the country legally was simply not an option. But, as before, my father had a plan. Step one was to get us prepared. "We must be ready to leave quickly. At the drop of a hat," he explained to mother and me. "Get everything ready for the road and put it together in a place where we can grab it and go in a hurry."

A large steamer trunk was secured, and we filled it with the items we were unable to carry, but did not wish to leave behind. The little items we were able to tote with us were bound up and placed near the door, so that when opportunity knocked, we would be prepared.

Of course, we could not get back to Poland as we had left her, by horse-drawn wagon. The roads were impassable, so we had to look to the trains. But there was a problem. Trains very seldom stopped at Stantzia Alga. When they did, all passengers boarding and arriving were carefully scrutinized. With no travel documents, we stood no chance of boarding a train legally.

But my father was determined to get us aboard in one way or another. And it had to be aboard the right train. The Tashkent to Moscow Limited was the one that would deliver us to our first destination. But getting it to stop in Alga would not be easy.

My father's plan was for him to first travel alone by foot some fifty kilometers southward to the next major town of Kandyagash, where he knew the Moscow train regularly stopped. He would bribe the conductor, board the train and convince him to make a clandestine stop at Alga to pick us up. My father said good-bye one morning and told Mama and me to take our *pecklach*, our hand luggage, and to be at the train station at 4 AM ready to board the train.

Mama arranged to have the big steamer trunk we had packed with our family treasures shipped to our destination of Lvov. Of course, we never saw the box again. I suspect that some of our family heirlooms are today still decorating the station house at Stantzia Alga.

We said good-bye to our mud home. Despite the primitive conditions and daily deprivations, this place had been an adventure for a young boy, and more importantly, it had been a sanctuary for our family. Even at this point, months after the war's end, we had no conception of the inferno that had just engulfed European Jews – an inferno from which we had barely managed to flee.

Mama and I sat patiently in the dark of the deserted railway station thinking similar thoughts. When will we be able to stop running? When will we have enough food to eat? When will I be able to attend school? When will we be normal citizens and not always be scurrying from here to there like mice in a dark alley?

Our thoughts were interrupted by a distant beacon cutting through the dusty darkness, followed by the unmistakable "whoot-whoo" whistle of the approaching Russian locomotive. We grabbed our packages and stood on the platform, clutching each other tightly as the locomotive swiftly pulled in. The familiar scent of the steam boiler filled our nostrils. Would it stop this time, or keep chugging through as it usually did? Just as we heard the metallic "Skree" of the brakes, we spotted Tatu hanging half out of the open boiler car door.

"Jump in. Come on. Throw me the *pecklach*. Quick. Quick!" One big tug and I was on board. The train was off after having stopped for perhaps only forty-five seconds. The train was crowded with sleeping passengers on their way to Moscow, and somehow Dad had found a little space for us. We were on our way.

After an uneventful three-day journey, the train pulled into the Great Station of Moscow. Coming from primitive Alga into what was still a formidable and quite extraordinary capital was unforgettable. While we only stayed there a few days, memories of Moscow have remained with me to this day. Of course, the Kremlin and Red Square are vivid in my memory, but so is running alongside a speeding trolley car and hitching a free ride. Perhaps we were supposed to be pitiful refugees, but I felt like a tourist taking in the sights and smells of my first big city.

We were more or less encamped at the train station each day while trying to make a connection to take us westward to Poland. We finally wound up "riding the rails," hopping aboard empty freight cars like hobos, as we slowly made our way back from Moscow to Lvov. We joined up with "fellow travelers" – Ukrainians, Latvians, Jews and Gypsies – in open-air camps for the night, stretching out against a coal pile as the rhythm of the rails rocked us to sleep.

The traffic flowed west, always west, and the further we traveled, the more refugees joined us on the trail. The mood was upbeat and optimistic. The war was over. Enjoy the freedom. Start life anew. We were in that short post-war period before the Iron Curtain had yet descended. Fortunately, crossing out of Russia was not yet the death-defying deed it was soon to become.

We frequently hopped a boxcar with no idea where it was heading, and hence wound up dead-ended on a rail spur. My father would often try to flag down a passing westbound train. "C'mon, hook us up!" he would shout at the passing conductor. "Hook us up. We need to go west." Sometimes they would feel sorry for us and agree, but usually, we would grab our belongings and look for the closest road. When we couldn't ride, we walked. And when we couldn't walk, we rested. Our destination was always the same: the next train station, where we would wait for another westbound train. My mother was fanatical about our staying together.

"Don't wander off, Hetche," she would admonish. "Stay close by because we don't know when the next train is coming, and G-d forbid we should get separated." Many families were, in fact, split up in just this way.

While we tried to find covered boxcars in which to ride, we were most often in open coal cars or flatbed wagons that offered no protection from the elements. We would often wake up soaking wet in the middle of a rainstorm. I soon thought nothing of it and learned to sleep, wet or dry.

Hunger, our old companion, was still traveling by our side. Whenever we pitched camp, I would run to find the closest potato field and dig up a few gleaned potatoes. I was skilled at building a fire in a hurry and was soon boiling the potatoes for the three of us, and often for several more hungry travelers.

My father was known as a charismatic go-getter. He was constantly attracting an ever-changing entourage of homeless hangers-on. His confidence and proud demeanor served as a tonic for these badly beaten souls who had endured so much and had survived with so little.

One such character who remains vividly in my memory is a Polish professional soccer player from Lvov. He was terribly undernourished, and my mother, feeling sympathetic, took him under her wing and made sure he received sufficient food. As soon as he was fed and feeling stronger, he took off without warning, and we never saw him again. In this way, many fellow vagabonds floated in and out of our itinerant lives during these long summer weeks on the road.

Religious observance while we were on the move was, of course, out of the question. While my mother strictly adhered to the Jewish dietary laws during this period, none of us was able to avoid violating the Sabbath sanctions against travel and other types of work. But since we were fleeing for our lives, this fell under the rubric of *Pikuach Nefesh*. Despite this, I recall how Mama would remind us each week that "Today is *Shabbos*," just so we wouldn't forget about it.

Before leaving Alga, we had received a letter from Munjee. He wrote that soon after leaving home, he had been transferred by the Red Army to the Polish Army, and that he was safe and stationed in Poland. Regarding the fate of the rest of our family, we were only getting a trickle of information. As we made our way westward, we would hear, with increasing regularity, about the fate of the Jews we had left behind. A horrific picture started to emerge as we listened to fellow travelers talk about gas chambers and a place called Auschwitz. As the realization sunk in that most Jews who fell into Nazi hands were murdered, we became more and more anxious about finding our family members.

"Look at the faces, Hetche," Mama would instruct. "Look at everybody we see. Maybe we'll see someone from home." In particular, I searched for my favorite uncle, Psachya. He had ridden his bicycle to Buczacz, and I suspected he might have survived the onslaught. He did not. He perished, along with his wife and little baby girl, Yonah.

Initially, we could not believe that the Nazis had killed every Jew in our *shtetl*. We knew that some had to have survived. They simply could not have killed them all. We knew that something horrible and unbelievable had taken place during the war, but, after all, ours was a big family. Some must have gotten through as we did. We were determined to find them. Our destination became Lvov, the closest big city, and from there we planned to return to Bohorodczany and reunite with any surviving family members.

After a few more days we finally reached Lvov and, once there, we immediately set off for our *shtetl*. But we were stopped – stopped by other Jews in Lvov who told us the grisly truth: "They're all gone. Don't go back. There's no one left. And if you do go back, the Ukrainians will kill you, too."

Slowly, piece by piece, we were able to patch together what had happened to our family, and to the entire Jewish community we had left behind in Bohorodczany.

Just four days after our departure, on July 2, 1941, the Nazi-allied Hungarian army, under German command, entered and quickly occupied Bohorodczany as the Russians fled the city. The German army followed and soon established a ghetto, into which all of the town's 2,500 Jews were ordered to relocate. Through deportation, deprivation and disease, their numbers were reduced to 1,200 in less than one year. On June 16, 1942, the remaining Jews were marched to neighboring Stanislawow, where a recent *Aktion* had reduced the Jewish ghetto from 40,000 to less than 10,000.

The Jews of Bohorodczany were confined to a derelict building called Rudolf's Mill. This spot was to be the killing ground. The 1,200 surviving innocent men, women and children of my *shtetl* were lined up and murdered like sheep in a slaughterhouse. Their former Ukrainian neighbors carried out what, by this time, had become a routine bloodbath. The victims' bodies were taken to a nearby cemetery and dumped into a large communal grave.

How could it be? Zayde, Lonka, Vuitche Psachya...all cruelly murdered? Why? What had they done to deserve such a punishment, other than failing to flee in the face of danger? I slowly came to realize exactly what my father's quick thinking and resolute action had meant in terms of saving our lives. Had my father not decided to run, and had my mother not agreed to our joining him, we would certainly all have been killed. The Hasten name would have disappeared forever. In terms of my brother and me, father had not only given us life, he had preserved our lives, and I will always be in his debt. While I never expressed my feelings of gratitude to him during his lifetime, I did say "Thank you, Tatu, for *shlepping* us out of that place," when I poured my heart out at his funeral many years later.

While he certainly had every right to do so, I do not recall my father ever gloating or pointing out that he had been proven correct about his decision to leave our town ahead of the German advance. In the face of so much misery and mourning, there was little room in his heart for such petty vindications. My mother, however, had to admit that Dad was right, and sometimes, years later, I would use this fact when encouraging her to do something she did not wish to do.

"I know you don't want to go there, Mama," I used to chide. "But you didn't want to leave Bohorodczany either, and later you were very glad that you did."

The enormity of what had happened to Zayde, to Lonka and to the rest of our family did not sink in right away. I remember lying awake on my cot during the night, trying to sort it all out, to somehow shape some sense into what had happened.

Shock melted into anger. How dare these arrogant Nazi bastards wantonly murder defenseless old men and children? My anger extended to Jews as well. How could we have left ourselves so wide-open and so defenseless? Through our miserable vulnerability, we invited the enemy to slaughter us! My rage often brought me to tears, and I began to assail others with my angry outbursts. Looking back, it was through this cathartic quest for answers to the unanswerable that some of the core aspects of my personality were forged. I came through this period a changed person. My innocence had been burned away, but I had gained something of enormous value: a new personal philosophy that can be summed up in two words: Never Again!

These words said so much to me then, and they have grown even more meaningful over the ensuing decades. In later life, I came to believe that, since history has taught us that weakness invites disaster, we, as Jews, can "never again" afford to place ourselves into such a defenseless position. It is this fundamental principle that has led to my life-long devotion to Zionism and that accounts for my opposition to those who would have us appease our enemies, be it Stalin or Arafat. When I see today's Jewish leaders making the same mistakes in the 21st century that we witnessed and paid for so dearly back in the 1940s, I have to ask myself: *What does "Never Again" mean to them?* and *When will we ever learn?* Apparently these leaders don't understand Benjamin Franklin's exhortation: "Make yourself into a sheep and the wolves will eat you."

Over the ensuing years, as my political awareness grew, I began to gain a more profound understanding of this line of thought. I came to comprehend that the banner of "Never Again!" must be firmly planted into a foundation of Jewish strength. As an adult, I concluded that this foundation of strength must contain three core pillars.

The first pillar is spiritual strength. Judaism, which is more than merely a religious discipline, must be grounded in the spiritual teachings of our heritage. Our strength must flow, first and foremost, from the Torah. The Torah provides the basis for our existence as a people and a framework of law under which to carry out that existence. A Jew ignorant of Torah can never be a truly strong Jew.

The second pillar is physical strength. The Torah's parchment offers precious little protection against missiles, bullets, and bombs. We are obligated to protect ourselves, by military means, from what has been shown time and again to be a hostile and often savage world.

The third pillar is intellectual and political strength. To make sure that the words "Never Again!" resonate with truth, we must achieve strength in the research laboratory, in the university, and at the negotiating table. We must be clever, and we must be capable of forging alliances with strong partners who will offer protection when we are threatened. It was firmly astride these three pillars, and under the rubric of "Never Again!" that I came to understand my place as a survivor and a Jew.

But when I was a youth in post-war Poland, these thoughts were still being formulated. Even though my immediate family was alive, our future was anything but certain. We had survived, but exactly what sort of survivors were we? In the normal world, when someone survives a near brush with death, his family and neighbors rejoice as the survivor resumes his normal life. But we were strange survivors indeed. Everyone in our family had been murdered. Our neighbors were threatening to kill us if we dared to return home. We felt like shadows or phantoms. We had only our bodies, our flesh, which had somehow managed to avoid being consumed by the flames. Everything else that defined us, that supported us, had been burned away. Many Jews who were faced with this numbing realization became despondent and aimless. Some felt they should have died along with their loved ones and that they had survived only by some fluke. To these poor souls, the future held little meaning, and they soon descended into lives of despair as Poland fell increasingly under Soviet domination.

But this path was not for us. We had survived because we used our wits and our courage. We made our own fate, and we would continue to do whatever was necessary to ensure our safety and well-being. This was the attitude that I learned from my father and that I still maintain today.

In Lvov, we were informed about the fate of the city's Jews — how they were rounded up, marched into the forest, and machine-gunned into mass graves. We heard how the Nazis were ably assisted by the local Poles who gladly carried out much of the dirty work. Despite being in the presence of these murderers, we felt relatively safe in Lvov since there were large numbers of returning Jews like ourselves, and we felt strength in numbers.

But for a Jew to venture into the provinces was considered highly dangerous. In the smaller towns and villages that had been rendered *judenrein* by the Nazis, the local residents – who had profited by grabbing Jewish homes, businesses and other property – did not expect any Jews to be coming back. When some survivors did, in fact, attempt to rejoin their pre-war community, they were met with overt hostility by locals intent on "finishing the job" for Hitler. A key example of this atmosphere was the atrocity known as the Kielce Pogrom.

Prior to the war, one-third of the western Polish city of Kielce's population of 75,000 was Jewish. Most were deported to the Treblinka death camp and murdered there in the summer of 1942. When the war ended for Kielce in January 1945, no Jews remained. But gradually some 200 straggling, skeleton-like survivors returned from the camps and from the forests where they had been hiding. Rather than seeking out revenge against those Poles who had assisted the Nazis in exterminating the Jews of Kielce, most Jews confined themselves to living together in a single building, where they worked and waited for passage to Palestine.

On the morning of July 4, 1946, eighteen months after the city had been liberated from the Nazis, rumors began to circulate throughout town. The rumors were of "blood libel" – the oldest and most primitive manifestation of classical anti-Semitism. The rumors held that at 7 Planty Street, the building housing the Jews, Polish children were being killed on a regular basis by Jews intent on using their blood in the manufacture of *Matzoh*, the Passover bread. The fact that this rumor surfaced in July, two months later than Jews customarily bake *Matzoh*, did not deter it from spreading like wildfire. Soon, a crowd gathered at the building and began openly massacring the Jews. Forty-two were killed and nearly a hundred were wounded. Participating in the mob attack were Poles from all walks of life: peasants, factory workers, housewives, soldiers, students, and members of the intelligentsia. Thousands either took part in the carnage or stood as mute witnesses.

Thanks to Soviet repression, the world did not fully learn about the Kielce pogrom until recently, but to the Jews attempting to reestablish themselves in Eastern Europe after the war, the word spread quickly and the message was a clear one: You can never go home again.

Hearing of similar incidents convinced us that returning home was out of the question, and that we would have to try and get by in Lvov. We found a small apartment and began to rebuild our lives. Eventually, a synagogue was opened, and I finally had the opportunity of participating in the service as an adult by being called to the Torah. I suppose this was my de facto Bar Mitzvah, although there was no celebration of any sort, just me and my father going to *shul* on a Thursday morning. I was given an *aliyah*, and a few congregants shook my hand and wished me a *Mazel Tov*.

Schooling at this point was unavailable, and, of course, we had to make a living. I again sought out the marketplace to buy, barter, or sell whatever I could, in order to help provide for our needs. The marketplace represented the last flicker of free enterprise under the fast encroaching Soviet way of life. The local police, acting under Soviet directive, would regularly head for the market to round up "profiteers" and "hooligans" and would usually target a particular group. One day, the police decided to single out teenagers. They surrounded the open-air marketplace, pulled out all the teenagers, me among them, and placed us all under arrest. A mousy little Ukrainian police sergeant approached me and pointed his pistol at my belly.

"What are you doing here?" he squeaked.

"I'm trying to find some food for my family, officer," I replied.

"Why don't you shop in the government stores?"

"I tried and found them empty," was my reply.

"Ah ha. *Spekulant*. Come with me," he ordered and motioned with his gun.

The round up netted dozens of young Poles, Ukrainians and Russians, but, as far as I knew, I was the only Jew in the group. We were all transported to the police station for questioning. I was placed in an isolated cell, where I sat and waited for several hours. During my wait, I could hear the sounds coming from the adjacent interrogation rooms. I heard shouting, sobs and cries of pain as wooden sticks cracked against flesh. I naturally became alarmed and was certain that this was it. They were going to come into the room and beat me to death!

Finally, a Russian police captain entered and began with routine questioning. "Who are you?" "What are you doing here?" and so on. I answered nervously, but truthfully: "I arrived in Lvov last week with my parents. We are trying to get back to our hometown of Bohorodczany. I was in the marketplace looking for supplies for the journey,"

The captain stared at me, not because of what I had said, but because of the way I had said it. I was speaking to him in perfect Russian.

"Where did you learn to speak such good Russian?" he asked. "Are you a Russian?"

"No, I'm not, but I just came from Russia."

This fact gained his interest and he began to press me for more details. I was happy to oblige since, while he was asking, he wasn't beating. The interview went on for hours as I explained how we got to Kazakhstan and how we made it to Moscow and then to Lvov.

In the end, they never laid a finger on me. I was released late at night and told to stay away from the marketplace and to do my shopping only in government-owned stores. I wanted to tell them that there was nothing to buy in these stores, but I held my tongue and made my way back home to my very worried parents.

Once our lives stabilized in Lvov, our next task was to reunite with Munjee. We knew from his letters that his Polish Army unit was stationed in Wloclawek, near Warsaw. We decided to move to Wloclawek, in order to be close to him. We packed up our few belongings and caught the train to Warsaw. We arrived soon after in Wloclawek and enjoyed an emotional reunion with Munjee at the town's Jewish community center. After we embraced and kissed, Munjee told us of the fighting and his years of service in the Polish Army under the most extreme conditions. He had fought valiantly to liberate Warsaw and had become a passionate firebrand. Now, all he could talk about was Palestine and how we needed to go there to fight the British for a Jewish homeland. In my eyes, he was a true hero, and it was good to have my big brother close by again.

Of course, talk of a Jewish homeland in Palestine was the all-consuming topic among many young Jews returning after the Holocaust. In fact, in Wloclawek, I had joined a laborite Jewish Zionist group known as *Hashomer Hatzair*. I recall that our group was once addressed by a Jewish representative from Palestine named Barzilai, who described Kibbutz life to us in great detail. He urged us to get to Palestine in any way possible, in order to help build the Jewish homeland. After statehood in 1948, Barzilai, a talented musician, became Israel's first ambassador to Poland.

Our finding an apartment near the army base permitted Munjee to visit us regularly. After many months, his unit was demobilized and he moved in with us. I recall how Munjee and I washed dishes in the little dairy café my father soon opened. As we washed the dishes daily, we would dream about the warm sunny life on a Kibbutz. It was at this point that a tragic and transforming event took place.

It was shortly after the July pogrom in Kielce when a similar incident was averted in our community. One afternoon, crowds of Poles started to gather in the Jewish quarter of Wloclawek. They descended upon the town's only kosher butcher shop a few doors from our café. Rumors had been circulating around town all day that the finger of a Christian girl had been found in the meat provided by the kosher butcher. It was another classic blood libel myth that was rooted in centuries of church-sponsored anti-Semitism. How the religious orientation of the severed finger's owner was determined, I do not know.

Amid shouts of "Kill the Yid!" and "Blood Butcher!", the crowd edged forward toward the entrance to the shop. Finally, the butcher, a burly, broad-shouldered man, emerged brandishing an axe.

"Listen to me," he shouted above the noise of the mob. "I survived the death camps, and I am not afraid of you. Any one of you that sets foot across my doorway will have to deal with this!" He waved the axe high above his head. "I'll chop you to pieces if you set foot in here."

At this, the mob backed off and finally dispersed. My father and I witnessed the whole scene, and we became convinced of two things. First, like most cowards, the anti-Semites in this town would retreat at the first sign of any real resistance. Secondly, we understood, as did the more than 200,000 Jews who had just returned to Poland after the war, that this country could no longer serve as our home. Almost all of these 200,000 surviving Jews wound up leaving Poland, a country that only six years before was home to the largest Jewish population in the world (three million).

It took a little time, but eventually even the victors began to understand that most Jewish refugees could never go home again. Since the American occupying forces in Germany and Austria were able to successfully repatriate almost all non-Jewish DPs (displaced persons), they tried, sometimes forcibly, to do the same with Polish Jewish refugees. After all, Poland was the country of their birth, their language and their culture. But after Kielce, and after a group of Jewish repatriates came back to Germany badly wounded, the Americans and the rest of the world began to understand that the problems facing Jews in Poland did not die with Hitler.

We had spoken of leaving Poland before. My father understood, as did I by this time, that living under a Soviet-dominated regime was going to be tough. But initially our culture, our language, and our memories of a better time created an inertia that, for now, kept us in Poland. It was the incident at the butcher shop that was the final straw. At last we came to realize that staying in Poland condemned us to a life of disquiet and danger. After all, what was really keeping us here now? The roots that tied us to this part of the world had been cut off, one-by-one. And so, with the inertia overcome, our family once again prepared to join the flotsam in the maelstrom that was post-war Europe.

We had come back, but we had not come home. The darkness that engulfed us that June of 1941 had not lifted as we had imagined it would. We would have to keep moving a bit longer and a bit further before we could hope to reach the dawn.

Chapter Five

Placed Among the Displaced

T HE UNDERCURRENT of Zionism flowed freely in our family. Emanating from its source, the centuries-old yearning for a return of Jewish sovereignty, this current was fed by wellsprings of Jewish tears and longing whenever and wherever the Diaspora demonstrated the weakness and vulnerability of a nation with no land to call its own.

In the 1930s, my father had met and become an admirer of Ze'ev *(Vladimir)* Jabotinsky, the Zionist leader who declared that European Jewry must reclaim the land of Israel from the Arabs and the British. My father would attend Jabotinsky's public speeches and hear him declare that "Jews must liquidate the Diaspora before the Diaspora liquidates the Jews" – an amazingly prophetic declaration.

While we received the love of Zion with our mother's milk, as a practical matter, immigration to Israel under the British mandate was not something our parents seriously considered. We grew up amid taunts from the local Poles: "Jews – Go Back To Palestine!" While a number of Jews did exactly that, for the vast majority of Europe's Jews, neither the cries of the Zionist nor the Jew-baiter were sufficient to mobilize us into action.

In post-war Poland, young Jews spoke constantly about getting to Palestine in one way or another. But doing so with no money, no papers and against a British quarantine was a formidable challenge. It was within this atmosphere that the *B'richa* conducted its activities. The *B'richa* was an underground organization run by the Jewish Agency. It was involved in smuggling Jews out of Eastern Europe and into Palestine, where they would join the *Hagganah* and become trained as soldiers. This process was known as *Aliyah Bet*. *Aliyah Aleph* was the term for entering Palestine through normal channels, while *Aliyah Bet* referred to the secondary stage of getting Jews to Zion by any means available.

At this point, I was only fifteen and too young to join this underground flow. While I toyed with the idea of entering Palestine to fight for a Jewish homeland, I could not abandon my parents. This was particularly true since my father's health was deteriorating.

Once the decision was reached to leave Poland, my father wasted no time in making preparations. We smuggled ourselves through the woods across the Polish/Czech frontier in the dead of night. After paying off both the Polish and Czech border guards, we traveled to the appointed spot, where we joined roughly three dozen other Jews in the woods to wait for the signal to cross.

Twice we were summoned to the crossing, and twice we were sent back because the right border guard was not yet on duty. Finally, several hours later, on the third try, everything worked and our group was permitted access into Czechoslovakia under the watchful eyes of the border guards. As a final farewell to Poland, or perhaps a final indignity, one of the Czech guards made an announcement: "As you leave, I want you to give me all your cigarettes," he bellowed and took off his peaked cap and held it out.

Passing refugees were required to empty their pockets and dump their cigarettes into the guard's overflowing cap. My last image of Poland was of a smirking border guard counting up his booty of cigarettes.

Once we got past this guard, I knew we were safe. On the Czech side, we were greeted by Jewish Agency representatives who loaded us onto waiting trucks destined for Bratislava. In Bratislava, we found ourselves in a huge transit camp, whose major activity was sorting out the post-war chaos.

Conditions were terrible. Many hundreds of Jews from all over Europe were crowded into bomb-ravaged buildings. We slept, when it was possible to sleep, on army cots, and we ate whatever we had brought with us. The atmosphere was that of a rescue shelter or evacuation center after some great calamity or disaster. We were evacuees whisked from a storm of anti-Semitism that has not fully subsided to this day.

I don't ever recall feeling a touch of regret about leaving my homeland behind. Polish hatred had cleansed my heart of any vestige of nationalistic feelings. Through no choice of my own, I no longer felt myself a Pole. Perhaps I had never been one. But I was definitely a Jew, and I knew I would remain one forever.

After a few days in Bratislava, a group of us were directed to head toward the Austrian border on foot. We were shuffled quickly across the border and used trains, buses and jeeps to travel to another transit camp near Vienna. It was here that we joined the flood of displaced persons in the war's backwash. We did not realize it at the time, but we were part of a major chapter in Jewish history.

By VE Day, May 8, 1945, the war had created over 100,000 Jewish displaced persons (DP's) liberated in the western Allied-occupied zones. These Jews, along with those soon to join them from eastern Europe, were the *She'eirit HaPleitah*, the surviving remnant. They had endured the extermination camps, the forced labor camps, the ghettos, the death marches and more. While the Allies made attempts at repatriation, most Jews could not, and would not, return to their Holocaust-haunted homes. Instead, they were collected in a series of DP camps in Allied-occupied western Europe, and it was within these camps that a national consciousness with a political agenda was incubated. The agenda was a simple one: national redemption. The surviving remnant must emigrate from the ashes of Europe back to the soil of Palestine and there establish Eretz Yisroel, a new Jewish homeland.

For us, as for the other surviving Jews from Eastern Europe and Russia, conditions continued to deteriorate. Fleeing from ongoing anti-Semitism and encroaching Soviet domination, our family joined the more than 100,000 other Jews pouring into the Allied DP camps. By the end of 1946, there were roughly a quarter million Jews housed in the camps, with 45,000 of us located in Austria. This influx of mostly Polish Jews changed the demographics of the DP Camps. While originally made up of single stragglers, the population after 1946 consisted mostly of family groups like ours.

Our eventual fate, as well as the conditions under which we lived, became an international political issue. In particular, at the former concentration camps that were, by then, being administered by the US Army, decisions had to be made about how to deal with the pathetic, starving victims. The army provided medical attention and food, but it was unable to conduct repatriation and continued to intern the survivors as prisoners in the camps. Aside from the fact that the US was not carrying out gassings, it appeared that the army had simply taken over the role of the Nazis.

Receiving word of these conditions, President Truman dispatched Earl G. Harrison as his personal envoy to investigate conditions in the American Zone camps. He described the camps as awful and blamed the military administration for the disgraceful state of affairs. He was convinced that the only solution was for the British to immediately grant 100,000 entry permits into Palestine and make them available to all Jewish DPs.

Truman agreed with the report's findings and worked to persuade the British to increase Jewish immigration into Palestine. The British, concerned about arousing Arab animosity and disrupting their flow of Middle East oil, never agreed to raise the Jewish quota above the standing 15,000 per annum level. Despite a half-century of lip service in favor of a Jewish homeland, starting with the Balfour Declaration, it was clear to the British that Arab oil was more valuable than Jewish blood.

To me, this was no surprise. I recall my father telling us: "Jabotinsky said that no one is going to hand the Jews a state on a silver platter. If we want a Jewish homeland, we must be prepared to fight for it and shed Jewish blood." How true. How sad.

Conditions in the American Zone camps improved vastly after the issuance of the Harrison Report. Jews were afforded a special status and were no longer grouped together according to their prewar nationalities. A special advisor on Jewish affairs was appointed at the US military headquarters in Germany. The care and well-being of the DPs was entrusted by the military to United Nations Relief and Rescue Association (UNRRA) and its successor, the International Refugee Organization (IRO). These groups provided the basic necessities of life, as well as coordination of the various social welfare agencies active in the camps.

At the Vienna transfer center, we were placed on trucks and driven to a DP camp called St. Marein in the British occupation zone of Austria. The barracks of St. Marein were our home for the next several months. Conditions were somewhat better, and an air of normalcy was beginning to emerge as people attempted to establish the routines of day-to-day life. I was even able to begin attending classes and playing soccer with other youngsters my age.

I recall representatives from all sorts of agencies and organizations offering help and recruiting members in the camps. The Jewish Brigade Group from Palestine told us of their role serving under the British during the war. The global Jewish relief agency known as the Joint Distribution Committee was highly active, visibly directing basic aid such as clothing, toiletries and food to the needy. ORT *(Obschestvo Remeslenovo i zemledelcheskovo Trouda,* meaning The Society for Trades and Agricultural Labor) was on the scene establishing vocational trade schools as well.

As always, my father was not one to be easily content with his situation. While conditions were tolerable in the British DP camp, he felt uncomfortable being under the supervision of a regime that was at the same time responsible for suppressing Jewish immigration into Palestine. While on the one hand serving as our liberators, the British had greatly disappointed all of us. We witnessed how they disregarded their own Balfour Declaration, which had called for the establishment of a Jewish homeland decades earlier. We felt betrayed by the British, whose policy of Arab accommodation and acquiescence resulted in the creation of an enormous barrier to our hopes of leaving the ashes of Europe behind and starting a fresh life in *Eretz Yis-rael*. I also suspect that Dad already had, in the back of his mind, the idea of immigrating to America. Whatever his motives, after a few months at St. Marein, he arranged to have us transferred to the Ranshofen DP camp near Braunau am Inn in the US Zone near the German border. Braunau is known as the birthplace of Adolf Hitler. Today, no monument marks this spot. In fact only two words appear over the doorway of Hitler's birthplace: "Never Again!"

Conditions at Ranshofen were substantially better. Instead of living in barracks, we were housed in three-story brick buildings. We remained in Ranshofen for several months until it was eventually closed down. While others were repatriated or emigrated to Palestine or other countries, we did not yet have a specific destination. Hence, we were shifted to yet another DP camp in the American Zone called Ebelsberg, near Linz, Austria.

The years spent in Ebelsberg were undoubtedly the most formative and influential of my life. Long-term friendships were forged as my world out-look was being molded. I soon fell in with other young survivors whose lives, like mine, had been scoured like the blade of a knife. All entangling links to our former existence had been broken by the war. As a result, and perhaps driven by a sense of guilt, many were filled with a sort of bluster or bravado. The over-arching attitude, not surprisingly, was "Never Again!" Never again will we be led like sheep to the slaughterhouse. If we are attacked again, we will be on our feet and not on our knees. I shared these sentiments, despite the obvious fact that we could not possibly be the captains of our own des-tiny while languishing in a DP camp.

There was little overt despair over lost loved ones, and there were only occasional flashes of revenge or retribution against the perpetrators. Occasion-ally, one Jew would denounce another as a "kapo," a camp collaborator who, in order to save his own skin, provided assistance to the Nazis. I saw with my own eyes how the unmasked kapo would meet with swift justice at the hands of survivors who made certain he would "Never Again" see the light of day.

We attempted, as best as we could, to memorialize the dead somehow. We had no graves to visit. Because most of us did not know the exact date our loved ones had perished, *yahrtzeit* prayers were next to impossible. Our camp was near the notorious Mauthausen concentration camp where 36,000 prisoners were worked to death in the nearby stone quarry. I recall a camp ceremony during which ashes from Mauthausen's crematoria were placed into a glass box, so the remains could be transported to Palestine. My father was one of the speakers at the ceremony, and he helped to seal the box for shipment. Years later, after my father's death, I visited the Yad Vashem Holocaust memorial in Jerusalem and saw the same box on display. Today, it serves as a link to the victims of the *Shoah* and, for me, as a tangible link to my father.

The political milieu in the DP camps was characterized by layers of complexity and competing cross-currents. The youth group I had originally joined in Wloclawek, *Hashomer Hatzair*, like the Socialist group *D'ror*, was aligned with the leftist ideologies advocating a bi-national state in Palestine. While this faction represented the majority, I soon switched to *Betar*, the youth group of Jabotinsky's right-wing Revisionist Party. *Betar* (an acronym for *Brit Trumpledor*, named after the one-armed Russian martyr who gave his life defending the land of Israel against Arab attack) believed that Jews needed to reclaim the ancient land from whoever now held it, be it Arab or Englishman, in order to establish a modern Jewish state.

It was at this point that I first heard about a man named Begin. His name was whispered with reverence throughout the alleyways and backrooms of all the Jewish DP camps. Menachem Begin was the leader of *Etzel* – the *Irgun Zvai Leumi*, the Military Nationalist Organization, or simply the *Irgun*. *Irgun*, along with the *Hagganah*, comprised the core of Jewish resistance to the British colonial government in Palestine. Both groups were considered illegal by the British. But since the *Hagganah*, whose Jewish Brigade had served under the British during the war, was viewed as the less extreme of the two, its activities were somewhat tolerated by the authorities. The *Irgun*, however, was viewed by the British as an underground terrorist organization. During the war, the *Hagganah* had advocated restraint and cooperation in dealing with the British and the Arabs. The *Irgun*, conversely, adopted a more militant position and vocally called for an immediate revolt against Britain while the war against the Nazis was still being waged.

The *Irgun* was founded by Jabotinsky in Palestine in 1931 as a non-Socialist military arm of the Revisionist Party, whose policies called for the creation of a Jewish state, by force if necessary, on both sides of the Jordan. Despite their calls for liberation from the British, the *Irgun* had actually worked secretly with the British against the common Nazi enemy. In fact, one of the *Irgun*'s first leaders – the mysterious military genius

David Raziel – was killed while conducting an underground mission to Iraq in behalf of the British army. The loss of Raziel in 1942, shortly after Jabotinsky's death, took a heavy toll on the *Irgun*, as did the split in the group led by Avraham Stern. Yaakov Meridor was chosen to head the organization, but he was not successful in revitalizing it. Begin, a senior and charismatic *Betar* leader from Poland, who had just recently arrived in Palestine, was persuaded to take over the reins from Meridor in December, 1943. He immediately undertook a tactical campaign of revolt and resistance, which eventually succeeded in driving the British out of Palestine.

During the critical years of 1946 and 1947, the British had placed a price on Begin's head, and this fact only made him more of a hero to our *Betar* group. Begin and the *Irgun* were whipping the British in Palestine. Stories of his activities filled us with an entirely new emotion: Jewish pride, or what Jabotinsky referred to as *Hadar*. While I was brought up by my father and grandfather with a strong sense of pride in the history of the Jewish people, this was different. My newfound pride arose from what my fellow Jews were doing in Palestine right now…not 2,000 years ago.

Begin's voice was an inspiring call to arms to all the displaced and dispossessed young Jews of Europe. "You are the Hebrew soldiers," he would declare. He would often repeat Jabotinsky's well-known admonition: "The blood of the Maccabees flows in your veins!" Begin's words held a resonance that went beyond mere youthful romanticism. There was a flavor to his rhetoric that transcended our recent history and tapped into the most basic ancient roots of the Jewish people.

On February 1, 1944, Begin's well-known "Proclamation of the Revolt" was first distributed by leaflet throughout Palestine, after having been broadcast over the *Irgun*'s clandestine radio station. *Betar* groups like ours circulated the Proclamation throughout the DP camps. With my glue bucket and *Rak Kach* posters, I became known as a prolific pamphleteer. I would often show up in class with hundreds of such leaflets stuffed under my shirt. An excerpt from the Proclamation:

Hebrews!

The establishment of the Hebrew Government and the realization of its program is the sole way to rescue our people, to save our existence and our honor. We will go in this path, because there is no other. We will fight. Every Jew in the homeland will fight.

Hebrews!

The fighting youth will not be deterred by victims, blood, and suffering. It will not surrender, it will not rest, as long as our days have not been renewed as of old, as long as our people is not assured of a homeland, freedom, honor, bread, righteousness, and justice. And if you will surely aid it, then your eyes will soon see in our time the return to Zion and the renaissance of Israel. This and more may G-d grant us!

Excerpt from the Proclamation of the Revolt, 1944

The Insignia of the Irgun Zvai Leumi

While our family never fit the stereotype of the eternally victimized *shtetl* Jew, since we had too much Jewish pride for that, I still felt that Begin and *Betar* represented a metamorphosis. A tough new Jew was emerging from the ashes – one filled with pride and a love of Zion, ready to fight to reclaim and defend our rightful homeland. A Jew not bound by the tired, failed ideologies of Socialism. A Jew no longer willing to suffer the bigot and the anti-Semite. This was the Jew of the future. This was the Jew I became, and this is the Jew I remain to this day.

Our pride was reinforced daily thanks to the interaction with the surrounding Austrians. We understood that Austria had given birth to the most virulent strain of Nazism. We knew that not only Hitler, but Eichmann and many other Nazi fanatics were Austrians. Our *Betar* group would often come in contact with young Austrian men at the soccer games we attended. These encounters would sometimes explode into fist fights and worse. I recall our hubris, as a mere dozen of us would come face to face with thousands of Austrians at these soccer matches. We would confront them and taunt them: "We are still here. You didn't kill us all. We're not afraid of you and we're here to kick your ass!" This wasn't hollow boasting. We were really not afraid any longer. The Austrians and the Germans were now the defeated people facing the dead end of history, and although we were the ones in the camps, we saw ourselves as the powerful wave of the future.

Another factor that contributed to our fearlessness was the fact that we were being trained in weapons combat by the *Betar* leadership. I carried a pistol and regularly underwent target practice and small arms drills in the forests near the camp. We knew we were being trained to fight the British, the Arabs and anyone else who stood in the way of a Jewish homeland in Palestine.

In effect, we also became the protectors of the camp. We had our own Jewish police force that maintained order in the enclave. I recall how, at one point, a busload of Austrian police streamed into the camp looking for a fugitive who they believed was hiding amongst us. We gathered in the street and blocked their advance. "Stop. Turn around and get the hell out of here!" we proclaimed. "You have no authority in here. We are the authority in this camp, not you." I don't believe they knew that we were armed, since we kept our weapons hidden, but they were convinced. They backed off, turned and departed, never to set foot into the camp again. I know that, to a man, we were all prepared to use our weapons to defend the camp from the Austrians, if push had come to shove.

We shared a certain bravado and toughness born from our recent common experiences, and also from a certain unnatural selection process. We were the only Jews from our town who had found the wherewithal to pack up and flee the advancing Nazis. Those who did not share this tenacity were all gone. Similarly, while survival during the Holocaust was mostly a matter of luck it also required a certain toughness and resilience. The young people of the camps all shared these qualities, since those who did not...those with timid personalities or poor survival skills, had all been burned away in the crucible of the Holocaust. And it was these same tenacious qualities that we observed and so admired in Begin and his philosophy. It is safe to say that he was my hero, and I was prepared and anxious to follow his leadership.

While my peers and I emerged from the Holocaust ready to take on the world, there was also a sizable contingent that clung to their classic liberal beliefs. This so-called "intellectual" faction advocated a naïve support for a bi-national secular state in Palestine that would somehow share sovereignty with the Arabs under a democratically elected government. They were of the school that didn't want to make waves. They urged *havlagah* (restraint) in dealing with the British and the Arabs. The intellectual faction wished to hold more discussions with the British to persuade them to issue another White Paper that would allow for more Jewish immigration into Palestine.

They did not understand the realities of the situation. They did not see that Britain had absolutely no incentive to comply with Jewish requests issued from a position of weakness – particularly when doing so would endanger their relationship with the Arab majority in the region.

I personally rejected the prevailing politics of accommodation. I believed, and I still believe, that this is the path of weakness, and that this path leads directly to Auschwitz. In order to effect change, Jews, or anyone else for that matter, must be able to operate from a position of strength. Become strong and the world will listen. Remain weak and the world will insure your silence.

The prevailing liberal attitude was reinforced by the Jewish population in Palestine, under the leadership of the Ben Gurion-led Jewish Agency, which was exporting its doctrines to the camps. The camp schools were filled with Jews from Palestine who spread this liberal dogma. But we weren't buying it. I would often come into conflict with these teachers who spotted my right-wing *Betar* leaflets when I attended class after having been up all night emblazoning the walls and fences of the camp with posters and graffiti slogans. *Rak Kach*. Only thus. Both sides of the Jordan. Resistance, not restraint.

By age sixteen, I was anxious to arrive in Palestine and join the ranks of the *Irgun* fighters under Begin's leadership. But there were several problems. First and foremost, the British were not permitting any sizable legal immigration. As mentioned, the Jewish Agency had established the *B'richa* that was conducting illegal refugee smuggling into Palestine in a program known as *Aliyah Bet*. However, politics ruled the *B'richa*, and they were unwilling to permit *Betarim* (right-wing youth) to join the underground stream. Obviously, they were not inclined to import Jews whom they regarded as likely troublemakers and eventual political opponents. So, we waited along the sidelines as world events came into play. The courageous efforts of the *Irgun* and the *Hagganah* were taking their toll on British patience in Palestine. Incidents, such as the case of the Exodus, an immigrant transport ship denied entry and sent back to Europe by the British, were changing world opinion about a Jewish homeland. These factors, coupled with a growing awareness of Nazi atrocities coming to light, helped to generate an atmosphere of sympathy for the Jewish plight. In November, 1947, Britain accepted a United Nations resolution calling for the end of the mandate in May of the following year.

When May arrived, the earth-shaking news that the UN had approved the partition of Palestine into Jewish and Arab states set the DP camps aflame with excitement. The partition was to go into effect on the day the British flag was lowered, and at that moment, the new State of Israel was born, creating a politically sovereign Jewish nation for the first time in close to 2,000 years. Of course, this act also marked the beginning of the War of Independence, as all of the Arab states in the region mobilized armies and attacked the new nation in its birth throes. Our joy was boundless, and our desire to run to Israel's side was almost overpowering.

My brother yielded to that desire and announced his plans to join the fighting. Munjee was now known as Mark, and he had grown into an assertive and passionate Zionist. Like me, Mark was aligned with the *Irgun*, and it was through them that he arranged his passage. Separate from the *B'richa*, the *Irgun* had its own underground smuggling operation in place, albeit on a smaller scale. In June 1948, Mark said good-bye to us and took off for Port-de-Bouc, France, where the *Irgun* had arranged for his secret passage to Israel aboard the freighter Altalena. The Altalena, loaded with fighters and military equipment, was shelled by Ben Gurion and the Israeli military. Its story has been well-documented and I will not expound upon it here. Learning of this disgraceful incident through Mark's letters convinced me even more of the correctness of our position in supporting *Betar*. I had expressed a strong desire to join my brother on his journey to Israel, but I was not old enough. The *Irgun* had established eighteen as the minimum age for passage aboard the Altalena. At 17, I was too young to join Mark, so I remained behind, stuck and still waiting in the camp with my parents.

Although, as a *Betar* member, I now found myself in the political minority, the one issue that united the prevailing right and left wings was Zionist fervor. We all wanted to leave Europe and the Holocaust behind and make *Aliyah* to Israel. Regardless of where we stood on the political spectrum, we were filled with a zeal to demonstrate our newly found toughness by standing up to the Arabs. We understood that the only way to regain respect in the eyes of the world, the only way to forever bury the stereotype of the Jew as history's perpetual victim, was to stand up and fight for a Jewish state. Even if we failed, it would still show the world that Jews were willing to risk their lives for the establishment of a Zionist homeland.

Eventually, it was this mindset that accounted for Israel's success in its War of Independence. To the 600,000 Jewish inhabitants of the new State of Israel facing the twenty-two million strong Arab enemy, the numbers didn't matter. They fought as if they had nowhere else to turn if they lost, because, in fact, they did not. They fought as if they were trying to violently shake off the image of the cowering *shtetl* Jew. Because, in fact, they were. They fought as if they had already seen the consequences of defeat, known as Auschwitz, and as if death in battle was infinitely more attractive.

In the midst of this highly charged environment, I suddenly found myself facing an enormous dilemma. My father, always one to swim against the tide, had put our names on a waiting list for immigration. Not to the new State of Israel, but to the US – to America!

The shock and disappointment I felt at this development was profound. My mother went along with my father's decision, but I did not. I was a minor, still tied to my parents, but my heart was in Jerusalem, not in New York. I was overcome with shame as I revealed this traitorous act to my pals and buddies, most of whom were heading for Israel. I considered running off and joining Mark, but I could not abandon my parents. In particular, one of the factors driving my father's desire to go to America was his health. Although it had not yet been diagnosed, he was suffering from emphysema, and he correctly understood that he would receive far better medical attention in the US than in Israel.

Mark was our war correspondent, and his letters kept us up to date on conditions. The *Irgun* and *Hagganah* had merged into the Israeli Defense Forces, which still serve today as the core of Israel's military establishment. Their ranks filled with young survivors of Hitler's death machine, the IDF led Israel to an historic victory in 1948. My brother fought bravely for the liberation of Jaffa and served in the infantry during combat in Jerusalem. I still regret not being on hand to savor the sweet taste of triumph washing away the taste of Holocaust ashes from my mouth.

After Israel had gained her independence, the letters from Mark explained that he was now not only demilitarized, but also growing demoralized. His letters grew more and more despondent as he searched for work and the basic needs of life in war-ravaged Israel. He painted a desperate picture of people living on the beaches in flimsy shacks. The economy was non-existent, with precious little social welfare, widespread hunger and even cases of starvation. Because of his right-wing politics, Mark was something of an outcast under the new labor-led Israeli government. He did not see a promising future for himself in the new socialist-led state, and he soon began to speak of returning to Europe.

The picture we received from Mark served to convince my father even more that he was correct in seeking passage to the US. While I still harbored strong Zionist feelings during these years, and while I still felt that I was being held somewhat against my will in the camp, I came to understand that Dad's position was right. And he needed me at his side if we were to be successful in forging a new life for our family in America. I was brought up to respect my parents, so I stayed at their side for nearly five long years as we awaited word from the American embassy.

As we languished and lingered those last several years, the camp population diminished due to repatriation and emigration, and we once again had to be relocated when the Ebelsberg camp was liquidated. We next found ourselves in a nearby camp known as Asten, outside of Linz, billeted in former military housing units. We were given a small apartment with a bathroom at the end of the hall. We had come a long way from the public cesspools of Alga.

It was during those years that, like all young men, I began to mature physically and intellectually. I look back upon myself during those post-puberty years as being perpetually in love. The young women of the camps, like all of us, had had their souls rubbed raw by the war. Many were hungry for some sort of emotional stability and fell easily, perhaps too easily, into romantic liaisons. Going out with a young lady on a date gave us a sense of normality, of how life was before the war. We would go to the cinema or a camp theater performance and try to make small talk, although the conversation would always wind up on the same subjects: Palestine, the *Irgun* and eventually, Israel. While I saw myself as a zealot, I'm sure some of my dates must have thought me something of a bore.

I filled my days, and many of my nights, with my underground work. Before Israeli independence, spreading the message of the *Irgun* took precedence over my schoolwork, and this fact led to problems. As stated, the school teachers were, for the most part, Jews of a decidedly left-wing bent. My politics were well-known, and this led to run-ins that eventually labeled me as something of a truant and delinquent. Showing up late for class with *Rak Kach* leaflets stuffed under my shirt was a sure way to gain the animosity of the teachers. One incident stands to illustrate my state of mind at this point.

My science and mathematics teacher, one Mr. Elephant (yes, that really was his name) was a rather strict disciplinarian. His students were required to stand whenever he entered the room and when he exited. He was aware of my right-wing activities, and I was often singled out when Mr. Elephant wished to make an example of someone. After some minor infraction, Mr. Elephant insisted that I bring my parents to the school the following day to consult with him about my deportment. I did not convey this message to my parents. When they failed to appear, Mr. Elephant insisted that they be summoned for the following day.

When, after several days, my parents did not show up, Mr. Elephant became enraged at my defiance and ordered: "Out! Get out of my classroom and only return with your parents!" When I did not budge from my seat, he dismissed the class and ordered me to stay and stand by my desk. As soon as my classmates had departed, I immediately sat back down, an act which Mr. Elephant correctly interpreted as disrespectful. "Just what I expected from a delinquent like you," he bellowed as he grabbed me by the lapels and dragged me to my feet. I drew back my arm and was ready to fight, when he backed down and commanded me to accompany him to the principal's office. Once there, Mr. Elephant demanded my immediate expulsion from the school, since I was obviously a fanatic sociopath. The principal sent me home and said he would get back to me after things cooled down.

Meanwhile, my classmates rallied to my support. They encouraged me not to retreat and supported my defiance of Elephant. Encouraged by this show of solidarity, I organized a mini-rebellion. We all marched on the principal's office and told him that if I were to be expelled, all the other students in my class would organize a boycott and shut down the school.

The principal called a meeting of all the parents and, of course, Mr. Elephant was on hand. The teacher had obviously been chastened, since his demeanor was that of a changed man. The principal announced that classes would resume as normal and that all students were expected to attend. He and Elephant assured us that students would be treated with respect in the future, and in fact, it was so. I eventually became one of Elephant's top students, and in very short order, we became close friends. I learned a great deal of math and science from Mr. Elephant, but I also learned that sometimes a little friction can create enough heat to produce a warm and lasting friendship over time.

My delinquency extended beyond the classroom. I had become adept at an arcane skill that literally served to open many doors for me in the camps. I soon developed a reputation as the camp's premier lock-picker. Once I had a piece of wire in my fingers, no lock in the area was safe. But it was not for thievery or any sort of personal gain that I employed this skill. It was only used for the cause. After breaking and entering a locked up theater during the night, our crew would decorate the place with *Irgun* posters and slogans in order to spread our message to the public. My buddies and I would go from building to building plastering them inside and out with our succinct message: Only thus! Today this might be viewed as vandalism or graffiti, but as young idealists, we were on a crusade to mobilize a people and move it toward statehood. Compared to the incomprehensible crimes that had been perpetrated against us, our petty misdemeanors seemed rather tame.

In addition to the skills I learned on the street, I was fortunate to benefit from the vocational training made available in the camps through ORT. ORT's mission was to rapidly imbue Europe's young refugees who, like me, had been denied a normal education. With marketable crafts and skills, we would be enabled to start earning a living. ORT offered classes in auto mechanics, jewelry making, cooking and so on. I was an accomplished tinsmith and had experience working with metal, so when I saw a class in engraving being offered, I immediately signed up.

An elderly Austrian gentleman, Herr Müller, who had served as the royal engraver for Emperor Franz Joseph, became our teacher. He invited me to his home one day and showed me some samples of his exquisite work. I fell in love with engraving and soon began working very hard to improve my style and technique. During the year that I spent under Müller's tutelage, I became highly skilled at creating decorative filigree for jewelry, trophies and the like. Müller offered strong encouragement. He would take me aside after reviewing my work and tell me, "You are going to be very good at this someday." As it turned out, it was my engraving skills that landed me my first long-term job in the US and launched my business career. I will always owe a lifelong debt of gratitude to Herr Müller, and particularly to ORT, for providing me with the opportunity to learn this splendid craft.

I also used my time in the camps to develop other artistic skills, such as music. My love of music grew out of an episode that took place back in Kazakhstan when I was twelve years old. I was lying on my bed when a passage of the most soulful stringed music in the world reached my ears. I immediately ran outside to find its source. The music was emanating from a neighboring building. I entered the building and followed the melody to the correct room and walked in. And what I discovered shocked and amazed me. Sitting on the floor was a hugely deformed midget playing a bowl-backed mandolin. The instrument was almost as large as his misshapen body. He was accompanied by a guitarist and vocalist, and they were performing a repertoire of Russian folk songs. The little mandolinist was unable to hold the instrument to his body in the normal manner and, instead, laid it on the floor as he plucked and fretted it, using only two fingers from each deformed hand. He was also able to brilliantly play the guitar in this unusual fashion. *This is impossible*, I thought. *Such beautiful music being produced by such an unattractive little man.* I was totally fascinated, and by the end of the day, I had fallen in love with this music and wanted to make it my own.

I pestered my father for months until he finally relented and purchased a mandolin for me. It was old and in poor condition, but to me, it was a gift from G-d. I worked at it daily without fail until my fingers were calloused and bleeding. I worked out all the Russian folk melodies by ear, mostly by imitating the midget mandolinist, and I was soon entertaining my parents and their few friends in Alga. I was not interested in lyrics or in playing accompaniments. I loved melodies and played them exclusively. Sadly, the mandolin wound up in the lost steamer chest, and my musical career was put on hold once we left Kazakhstan.

After we had settled in the camps, Dad recalled how I was musically inclined and how much pleasure my music had afforded our whole family. The mandolin was not a serious instrument, however, and he wanted me to attend the conservatory and study music properly. So, he located and purchased an old violin for me. The violin has the same four strings, and is tuned to the same notes as a mandolin, so the transition was relatively easy, once I mastered the use of the bow. My father enrolled me in the Brückner Conservatory of Music in Linz, where I studied violin and music theory for about six months. I learned to read music and became something of prodigy in a very short time. My instructor told me: "You have the talent to become a first-rate violinist if you choose to. But you must practice at least three hours per day without fail."

At this same period, however, I became seriously interested in sports, especially in soccer. Soccer practice took place after school, which directly conflicted with my music lessons and daily practice time. So, I had to make a difficult choice. For a time, I stayed with the violin, but after a few months, the weather turned warm and I began to question my decision. *Am I going to give up soccer, give up playing outdoors and competing with the other boys in order to stand here alone in my room all day dragging this bow across the strings?* I asked myself. The world of music suffered a great loss that day, I'm sure, when I decided to forego my violin studies for the soccer fields of Ebelsberg.

As the months went by, I became resigned to our family's plans. I knew I had to shift my focus towards our life ahead in America. I began to study English and to set aside my Zionist dreams. By this point in my life, I had learned the value of being adaptable. I began to mature from the young DP camp commando into a serious 19-year-old determined to become success-ful in the land of opportunity.

By the end of 1950, most of the DP camps had been closed, and we were one of the few remaining families still awaiting resettlement. But we never gave up hope. Finally, in January 1951, the word we had been await-ing arrived. We were granted permission to set sail for America under the Polish immigration quota. Our family was instructed to report to the port of Bremerhaven in sixty days to board the ss General Muir bound for New York harbor. But another obstacle was awaiting us.

As soon as we arrived in Bremerhaven, my father took seriously ill. He was hospitalized with a severe case of pneumonia, and we feared not only that we would lose our passage, but that we might, in fact, lose Dad. He had been a heavy smoker in his youth, and this bout of pneumonia was brought on by the early stages of emphysema.

We were put up in transit center barracks, and I was given a new pair of shoes by the Joint Distribution Committee. I remember wearing those shoes out by marching several times each day back and forth to the hospital.

"Tatu, you've got to get better," I would plead. "We've waited five years to go to America, and now we're going to miss the boat." I also implored his doctor, whose written release was required before my father would be admitted on board: "You've got to release my father. We've got to get on that boat!"

I don't know if my pep talk did any good, but on the last day before we were scheduled to set sail, the doctor signed the release. On the following day mother and I assisted my very weakened father as he made his way on board. The ship was an aging military supply ship with only a few staterooms and bunk-bed dormitories set up, one for men and one for women, in ship's steerage. Dad spent the entire passage crowded into the bowels of the ship on a cot below decks. His chronic seasickness was complicating his recovery. I would try to bring him special food that would not upset his stomach. To accomplish this more easily, and to gain access to better food than was available to the rest of the passengers in steerage, I secured a job in the ship's galley. I was strong and tough and could quickly load and unload the many crates, boxes and bags of food supplies.

Many of the other refugees on board were also feeling seasick and would ask me to smuggle out onions (an old world remedy for *mal-de-mère*) for them to eat. Their condition seemed to improve, although their breath got worse. It was there in the ship's galley, amid the dirty dishes and garbage, that I first came into contact with real Americans and got a whiff of a new and exciting way of life.

Those dozen days on board the ss Muir represented my first heady exposure to American-style liberty. I met African-Americans for the first time and was quickly charmed by their easy manner. They were quite muscular, as was I by this point, and we would engage in friendly arm-wrestling bouts to fill the time. The spirit of freedom evident among the entire crew was infectious. I got a taste of what living in a free society was all about – and I thought it tasted great! I made up my mind that if I concentrated and worked hard, I could achieve great things in America.

Even before my arrival, I felt that America was the place I had been looking for all of my life. I envisioned it as a place where people were normal and things made sense, where everyone, even the government, behaved logically and with compassion. I had always felt that my life, and the world I inhabited, had somehow been unnatural and inverted, and that somewhere in the world there must be a place where things worked the way they should. The same American Dream that had lured millions to its shores was now beckoning me. I may not have been one of those huddled masses, but I was definitely yearning to be free.

It was these thoughts that coursed through my mind as I stood on the wind-swept deck on the afternoon of April 10, 1951, alongside hundreds of other refugees, as we glided into New York harbor and I first set eyes on that beautiful lady with the lamp.

Chapter Six

New Home, New Hope

IT WAS A PUZZLING, yet exhilarating feeling that I couldn't quite explain. I had never before set foot in the States. Yet, as we gazed upon the Statue of Liberty, I immediately felt at home. In fact, after fifty years, I still feel at home. I get goose bumps thinking about those first dramatic moments in this beautiful new land. I recall looking up and seeing a dirigible in the sky for the first time in my life. I assumed it was there to welcome us to America.

I did not bring along too many naïve notions about *de goldeneh medinah*. I knew that America was a rich country, but I also understood that I would be working very hard. I would be the sole or primary breadwinner for our family, and I had a lot of education to catch up on. In my enthusiasm, however, I became convinced that in America, I could accomplish anything I chose.

Once disembarked, we were met by a HIAS (Hebrew Immigrant Aid Society) representative who quickly escorted us through customs and immigration. We witnessed scenes of tearful emotion as war-torn families were reunited at the dock. But unlike them, we had no one to greet us. We had no ties to America at all, and this fact had contributed to our long delay in entering the country. We bypassed Ellis Island, whose immigration processing facility had recently been closed, and headed straight for the dock on the mainland.

Back in Austria, where my father had first discreetly applied for immigration at the US Consulate, he was asked where in the US he wished to reside.

"In New York," he replied.

"I'm sorry, Mr. Hasten, but New York is full," replied the clerk. "There are too many immigrants there already. Do you have a second choice?"

"No, not really. How about some place where the weather is like in Poland?" said my father after a bit of reflection.

"Well, let's see. Poland is pretty cold, so why don't we send you to Minnesota. It's plenty cold there."

Dad agreed.

So, without time to see much of New York City, we were packed off by train to Minneapolis by the Jewish resettlement agency. On route to the train station we were given some cash and I saw American currency for the first time. I recall being puzzled by the fact that a nickel was bigger than a dime but was worth half as much. *This country will take some getting used to*, I thought.

After an overnight train ride, we arrived in Minneapolis. There we were met by a German-speaking representative of the Jewish Family and Children's Service, a Miss Berman. A single woman in her thirties, Miss Berman's job was to assist new Jewish immigrants in getting on their feet in Minneapolis. Her first step was to give us a ride in her car for a quick tour of the city. I stared from the window of the big sedan as she pointed out a synagogue here and a grocery there. Although I tried to act blasé, I could barely contain my excitement. Our final stop was a dilapidated hotel where I was brought down to earth. This was to be our temporary digs. It was a run-down dump, but the lobby held a device I had only heard about until now. I'll never forget my first glimpse of the gray, ghost-like figures moving across the tiny television screen. I had never seen TV before, and I found it completely fascinating.

After a few nights stay in this seedy flophouse, Miss Berman drove us to our new apartment. It was a second floor walk-up with a private bathroom located in a small building at 1912 Glenwood Avenue. The apartment contained a few pieces of donated furniture, and Mama quickly went to work turning it into what would be our home for the next few years.

My first priority, of course, was to find work. Finishing my schooling would have to wait until I was able to earn enough to put food on the table. I recall sitting down with Miss Berman and reviewing my qualifications and education for an employment form she was completing. The form's first question, naturally, asked for my name. My family and friends called me Hetche, but the first name on all my documents was Hertz.

"You know, Hertz, that name sounds a little too German for America," explained Miss Berman. "Would you consider changing it?"

"I guess so, but I'll have to ask my parents," I replied. "Change it to what?"

"I don't know. How about Harry?" she suggested.

"No. If I call myself Harry, everyone will think I'm trying to be the president," I responded. "Any other names?"

"Well, we could try Herman, but that's also rather German-sounding. You know, I've always liked the name Hart."

"Heart? Doesn't that mean *Herz*?" I asked her in German.

She explained about the difference in spelling and pointed out that a hart was a stag or a male red deer. I liked that image and I liked the sound of the name at once.

"Okay. That's fine. Let's put down Hart. Hart Hasten," I declared. "I'll make sure my parents don't object."

As it turns out, the name was highly appropriate for another reason. My actual Hebrew name is Naftali, for one of the original twelve tribes of Israel described in the Torah. Each tribe had a trademark or logo emblazoned on its tents and shields. The logo of the Naftali tribe was the male deer, or hart. I soon adopted Hart as my first name and began using N., for Naftali, as a middle initial. Some five years later, when I applied for US citizenship, I legally changed my name to Hart N. Hasten.

The resettlement agency had found a manual labor job for me and I began work within a few days. I was hired as a presser by a small company owned by a pair of Jewish brothers named Barnett. I operated an electric hand iron and was paid eighty cents per hour. The company manufactured and distributed a line of women's coats. Originally they had asked if I could work as a maintenance man, but since I knew no English whatsoever, this job was out of the question. They did agree to train me on a commercial clothing press, where I could perform piecework and where language skills were not so critical.

Barnett's coat factory was a sweatshop in the sense that working conditions were dirty and hot. We perspired profusely, regardless of the weather outside. I, of course, had been raised to work hard and quickly, and that's exactly what I did. My strong work ethic soon caught the attention of both the ownership and of the union shop steward. After a few weeks on the job, I was approached by the union representative.

"What are you doing, Hart? You're working way too fast," he admonished.

"What do you mean?" I replied, not understanding.

I didn't fully appreciate the role of labor unions and was puzzled by this plea to slow down my work.

"You're making it hard for the rest of us," he explained. "Once Barnett sees that you can press that many coats per hour, he'll want all of us to do the same thing. Just take it easy and you'll be fine."

Well, I didn't like this one bit. If the other pressers wanted to be lazy, why should I go along with them? The union steward's words had the exact opposite effect. Instead of slowing down, I now began to work even faster. I soon gained the animosity of many of my co-workers. However, my stepped up productivity also earned me the attention of the younger Mr. Barnett. He took me aside about a week later and told me, "You're doing a great job, Hasten. Starting next week, we're giving you a ten cent raise."

This was great news. With an additional five dollars each week I could stop accepting the resettlement stipend we had been receiving from the Jewish Federation. It was more than merely the money. This raise signified our ability to stand on our own financially in our new adopted homeland. I could hardly wait to tell Miss Berman the news.

When the next payday arrived, I was dismayed and disappointed to find that my pay had not been adjusted. I showed my check to my father, who said I should speak up to the boss. I went to Mr. Barnett's office and told him that my pay was still at eighty cents, not ninety cents per hour as he had promised. "Oh yeah, yeah. Next week. You'll get the raise next week." Next week came and went and still no raise. I again spoke up and was again promised a raise the following week, but it again failed to materialize. Every week I'd look for that dime raise while I continued to work every bit as hard. This routine went on for over two months until it became clear why the company was reluctant to raise my salary. Their business was going through a decline, and being the newest hire, I was soon laid off.

What happened next could be characterized as a defining moment for me. Three days after being laid off, as I dejectedly scoured the daily classified ads looking for a new job, I heard my landlord downstairs yelling that I had a phone call. I ran down to his apartment and picked up the receiver.

"Hello, Hasten. This is Mr. Barnett." I recognized my former boss's voice. "We just got in a big order and I need you back at work. We'll put you back at ninety cents. When can you come back?"

"I'll call you back," is all I could say.

I ran upstairs elated. "Tatu. Guess what? That was Barnett. They want me to come back to work and they're giving me the raise!"

My father looked at me for a moment and then spoke firmly: "You are not going back there, Hetche. Those people are *gannofs* (thieves). They are exploiters, and you should not have anything to do with them."

I couldn't believe my ears. "But, Tatu. We need the money."

"Forget about it, Hetche. You're not going back there. There are other jobs out there where you could work for decent people. These sweatshop exploiters pay you with promises just to keep you working and then get rich, thanks to your labor." Dad was no socialist, but his words rung true, and I agreed not to accept the offer, although it meant serious financial hardship.

My father had tried to go to work himself. The agency had found him a job in a leather production factory, but after only two weeks, he collapsed on the job and had to be driven home. He never returned to work after that incident.

The next day, after Mr. Barnett's first phone call, he called again.

"Why didn't you report for work?" he wanted to know.

"I decided I wasn't coming back. I'm going to find some other type of job," I explained. When he insisted on knowing my motives, I revealed the truth: "Two months ago, you promised me a dime raise, but you never gave it to me. That's the reason," I admitted.

"Oh. Don't worry about the dime. We're going to give you much more money than that." "First thing is we're going to pay you by the week, and we're going to give you $50 per week salary."

This was great! Fifty dollars! I had been earning about $30 per week on an hourly basis. I immediately ran and told Dad the good news. "Tatu, they called me back and they agreed to give me on a weekly salary and to pay me $50 per week!" I was overjoyed. This was double what I was making originally.

"You are not going back," declared my father. "Not for $50. Not for $50,000. You are not going to work for crooks."

The following day, they called again, and again I declined. This badgering went on for about a week, and each time they raised the salary offer. They finally got up to $75 per week, which was a respectable wage in 1951. As the offers got more generous, my father took this as further proof of their duplicity.

"You see. Now you see what they were doing?" he exclaimed. "They had you in a job that was worth $75 per week and instead were only paying you one third of that. Do you see what exploiters these bums are? You're never going to work there ever again!"

This had turned into a matter of pride, and despite the fact that we needed the money, no amount of it would lure my father away from his principles. It never occurred to me to defy the man and return to work against his wishes. In fact, out of respect for him and his opinion, until I got married, I would turn over every paycheck I received directly to him.

As it happened, not returning to the coat factory turned out to be one of the best decisions of my life. It forced me to seek out other employment and led me to the next stop in my career – a step that lasted over thirteen years.

So, with my pride and principles intact, I went back to searching through the help wanted section of each day's newspaper. My English was a little better now and I could understand most of the words in the ads. One day, my eyes fell on a particular ad that caught my attention: "The Bemis Bag Co. packaging division is seeking an experienced engraver," it declared. The word "engraver" is what interested me. I had been trained by Herr Müller in Austria as an engraver and still had samples of my work. *This might be worth a look*, I thought. I placed the call and was asked to report for an interview on the following day.

When I got to the Bemis employment office, I met with the foreman of the engraving department, Al Anderson. I soon discovered that the type of engraving this company dealt with was far different from the jewelry and plaques I had been trained to inscribe. The Bemis Bro. Bag Company was over one hundred years old, and it was one of America's first and foremost producers of feed and food container bags, as well as other forms of product packaging. Anderson's department handled the production of engraved metal plates used in the printing process. Despite the fact that my samples were engraved jewelry, not printer plates, I nevertheless pulled them out and laid them out on Al's desk.

"Oooh. You have talent. I can see that," said Al as he examined my work. "We can train you to transfer your talents to printer plates. I have to warn you that as the new kid on the block, you'll be the one to operate the freight elevator. If you've got no problem with that, I can start you right away at ninety cents per hour." I gladly agreed and was soon earning, as well as learning the engraving trade, although most of my time during those first weeks was spent aboard the freight elevator.

I became a part of the package production team, along with designers, graphic artists and printers. I learned how to make rubber plates and mats. Each four-color job required up to four hand-engraved metal plates needed to produce the artwork image. It was precise handwork, but I never tired of it. I was also trained in hand typesetting: putting together galleys of type and slugs to form the packaging text. Advances in technology have mostly eradicated the need for the skills I acquired during this period, but I still hold a great fondness for the arcane crafts of typography and plate-making done by hand the old-fashioned way.

I loved my work intensely and became highly adept at even its most minute aspects. I started gaining a reputation as a perfectionist. I received regular hourly pay raises as I learned every phase of the operation and developed a strong loyalty to my employer. One day, I was called in to speak with Al Anderson.

"You're doing an exceptionally good job, Hart," Al said warmly. "We've never had a plate-maker here as good as you. We've talked it over and decided we're giving you a quarter raise."

This was amazing news. Nobody ever got a raise that big. And unlike back at the coat factory, this time it showed up on my next paycheck. My rate had jumped from $1.25 to $1.50, and I was learning that, in America, hard work really did pay off.

Then a strange thing happened. I once again had a run-in with the union. The chief union steward at Bemis was a man named Tracy Chase. When I reported to Mr. Chase that I had received a twenty-five cent raise, instead of being pleased, he acted upset.

"A quarter raise? Nobody gets a quarter raise!" he groused. He was evidently unhappy that the biggest hourly pay increase ever awarded by the company had not come about through union collective bargaining. He was afraid that if workers discovered they could successfully snare big raises on their own, they would soon figure out that they could do without labor unions and the weekly bite they took out of each worker's paycheck.

Chase's reaction to my good news shocked me and made a strong impression. I began to understand that labor unions did not represent my point of view or my values. I began to regard the union as a "con game" preying on uneducated workers, serving as a champion of mediocrity and an enemy of efficient business practices. After thinking things over, I sought out Chase and confronted him:

"I thought you union guys were supposed to look out for me. But instead, you're only interested in collecting your dues!" I let him have it. "Yes, I got this raise by working hard, not by threatening to go out on strike. And I got this raise just for me, not for all the other plate-makers, because I deserve it and they don't! I am so angry at you and your union that the first chance I get to get out of this damned union, I'm going to grab it." And, when the opportunity arose, that's exactly what I did.

We were finally off the welfare rolls and getting accustomed to our new life. Although my father was permanently disabled and possibly eligible for some sort of government subsidy, once I had secured a steady job, we received no further assistance. I began to feel very secure in my job, thanks to all the praise that was being heaped upon me for my workmanship. I soon began to spread the word that I was ambitious and was interested in joining management.

Because of my youth (mid-20s) and relative lack of seniority, it came as something of a surprise when an opportunity did, in fact, come along to join Bemis' management team. Al Anderson told me that I was the best plate-maker in the history of the company, and that he wanted me to become his right-hand man. I was soon appointed to the post of Assistant Foreman and placed on weekly salary. Although I did not receive any equity or stock options, this promotion opened up new doors for me and moved me quickly along my eventual career path.

After a short time, I purchased my first car, a 1947 straight shift Chevy jalopy, and I recall teaching Dad to drive my car, in an effort to get him out of the house more often. My parents spent their days learning English and becoming involved in community life through the synagogue where Dad attended daily services. But Dad's principles managed to get him into some difficulty at this first synagogue.

One day, after services, he overheard the synagogue's Romanian-born Rabbi whisper to one his assistants, referring to his congregants: "Don't worry. My *ferdelach* (Yiddish for horses) will pull the load." Well, this patronizing comment enraged my father. He resented being thought of as part of a mindless herd by this Rabbi. "Am I a horse?" he asked angrily. "What sort of Rabbi is this who calls his people horses?"

Dad wasted no time in locating and joining another Orthodox synagogue led by a Rabbi Chaim Ginzberg. Rabbi Ginzberg was a man of great learning and tremendous compassion. Soon, he and my father embarked on a profound friendship that lasted the rest of my father's life. Rabbi Ginzberg remained a close family friend until his death in 1999.

When the Romanian Rabbi learned that one of his horses had bolted and left the corral, he was highly displeased. The Rabbi dispatched a couple of his synagogue goons to pay my father a visit. I recall staring at these tough-guy Jewish mafia-types standing toe-to-toe with Dad in the center of our apartment.

"You know, Mr. Hasten, you're not a citizen here yet. And you're not acting the way a good American citizen should act," one of them said in Yiddish with a barely repressed sneer. "You know, Mr. Hasten, we could make things difficult for you when you try to become a citizen. Think it over."

This bit of extortion did not go down well with me at all. I was filled with the ideals of my new-found American freedom, and this whole scenario was so "old world" and so entirely out of place. I immediately shot up and began shouting in English: "What in hell? Did you just threaten my father?" I stormed and grabbed the one that did the talking by the arm and escorted him to our front entrance. I made as if to throw him down the stairs. "Both of you. Get out of here right now and don't come back. We want to have nothing to do with you or your Rabbi." I was incredibly outraged and amazed by the irony. After having survived Nazi death squads, Communist totalitarianism, and all of the privations of war, we were now being pushed around by some two-bit Rabbi and his thugs here in America. This was a clear case of "Never Again!," although I never imagined that I would be directing this attitude toward other Jews in America. My failure to be cowed by these bullies did the trick and we never heard from them again.

Most of the friends that we made in Minneapolis were American-born, and as a result, we were becoming culturally assimilated into this country's Jewish way of life. That's not to say we abandoned our old religious observances. We still kept kosher in our home. My mother would not drive on Shabbos. I took off from work on Jewish holidays. But we became Americanized in terms of our tastes, our diets, our appearance, our enthusiasm for sports and a thousand other ways. I didn't really appreciate this phenomenon until I visited some old friends from the DP camps that had re-settled in New York. I could quickly see that most of them had mentally never left Europe. They spoke only a little heavily-accented English. Most took no interest in American sports or community affairs.

As I spent more time with them, I discovered that, for the most part, I had very little in common with them anymore. There was a particular young woman whom I had known in the camps. All of us had admired her because she could speak fluent English. Whenever an American or British dignitary visited the camp, she would escort him or her and serve as interpreter. I assumed that her English was perfect. I'll never forget my shock when I met her again several years after we had both immigrated to the US. I couldn't get over how heavy and pronounced her accent now sounded. Her English pronunciation was unimproved from her days in the camp, since here, imbedded in the Polish immigrant community, English still remained her secondary tongue.

Unlike some Jewish enclaves in the US, our Minneapolis community was not insulated from the surrounding world. In fact, there was a conscious effort on the part of many post-war immigrants to shed the mantle of the *shtetl* Jew. They believed that it was the isolation and cultural detachment of European Jewry that may have hastened the onset of the Holocaust. I, for one, wanted to become a full-blooded American. I loved all things American, including the English language – full of strange poetic idioms and idiosyncrasies.

My first formal schooling in America was in the form of the English classes offered to all new immigrants. I knew little English at first, and these free lessons, where I studied alongside new Americans from Mexico, China and elsewhere, were extremely beneficial in laying a basic groundwork for further study. While my language skills were improving, I recall an early incident that illustrates the problem I had with English idioms.

I was standing in the locker room at Bemis getting dressed after a shower and had placed my towel down on the bench. Another worker came by and indicated he wished to sit on the bench and, pointing to my towel, said simply: "Do you mind?" I understood the word "do," and the word "you." I understood the word "mind" as meaning "brain." But I was not familiar with the expression: "Do you mind?" So, wishing to be agreeable, I simply nodded my head and said "Yes." The co-worker took this to mean that "Yes, I *did* object to his sitting on the bench," while I meant to communicate: "Yes, it's okay with me if you sit here." This misunderstanding led to a brief flare-up of tempers, and it taught me that I must begin memorizing English idioms. Actually, I've been collecting them ever since.

The only discrimination I experienced during this period, due to my immigrant status, originated from some of the American-born Jewish girls I was trying to date. I did get more than my share of rejections from these princesses who did not wish to be seen escorted by a *"greener"* (greenhorn) like me.

After a few months of English classes, I began picking up the language quickly, and I was anxious to resume my interrupted formal education. I enrolled in West High Evening School in a High School Equivalency program and attended class every evening after work. I was a diligent student and was rewarded with top grades. One time, a particular left-wing teacher, who lectured us constantly about the dangers of Senator Joseph McCarthy, awarded me an A minus for the semester. Upon seeing the grade, I immediately ran to the teacher's office:

"Why do I have an A minus? Why not an A?" I asked.

"An A minus is a very good grade. This is not an easy course," he replied.

"Yes, I understand, but what would it take for me to get an A instead of an A minus," I pressed.

He thought for a long time and finally said he'd review the matter and get back to me, which he never did. I got the message that the only way I could get a top grade in this fellow's class was by becoming a member of the Socialist Party.

I worked diligently at my studies aimed at obtaining a high school diploma. I never succeeded in getting that diploma because I left high school a year before I would have had the requisite credits for graduation. I dropped out, strangely enough, because I was accepted for admission to college. Without the benefit of a high school diploma, I managed to begin my matriculation at the University of Minnesota Institute of Technology in 1955.

As stated, I was in a hurry to catch up on my interrupted education. I did not feel like waiting another year to complete my high school studies, given the fact that I was already 24 years old and anxious to obtain a college education. I understood that becoming an engineer would further my career, so I decided to sit for a battery of entrance examinations offered by the university.

While my test results did qualify me for acceptance into General College, they were not sufficiently high enough to assure my acceptance into my primary choice, the Institute of Technology.

"Hart, your scores are very good," my advisor told me, "but they need to be exceptional to get into MIT. Without a high school diploma, and with these scores, my advice is to enroll in General College and then move on to MIT after that."

"But that will mean another three to four years. I can't wait that long," I pleaded. "I want to become an electrical engineer, and I need to get in now. What would it take to get me accepted today?"

"About the only way is for the Dean to make an exception for you," he said.

I promptly made an appointment to see the Dean. I took along my grade transcript from high school, and he quickly noted that I received A's in all my classes. I pointed out that there were no "creampuff" courses. I had enrolled in mostly math and science classes because I was very anxious to become an engineer. I explained that I did not have any more time to waste on high school courses, that I was the sole supporter of my family, and that I needed to enroll at MIT to further my training and my career.

The Dean displayed an immediate interest in my immigrant background. He peppered me with questions about my experiences during the war and how our family made its way to Minneapolis. He also asked about my career goals.

"I wish to become an electrical engineer," I responded.

"That means you'll have to work very hard," he said.

"That's one thing I'm not afraid of," I said.

I could tell that the Dean had an understanding and an appreciation of the post-war immigrant experience, and that I had made an impression on him.

I don't know if it was my spunk, my chutzpah or just my lucky day, but after our meeting, the Dean agreed to issue permission for me to enroll at the Institute, despite my lack of proper credentials. I actually carried a special permit signed by the Dean that I could present if ever I was challenged. I recall proudly displaying the permit to a number of my jealous immigrant friends who had also sat for the entrance exams. Most had failed entirely. A few, like me, had succeeded in obtaining grades only sufficient for entry into General College. Several tried, without success, to replicate my accomplishment by also going before the Dean. My acceptance at MIT bolstered my self-confidence and made me feel, for the first time since I had arrived in America, as though I were moving ahead of the pack.

I began my studies, attending evening classes with a full credit load, while working full-time, and often overtime, at Bemis. The workload was enormous and left little time for such secondary activities as socializing or sleep. I recall yearning for just a little extra time to do my homework and reading. I used to fantasize about being assigned to work as the plant's night watchman. That would have been ideal! I would have had plenty of time between my rounds to keep up with my studies. If the job had paid more, I would have applied for it.

I excelled at my courses in electrical engineering, and the Dean's words proved correct. I was required to work very hard. But after two years of study at MIT, a transformation began to take place within me. I began to take notice of the lifestyle of most of my fellow engineering students. Today, these fellows would be classified as "techno-geeks." They were mostly a bloodless lot, clutching their slide rules like precious security blankets, enjoying little or no human interaction whatsoever. The longer I continued in this milieu, the more distasteful it became to me. As my language skills advanced and as I became more acclimated to American life, I discovered that I thrived on human interaction. With each passing day, I became more disillusioned with my chosen course of study. I imagined myself spending life as a faceless engineering drone confined to some isolated laboratory. I needed a way out. And it was soon to arrive.

My superiors at Bemis were very cooperative in permitting me to integrate my studies into my work schedule. I was able to report for work during different shifts, depending on how my class schedule was structured. But this was about to change. In 1957, I was offered a management position to head up Bemis' entire paper division. I was told that if I accepted the job, my schedule could no longer be so flexible. I would be in charge of all three production shifts, and I would be expected to be available around the clock. I would be called upon to be on site during various hours of the day and night. In addition, I would be required to attend out-of-town management seminars and to visit various Bemis plants around the country.

This travel, as well as my added responsibilities, would drastically conflict with my continuing studies. I knew I had to make a choice, and it was not really a difficult one. On the one hand, there was the prospect of complet-ing my studies, earning my engineering degree and then joining the ranks of America's "wire-heads." On the other hand, there was a road leading toward tremendous advancement opportunities where I would be well compensated and called upon to exercise my developing "people skills." I decided to curtail my studies and accept the management post. While I did experience some remorse about letting the Dean down after he had displayed such confidence in me early on, I am certain that he would understand how my ambition steered me toward this decision.

As my family and I began to build a life here in America, I became ever more aware of how my father had wisely guided us. Had it been up to me, we would have followed our Zionist passions to Israel as my brother had done. While I felt some regret about not settling in Israel, I realized that under the Ben Gurion-led labor regime, my opportunities for advancement would be severely limited. The Laborites made life very difficult for those Jews who did not share their political point of view, or their European heritage. Their notorious treatment of Sephardic Jews during this period has left scars that are still visible today.

Mark had run into this harsh reality. He wound up leaving Israel and, unable to enter the US due to immigration quotas, he relocated to Canada in 1952 and settled in Montreal.

We would follow events in Israel very closely, and when war erupted in 1956, I was strongly torn between rushing to aid Israel's defense and remain-ing with my parents in the US. Somewhere along the way, I emerged as an essential American. To this day, despite my fierce loyalties to Israel, I view myself as an American citizen and, at the risk of sounding corny, an Ameri-can patriot. Aware of my deep ties to Israel, friends sometimes ask, "Which country do you like better, Israel or the US?" I always respond that this absurd question is like asking a child to choose between the love of his mother or his father. While Israel has no stronger advocate than me, in my bones and in my heart, my identity is American.

My parents were also adjusting well to life in America. My mother kept a kosher home, and both my parents strictly maintained the Sabbath. My rigorous schedule, however, made my Shabbat observance less than total. This lapse on my part resulted in my mother dispensing heaping doses of Jewish guilt on my head, as she would always feign surprise at my lack of observance: "What? You're going to work on Shabbos?" she would exclaim as she saw me leaving the house on Saturday morning for the fifteenth time in a row. I was able to compartmentalize my religious and secular lives, and I had no difficulty resolving these matters. There's a Yiddish expression which delineates the sacred from the profane that characterized my outlook: "What is due to G-d is G-d's, and what is due to the people is the people's."

While my level of religious observance was lower than that of my parents, there was still a clearly defined boundary, a line over which I would not cross. I would never, for example, consider marriage to a non-Jewish woman. I could never imagine myself living in a non-kosher home. And, as might be expected, my level of observance increased over time, and it became more intense after I married and became a father.

At this stage of the game, my major concern was getting ahead and achieving some level of financial stability for my family. This priority became evident very early on through an episode that took place some six months after our arrival in America.

It was shortly after I purchased my first car that my mother became suddenly and severely ill, complaining of terrible pains in her back and abdomen. We had already started visiting Dr. Goldman, a Jewish general practitioner to whom the resettlement agency had referred us, so we rushed Mother to his office immediately. Dr. Goldman examined her and informed us that she was indeed very ill and needed to go to the hospital without delay. I bundled her up and drove her to Mt. Sinai, the major Jewish hospital in Minneapolis. I rushed in and headed for the admissions desk. I explained to the clerk that Dr. Goldman had sent us. The clerk stared at me blankly and then informed me that the hospital required a one hundred dollar deposit before admitting any new patients.

"But I don't have a hundred dollars," I replied, somewhat stunned.

"Well, then we can't admit her," was the reply.

"But you don't understand," I pleaded. "This is my mother, and she's very sick. Dr. Goldman said to bring her here." Although my English was not the best, I'm sure I was making myself understood. Despite my protests, the clerk kept insisting on the $100 deposit. When I saw that I was getting nowhere, I asked for directions to a pay phone and immediately called Dr. Goldman.

"Dr. Goldman, this is Hart Hasten. I'm here at the hospital with my mother and they want a hundred dollars to let her in," I explained.

"Well, give them the hundred dollars," he advised.

"I don't have a hundred dollars. I haven't been in the country long enough to save that much."

I began to regret my decision to buy the car the week before even though I desperately needed it to get to work.

Dr. Goldman advised, "If you don't have the money, then take her down to General Hospital. They don't require any deposit there."

At that time, I didn't know one hospital from another. "Is it okay to take Mother to this General Hospital?" I asked.

"Oh, sure. They have very good doctors down there," Goldman said.

"You mean you won't be her doctor?" I asked.

"Oh, no. I don't practice at General. Only at Mt. Sinai."

"But, Doctor," I pleaded, "I want you to be her doctor. Isn't there anything you can do so we can stay here?"

"I'm afraid not. But don't worry. She'll be well cared for at General."

Goldman's attitude was: You're an immigrant. You have no money. Go to General. Come back to Mt. Sinai after you've got a few bucks in your pocket. I will never forget his condescending tone and arrogant manner. I discovered that night that having money in America could mean the difference between life and death.

We trudged off to General Hospital where Mother was indeed admitted at no cost. She was assigned a bed in a huge ward filled with the city's less fortunate patients. I spent the morning with her and then left her to head back to work. That afternoon, I returned to the hospital to check on her. As soon as I arrived, she lifted her gown to display her abdomen covered with ugly black and blue bruises.

"What happened to you, Mama?" I asked her in Yiddish.

"Everyone is coming along all day and poking and prodding me like crazy," she managed to explain, on the verge of tears.

"Well, did you complain to the nurse?" I inquired.

"I tried to. I think she said that this is General Hospital, and all the interns and medical students come here to learn. Each one has to poke into my stomach so they should learn how to become good doctors."

I didn't care for the thought of my mother being used as a medical guinea pig, but I couldn't think of what to do about it. My mother's treatment continued to upset me as I returned to work for my next shift. I could not get the image of her being mistreated out of my mind, as I attempted to complete my workday.

After my shift ended, I returned quickly to the hospital again and saw that Mother was in no better shape. She was still being abused by the teaching staff. Worse than that, I could tell that she was worried about my welfare. I again felt like that frail sickly boy lying in his typhus-ridden bed back in Alga. It all came rushing back. I thought of how much she meant to me and how I was letting her down. It was then that I noticed a red tag on her chart at the end of her bed.

"What's this red tag?" I asked a passing nurse.

"Oh, that means she's been marked for surgery. She's going to be operated on tomorrow morning," explained the nurse.

"Did she give you her permission for the operation?" I demanded.

"This is General, sir. The papers you signed when we admitted her say we don't need any further permission. We're going to operate on her in the morning and that's that," barked the nurse as she walked off.

I thought of my mother lying in her bed, with her abdomen covered with bruises from all the "topping" she had endured. I looked around the ward and became disgusted with the uncaring medical staff in their starched white caps and their starched white arrogance. No compassion. No humanity. My mother could not even speak to the nurses to complain that she was being mistreated. She could only *"krechtz"* (moan). I became convinced that if I didn't do something quickly, my dear mother would certainly die in this place.

I phoned Dr. Goldman again and again until I finally got through to him. I was shaking as I tried to control my anger.

"Dr. Goldman," I pleaded, "this is not a good hospital. Mother needs to go back to the Jewish hospital. It's better at the Jewish hospital."

"Like they told you, they won't accept her without the hundred dollars. I'm sorry."

He was about to hang up, and I was convinced that just one phone call from him to Mt. Sinai Hospital would have secured a bed for my mother. But he was heartless and simply didn't care. His job was providing basic medical care for immigrants being resettled by the Jewish Federation. It was just a job, and he wasn't about to put out any extra effort. My anger suddenly erupted.

"Dr. Goldman. Let me tell you something. Maybe I don't have the hundred dollars today, but someday, I will have money, and I will never ever forgive the way you treated my mother." I was enflamed and the words tasted acrid as they passed my lips. "If anything happens to my mother, I will hold you responsible."

He said nothing and hung up the phone. I was getting desperate. I decided that I had to get Mother out of there. These butchers were not going to learn their surgery skills on her body, and that was final! I next phoned my father.

My father, at this point, was quite ill himself and was not able to accompany me to the hospital. I explained that I had to get Mother out of General and into Mt. Sinai, but I needed a hundred dollars.

"I'm sorry, Hetche," he said softly, "but we don't have a hundred dollars."

I will never forget the evident anguish that encased his words as he uttered them softly to me.

"What are we going to do, Tatu?" I asked after a pause.

"Well, all I can think of is Marvin. Marvin Kohnen, the barber."

I knew Mr. Kohnen and had frequented his barber shop on Plymouth Avenue. He was a genial fellow "greener" who became one of our early friends in Minneapolis. But did I know him well enough to borrow a hundred dollars? We had no relatives to call upon, so Marvin seemed to be our only hope.

"Marvin is such a nice man, he's been in this country for a while. Maybe he can help us now," suggested Dad. It was evening by now, and I again left Mother's bedside and rushed over to Marvin's house. I knocked on his door and he answered quickly.

"What is it?" he said, as soon as he saw the anxious expression on my face.

"I need a hundred dollars," I blurted without preamble. "It's my mother. She's going to die if we don't do something." I quickly ran down the situation and he seemed to understand fully.

"Come in, Hart," Marvin said, and then directed me to sit down at the kitchen table.

He stepped out and returned with a handful of cash. He sat down across from me and started counting one-dollar bills out on the table. Many of the bills were crumpled and sprinkled with hair clippings. I calculated that this sum was probably a week's income for the man.

"You know that I'll pay you back, Mr. Kohnen," I swore sincerely.

"Don't worry about it. Pay me when you can," he said.

I thanked him a few more times and then rushed back to the hospital with the bills stuffed into my pockets.

Back at General, I phoned for an ambulance to transport my mother back to Mt. Sinai. I did not wish to risk driving her in my car again. It was around 11 PM when the paramedics arrived with their stretcher and I pointed out my mother to them. Just as they began to move her from her bed, a nurse came running down the ward.

"Just what do you think you're doing?" she demanded.

"I'm taking my mother out of here," I replied calmly.

"You can't take her. The doctor didn't discharge her yet!"

"Get out of my way!" I stated forcefully. "My mother is not a guinea pig, and you are not going to experiment on her!"

I had seen the results back in the DP camps of what so-called Nazi doctors had labeled as medical experiments. While I might have been over-reacting based upon this memory, I nevertheless regard my decision to pull mother out of that dismal place as definitely the right thing to do.

I followed the ambulance in my own car and burst into the admissions office at Mt. Sinai brandishing my pack of one-dollar bills. I spread the bills on the admission clerk's desk and asked her to admit my mother, which she did immediately. After parking the car, I took the elevator to Mama's floor and walked into her brightly lit room.

"*Ich fiel shoin besser*! (I feel better already)," she exclaimed and I could see that her whole attitude and demeanor had improved greatly. She was given a thorough examination the next morning by the chief resident, who diagnosed her condition as diverticulitis and recommended a treatment course of only medication. No surgery was ever recommended or performed.

After a few days, Mother was released, and within a few weeks, I had saved enough money to pay back Marvin in full. Not surprisingly, I developed a warm, lasting relationship with Marvin and became something of a Dutch uncle to his two children.

Fortunately, my mother recovered fully from her illness, and although our family eventually obtained health insurance coverage, I made a promise to myself to always keep money set aside for emergencies. I had learned something important about the American attitude towards money, but moreover this incident served as a true wake up call for me in other ways as well.

It is this type of transfixing experience that can mold a boy into a man. I was shaken by this to my very core. I saw clearly for the first time that my poor mother – who had given birth to me, who had saved me from destruction repeatedly in Kazakhstan, who had slaved and suffered to put food in my mouth – had been denied medical treatment because some doctor thought she wasn't good enough to stay in a Jewish hospital! The scales fell from my eyes as I saw our situation clearly for the first time. And what I saw filled me with anger and outrage.

To this day, the thought of that arrogant SOB still upsets me. Who in the hell was he? In fact, where was he when we, along with millions of other fellow Jews, were fighting for survival in Europe? He was comfortably collecting his fees for treating poor, dirty refugees for the Jewish Family Agency, all the while looking down his nose at us. What gave him the right? Where did he earn his claim to arrogance?

Another important lesson arose from this incident that has stayed with me ever since. Standing in that hospital waiting room with a sick mother, penniless in a strange land, I knew in my gut the gripping feeling of naked fear and helplessness. It is the recollection of this feeling that enables me to empathize with those who have asked for my assistance over the years. While I have tried to fulfill the commandment of *tzedakah*, which requires every Jew to help those in need, it is because of this incident that I do so not merely out of obligation, but also to satisfy a personal angel that has resided in my heart ever since those difficult days.

Sadly, there were other poignant lessons I was taught during those early years in America. I soon discovered that anti-Semitism was not something I had left behind when we sailed across the Atlantic.

During my first months at Bemis, my studious habits had caught the attention of one of the senior engravers, Frank Bleifus. Bleifus had served in the Pacific with the US Navy during the war, and he would often share his wartime stories with us.

"Hasten, you like books, don't you?" he asked me one day.

"I'm trying to learn English better. That's why I'm reading all the time," I told him.

"Well, I've got a great book for you," he proclaimed. "It's called *The Caine Mutiny*, and it's all about life on a battleship in the Pacific during the war. It is the greatest book ever written. No joke."

"Who wrote it?" I asked.

"Some sailor named Wouk. Herman Wouk. Check it out." Bleifus also characterized Wouk as "the greatest author that ever lived."

After listening to Bleifus' repeated entreaties for me to read this extraordinary book, I finally relented and found a copy at the local library. I checked it out and began the difficult task of reading it. With my limited English skills, it was a challenge. I kept my German-English dictionary open and was kept busy looking up words such as "conn" and "ordnance." I finally got through it and agreed that it was indeed an excellent story and well-told. But, after reading all the great Russian classics and most of Shakespeare in my younger years, I would hardly call this the greatest book ever written. I informed Bleifus that I had finished the book and he couldn't wait to discuss it with me.

"I can tell you right away, Frank, it's not the greatest book ever written. But it's a good story and very interesting. Why do you think this book is so great?" I asked him.

"Because it's all so true. It's exactly as I lived it during the war. That Captain Queeg character, he was my captain. He behaved just as nutty as the captain on my ship."

"What about the Jewish lawyer character?" I asked him. "His name was Greenwald. After winning the case, he gets a little drunk and tells the ship's officers: 'I'm not on your side here when you attack the military. The Nazis were making soap out of my relatives, and it was these soldiers who defeated them.' What did you think of that character?"

"Oh, Hart. Don't you understand," he said with a knowing smirk. "The book publishing business and the movies and the theatre, they're all controlled by the Jews. This book never would have gotten published, unless the author put in something favorable about the Jews."

I was taken aback. Frank was aware that I was Jewish, and this fact did not seem to restrain him from sharing his "common wisdom" brand of anti-Semitism with me. I resented this and decided to look into things a bit further. I started doing some research at the library to see if there was any truth to what Bleifus was saying. In the process, I came across a review of *The Caine Mutiny* in *Time* magazine. The review contained a fact that stunned me. I had to read it over several times to make sure I had it right. The reviewer explained that not only was Herman Wouk a Jew, he was an Orthodox Jew who had served in the US Navy during the war. Armed with this fresh ammunition, I rushed back to Bleifus. "So, you think this is the greatest book ever written?" I asked.

"Yep, that's right," he said.

"Greatest author who ever lived?" "That's right."

"Well, what if I were to tell you that the author, this guy Wouk, is Jewish?" I asked, hypothetically stringing him along a bit.

"He couldn't be Jewish. There were no Jews in the Navy," he declared matter-of-factly. "Wouk had to be in the Navy. Therefore he couldn't be Jewish." Bleifus seemed satisfied with this bit of pure logic.

It was about to crumble, however, when I told him quietly: "I'm going to surprise you. Wouk is Jewish. Not only that. He's an Orthodox religious Jew. He wears a yarmulke all the time. It's all here in *Time* magazine. Read it yourself."

Bleifus was crushed, and for the first time, speechless. He refused to speak to me for many weeks thereafter, and after we did resume speaking to each other, the subject of *The Caine Mutiny* was buried at sea and never brought up again.

Ironically, many years later, I met Herman Wouk and got to know him. I shared this story with him, and he was particularly amused by Bleifus' blanket statement that there were no Jews in the Navy. He pointed out that it was common practice for Jewish boys in the military to keep their Judaism under wraps during the war.

This didn't surprise me, since I had run into the same practice during my early years at Bemis. My religion was never an issue at Bemis and while I was the only Jew to serve in a salaried management position, there were a few Jews among the company's hourly rank and file. I had befriended one fellow, a plate maker named Louie Miller. Louie was an American-born Jew who would sometimes give me a ride to work. He had one of those new push-button car radios that I would admire each time we'd ride together. Louie made it clear that he did not wish to be known as a Jew at work. I recall turning down the radio and asking him why.

"Louie, why don't you want anyone to know that you're Jewish?"

"Look, Hart," he said, "I've lived in Minneapolis all my life, and I know how much anti-Semitism is out there. Being a Jew doesn't get you anywhere in this town. So please don't tell anyone that I'm Jewish, okay?"

The strange thing was that, despite Louie's efforts, everyone knew the truth. I would always take time off work to attend synagogue during the Jewish New Year season for Rosh HaShanah and Yom Kippur. After my return, my co-workers would invariably ask me: "Louie doesn't think we know that he's Jewish, but we do. Why didn't he take off from work for the Jewish holidays, too?" This inconsistency was quite puzzling to my colleagues. Why is one Jew required to miss work for religious reasons while another is not? Why does one Jew hide the fact of his Judaism and another does not?

What they did not understand, and what I did not fully understand until much later, was that Jews like Louie were reacting to a lifetime of exposure to the sometimes subtle, sometimes overt, institutional anti-Semitism. While some of these attitudes were undergoing change in post-war America, thanks to movies like "Gentleman's Agreement" and others, anti-Jewish discrimination was still the rule at many US workplaces. I'm happy to say that this was never the case at Bemis. In fact, I soon discovered that non-Jews held much more respect for a Jew who is proud and knowledgeable about his religion than one who tries to sweep it under the rug.

Over the years, I observed that many American Jews, who attempted to cope with living in a Christian dominated society believe that the best way to gain acceptance is by minimizing their distinctiveness and attempting to blend in at every turn. In an effort to become like the *Goyim* (non-Jewish nations), many Jews would abandon our practices in the name of "good relations." This road never held any attraction for me. I observed that a non-Jew, educated about his own Christian faith, will have little respect for a Jew that knows nothing of his own heritage. Hence, I came to the conclusion that the best defense against the anti-Semite is an educated Jew. From education emerges pride, and it is this pride that will earn the respect and eventual acceptance by the non-Jewish community.

Along these lines, many Jewish young men in those days made it a practice to date only *"shiksas,"* or non-Jewish women. By contrast, I dated solely Jewish women, and despite my heavy workload, I still managed to find the time for some romance. I preferred to go out with American-born women who would serve to further my acclimation to American life. I became involved with a lovely girl from St. Paul. She was a warm and disarmingly beautiful girl who fell in love with me and wanted very much to get married. But marriage was simply out of the question for me at that point. I explained to Lois that my family depended on me as the sole source of income, and that I was also carrying a full load at college. This left me with no time to devote to a wife and family.

I did, however, find the time during this very hectic period of my life, to devote some energy to those who had assisted us. I felt a great sense of obligation to the Jewish Federation and the social service agencies that had aided us in resettling in America. It was for this reason that, shortly after obtaining regular employment, I made my first charitable contribution to the Federation. It was only $5, but it represented a day's wages at the time. I also went door-to-door around the neighborhood each year and asked for donations from other immigrants. Despite the fact that I have been a strong Federation supporter during the intervening decades, I don't feel I will ever fully repay the debt I owe them for their assistance at a time of great need.

In addition to my other responsibilities, I had also become a landlord. I had managed to save enough money to purchase our home. The house was a duplex, and the other unit was rented out to two elderly sisters, former schoolteachers, Elizabeth and Maude Kramer. It was my job to collect the rent each month, as well as look after all the maintenance needs of their apartment. The Kramer sisters were tidy, charming ladies who took a liking to me. They once told me that I reminded them of Jesus Christ! I don't believe they were old enough to have known Christ personally, so I presumed they were speaking figuratively.

Marriage seemed an unlikely prospect for some time to come, mainly for financial reasons. I recall being overjoyed that I had managed to rent out some storage space in my garage for five dollars per month. This meant an extra sixty dollars per year. When my brother first arrived in Montreal, he also needed some financial help until he could get himself established. He contacted me and I agreed to mail him $300. I wanted to make sure he received it, so I purchased a money order, and went to the Post Office and asked how to go about sending a registered letter.

"I want to make sure he gets this. It's very important," I explained to the uninterested postal clerk. "How do I send this so he has to sign for it?"

"Don't worry about it," she said laconically. "Just send it regular and it'll get there fine."

"No, you don't understand. This is very important. I have to be sure he receives it."

"He'll receive it. Just put a stamp on it and throw it in that box over there."

This exchange went back and forth for a while, until I became so angry that I finally relented. I licked and sealed the envelope, put a stamp on it, and threw it into the outgoing mail bin.

A few days later, on the following Sunday, I had cooled down sufficiently to review my actions at the post office. I suddenly realized that in my anger and haste, I had failed to place an address on the envelope! I immediately panicked.

I tried to phone the Post Office, and after repeated attempts, someone finally picked up the phone. I explained what had happened and asked what becomes of letters that bear no address.

"Oh, we have a place where we keep all non-addressed mail," he informed me.

"Thank G-d. Could you please take a look and see if my letter is in there?" I begged and went into a detailed description of the envelope and the contents.

"Well, today is Sunday, and I'm not even supposed to be in here, you know."

"You don't understand," I implored. "This is an emergency. You must go and look."

After a bit of cajoling, I persuaded the fellow to go and look. Miraculously, he retrieved my letter. I instructed him to open it.

"I'm not supposed to do that!" he said.

"But it's my letter, and I'm giving you my permission. Open it up and you'll see the money order with my brother's name and address. Just copy the address from the money order and write it on the envelope. Then, seal it back up and send it out. Okay?"

"Well, okay, I guess, but I really shouldn't be doing this," he said, and then did it anyway; Mark received the money order a few days later.

It was during those very busy times that I met an extraordinary young woman who was destined to become my future sister-in-law. One of the families in the predominantly Jewish north side neighborhood of Minneapolis was the Rabatniks, and I got to know their very attractive step-granddaughter. Anna Ruth Robinson had grown up in Texas and had moved to Minneapolis after the war when her father remarried. As mentioned, I was simply too busy at that time to get seriously involved with anyone, but I could see that Anna Ruth was someone very special. By this time, Mark had moved to Montreal, and I thought that he and Anna Ruth might make a good match. I gave her my brother's address and urged her to write to him. "If you like me, you'll love my older brother. He's just like me, only more so," I told her.

They began corresponding, and after a few short months, Anna Ruth announced that she was going to Montreal to meet Mark, since he could not obtain a visa to enter the US. She took off alone to meet a man she had only known through his letters and an occasional telephone call. One week after her arrival, her family and ours received the surprising news. Mark and Anna Ruth had eloped and were now married. While my parents were disappointed at not being able to see their older son stand under the *chuppah* (wedding canopy), they knew Anna Ruth and were very pleased at the news. Anna Ruth's family, however, was not particularly thrilled that their granddaughter had run off and married some "greener" with an unknown past and an uncertain future.

The marriage enabled Mark to enter the US, and the couple settled for a short time in Minneapolis before moving on to Texas, where Mark enrolled at SMU. Anna Ruth's family's fears were soon overcome, as they came to know and to admire Mark.

Mark and Anna Ruth's marriage has endured for almost fifty years and has produced, as of this writing, four children, eighteen grandchildren and a great-grandson. It is one of the truly great marriages of all time, and I am proud that I played a role in making it happen.

Like many immigrants to the US, I simply could not wait for my opportunity to become an American citizen. My five-year wait ended on April 10, 1956. In anticipation of that day, my parents and I all completed the appropriate applications and signed up for special civics courses designed to teach immigrants enough about American history and government to enable them to pass the citizenship exam.

Our instructor alerted us that, in addition to the written exam, the judge conducting the swearing-in ceremony often liked to toss random questions to the candidates, in order to test their actual knowledge. Evidently, some immigrants memorized the answers by rote without actually understanding their meaning.

When the day came, I was ushered into the judge's chambers, along with about a dozen other candidates hailing from various nations. As we had been warned, the judge began peppering our group with questions like: "How many branches make up the federal government?" and "Can you name the Speaker of the House of Representatives?" Those who were unable to answer the judge's questions correctly were instructed to take the exam again in sixty days.

When my turn arrived, the judge stared down at me sternly and asked a rather bizarre question: "Young man," he said with a slight twinkle in his eye, "can you tell me the meaning of the term 'ex post facto'?"

This threw me. The question came out of the blue and had nothing to do with American government or history. In fact, it was a question about the meaning of a Latin phrase. It wasn't even about English! I thought about it for a moment and concluded that the word "post" meant "after," and I guessed that "facto" meant "fact."

"It means 'after the fact,' your Honor," I finally replied.

"That's right. That's exactly right," the judge said sounding a bit disappointed that he was unable to trip me up.

Those who remained were then asked to rise en masse, raise their right hands, and repeat the citizenship oath that transformed us into full-fledged naturalized US citizens. As refugees for the past fifteen years, my parents and I had not been citizens of any nation since the night we fled from Bohorodczany back in 1941. The impact of once again having a true homeland was overwhelming. I was swept with feelings of pride and gratitude, and with something else that can only be termed "sweet survival." I was here, an

American citizen, standing on American soil, despite typhus and despite the Nazis and despite everything! I shall not die and I did not die. I had lived to see this day, and what a sweet, sweet day it was.

America, with all her seductive opportunities, was clearly opening its tents for me. By the end of the decade, I was, for the first time, able to allow myself some measure of optimism. I saw myself able to not only keep my head above water financially, but also to see a progressively positive course ahead of me. This road, however, was soon to take an unexpected turn – a turn toward California and toward love.

My father
Bernard (Berish) Hasten

My Mother
Hannah Hasten

With young Holocaust survivors at the
Jewish Community Center in Wloclawek, Poland

After the war in Wloclawek.
A visit from Yisrael Barzilai, a prominent leader of Hashomer Hatzair
in Palestine and the future first Israeli ambassador to Poland

At age 15 in Ebelsberg,
Austria, D.P. Camp

My father (center, in hat) participating in a memorial
for the victims of Matthausen extermination camp

(Note box containing ashes of the victims bound for the new State of Israel)

In my soccer playing days in Minneapolis at age 21

With my sister-in-law, Anna Ruth,
my brother, Mark and my parents

My uncle
Psachya Halpern

My uncles,
Joseph and David Halpern,
Buenos Aires, Argentina

Simona
and Hart N. Hasten

My children:
Bernard Hasten,
Joshua Hasten
& Renée Halevy

My grandchildren:
Benny Hasten, Ely Halevy, Samantha Hasten, Hannah Hasten, Leny Halevy,
Erica Hasten, Dorayah Halevy, Shane Halevy, Adin Hasten, Joseph Hasten

With UJA delegation and former Israeli
Prime Minister David Ben-Gurion

With Prime Minister Yitzhak Rabin

MK Menachem Begin, the leader of the loyal opposition party in Israel, addresses a group at our home

With Rabbi Chaim Ginzberg and godfather, Menachem Begin, at my son, Josh's bris

My mother-in-law, Miriam Braunstein, godfather Menachem Begin and my mother, Hannah Hasten at our son, Josh's bris

Rabbi Chaim Ginzberg; Mohel Michael Aronson; my brother-in-law, Ernie Braunstein; my mother, Hannah Hasten; and godfather (sandek), Menachem Begin at my son, Josh's bris

Menachem Begin visits the
Hebrew Academy of Indianapolis

With newly elected Prime Minister, Menachem Begin and
Ya'akov Meridor. The two Irgun Zvai Leumi commanders

With Aliza and Menachem Begin

With Prime Minister Begin in his office

Prime Minister Begin
congratulating me after my
receipt of the Jabotinsky medal

Prime Minister Menachem Begin
with his daughter, Hasia
and my wife, Simona

With Simona and Prime Minister Begin
with his godson, Josh Hasten

Prime Minister Menachem Begin with his godson,
Yishayahu Alexander (Joshua Hasten)

With Menachem Begin, David Hermelin
and Yehuda Halevy, introducing Begin prior to
his final address as Prime Minister in the Chagall Hall
of the Israeli Knesset

With Foreign Minister Moshe Dayan

With former Foreign Minister
Abba Eban

Introducing Prime Minister
Yitzhak Shamir

With Prime Minister Yitzhak Shamir, UN Ambassador
Benjamin Netanyahu and Freda and Harry Hurwitz

With Prime Minister Yitzhak Shamir
and Ambassador Meir Rosenne

With President Ronald Reagan

Chapter Seven

Love, American Style

IN 1960, I finally traded in my beaten-up 1947 Ford for a bright yellow 1957 Chevy Impala. My circle of friends included mostly young, American-born Jewish men and women, and I was known as something of a rising star at Bemis. After ten years in America, at age 29, I decided that I could finally do something unbelievable: I could take a vacation.

I teamed up with two of my bachelor buddies, Jerry Rubin and Sonny Streitman, and in April of 1961 we set off in my Chevy for a three-week trip to Los Angeles. A number of our friends had relocated to Southern California and had written to us about the sunny way of life they enjoyed there. We wanted to see it for ourselves.

The drive across America's newly-constructed highway system was a pleasure, although Sonny and Jerry didn't get along too well, and I often had to serve as an intermediary. Jerry wanted to stay at a motel during our visit and Sonny preferred the economies of staying at the YMCA. They quarreled about it constantly to the point that I had to step in. I found a discount motel on La Cienega that was plain, but clean, and only cost us three dollars more per night than the Y. This seemed acceptable to both, although they soon found other subjects to quibble about.

Once we hit LA, we teamed up with a fourth buddy, Larry Gozansky, who had moved to California from Minneapolis a few years earlier. Larry was a first-rate amateur musician and knew a lot of the Jewish girls in the LA singles crowd. He directed us to the popular nightspots each evening, where we'd enjoy dancing, making new friends and exploring life in the LA fast lane.

One evening, Larry had taken us to a Jewish singles dance at the local Jewish Community Center. We were sitting and chatting with one of Larry's friends, Sam Dreyfus. Naturally, the subject turned to Israel, my favorite topic. We discussed the current political situation, and Sam listened politely to my opinion of the Ben Gurion regime. But Sam was one of those fellows who could turn any conversation back to his favorite topic – girls.

Sam turned to me and said: "You know, you really ought to meet a girl I know who used to live in Israel. She's very pretty and lives over near Fairfax Avenue. You really should meet her."

"I don't know. We've got plenty of girls right here. Anyway, we're driving back to Minneapolis in a few days."

"No. You really have got to meet this girl," he persisted.

"Okay, already, why not. What's her name?" I asked.

"Her name's Simona, but I don't have her phone number. I do have her friend Batya's number," Sam explained. "Just give Batya a call and ask her to give you Simona's phone number." He scribbled down a number and shoved it into my hand. "Just call this number and ask for Batya. Batya will give you Simona's phone number. Do it, Hart. You gotta meet this gal."

It seemed like a long way to go for a drink of water, when we were swimming in a big fresh water lake, but to pacify him, I said, "Okay, okay, I'll call her." I shoved the note in my pocket and promptly forgot about the whole thing. A few days later, on our last Sunday in LA, I was in our motel room and came across the phone number in my pocket. *What the heck,* I thought and dialed the number.

"Hello, may I speak to Batya, please," I said.

"Who's this?" came the gruff male reply.

"My name is Hart Hasten and I'd like to speak with Batya. Who am I speaking to?"

"This is Batya's uncle."

"May I speak to Batya, sir?" I asked.

"What do you want to speak to her about?" he asked.

"I need to get someone's phone number," I replied.

"Whose number do you need?"

This fellow certainly is nosy, I thought.

"I'm trying to get in touch with a girl named Simona Braunstein. Do you know her?"

"Yes. I know Simona. Why do you want to talk to Simona?"

I was getting a bit annoyed at this point.

"I would like to ask her out on a date, if you must know," I said just a bit shrilly.

"What about Batya? Maybe you'd like to take her on a date instead?"

I couldn't believe this guy.

"Look, would you just let me speak with your niece, please?"

He finally gave her the phone, and after I explained myself to Batya, she agreed to give me Simona's phone number. I dialed her up immediately and introduced myself quickly. I stunned her a bit when I announced that I was coming over to her house to meet her.

"What do you mean you're coming over? Who are you? " she shot back. I explained again that I was from Minneapolis, that I was a friend of Dreyfus', and that I didn't have much time left in LA. I didn't know if she was impressed with my cheekiness, but she agreed to see me. "If you want to come over, come over," she said in a blasé tone.

As on most Sundays, I hadn't bothered shaving, and I was dressed very casually. I thought of cleaning up a bit, but then decided to just drive right over to the home she shared with her mother and step-father. Her mother came to the door, and I could sense immediately that the woman liked me. In fact, she couldn't get enough of me. She was extremely inquisitive, wanting to know details about my family and business activities.

"Oh, you're from Europe," she said. "Where does your family come from? No kidding?" After a brief interrogation, she told me about how her family came from Bucharest in Romania, and how they had lived in Israel before immigrating to the US. I believe she was taken with me because she had a higher regard for European men than for either the American or Israeli-born fellows her daughter had been bringing home.

After about ten minutes of this, Simona came in and we were introduced. I don't believe either one of us made a big impression on the other. I looked rather scruffy and, while she was very pretty, I didn't see anything special about her. After a bit of small talk, I suggested we go for a walk and get to know each other.

We walked around Fairfax Avenue for perhaps an hour, just making polite chit-chat. I learned that she was born in Bucharest and had lived in Nagy Varad in Romania. She spoke Romanian, Hungarian, Yiddish, Hebrew, English and Spanish. And she spoke them well. We discussed her life in Israel, and I told her about my Zionist background. While I wasn't exactly taken with her, I enjoyed her direct and sincere manner. She spoke her mind freely, with an irrepressible innocence that I found charming.

"My mother just likes you because you're from Europe and not an Israeli. It takes more than that to impress me," she said, giving me the once over.

I found out later that she thought I was rather arrogant and cocky, which I probably was.

"Well, to tell the truth, the only reason I called you is because Dreyfus said I should meet you, since you used to live in Israel," I admitted. "I'm always giving him my opinions about Israel and the Middle East, and I guess he thought you'd find this subject interesting."

"Tell Dreyfus that I'm used to men shaving before they go out on a date with me."

She was letting me have it, but I kind of liked it. I walked her home and said good-bye, figuring that we would not be in touch again. But then a funny thing happened. The next day, April 23rd, was my thirtieth birthday. I was sitting around the motel thinking that I'd like to do something special to celebrate. Going over in my mind all the people I had met during our visit, I could not think of anyone with whom I cared to spend my birthday celebration, with one exception: Simona. I was fed up with hanging around my friends and their non-stop bickering. I just wanted to spend a quiet evening with someone I could talk to. So, I phoned Simona and asked her to join me for dinner and dancing at a posh spot on Sunset Boulevard. I told her that the nightclub was featuring some terrific dancers and a great jazz band, and that I would even agree to shave beforehand.

It was a splendid evening. We began to warm up to each other, and it was becoming clear to me that I would rather be with Simona than with any of my other friends, male or female.

We were slated to leave LA on Thursday, and I knew I wanted to see her again before going back to Minnesota. I picked her up on Wednesday, and we began to relive the wonderful evening we had shared a few nights before. But then the magic started to wear off and, before long, we were quarreling about some silly subject. We were both headstrong and stubborn (*we still are!*), and neither of us would yield the point. So, we said good-bye on a downbeat note, both of us thinking that this was undoubtedly our last encounter.

The following day, I bid farewell to the City of Angels and hit the highway back to the Midwest. During those long, all-night driving stretches, I found I could not erase the memory of Simona from my mind. With each romantic song that played on the radio, I saw her lovely face. This was something new and surprising to me. I was no moony teenager. I was a 30-year-old Jewish bachelor and no stranger to affairs of the heart. Yet, the feelings that gripped me during that long drive home were completely unique and indescribably sweet.

Somewhere past Denver, I decided to try and put my feelings down on paper. I wasn't too happy with the way it turned out, but I mailed my thoughts off to Simona in a letter. As soon as I reached home, I decided to follow up with a present. I had concluded, after due deliberation, that she was probably right in that squabble that had marred our last day together. I wrote her an apology and asked that she accept it, along with a bracelet I had purchased as a peace offering.

Simona and I corresponded over the next few weeks, and it appeared that she had forgiven my transgressions. Soon she began sounding more affectionate in her tone. Over Memorial Day weekend, I was sent, by Bemis, to a management seminar in St. Louis. The seminar ended on Friday morning, and I had three days remaining before I had to report back to work. With the free time on my hands, I decided to look up my old friends and *"landsmen"* (countrymen), the Hipschmans. I invited Sam and Clara to join me for lunch at my hotel. As far as I knew at the time, Sam and Clara Hipschman were the only other Jews from Bohorodczany to have survived the Holocaust.

Over lunch, Sam and I talked about the reasons for his survival. He was in the military at the time the Germans overran our hometown and was therefore stationed elsewhere. The stories of his miraculous survival could fill another book. (Sadly, his story will have to be written by someone other than Sam, since he passed away, at age 84, during the writing of this book.)

After bringing Sam up to date about my parents, my brother and myself, I revealed to him my current feelings about Simona. I told him that I had met a lovely Jewish girl during a recent trip to Los Angeles, and that I thought I was falling in love with her. It seemed that Sam could see directly into my heart. He hunched over and said seriously, "Hetche, it's obvious how you feel about this girl. You've got a few days off right now. Why not go pay her a visit?"

"I have to be back at work on Tuesday in Minneapolis," I explained.

"So take a plane," offered Sam.

Great idea, I thought.

In 1961, airlines were just beginning to offer prop-jet service, and TWA had a non-stop flight from St. Louis to LA that afternoon. I rushed back to my hotel and made the travel arrangements. I then phoned Simona and told her I would be in LA that evening and asked her to pick me up at the airport. I'm not sure if this move impressed her with my sincere devotion or with my impetuous spontaneity, but in either case, she seemed very excited that I was jetting halfway across the country just to spend a few days with her.

Thanks to the time difference, I arrived in Los Angeles one hour before the onset of the Sabbath. As I disembarked, I was disappointed to find no one waiting for me at the airport. I called Simona from a pay phone, and she explained that she had been to the airport earlier with her older brother,

Joe, and had evidently gone to the wrong gate. When I didn't appear, Joe, rather than investigating the matter, insisted they go back home. I hailed a taxi, and before long, we were in each other's arms.

Simona's mother was so warm and genuinely effusive. She was obviously impressed with my actions and couldn't stop dispensing hugs, kisses and non-stop food and drink. Mrs. Braunstein had laid out a delicious Shabbat meal, which included a traditional menu plus an assortment of Romanian delicacies.

Simona and I did find the opportunity to be alone, and I used the time to open my heart to her. I explained that I had fallen in love with her and that I felt differently about her than about any other woman I had ever known. Even though she was only twenty-one years old, Simona knew her mind. She told me that she liked me because I seemed more mature and settled than the other men she had dated. She appreciated the bracelet, and she was certainly impressed with my decision to fly to her side, but she needed some time to think things over.

Simona's level-headedness seemed to complement my impulsive nature. She was working as a medical assistant in a doctor's office and was scheduled to receive some vacation time soon. I insisted that she come to Minneapolis to meet my family during her vacation. By this time, my brother and sister-in-law had left Texas and had moved back to Minneapolis. I pointed out to Simona that she could stay with them during her visit. She discussed it with her stepfather and her mother, and then agreed to visit.

After arriving back home, I sent Simona an airline ticket and she flew to Minneapolis in mid-June. I showed her the city and introduced her to everyone as my "girlfriend." This was really the first time we were able to enjoy long stretches of time together. We went on picnics in the country-side and really got very romantically involved. Although there was no formal proposal, we both gradually came to regard our engagement as a fait accompli. The transition from girlfriend to fiancée was almost completed when, at Simona's suggestion, we purchased a small diamond engagement ring. But I knew there was one more step that I needed to take in order to make it official. I had to talk to my father.

I opened with, "So, Tatu, what do you think of Simona?"

"A wonderful girl. A true beauty," he replied. "Can we talk 'tachlis' (talk turkey)?"

"Sure," I said.

"You like her? I mean, you really like her?"

"I sure do, Tatu," I replied.

"Then you ought to be married. But first, I want to talk to her mother. Dial up the telephone, Hetche," he instructed.

I did as he asked and soon had Simona's mother on the phone. I handed the receiver to Dad and he introduced himself in Yiddish.

"Well, it looks like the kids love each other," he said bluntly. "I am too sick to move from here, Mrs. Braunstein, so I would be very grateful if you could find the time to come here to Minneapolis to discuss the *'shidduch'* (match) and let's *'shreib t'noyim'* (write a marriage contract)."

They worked out the details, and within a few days, Simona's mother arrived in Minneapolis. She was introduced to my parents, and the three of them quickly went to work on planning the wedding. They set the date, decided which synagogue, and determined who would pay for what. At the end of the conference, Simona and I were free to tell our friends and family that we were formally engaged. Although there was no actual wedding dowry, and despite the fact that Simona and I had met each other on our own, our nuptials still had many of the old-world trappings of a *shtetl*-style arranged marriage.

On July 30, 1961, some three months after our first meeting, Simona and I were wed by Rabbi Ginzberg and the most important partnership of my life was launched – a partnership that has lasted, as of this writing, for over forty wonderful years.

Our wedding day started out wet and rainy, but by the time the ceremony began in the afternoon, the sun had come out and was shining brightly. This was taken as a good omen by many of the 200 guests who watched as we stood under the *chuppa* (wedding canopy) and yelled *"Mazel Tov"* when I stomped on the traditional wine glass. We honeymooned at a lovely rustic resort in Brainard, Minnesota, filling our days with water skiing, canoeing and huddling around the campfire every evening in each other's arms.

I often think back to that fateful road trip and my two traveling buddies. I have not heard from Sonny Streitman since the early 1980s, but have stayed in touch with Jerry Rubin, whom we count among our good friends and who now lives in Las Vegas.

Jerry's career was in social work, the field in which he earned a PhD. After some years of practice, he entered social work education. He was department chair and taught classes in the School of Social Work, University of Nevada, Las Vegas, for twenty-four years, before retiring in 1998.

Simona and I settled into a small apartment near my parents' home in Minneapolis. This was the first time in my life, at the ripe age of thirty, that I was not living under the same roof with my parents. Surprisingly, this major change did not require much of an adjustment on my part at all.

While I was initially opposed to Simona's going back to work, we soon discovered that being solely a homemaker did not suit her. She explained that she needed a certain amount of professional fulfillment in her life, as did I, and I easily understood this need. And besides, we could use the extra income.

Simona soon found a job in Minneapolis similar to the physician's aide position she had held in Los Angeles. Amazingly, the employment agency found her a job assisting two physicians, the Gordons, husband and wife, in a family medical clinic located directly across the street from our apartment. It meant Simona could walk to work, but I was annoyed that we were forced to pay an agency for finding a job located right in our own backyard.

My own career was progressing rapidly, and I imagined that I would continue my advancement within the company until my retirement. But this was not to be. I guess you could say that I became infected with that most American of conditions known as the entrepreneurial bug. It was a condition whose symptoms would change my life more radically and more profoundly than I ever could have imagined.

Chapter Eight

The Bemis Years

By 1961, I was earning a $7,900 annual salary and had advanced to a key management position with Bemis as the foreman of the plant's paper operation. Complex production problems were thrown at me, and I would be required to find effective solutions. I had advanced from the engraving division and was serving as the supervisor of the entire Paper Department, which employed about twenty women and five male pressmen.

The Paper Department was an around-the-clock operation, with bag production taking place day and night. I took my responsibilities very seriously, and I felt that I should be present during all three shifts. This created an extremely rigorous workload, and I began to wonder if I had made a mistake by leaving my secure hourly position and joining the ranks of management. I was still attending electrical engineering classes at MIT while working three shifts per day. It was simply overwhelming. I knew I needed to have a talk with my boss, plant supervisor Stan Peterson. Stan, like many members of Bemis' management echelon, was of Swedish descent. He was a former football player and did not hold a degree. He was an exceptionally effective manager, thanks to his strong "people" skills. I learned a great deal from him about how to motivate those working under me to excellence.

Every day on the job, I had to restrain myself from walking into Stan's office and saying, "That's it, Stan. I can't take this anymore. I want my old job back in engraving. This is just too much!" But for some reason, I never knocked on that door. Instead, I pushed on, often walking the floor at 3 AM thinking to myself: *What am I doing here? I should be home with my wife or studying for my classes.*

This was perhaps the most demanding and difficult time during my tenure with Bemis. But then, after three months of doubt and tribulation, something strange happened. A veil parted, the fog lifted, and I suddenly understood clearly what my role was to be. The anxiety I had been experiencing was due to my being thrown into a sink-or-swim environment. I now looked around and discovered that I was swimming smoothly and would not be sucked down the drain. For the first time, I had a clear understanding of my job mission and how I was expected to carry it out. Almost overnight, I started to "get it."

There was a casualty to this epiphany, however. I recognized that if I was to devote myself fully to my career, I could no longer continue my full-time studies at MIT. Thus, while my career advanced rapidly, it did so without the benefit of an engineering degree.

Once I came to the realization that I could properly do the job expected of me, I immediately began thinking of ways to improve the production operation. I began to devise methods that would streamline the traditional workflow and introduce some rather dramatic efficiencies. In order to carry out these improvements, I needed the full cooperation and support of our workforce. I soon developed a certain management style based on team communication.

I had spotted some unused floor space on the 6th floor where the Paper Department was housed, and I decided, on my own, to transform it into an employee conference room. This was a novel idea at Bemis at the time. On a rather regular basis, I would announce production meetings. At the appointed time, I would shut down the entire production line and all of the equipment, and then ask the crews to sit around the conference table. I would provide doughnuts, sodas and coffee, and I would invite and encourage brainstorming.

"Listen, people," I would begin, "our waste is way too high. We are wasting over six percent, and I am convinced that we can bring that number down to one percent or below. Anyone got any ideas how we do it?"

I know that in today's manufacturing environment of quality circles, and after the influence of Japanese production practices, my innovations do not sound particularly revolutionary. But in 1961, the practice of asking a production worker how to become more productive was not common at all. Many of these folks had been on the job for decades, robotically following their directives. Until I came along, no one had thought to ask *them*, the front line troops, if they had any thoughts on doing things better.

As was to be expected, I tapped into a huge reserve of pent-up criticism and frustration. In the area of waste, for example, one pressman explained to me how he could tell that a press run was faulty *before* it was run. He would routinely run it anyway, knowing full well that it would wind up being dumped. Why? Because that was the standard procedure, and he did not have the authority to change it. Simply listening to what this fellow had to say resulted in cutting our waste percentage in half overnight! Of course, there was a lot of chaff among the wheat. Many workers consumed time at our meetings simply venting their frustrations and I had to be alert not to permit these meetings to degenerate into general gripe sessions. But that's how I saw my role. It was up to me to listen carefully and determine which ideas rose above the general noise level and were worthy of further pursuit. We would cover all areas of the business – from equipment speed to safety practices. We even discussed how to keep the restrooms more tidy.

Listening, however, is not enough. If all a manager does is listen politely, and nod his head sympathetically, but then fails to deliver any follow-up action – all he succeeds in doing is raising false expectations. On the other hand, if the crew observes that some of the innovations suggested at these sessions are actually put into play, the effect can be dramatically positive. Plant workers were now viewing themselves not as mere mindless ciphers, but as having some level of control over their work environment. This resulted in a big morale boost and emergence of a quasi-proprietary interest among the crew that was based on ego, as well as money. A pressman, for example, who had suggested a cost-cutting procedure on his line, wanted it to succeed, not only because it would result in bigger profits and thereby bigger bonuses, but also because he wanted to be proven correct.

All of these grass-roots management methods could not fail to attract the attention of the company's so-called efficiency experts: the industrial engineers. I recall how the two IE (industrial engineers) guys were shocked, on entering our area, to see all of the equipment shut down at 10 AM and all of the crew sitting around a table eating doughnuts and drinking coffee. When the IE fellows objected, I simply informed them that we were having a meeting and would be back in production in thirty minutes. This was unheard of at the time, and the two of them scurried off to report my outrageous act to their boss, the plant superintendent. My phone was soon ringing.

"Hart, this is Frank. They tell me you've shut down production down there. What's going on?"

"Did you see last month's production report?" I countered. "All of our increased productivity and reduced waste was the result of ideas we cooked up at a production meeting. We're having another such meeting right now, and I'd like to keep having them on a regular basis."

"I see. Well, could you write me a memo about this and I'll get back to you."

"Of course," I replied. "Oh, by the way, please keep those IES off my floor from now on, will you?"

Frank's response was not surprising, given his "hands-off" management style. Rather than dealing with issues directly, he preferred to sit at his desk drafting memos and sending them out hither and yon. I was a daily recipient of his memos. At first, I would sit down and dutifully prepare a written reply. But, after a while, I realized that his memos were not based on reality, and dealing with them only got me more and more frustrated. Eventually, I simply stopped responding to them and he stopped writing them. Frank even admitted to me that he was a trained technical writer and preferred writing to doing anything else. He was obviously in the wrong job, and it wasn't long before upper management came to the same conclusion.

In addition to the brainstorming sessions, I also implemented a system of incentives that served to reward an employee who was able to significantly increase his or her rate of production. If I felt that an employee was doing an outstanding job, I would go to bat for him or her and persuade upper management to grant a pay raise. In this way, I developed a strong rapport with my workforce. Essential to maintaining this rapport was a high level of credibility. If I said I was going to try an efficiency method, I did it. And if I said, "I'll get you that raise," I always came through. These practices formed the foundation for a fierce loyalty among everyone working under me. I found that I was able to build upon this foundation and take our department to new levels of achievement.

Meanwhile, at home, the cycle of life continued. Simona and I had decided to give up our apartment and had moved in with my parents. This made it easier for us to care for Dad, whose health was in a tailspin. By age 66, his trips to the hospital were becoming more and more frequent. The doctors explained that his chronic emphysema was incurable and would eventually result in his death. I regarded my father's deteriorating health as a direct result of the deprivations he suffered during the war. How many times had he sacrificed his own well-being in order to assure the safety of his wife and children? How many times had he given up his bread to us and gone hungry so that we could eat? All those years of fear and hunger were finally catching up with him.

In the end, my mother, brother and I were with him in the hospital. He was no longer conscious, and we could tell from his labored breathing and general disposition that these were his final hours. We were gathered at his bedside when a nurse entered the room and asked us to step out while she changed the bedding. By the time we re-entered the room, some three minutes later, Tatu had died quite peacefully. While his death came about much too soon, he died in the manner of a *Tzadik* (a righteous Jew) with no rancor or trauma, but with a gentle kiss from G-d.

I spoke from my heart and soul at my father's graveside. I told about how he had "shlepped us through thick and thin." I spoke of how all of us owed our lives to his courage, his intelligence, and his indomitable spirit. It is this spirit that I believe I have inherited from my father – a certain tenacity and persistence of purpose that compels me never to give up, regardless of the odds against me. It is this quality, I announced, that I would hope to pass on to any children I might be granted.

A few weeks after the funeral, as if G-d had been listening, we received the good news that Simona was expecting. Our first child, Renée, was born in January 1964. Her sweetness and beauty quickly helped to sweep away the despair after my father's death.

This was an exciting time for me professionally. I was cutting my teeth as a manager, and I was able to quickly see the results of my efforts. We could tell very soon if a new idea was going to work or not. This constant feedback, both in production methods and in management techniques, helped me to learn quickly how to harness that most important resource of any operation: the human element.

One incident that remains with me involved the acquisition of a five-color press. Our department needed this sort of machinery because we were frequently required to produce five-color artwork. To accomplish this on our four-color press meant running the whole job twice – a time-consuming and expensive practice. I received word that a five-color press was no longer being used and was available at a Bemis facility in Kansas City. I flew to Kansas City to look it over and determined that it would be perfect for us.

"I want this press. Send it to me," I told the superintendent, and he agreed.

My first order of business on returning to Minneapolis was to bring in some engineers and figure out how to reinforce the flooring to securely support this very heavy piece of equipment. It took several months to apply the reinforced concrete, to move existing equipment, and to prepare the space for the arrival of the new press. All of this, by the way, was being done without the knowledge of Frank, my boss. The fact that I could pull this off demonstrated how out-of-touch Frank was with day-to-day operations.

Finally, one sweltering Friday, the equipment was delivered to the plant and left on the loading dock. Frank spotted it and came over to me.

"What's that equipment out on the dock?" he asked.

"That's a five-color web press I had transferred here from Kansas City," I replied.

"Where are you going to put it?"

"In our department on the sixth floor. I've strengthened the floor and picked out the best spot. Come on up and I'll show you."

Frank looked over the space and concluded that I was making a mistake. He whipped out his trusty slide rule and paced off the space.

"You don't have enough room here, Hart," he announced.

"But, Frank, we measured it. It will fit just fine."

"No, you're wrong. You do have enough room in the back. You need to put the thing in the back. Okay?"

"Frank, why would I want to put it into the back? It belongs right here in our production line. Everything is right here," I explained patiently.

I rolled out the floor plan that I had designed and showed him exactly how the new press would fit smoothly into our workflow.

"I disagree, Hart. It needs to go in the back," he insisted.

I don't know if it was the steamy temperature or just my frustration boiling over, but I was at the end of my rope. We had worked and planned for months to bring this off, and I was not about to let some slide-rule-toting slacker sabotage our efforts.

"Frank, there is no way this press is going in the back. Now get the hell off my floor because you're wasting my time!" I exploded.

"Don't forget that I'm your boss and I can have you fired!" he shot back.

"So do it. That's up to you, but I am not going to move the location of this press!"

Frank stared at me wide-eyed, turned and walked off quickly.

Over the entire weekend, I wondered if my hot temper would wind up costing me my job. I was, after all, the only Jew in management, and one of only a handful of Jews in the whole company. I also did not attempt to conceal or downplay my Judaism in any way. While this fact was never an overt issue during my years at Bemis, I was still concerned that my behavior might afford my superiors the opportunity to "get rid of that loud-mouthed Jew." At the same time, I was secure in my position, since production quotas had risen steadily since I had taken over. On top of that, I was right, and I believed I could demonstrate the correctness of my position to anyone reviewing the matter.

As expected, first thing on Monday morning, I was called down to Pete

Mulvaney, the plant manager's, office. Frank was waiting in Pete's office when I arrived.

"You know what this is all about, Hart?" Pete started.

"Yes, I do, sir," I said.

"I understand you had some words with Frank on Friday."

"Yes. Yes, I did."

"Why don't you tell me what you have in mind about this press," he said patiently.

I laid out my floor plans and templates across his desk and went through the whole story of how I obtained the press in Kansas City and reinforced the flooring to support the machine. I pointed out how the new machine would enable us to boost our efficiency and thereby our revenues.

"What about all that, Frank?" Pete asked.

Frank characteristically began brandishing his slide rule and busily started making rapid calculations. Slide. Click. He mumbled that his figures did not support my assumptions.

I pled my case further, pointing out the proximity of my location to the elevator and my ability to view the press's operation from my office. Placing it in the back would take it out of my direct view.

Slide, click, slide. Again, Frank consulted his slide rule and said, "According to my numbers, the number of linear feet from the elevator remains constant in either scenario."

With every point I would raise, Frank and his slide rule would counter with some sort of mathematical mumbo-jumbo. His attitude was that "I must be right because I have the slide rule and you don't." Finally, Pete had had enough.

"Frank, why don't you take that goddamn slide rule and shove it up your ass!" he bellowed. "Hart is right and you know it. This meeting is over!"

The press was placed where I had designated it to go, and it immediately began to perform exactly as I had predicted. This victory caused my stock to go up in the eyes of top management and led to my taking on a new assignment that would change my life forever. Meanwhile, Frank and his slide rule were soon fired.

As the productivity of our department continued to improve, my reputation as a company trouble-shooter was rising. So, I was not surprised when I was approached by top management in October of 1963 about a Bemis plant on the south side of Indianapolis. The plant was losing money, and they did not understand why. They wanted me to visit the facility, study its operation, and file a detailed report with recommendations on how to turn it around. Of course, I agreed.

The Indianapolis plant was larger than the one in Minneapolis, employing around two hundred full-time workers. The plant produced its own ink onsite and owned more and better quality equipment than we did in Minneapolis. In addition, their customer base was better than ours, both in quantity and quality. Both their management and their workforce were at a higher skill grade than ours. With all of this going for it, no one could understand why the plant was losing money. This puzzle was baffling headquarters, and it was my job to find the solution.

What I found was rampant mismanagement and poor judgment at every turn. I recall that during my first day onsite, while taking a tour of the plant, I walked by a large blackboard in the middle of the largest department.

"What's that?" I asked my guide, pointing to a list of names scrawled on the board.

"Oh that's the Goof Board," he explained. "Those are the names of people who screwed up and wound up costing the company money."

I couldn't believe this! *How totally wrong-headed,* I mused.

I decided that my first recommendation for the troubled Indianapolis plant was to replace the Goof Board with a Gold Board that named those employees who had performed exceptionally well and managed to save the company money.

I then observed that the superintendent of the plant had let the place fall into complete disarray. There was filth and trash everywhere. The restrooms were unbearable and there was litter underfoot at every turn. Employees were permitted to eat wherever they chose, including at their posts. As a result, mice and rats ran rampant throughout the plant.

I filed my report, listing the many inefficiencies, the poor housekeeping, and the many questionable management practices that I had observed. I assumed that top management would take it from here and that my job was done. A few days after my report was filed, I received a phone call from headquarters.

"Hart, we've looked over your report about Indy and we agree with all your findings. We need to have a change of management there and we need to do it right away."

"I agree," I said.

"Good. Because we believe that the best person to take over that plant is you. How soon can you move?"

I was a bit stunned and I didn't quite know what to say. I really did not wish to leave my mother. In addition, Simona was pregnant with our first child. I asked for some details and then said I would have to discuss it with my wife.

The following day, I received a call from one of the top principals at Bemis. He again stated how important it was to the company for me to take over the Indy plant. He made it sound like the whole future of the business depended on my move. But I was resistant. I pointed out that my mother, my brother and his family were all living in Minneapolis, and that they depended on me in many ways. I mentioned that we had a baby due in January, and that planning a move to a new city would be very tough on my wife at this time.

They became persistent. Evidently, top management was envisioning me as the man on the white horse. According to them, I was the only one who could rescue this plant, so they began to turn up the pressure. They offered to increase my salary to $9,500 for the coming year and to cover all of my moving expenses. Finally, they said, "Look, Hart, just agree to run the place for one year. If you can't turn it around by then, just bring us back the keys." I was impressed. They were prepared to shut down a multi-million dollar operation if I did not agree to take a crack at it. After much discussion with Simona, I finally relented.

It was assumed that since I knew how to make money for the company in Minneapolis, I could do the same once I got in the saddle in Indianapolis. In this regard, I made a rather foolish remark that was later to come back and haunt me: "My success is based on managing people. People are the same all over."

One of the first things I discovered after taking over the Indianapolis plant was that people were definitely *not* the same all over. The workforce in Minneapolis was made up of Norwegians, Swedes and Germans who had come off the farms and enjoyed a very strong work ethic. The employee turnover rate in Minneapolis was nearly zero. In Indiana, everyone was from somewhere else. Many were from Kentucky and Tennessee, and most had poor work habits and were plagued by unstable families with drinking problems and the like. Therefore, the turnover rate in Indianapolis was very high. This meant that most of the employees had been hired during the past year. I could see that I had my work cut out for me.

Fortunately, Bemis had given me free reign as superintendent, and I quickly went to work putting into place those changes I felt could return this plant to profitability. I began by setting a tone and getting the message out to all employees that I was interested in rewarding and recognizing excellence. After getting rid of the Goof Board, my first order of business was to sit down with the union leadership and explain that they could expect me to be very strict and very tough, but very fair. Theirs was a powerful union with the ability to shut down the plant in a heartbeat. They pursued grievances aggressively and had become used to little resistance coming from the superintendent's office. I placed them on notice that things were about to change. Grievances with no merit would be aggressively rebuked, and contract negotiations would be based on fairness to all parties. I'm pleased to say that I won the respect of the union leadership and never had to endure a strike or walk-out during my tenure in Indianapolis.

As mentioned, the place was worse than a pig sty when it came to cleanliness. I even observed ladies jumping up on tabletops in the lunch room to avoid the mice scurrying about their feet. These conditions were more baffling in light of the fact that there were company-wide janitors on staff! In Minneapolis, we had no janitors. Each department kept things tidy in its own area. Here, in Indy, everyone felt clean-up was the janitor's job…except for the janitors! The solution seemed obvious. Get rid of the janitors! But first, I had to train people to clean up after themselves. Employees were in the habit of opening a candy bar and just pitching the wrapper on the floor. This had to stop.

I went out and personally bought fifty brooms and called a meeting of the fifty workers in a particular department. I passed out the brooms and addressed the group.

"Some of you haven't met me yet. I'm the new superintendent…also known as the new broom. I intend to clean things up around here in every way. Where I come from, in Minnesota, we don't have janitors to pick up after us. We do it ourselves. And starting today, that's the way we're going to do it here."

After setting into motion a housekeeping program in every department, I re-assigned the former janitors to more skilled, productive jobs. This action, naturally, did not sit too well with the union. I was soon approached by Jeremiah, a janitor whom I had now put to work as a baler operator. Jeremiah, along with the union steward and the union president, all came to see me about a grievance they were filing to protest Jeremiah's re-assignment.

"Mr. Hasten, Jeremiah wants his old job back as a janitor," said the union steward.

"I'm sorry, but that's impossible," I explained. "The job has been eliminated. But we have found Jeremiah another job at a higher rate of pay. So, what's the problem?"

"Jeremiah has been working as a janitor at this plant for fifteen years," said the union president. "He doesn't want to be a baler. He likes being a janitor. That's what he's used to, and we agree that's what he should be doing. We are prepared to file this grievance unless you agree to reinstate Jeremiah at his former position."

By this point, I was fuming. On top of that, no one had heard from Jeremiah. I had a hunch that he was being used as a pawn by the union. I surprised everyone in the room when I suddenly jumped to my feet and looked straight at Jeremiah.

"Jeremiah, damn it!" I yelled. "Who says you have to be a janitor just because you're colored? I'm giving you an opportunity to make an extra fifty cents an hour and to learn a skill to boot. What's wrong with you? You want to remain a janitor because you're colored and they have you convinced that that's all you can do. Damn it, Jeremiah. I believe you can be something more than a janitor. I believe in you. I believe you have as much ability as any of those white machine operators. Don't let these union guys brainwash you. I'm handing you an opportunity to be something more. Please don't disappoint me."

Jeremiah got up without a word and returned to work. The union fellows were speechless. They didn't know just what to make of my little pro-civil rights speech, but in those days, following the assassination of John F. Kennedy, the country's mood was highly sympathetic toward the black civil rights movement. To go counter to this would have appeared unpatriotic at the time. The union boss understood this. He turned to the steward with his decision.

"You know, Mr. Hasten is right. Jeremiah *is* making more money and *is* improving himself here. Let's drop this one."

But they did not give up that easily. The union devised other strategies to test me and find out what I was made of. One incident, which took place about three weeks after I took over, comes to mind.

We had received a large order on a tight deadline. In order to make it happen, we had to work over the weekend. I scheduled an overtime crew to come in on Saturday. I knew the union guidelines backward and forward, and I was aware that they required me to call in those employees with the greatest seniority whenever overtime work was available. But on this date, the person with the highest seniority did not get called. Instead, in order to keep costs down, I extended the overtime opportunity to someone at a lower pay rate and with less seniority. The more senior employee, who had been overlooked, immediately filed a grievance. Even though the alleged offense had just taken place on Saturday, the employee and the union president were waiting for me in my office first thing on Monday morning. They presented me with a written grievance and announced that they were going to file it immediately. I told them to come back that afternoon after I'd had a chance to look into the matter.

The whole thing looked fishy. First of all, where was the verbal grievance, as called for in the rules? Secondly, how did they get this matter investigated and decided on so quickly? I began asking some questions and learned that, even if I had called in the most senior employee, she would not have been able to come in on Saturday since she was out of town. I called them back into my office and decided to defend myself with a strong offense:

"You know that you folks are the reason this plant is going down the drain," I said accusingly. "The company makes one error and you're ready to jump on it with both feet. You don't even give us the benefit of a verbal complaint, as the guidebook calls for. Instead, you conspire and waste no time in mounting an attack. Where is your loyalty to Bemis? You know they sent me here to turn this plant around. Now I see why this place is in the red. It's because of people like you who don't give a damn if Bemis makes any money or not."

At this point I took their written grievance, tore it up into shreds and pitched it into the wastebasket. Their jaws dropped and they were at a loss for words. I went on, and what I said next shocked them even more.

"Yes, you are absolutely right. You do have a legitimate complaint. We should have called you in first. We didn't do that, and it was a mistake. But you know that this plant lost over $600,000 last year, and it cannot afford to pay any overtime to you, the highest-paid person on the crew. So, because I care about the welfare of our company, I called in someone who is at a lower pay scale. That was my mistake, and I'm prepared to pay for it."

I took out my wallet as I continued.

"I figure you lost about $8.50 in overtime pay. Here it is," I said as I handed her the money. "I can afford it. The company cannot. Now, take your money and get back to work. We've wasted enough company time on this matter already."

"Oh, no, Mr. Hasten," she said forthrightly, "I could never take your money." She got up to go, and as she was walking towards the door, I stopped her. "Oh, just one more thing," I said. "Were you home on Saturday? Could you have come in if I had called you?"

She looked sheepishly back and forth between me and the union president and finally looked down and shook her head.

"I thought so," I proclaimed. "Now get back to work. I don't ever want to see this type of grievance from you again, do you understand?"

I never had any problems with this lady again and I'm certain that the union came away with a clearer picture of whom it was they were dealing with.

I tried never to fire anybody – not only because I feared union reprisals, but also because I believed that everyone has certain talents, and it was my job, as a manager, to find the right fit for the right person. Sometimes, however, it was simply unavoidable. In the cases of the few employees I was forced to fire, I can honestly say that both the company and the employee were better off after they left. By way of example, the case of Richard comes to mind.

As I walked the floor of the plant, my eyes would invariably fall on a fellow who was constantly stopping his work and staring up at the ceiling. We had very high ceilings, and he seemed to be peering into the light fixtures and rafters as if he were looking for something. When I inquired about this strange behavior, I was told, "That's just Richard."

"Well what does Richard do?" I asked the foreman.

"Oh, he's been here about six months and he's assisting the machine operator," I was told.

"Well, what's he looking for up in the ceiling?" I asked.

"I don't know, but I'll have a talk with him about it," said the foreman. "I'll explain that he has to be productive and can't keep staring off like that."

The next day, I come out on the floor and there was Richard engaged in the same staring-into-space routine. I decided to take matters into my own hands and walked over to him.

"Richard, tell me," I said politely. "What do you see up there?"

"I know. I know. I know," he said sheepishly. "They told me. I got to be productive. I'll get right back to work."

He did so and stayed at his post for the rest of the day.

The following day, I came in and once again observed Richard walking up and down the aisles, far from his post, staring up at the ceiling intently. I called him into my office.

"Richard," I said sternly, "I've looked over your file. I see you have six children and that you're the only breadwinner in the family. As much as I hate to say this, if you keep this up, we'll fire you. This is my first warning. One more time and you'll lose your job."

"I know," he said. "I understand and I'll get back to work right away."

The next day, I observed Richard once again staring aimlessly upward and not doing his job. I immediately issued him a written "Final Warning," advising him that if he persisted, he would lose his job.

I handed him the notice and explained: "Richard, we're trying to turn this plant around. Everyone is expected to do his part. If you do this one more time, you'll be fired on the spot."

Richard was indeed observed doing the same thing a few days later. By this time, everyone in the plant was aware of the situation, so I was left with no choice. I instructed the office to prepare his final paycheck.

As I handed it to him, I said: "I feel very bad about this, Richard. I know that this is going to place a hardship on your large family."

"You don't need to worry about my family," he said with bravado as he walked out the door.

I surmised that the guy was a bit psycho and that I had done the right thing by letting him go. Firing Richard, while painful, helped to solidify my credibility, and I could already see the fallout from this incident benefiting the company. In a few days, Richard returned to the plant. My secretary announced that he was in the outer office and wished to see me. I didn't know what to think. Frankly, I was somewhat fearful of facing a recently fired employee with a questionable grasp on reality. There were a lot of nuts out there, and guns were easy to come by.

"Did he say what he wants?" I asked.

"Nope. Just says he wants to talk to you," came the reply.

I really did not want to see him alone in my office, so I went out into the hallway to face him there.

I took a chance, walked up to him and said: "Richard, what can I do for you?"

Richard turned and swiftly lunged at me with both hands. I stepped back as he grabbed my right hand with both of his and began to shake it.

"Mr. Hasten, I just came by today to shake your hand," he exclaimed.

"Why do you want to shake my hand?" I asked, puzzled. "I just fired you three days ago!"

"Come over here and I'll show you," he said, moving toward the open window and gesturing for me to look down to the street. I peered down and saw a taxi with the driver's door sitting open and the engine running.

"Mr. Hasten, that's my taxi," said Richard. "All my life, I wanted to own a taxi. Until you fired me, I never had the guts to go out and get one. Once you let me go, I had to do something, so I borrowed the money and bought this taxi. And I love it! I just wanted to thank you for giving me the push to go out and do what I really always wanted to do." He went on joyfully, "I never liked working indoors. I don't belong indoors. That's why I was always looking upward. I was looking for the sky. Thanks for helping me find the sky and finding my dream."

Richard waved good-bye as he jumped back into his taxi and sped off down the road.

This incident left me convinced that there is a right place for everyone in the organization, and sometimes, that place is outside of the organization.

As mentioned, one of the biggest problems I faced was in the area of housekeeping. I soon discovered that the general messiness was not entirely the fault of the work force. The same type of "efficiency experts" I had contended with back in Minneapolis had also implanted some of their bone-headed ideas here in Indianapolis. One such idea was to permit employees to eat on the job, thereby eliminating the need for a coffee break. The previous manager had stuck vending machines everywhere around the building. They were stocked with all sorts of snack foods and beverages. Employees were permitted to walk over to a vending machine at any time, purchase a candy bar, return to their station, and consume the candy. Meanwhile, candy wrappers and other trash littered the floor everywhere.

I immediately established an employee break area that housed all the vending machines in the building – along with tables, chairs and large trash containers. Employees were instructed to take regular breaks and to consume any snacks only in the break room. Eating on the job was strictly forbidden. With one notable exception, everyone liked the convenience of having all the vending machines in one place. And almost overnight, the place started looking much cleaner. The only chorus of opposition, not surprisingly, was emanating from the union. The union president marched into my office a few days after the "Great Vending Machine Revolution" and began shaking his finger in my face.

"There's going to be big trouble," he growled, "big trouble if you don't put those vending machines back where they were."

I stood up and faced him squarely. "Don't point that finger at me, mister. I'm going to clean this place up, with your help or without it. Instead of grumbling, you should be pleased that we're providing scheduled break times."

The fellow thought about this for a moment and then decided to back off.

While I did institute reforms that made working conditions better, by the same token, I insisted on total dedication when a person was on the job. Eight hours of work for eight hours of pay became my motto. Unfortunately,

I did have to cause some heads to roll in order to get this message through to everyone.

The printing operation functioned around the clock on three eight hour shifts – and I, of course, was in charge of all of them. I felt it my responsibility to be utterly familiar with all aspects of the production cycle during all three shifts. In this regard, I decided to make unannounced visits to the printing plant during evening and early morning hours. My first surprise visit to the graveyard shift took place early in my tenure at 3 AM. I walked into the building and was confronted with a deafening silence. There were no machines running, and I knew there were no meetings scheduled. I strolled in to the main department and observed the entire crew sitting around a table guzzling beer. They jumped up as soon as they spotted me, but it was too late. I fired them on the spot and made sure everyone knew about it the next morning.

I soon developed a reputation as being tough, but fair. And within six months, the plant had turned the corner and had stopped hemorrhaging money. While my work was exciting, challenging and rewarding, life in Indianapolis left a lot to be desired. I was putting in one hundred hour work weeks, and this left Simona home alone with a new baby in a strange city, with no support from friends or family. She was miserable and her unhappiness contributed to my own. We both very much wanted to return to Minneapolis when my one year hitch was up. We had not managed to become involved in the Jewish community at all. I did attend the orthodox synagogue, B'nai Torah, for my father's *yahrtzeit* (memorial) and for the High Holidays, but my stringent work schedule left no time for anything more.

My outlook at Bemis could not have been more sunny. I had succeeded in turning a money losing operation into a powerful profit center almost overnight. By November, 1964, I was earning $9,500 per year as a Level 13 Superintendent, and there was serious talk about making me a Manager, which under Bemis' organizational chart, was the equivalent of a divisional vice-president. I was headed beyond manufacturing and into sales and marketing. Despite all of these positives, a steady stream of dissatisfaction began to creep into my thinking.

My malaise began as I started talking to people who had been with Bemis for 30 to 40 years. After a point, these folks had become less and less productive as they slowed down and lost some of their youthful vigor and ambition. Many were in a dead-end rut, and it was often my job to try to find work for these fellows in order to keep them busy. Bemis preferred not to fire these senior staffers. At the same time, the career trajectories of these "elderly" execs were unmistakeably in descent. After a certain point promotions were replaced with demotions, and I dreaded it whenever I was required to carry out this unpleasant task. It was my onerous responsibility to sit on one side of a desk and tell a man thirty years my senior that he was being transferred to a less critical and lower-paying job. Suddenly, it became clear to me: this is where I'm headed. Someday, I'm going to be on the other side of this desk and some junior executive is going to be leading me out to pasture. It was an epiphany and the thought absolutely terrified me!

"Sure," I thought, "I'm working hard and achieving great things today," but I was just as sure that these fellows also worked hard during their younger years. I made up my mind that this was not going to be my fate. I went home to Simona and told her that at the first realistic opportunity, I was going to venture into my own business. I was not going to ripen on a corporate vine and then drop to the ground when all the juice was dried up. I was confident of my skills as a manager, and I knew I could transfer them easily into any business I wished to pursue.

To Simona, who always gave me her unconditional support, and to our friends with whom I would discuss my future business plans, I'm sure that I must have sounded like something of a dreamer. But I was a strong believer in the words of Theodore Herzl, the founder of modern Zionism, who said in reference to the establishment of a Jewish state fifty years hence: "*Im tirtzu, ayn zoo agadah.*" (If you will it, it is no dream.)

As our little family celebrated its first Indiana Thanksgiving, I could not help but give thanks to my late father. Just like years before, when my father became convinced that his only option was to get out of our hometown before it was too late, I was now also overcome with a similar, overpowering feeling. I had to get out – and the sooner the better. "*Im tirtzu, ayn zoo agadah.*" We had no idea, as we peered down the road ahead during that first Thanksgiving, how quickly and how strongly those words would soon guide our steps.

Chapter Nine

Testing My Talents

IN ADDITION to my anxiety over becoming a corporate burn-out, I was also harboring deep concerns about my job security. My friend and next-door neighbor would often serve as the sounding board for my various business ideas. He was an older man who had passed up numerous entrepreneurial opportunities because he did not wish to sacrifice his comfortable executive position at Western Electric, the city's largest manufacturing concern. His wife simply would not allow him to take the plunge and place their family's financial security at risk. So, he remained on the job at Western Electric until the day he was let go due to a general economic downturn. I swore a silent oath that I would never allow myself to be in a position where this could happen to me.

Fortunately, unlike my neighbor, I was blessed with a very gutsy and supportive wife. Simona's attitude was always: "If you're absolutely sure this is what you want to do, I'm here to help you do it." It was Simona's confidence and encouragement that gave me the "chutzpah" to take the necessary risks involved in establishing a new business. She will always enjoy my undying gratitude and appreciation for her unconditional support.

With each passing day, I became more and more convinced that I had to get out on my own. I became receptive to all sorts of business ideas. I pored over the newspapers and spoke of little else to my friends and family. I felt like the fellow in West Side Story who sang: "Something's coming, something good, if I can wait! Something's coming, I don't know what it is, but it is gonna be great!"

When the right opportunity finally did arrive, there was no bolt from the blue, no burning bush or other form of divine revelation. Instead, it was something as simple and innocuous as a new construction site that had cropped up on my route home from work. About nine blocks from my home, I noticed that a new building had just been completed and, in my frame of mind at the time, I was curious about every new business venture I came across. I pulled my car onto the gravel parking lot and walked in through the front door. A friendly chap approached me and introduced himself as Bill Wells. He informed me that he had just completed building this forty-four bed nursing home.

Bill explained that his background was in construction, and when he was unable to locate a suitable quality nursing home for his aged mother, he decided that he would build one himself. He told me how he had visited a number of local nursing homes and found that they all "stunk." They were mostly old-time boarding houses or converted hotels, and none of them was of sufficient quality for the care his mother needed. Mr. Wells had seen modern-style nursing homes in other cities, and he was convinced that there must be a demand for such facilities here in Indianapolis. He told me that, although he personally had no expertise in geriatric care, he had once owned a restaurant and knew how to run a kitchen. Mr. Wells was planning to man-age the nursing home himself, leaving the patient care coordination under the supervision of his ex-wife, Twyla. Twyla, an angular woman with a nervous laugh, had worked as a nurse's aid on a geriatric ward at a local hospital.

As we walked about the gleaming new facility, Mr. Wells continued to answer my endless stream of questions. He made sure I noticed the extra-wide corridors capable of turning a gurney a full 360 degrees, as he pointed out all the other modern amenities. There were no wards. Instead, each pair of rooms shared a common bathroom. He had truly done an amazing job of building a state-of-the-art nursing home, and I told him how impressed I was. I admitted my interest in starting a new business and explained how my wife had worked in the health service industry. I also pointed out that Simona's mother ran a small residential nursing home operation out of her home in Los Angeles. She had five or six extra beds and rented them out to elderly members of the Jewish community.

Since I lived in the neighborhood, I asked Mr. Wells if it would be okay if I stopped in from time to time to chat, and he gladly agreed. We shook hands and I wished him the best of luck with his new venture.

As it turned out, it would take a lot more than good luck to make this venture a success. After a few visits, it became apparent to me that Mr. Wells hadn't the faintest idea about how to run a business. He maintained no employee files, he calculated his own payroll, and he paid employees right up through payday. He didn't bother tracking his receivables and paid his bills as soon as they came in the door (*if he had the cash*), even if the vendor offered 30 day terms. His relationship with his staff was horrible. He hired only three nurses to provide three shifts of round-the-clock care. This forced him often to schedule them for back-to-back twelve hour shifts with no breaks for meals. I heard him deny a nurse's request for a day off, even though she had not had one in three weeks. Not surprisingly, Mr. Wells had a difficult time keeping adequate help on duty and was often reduced to performing much of the work himself.

Being something of a self-styled gourmet, Mr. Wells would invariably find fault with the menus prepared by the parade of cooks he hired. Whenever he was in charge of the kitchen, patients were forced to endure bizarre concoctions, such as sautéed calf's brains. He was his own secretary, and I recall him running down the hallway with a plunger in his hand, shouting, "My janitor quit this morning" as he ran by.

I would often stop in to see Mr. Wells after coming home late from work, around 9 or 10 PM. We would sit on the front porch of the nursing home and discuss his business affairs. He was steadily becoming more reliant on my advice as he discovered that I knew a thing or two about business management. I was also benefiting from the relationship, because I was gaining an inside peek into the workings of a business without having to invest any of my own money.

I tried to offer positive suggestions. When I saw his staff lined up at his office on a Friday afternoon to pick up their weekly paychecks, for a pay period that ended on Friday, I pointed out that he was paying for a half-day's labor which had not yet been performed.

"Mr. Wells, why don't you cut off the week on Tuesday or the previous Friday and give yourself a few days to make out a payroll," I suggested. "You won't be paying in advance that way, and you can certainly use the float. The impact on your cash flow over a year's time will be pretty dramatic."

He did not understand anything of what I was talking about. He was a hard-working guy, but he had no knowledge of basic business practices, and he was a disaster when it came to managing people.

Wells asked for, and I extended, advice in other areas as well. I helped him set up an effective billing system and designed an office organization structure that was simple and efficient. He was very impressed with both of these and did not fail to tell me so.

Over time, I became more and more convinced that I could operate this business without any difficulty…and that I could do a much better job of it than Mr. Wells was doing. Evidently, the same thoughts had crossed his mind as well. Finally, some six months after our first meeting, he laid his cards on the table.

"Hart, why don't you and I become partners?" he asked in a way that let me know he was dead serious. "You've got a good understanding of how to run things and I'm a pretty good builder by trade. We'd make a darned good team. I build 'em and you run 'em. What do you think?"

What I truly thought, at that point, I was not inclined to say. While I agreed that I had the right skills to successfully operate this business, I definitely did not care to be in partnership with Mr. Bill Wells. Wells was proposing that I put up some cash in exchange for a minority equity stake in the business. I suspected, correctly as it turned out, that Wells was strapped for cash and was tendering this offer in order to raise operating capital. Although the building held adequate space for forty-four beds, his occupancy had not risen above fifteen patients, and one of those was his own mother! Clearly, the business was sinking and the owner was looking for a lifeline to keep him afloat a bit longer. I'm certain that if I had accepted his offer, the lifeline would have turned into an anvil, and I would have been dragged down with him. I declined his offer, but at the same time I put a bug in his ear.

"No, Mr. Wells, I don't think bringing me in as a partner would work out. But if you're ever ready to sell the whole thing, then let me know and I'll make you an offer."

He listened to my answer, but declined to consider it.

"I don't want to sell it, Hart," he explained. "I've only been at this for a year. We've got fifteen beds filled, and we're growing. You've got to give things a little time. Think it over. Talk to the wife. This place is ready to take off. You and I could really do great things here."

This exchange went on for another six months. Wells, in complete denial about the course of his business, kept courting me to join him. I, of course, could see the true picture that he refused to face. The fact was that Wells was losing his shirt. He had yet to turn a profit, and, given his non-existent management skills, it was clear that he never would. I believed that all I had to do was bide my time, and before long, Wells would be calling me ready to sell out.

I explained my thinking to Simona and she was puzzled. Why would I want to buy a business that had lost money from the start? Shouldn't I be looking at businesses that had a good track record and were turning a profit? I explained that, except in extremely rare cases, successful businesses were not for sale. But more importantly, I had studied Wells' nursing home business very carefully. I had put together pro forma projections that had convinced me that if the facility could be filled up closer to capacity, it could make money – lots of money. I knew what his revenues were and understood that they would go up in direct proportion to the number of patients enrolled. In other words, thirty patients brought in twice as much revenue as fifteen patients, while forty-five brought in three times as much.

On the expense side, however, there were economies of scale at work. Doubling the patient population would only increase the overhead by forty percent. This meant that, in this business, profit margins rose dramatically as patient population grew. I determined that if I could get just twenty-eight beds filled, I could reach a break-even point. And if I could fill all forty-four beds, this nursing home would bring in an annual income roughly double that of my current salary at Bemis.

Of course, this raised the obvious question of why I presumed I would be successful in filling up these beds when Mr. Wells, after over a year of trying, had not been able to do so. The answer was simple: good management. Wells was so overwhelmed with cooking the meals, mopping the floor, making the beds and so forth that he didn't have the time to even answer the phone when a prospective patient called in. I planned to do things differently. I would assemble an effective management team that would afford me the time to carry out job number one: recruiting patients to fill our beds. I would not be distracted by all the grunt work that occupied Wells' time. Instead, I would be on the phone with doctors, convincing them to send me their elderly patients. I would do the one thing that Wells would never, or could never, do: launch a full-scale marketing effort aimed at filling up the facility. I believed that this would make all the difference in the world, and I'm happy to report that I was entirely correct.

I did not share these thoughts or my financial projections with Mr. Wells, although I did continue offering him my best management advice. I felt that any improvements he implemented would only serve to benefit me when I finally did get the chance to take over. I observed the weeks go by as Wells became more and more desperate and despondent over his situation. He was forced to move into the facility so he could keep working around the clock. He would cry to me continually about how he was unable to find any good staff, while never recognizing that you couldn't work people thirty days straight and expect them to remain on the job. Finally, the day I had been expecting arrived with a phone call. I picked up and heard Wells' hoarse voice on the line.

"Hart, you gotta help me," he pleaded. "I'm gonna have a heart attack and die right here if I don't get out. I'm working eighteen hour days, seven days a week, and it's killing me. You asked me to call you when I was ready to sell. Well, I'm ready. Let's talk."

We did talk, and I quickly learned what was really on Wells' mind. He was not looking to get out of the nursing home business entirely. He was just looking to recoup his investment and take a little time off. He believed that the business would stay in my hands just long enough for me to fail, at which point he would return in glory to save the day.

After some negotiating, we settled on a price for the entire operation. I would pay him a sum at closing and assume the mortgage payments on the building. Even after assembling all my savings, raising money from my friends and family, I was still short, and Wells agreed to take back a sales contract note in lieu of a portion of the purchase price.

He assessed me as being pretty green. I was in my early thirties, and while I knew a few things about management, I had no background whatsoever in patient care. He figured that, given my lack of experience, I wouldn't last too long in such a cut-throat business. Hence, he put together a very strict sales contract that entitled him to walk back in and re-possess the business if I so much as blinked the wrong way. For example, if a payment was only three days late, he was entitled to foreclose. This is exactly what he expected would happen. Wells extended the credit believing that the sales contract represented his ticket back into the business once I fell flat on my face.

Despite Wells' willingness to accept a portion of the purchase price on contract, I still had to come up with the bulk of the cash on my own. As I scrambled to put together the funds, there were four different individuals to whom I turned for assistance and guidance. They were my banker, my accountant, my lawyer and the executive director of the local Jewish agency. All four were absolutely uniform in their assessments of my prospects for success: "Forget about it!"

Starting with the last, Frank Newman had recently been named executive director of the Jewish Welfare Federation of Indianapolis. The Federation was then, and remains, the primary provider of social services to the local Jewish community. The Federation operated a Jewish old age home, known as the Bornstein Home, on the city's near north side. It was an aging building in a run-down neighborhood, and it occurred to me that they might be interested in upgrading. I approached Newman and suggested that, once I took over Wells' business, I could convert it to a kosher facility and sub-contract with the Federation to provide geriatric care for the Jewish community. Frank was about fifteen years my senior and spoke candidly with me.

"Hart, why would we want to take on a bigger facility when we can't fill the beds in the place we've got now," he explained. "Nursing homes are a dirty, ugly business. Take my advice, forget about nursing homes and find something else."

"Well, could you at least send some patients my way?" I asked.

"Why would we do that when our place is half empty?" he explained. "This is not the business for you, Hart."

I had also sought the counsel of my accountant. I had turned over all of Wells' financial statements, along with my projections, to Don Tekulve of the Max Cassen & Co. accountancy firm and asked that he review them for me. I recall pressuring Don constantly until he finished. When he finally called at 11 PM one evening to say that he had completed his review, I rushed right over to his house. I was hungry for some validation and was hoping that Don would deliver it. Don offered me a chair and I sat down facing him.

"Well, how does it look?" I asked anxiously.

Don stared at the floor and shook his head slowly. "Hart, you have no idea," he said methodically, "how awful this guy is doing. You're getting into a real sickbed here, and I strongly advise you…don't do it. If you do, you'll lose every nickel you put up."

"Thanks for the advice, Don," I said as I collected my papers and headed for the door.

Sadly, Don didn't get it either. I knew that Wells' operation was a mess and that he was losing money, but instead of focusing on my very conservative projections, Don only considered the business' past performance as a guide. He could not imagine how someone like me, knowing nothing about the nursing home business, could march in and hope to turn things around. I understood his skepticism. But I also knew he was dead wrong.

My next stop was a meeting with my banker. The branch manager at the Indiana National Bank where I had my family account was a fellow known by his nickname, Duke. Duke had always gone out of his way to be friendly toward me because he knew I headed up the Bemis plant. Bemis, with about $5 million on deposit, was one of INB's largest customers. Duke was always very interested in my activities, and I confided in him from time to time about my ambitions to branch off on my own.

"When the time comes, Hart," he assured me, "you come see me. I'll give you the best financing deal in town. You can count on it."

Naturally, when the day arrived, I did go knocking on Duke's door. I explained that I was planning to acquire an existing nursing home and that I needed to borrow a portion of the purchase price in order to close the deal.

I delivered all the necessary paperwork to his office and awaited his approval. For weeks, Duke would not give me a definitive answer. He kept instructing me to come back the following week while he gave his loan committee and business evaluation people an opportunity to study the request. This went on for about a month until finally my patience ran out.

"Duke, just tell me how much of the $20,000 I need you'll be able to loan me," I asked plainly, expecting that he would come through with at least a portion of it.

"Nothing," he replied just as plainly.

He gave me the usual rigamarole about nursing homes being too risky and rose to shake my hand as he showed me to the door. I was crushed. This fellow had sucked up to me for over a year and offered to do whatever he could for me, as long as I was with Bemis. Now, he figured that I would be leaving Bemis to run my new business, and my goodwill didn't count for much. Business was business, I was learning.

Finally, I turned to my attorney, Graham Bell, to review the sales contracts, mortgage assignment and other documents involved in the transaction.

"You cannot sign this contract," he stated emphatically. "There's no way. I'm not going to let you sign a contract that is so completely unfavorable to your interests. According to this thing, if you're late in getting your payment in by just three days, he gets everything back. Hell, the Post Office could hold up your check for three days and you'd be screwed."

"Well, I'm not worried about that one bit, Mr. Bell," I explained. "You see, I'm just going to pretend that the payments are due on the fifteenth of the previous month, and I'm going to deliver each payment to Mr. Wells in person."

"I'm sorry, Hart. I cannot, in good conscience, sign off on this contract as it now stands."

"I guess that means I need to find another attorney," I said calmly.

"I guess it does," he replied. So that's exactly what I did.

My next attorney was a fellow named Joe Quill. I had met Joe through his mother, who was a patient at the nursing home. Fortunately, Joe was familiar with the facility and understood my priorities a little more clearly. I think he also believed (*correctly, as it turned out*) that if I took over the home, I'd do a better of job of operating it, and hence, his mother would wind up receiving better care. We were able to formulate and execute the final contract with no difficulty. When I asked Joe what he really thought about the deal, he advised me candidly that I was paying way too much and that I should not give up my day job, just in case.

It appeared that no one saw what I saw when I looked at the facility. They saw a mismanaged white elephant that was consistently losing money, which it certainly was. But what I saw was the only specific-use nursing home facility in the city. While many were to follow, at that time, this was the only nursing home housed in a building that was built especially for that purpose. I saw the eight foot wide corridors and the intelligent room layouts. I saw a modern stainless steel kitchen capable of easily feeding forty-four patients and more. I felt in my bones that, if only these assets could be properly leveraged, this business had the potential of becoming a prover-bial gold mine. Unfortunately, no one, other than Simona, shared or even understood my vision.

Among those who were mystified by my decision was Craig Wooley, my immediate boss at Bemis. After turning in my three month notice, I took Craig by the hand and showed him the business I was buying.

"You're not serious?" he asked. "You're leaving Bemis to run this place? Woo, boy, are you ever making a mistake. By the way, I am refusing to accept your resignation. You are still responsible for the plant here in Indy. I don't have anyone else. I don't care if you only show up once a week, you are the only guy that can run this place. And you're going to remain on full salary."

I appreciated the financial cushion as I struck out on my own. I did stay around Bemis for a few more months after that, but effective December 31, 1965, my association with Bemis – the company that had nurtured me and taught me so much about American business practices over the past 14 years – was over for good. And there was nothing extraordinary about Bemis. They, just like thousands of other US companies, did not have a policy in place to train post-war immigrants in American business methods. They simply did so for their own self-interest. I received my education while Bemis received the benefit of my labor. In shaping me into an effective business leader, they were motivated by the same consideration that drives all of American indus-try, which is building value for their ownership. I don't believe I could have enjoyed a better grounding in management at any business school in the world than the one I was fortunate to receive at Bemis. The debt I owe this company can never fully be expressed, nor can it ever be repaid.

The fellow that did get repaid, on the other hand, was Mr. Bill Wells. For despite dire warnings from every quarter, or maybe because of them, my new business was a success from the very start. Within six months, we were one hundred percent occupied. My financial projections turned out to be incorrect. They were too conservative. My actual operating results were even better than I had imagined.

By following my business plan to the letter, things fell into place very rapidly. I put together a cohesive management team that was experienced in patient care, so that the quality of our service matched the strength of our modern facility. As I had planned, I spent the bulk of my time on the phone and in face-to-face meetings with doctors. I understood that, when it came time for a family to place a parent into a nursing home, the one person they relied on for guidance was their trusted family physician. If I could demonstrate to area GP's that we had the only nursing home in the state with hospital-style, modern, well-lit rooms and 24-hour care, they would flock to our doors. And that's exactly what happened. My pitch to local doctors was a simple one:

I operate the finest nursing home in town.

Ours is the only facility built from the ground up as a nursing home.

We have a Director of Nursing and a full-time RN on staff.

We have the finest nurses' aides, each personally interviewed and selected by me.

Among the many changes I instituted was a "ladies only" policy. We stopped accepting men as patients. This eliminated the need for orderlies, and it simplified the room assignments, since two ladies could share a bathroom while an unmarried man and woman could not.

All of our patients were private pay. We did not bill insurance companies or Social Security. And once we were completely full, we could start charging higher fees. I had not anticipated this in preparing my original financial projections, all of which assumed that rates would remain constant.

There were other bonuses to being in strong demand. We could actually operate at over one hundred percent occupancy. When I first spotted this, I thought we had made an accounting mistake. Our weekly revenue was more than the number of beds multiplied by the weekly rate! There were two main reasons for this apparent miracle. First, our waiting list was so tight that if a patient vacated a room in the morning, we could often get another patient moved in by the afternoon. This permitted us to collect twice for the same day. In addition, patients would often be required to visit the hospital for an in-patient procedure. Their families wanted to make sure that the patient's bed was still available when he or she got out of the hospital, so they would continue to pay for the room even while the patient was not there. This afforded us the opportunity to place short-stay patients into the same room temporarily, which resulted in double the revenue for the room.

The most ironic situation was that, once we had a waiting list, the same doctors whom I had solicited for patients during our first few months were now calling me looking for beds…and I had to turn them away. They often became indignant: "You came to me asking me to send you patients and, now that I do so, you don't have the room for them?" It was obviously time to think about expansion.

I recall receiving our first six-month financial statement from Don Tekulve at the same time we hit one hundred percent occupancy. The statements showed a very glowing financial picture. I immediately ran down to the INB branch to present our statements to Duke for his review and for a bit of "I told you so" gloating. He literally fell out of his chair!

"Hart, this is incredible," he gasped in total amazement. "How in the hell did you do it?"

"Simple. I worked my butt off," I replied.

"I owe you an apology, Hart," he said sincerely.

"Forget the apology. As you can see, we're full up and we got them busting down the doors," I crowed. "What I need is more money to expand."

This time, Duke smelled a winner and was anxious to talk about getting me that business expansion loan.

In an unbelievably short period of time, our nursing home, Colonial Crest (which was the moniker that Bill Wells had established), had developed a reputation as the finest facility of its kind in the state. I recall our first inspection by the State Board of Health. Mrs. Van Pelt was the inspector, accompanied by Ruth Bouk, the director of the agency. Van Pelt was an RN, and it was her job to examine the patients and determine the level of care they were receiving. After her review, she approached me and confided a personal opinion.

"You have the best facility in the state, Mr. Hasten."

"Write it down," I urged. "Please write that on the report, Nurse Van Pelt."

She couldn't do it, however. "I'm not allowed to write down personal opinions, I'm afraid," she said apologetically. "In fact, I'm supposed to find something wrong. If I don't, the agency will assume I'm not doing my job properly."

My strategy was working beyond my expectations. In six short months, I had taken a business that everyone agreed was a dead horse and had turned it into a cash cow. This involved paying attention to both sides of the ledger. On the one hand, I knew that our success depended on our reputation, which, in turn, was based on the high level of care we dispensed. To enhance this level of care, I put together the finest quality patient care team available. Unlike my predecessor, I did not have the arrogance to believe I could effectively operate the kitchen. Instead, I hired a dietician, Mrs. Porter, to carry out our meal planning. She was a professor of nutrition at a local university and a delightful person. Mrs. Porter was a tremendous asset and a wonderful teacher. She educated me about how to plan balanced meals around the seasons, how to keep track of calories, how to prepare meals for diabetics, and many more important food management skills. In addition, I was able to tout our facility as the only nursing home with a trained dietician on staff.

I noted an interesting phenomenon. Moves such as the hiring of a dietician and other qualified staff often resulted in an increase, not a decrease, in the business' bottom line. By devising meal plans months in advance, I was able to accurately project my food requirements and plan my purchasing accordingly. Mr. Wells had made it a habit to visit the grocery every day and paid cash at the check-out. When I questioned this practice, he informed me, "I want everything to be fresh for my patients." This reasoning didn't make much sense when I saw him buying canned vegetables, ketchup and other grocery staples.

With a meal plan in hand, I was able to begin purchasing in quantity from institutional provisioners. I was able to take advantage of the sales promotions they offered and to stock up on an item when necessary. In this way I was able to reduce the food cost per patient dramatically, while at the same time, increase the quality and nutritional value of the meals we served. It was a true "win-win" situation that was repeated in every aspect of the business.

I also upgraded the on-premise beauty salon in a spare room that I outfitted with a beautician's chair, sink and mirrors. Once each week, a beautician was available in the salon for hairstyling, haircuts, manicures, facials and the like for our patients. Since the patients paid for the services, except for the water used my only expenses were the initial cost of the fixtures and furnishings for the salon. The beautician would pay me a small commission, from which I quickly recovered my initial investment. But the true benefit was the enormous boost in self-esteem that this afforded our patients.

Family members coming to visit our patients would find them looking and feeling great. This created a high level of satisfaction with our facility. We were perceived as a place that not merely warehoused the elderly, but one that worked hard to provide a high quality of life for each patient. My desire arose from a genuine concern for the welfare of our patients, but I also understood that doing so reduced the guilt that a family member often feels about institutionalizing a parent. It may sound cynical, but if grandma's happy, the family is happy – and it's the family that pays the bill each month.

My key philosophy, which I worked to imprint on everyone on my staff, was that the "patient comes first." This may sound obvious, but this was not the standard of care being practiced in other nursing homes at the time. One example of how this philosophy was manifested was in the area of staff scheduling.

In visiting competing nursing homes, I noticed a particular pattern. These places were most heavily staffed during the times when staff was least needed. If you walked into a typical nursing home on a Sunday or holiday, you would find a skeleton crew on hand. And yet, this was precisely the time when relatives would most often come to call. This situation seemed entirely backward to me. I made sure, when hiring new staff members, that they were willing to work weekends and holidays.

I always made sure that we had extra staff on duty during holidays, and I insisted that the beauticians work extra shifts before Christmas, so that when families came to visit, their loved ones looked their best. I made it a point to stand at the front entrance and greet visitors every Sunday, and I made sure our best meals were served when I knew relatives would be join-ing us. Family members would come away, after a visit, deeply impressed with the high quality of care their loved ones were receiving. And it wasn't merely an act we put on for the benefit of patients' families. We really did raise the bar when it came to quality of care. Soon, the entire industry would be following our lead.

The reason for our success in capturing an early leadership role in this area was very simple. Good care was good business. When I took over the home, patients were being charged $8 per day for room, full board and services. As soon as we began raising the standards and offering more in the way of therapy and other services, we were able to begin charging more. And once the word spread – and it spread very, very quickly – we filled up to capacity, which, of course, enabled us to once again enhance our fees.

It did not take long for our competitors to catch on and start imitating some of our practices, but we managed to stay several steps ahead of them for many years to come. Meanwhile, patients benefited as the entire nursing home industry began focusing on quality of care issues.

In the very beginning, as I was still assembling my permanent staff, Simona and I would regularly carry out many of the day-to-day chores. Child care became an issue, since we really did not have the money for a full-time babysitter. Instead, I built a little playroom in the attic space of the nursing home just for little Renée. We outfitted the private playroom with toys, and we would check on her regularly throughout the day. Pretty soon little Renée became something of a familiar fixture around the nursing home.

During those early days, Simona would prepare lunch and dinner. Preparing breakfast seven days a week was my job. We really worked like galley slaves to make sure our patients were receiving the best of care. I understood that we were developing a reputation, and it was by this reputation that our business lived or died. That is the reason I became so concerned when, during our second week of ownership, I had a run-in with Mrs. Hopkins.

Mrs. Hopkins was the niece of a rather difficult, non-ambulatory patient, Mrs. Jenkins. I recall that Mrs. Jenkins had very delicate skin, and we had to continually keep turning her, so she would not develop bedsores or ulcers. I had staff members dedicated to this task and they were doing a fine job. The problem was that Mrs. Hopkins, her niece, was something of a wag, and word soon got back to me that she was complaining to other patients and to their families that the Hastens, who had just taken over the nursing home, were too young to know what they were doing. I was told that she was planning on taking her aunt out of the home and, not only that, she was encouraging other families to do the same. She had told everyone that she was watching us very closely and, sure enough, she was on hand every day, observing every little detail of our operation.

I smelled a crisis brewing and decided that I had to confront it before it got out of hand and destroyed my new business before it was even born. I found Mrs. Hopkins in the hallway headed for the laundry room and intercepted her.

"Oh, Mrs. Hopkins," I beckoned politely, "do you have a moment? I'd like to talk with you. Won't you please step into my office?"

As soon as she sat down in my office, I closed the door and turned to her immediately.

"So you think we're too young to run a nursing home?" I said with some defiance.

She ran for cover.

"I...I...I never said that!" she stammered.

"Oh yes, you did, Mrs. Hopkins. I heard it from several very reliable sources. And here's what I think: If you do not trust us with the care of your aunt, you should take her somewhere else right away."

"But I already paid for the week," she retorted. "I'm not going to lose that payment by taking her out before the week's up."

"We give refunds, Mrs. Hopkins," I assured her. "You won't lose a penny."

"Well, I don't know," she equivocated. "I guess I'll think about it. Let's just wait and see how it goes."

"No, I'm afraid you don't understand, Mrs. Hopkins," I said firmly. "If you wish to keep your aunt in this facility, then I must insist that you stop bad-mouthing us at once. When you walk out this door, I insist that you no longer tell people that we're too young or inexperienced to run this place. If I hear that you are continuing this practice, I will ask you to remove your aunt from our care at once. Am I being clear?"

Her jaw dropped and she was too stunned to say a word.

"Let me tell you a few things about myself, Mrs. Hopkins," I said more warmly. "I studied this business as an apprentice with Mr. Wells for a long time, and I know how to operate this home the right way."

I then ran down my credentials and impressed her with my achievements at Bemis.

"In the short time since we took over, haven't you noticed some positive changes?" I asked. "Did you notice that we have more staff on duty? I'm interviewing for a dietician, a full-time director of nursing and a new secretary. It is my goal to improve the overall level of care here."

"Well," she said after a pause, "we'll just have to wait and see about that."

"That's fine. You do that. And if there's anything you observe that we could be doing better, you come right back into this office and tell me about it. I promise to listen, and if it makes sense, I'll act on your suggestion. All I ask is that you discontinue your campaign of criticism. Do you think you can do that?"

"Okay, Mr. Hasten," she said finally. "I won't say another word to anyone but you."

We shook hands and she left. Within a few weeks, she was a changed woman. Every time we would meet in the hallway, she would offer the same apology.

"Oh, Mr. Hasten," she would beg, "you must forgive me. You were so right. You do give better care than Mr. Wells did. My aunt is much happier here since you took over. Please forgive me. I'll never say anything bad about you again."

This went on every day, and she got to be a bit of a pest.

"Okay, okay, already," I told her. "Forget about it."

In hindsight, the Mrs. Hopkins case may seem like a minor matter, but I still feel that had I not dealt with the situation head-on, her word-of-mouth campaign could have done irreparable damage. I knew that her complaints were unfounded and might even have been based on some level of anti-Semitism. I also knew that for my business plan to succeed, I had to develop a spotless reputation in the community and in the industry. Had her activities gone unchecked, she could have easily spearheaded a mass defection, and then I would surely have been finished...and all those nay-sayers would have been proven correct. A newly established business is innately susceptible to mortal attack. A problem that may constitute only a minor annoyance for a large, thriving company could easily spell doom for an embryonic entity like ours.

A case in point is the crisis I faced about a year after taking over the home. Mr. Wells, who was a self-described master builder, erred seriously when installing the building's heating system. As the weather turned cool in October, we fired up the boiler, only to learn that it was leaking badly. Unlike more modern sectional boilers that may remain partly functional in case of a leak, our boiler was not so designed. One leak meant we had no heat. A quick inspection revealed that the boiler could not be repaired and must be replaced – which was no easy feat, since it was put in place before the walls were built around it. Removing the leaky boiler required tearing down load-bearing walls, along with other feats of engineering. They told me it would take a week to remove the old boiler and replace it with a new sectional one.

"A week?" I shrieked. "We have no heat! It's October. I've got elderly patients in here. We can't be without heat for a whole week!" They put on two extra crews, worked around the clock, and agreed to finish the job in three days. I gave them the okay to do the work.

We had to keep the boiler problem under wraps. If patients and their families learned that we had no heat, they would have packed up and moved out in a heartbeat. I instructed the staff to claim ignorance about any heating problems.

"If a patient mentions that it's a bit chilly," I explained at a staff meeting, "bring her some more blankets." Whenever a patient commented about the cooler temperatures, I would respond with, "I'll go turn up the thermostat right away." This was no lie, since I did, in fact, turn up the thermostat, although I knew it would have no effect since we had no boiler. I thought of bringing in electric space heaters, but decided against it because of their poor safety record. I also felt that the sight of space heaters might alarm the patients.

Of course, we were lucky, as well. Had the weather turned much colder during those three days, we would have been sunk. As it turned out, a catastrophe was averted. We kept our patients toasty warm under the blankets, and we did not see a single defection. Had we not been so lucky, and had the outdoor temperature fallen, we would have been forced to close our doors and relocate our patients while the heating system was being repaired. There is no question in my mind that this outcome would have been the death knell for our new enterprise.

Another close call occurred a few months later when one of our patients was exhibiting jaundice and was diagnosed with hepatitis A by her private physician, Dr. Jones. Dr. Jones insisted that he had to report this case to the State Board of Health. I knew what this meant. If the patient was suspected of having a contagious disease, our facility would, in all likelihood, be quarantined. At this stage of the game, a health quarantine would effectively put us out of business...maybe for good.

I politely asked Dr. Jones, "Would it be okay if I had our staff medical director examine the patient?"

"By all means," he replied.

By this time, as part of my program of providing top quality patient care, I had already hired a medical director. Dr. Albert Donato was in private family practice and agreed to act as a part-time consultant for medical issues at our facility. Ours was the first, but not the last, area nursing home with a full-fledged physician serving as medical director. When Dr. Donato arrived, I took him aside and spoke to him gravely.

"Dr. Donato, I'm afraid it's Dr. Jones' intention to report this case to the State Board of Health. I would hate to see that happen, since they would be forced to close us down over this. Please examine her very carefully and let me know if calling the Health Department is absolutely necessary."

Dr. Donato nodded agreement and immediately went off to conduct his examination. After studying the chart, he observed that the patient had recently undergone a gall bladder operation. He concluded that the jaundice was the result of the operation and not due to hepatitis or any other type of contagion. I immediately phoned Dr. Jones with the good news.

"Dr. Jones," I exclaimed, "Dr. Donato is convinced that the jaundice is the result of her gall bladder surgery and not hepatitis. We'll keep her isolated and under observation, but we don't feel that a call to the Health Department is warranted."

Dr. Jones did not immediately wish to accept Dr. Donato's diagnosis. I placed the two physicians on the phone and listened as they debated the case. In the end, Dr. Jones reluctantly agreed to delay calling the Health Department and to wait a few more days to see what developed. Within that time, the patient fully recovered. No other similar cases surfaced, and Dr. Donato's diagnosis was deemed the correct one. I am convinced that, had I not acted quickly and brought in a second opinion, we would have been shut down.

The patient might have survived, but our fragile new business would, in all likelihood, not have been able to endure such an interruption.

During those early days, we got our first taste of dealing with demanding and difficult patients. Mrs. Shake was such a patient, and she was as tough as they come. The staff liked to dream up descriptive nicknames for many of the patients, and Mrs. Shake was known as "Stoneface" because of her grim demeanor. She was a rather self-absorbed widow of a prominent minister and did not feel she should be forced to eat her meals alongside the "common folk." Although we preferred that all patients eat their meals in the dining hall, our policy was "the patient is always right," so we honored her request and delivered each meal to her room. It was my duty to prepare Mrs. Shake's breakfast tray each morning.

Mr. Wells had given me some training in preparing breakfast, and I prided myself in the quality of every detail on the menu. If I prepared oatmeal, for example, there was never a lump to be found. My bacon was crisp to perfection and my toast was always the correct shade. Every breakfast was prepared to satisfy the particular tastes and preferences of each patient. Mrs. Shake's breakfast consisted of the following: a piece of fresh fruit; a glass of orange juice; a glass of prune juice; eggs over easy, firm and not runny; two strips of crisp bacon; two slices of white bread toasted to the exact shade of a manila envelope; black coffee, served boiling. In order to accommodate Mrs. Shake's insistence that everything be served hot, I would heat her plates and dishes on the grill before serving.

One sunny morning, the nurse returned to the kitchen carrying back the tray that I had just dispatched with Mrs. Shakes' breakfast. "What's wrong?" I asked. The nurse put down the tray and announced: "Mrs. Shake wants another breakfast." I pored over the tray trying to determine what caused her to reject what appeared to be a perfectly prepared breakfast. I prodded the eggs with a fork. They were just as she liked them. The toast was just the right shade. The coffee was scalding and the bacon was extra-crisp. Flawless.

I asked the nurse: "Why did she send it back?"

"Mr. Hasten, you always told me 'Don't argue with the patient,' so I didn't ask any questions. I just brought it back."

She had me there. But I was stumped. What was the problem? I could not conceive of how I could improve on this breakfast. I picked up the tray and headed for Mrs. Shake's room. Once there, I placed the tray on the side table and turned to her.

"Mrs. Shake, why did you send this breakfast back?" I asked politely. "What's wrong with it?"

"What's wrong with it? Why anyone can see what's wrong with it!" she exclaimed.

"Well, I'm sorry, Mrs. Shake," I said. "I've gone over each item and I cannot find anything wrong with it at all."

"First of all, the eggs are not right."

I took a fork and cut into the eggs and then said: "You see. They're firm, not runny. Isn't that the way you like them?"

"Okay," she allowed, "the eggs are okay, but the toast. Will you look at the toast? It's soaked. Soaked!"

I picked up the plate of toast, turning and examining each slice with scrutiny. She pointed to a corner of one piece. Looking very closely I could see that a spot of grease had been absorbed by the toast where it had touched the bacon.

"But, Mrs. Shake," I said. "it's only a drop of grease from the bacon. I really can't avoid that, you know."

"I don't care," she insisted. "I want another breakfast."

I put down the toast, went to the door, closed it and walked over to face Mrs. Shake. She was somewhat hard of hearing, and I would have to shout what I had to tell her. I did not wish for any of the staff to hear my next words.

"Mrs. Shake, I am not going to make you another breakfast. I cannot improve on this breakfast."

She remained impassive.

"Let me tell you something, Mrs. Shake," I said more forcefully. "It would be a sin to throw out this perfectly good breakfast. You're the wife of a minister. You, of all people, should understand what sin is all about." I could see that I was starting to get through to her, so I went on: "I think what's best at this point is for me to call your son to pick you up and find you another nursing home. It's clear that we are unable to please you here."

At this, her attitude took an about-face.

"Oh, Mr. Hasten, don't do it!" she pleaded. "Don't call my son. You know he recently had a heart attack."

I nodded.

"This would just kill him. Forget the whole thing. Leave the breakfast. I'll eat it."

Evidently I had said just the right thing.

I immersed myself in my new role as nursing home administrator. I got up to my elbows in every aspect of the operation. As stated, there were only fifteen patients onboard when I took over the reins. Within a few weeks, I knew everything there was to know about each patient and her family. I knew their idiosyncrasies. I knew what they liked to eat for breakfast and when they preferred to visit the bathroom. I am still able today, more than 35 years later, to recite all fifteen of their names and clearly picture their faces.

In order to achieve the level of patient care that I believed essential, it was often necessary to re-educate our nursing staff. Most nurses were "hospital-oriented" rather than "patient-oriented." They were fine when it came to dispensing medication and carrying out medical procedures, but looking after a patient's personal needs was outside of their territory. It was an ongoing struggle to change this mindset.

"You're doing a great job keeping track of the patient's medication," I recall explaining repeatedly to a Nurse Jarvis, "but what about her food? The patient has to eat or else she'll die. I don't want her to die. I want her to live. We make our living by making sure patients stay alive."

"But, Mr. Hasten," she replied, "I wasn't trained for that. I'm an RN. I'm not trained to feed the patient."

"I know that. But this is not a hospital. Here, everybody pitches in. You know that Mrs. Tangeman is a little senile, and you know that she needs some help getting started with her meals. If someone doesn't show her each time, she'll just stare at the plate and won't eat anything. Ten minutes later they'll take her tray away. After a few days of this, she'll starve. And if she starves to death, she won't be able to take any of your pills. So, just make it part of your job to feed her a few bites at the start of every meal. Okay?"

Nurse Jarvis never did give me her cooperation, despite several warnings such as this. In the end, I was forced to let her go in the name of quality patient care. "I don't think you belong in geriatric nursing, Miss Jarvis," I told her candidly as she departed. What Miss Jarvis was missing was something known as TLC...tender, loving care. This was a commodity we dispensed generously in the way we looked after each patient's personal needs and desires. We recognized that we were dealing with individuals who were in the sunset of their lives, and we saw our role as comforters and caregivers.

I was always amazed at how much I could learn from our patients. They had accumulated so much life experience that I could not help but pick up huge helpings of wisdom from them. I'll always remember the valuable lesson I learned from Mrs. Washburn during the first year of our ownership.

Mrs. Washburn, aged eighty-five, was recovering from a broken hip. She was alert and semi-ambulatory. We learned that she had a "boyfriend." Her paramour was a man of ninety-two who lived at another nursing home. Mrs. Washburn corresponded with him daily. She would entrust her treasured love letters to noone but me. Every morning, she would knock on my office door with a neatly inscribed envelope in hand.

"Here's the letter to my boyfriend, Mr. Hasten," she would say as she handed me the precious envelope. "Make sure you mail it."

"Of course, Mrs. Washburn. I'll mail it," I assured her. She was rather hard of hearing, so I had to shout my words back to her. "Don't worry. Don't I always mail your letter for you?"

"Well, you know, this is going to my boyfriend, and he'll get very worried if he doesn't get my letter," she would explain each and every day.

I would take the letter, signal a thumbs up and place it into our outgoing mail basket. Her gentleman friend would respond to her daily correspondence about once a week. This went on for months and months, and everyone on our staff was well aware and quite charmed by this nonagenarian romance.

Then one day it happened: The mail carrier returned one of Mrs. Washburn's letters to me as undeliverable. I stared at the envelope and saw the dreaded words: Recipient Deceased. What was I going to do? I was crushed. I was numb. How was I going to tell this lovely lady that the beloved man of her life had died? This was my first such experience, and I took it very hard, but I decided that it was my job to personally deliver the bad news. The first thing I did was alert the nurses.

"I'm going to go into Mrs. Washburn's room and present some very bad news to her," I told the two nurses on duty. "I don't know how she's going to react when she hears that her boyfriend has died, but I want you to be prepared with sedation and resuscitation equipment, if necessary. If we're not ready to act, in her condition, I'm afraid that news like this might prove fatal. I want you both outside her door when I go in."

I entered her room gingerly and left the door partially open. Mrs. Washburn was seated at the table writing her daily letter.

"Mrs. Washburn, I'm afraid I have some bad news for you," I said, placing as much compassion as possible into my voice. "The last letter you sent to your boyfriend came back marked deceased." I held the returned letter out to her.

"What's that?" she said, cupping her ear.

I tried again. A bit louder this time: "You know the gentleman you've been writing to all this time? He has passed on."

"What? Speak up, will you?" she yelled, screwing her face up tightly.

This time I yelled it out at the top of my lungs: "Mrs. Washburn. Your boyfriend. He DIED!"

She looked at me very matter-of-factly and said in a normal tone: "Oh, he died, did he? So, I won't have to write to him anymore, will I?"

She was totally blasé. She shrugged, put away the stationery, took the returned envelope from my fingers and tossed it into the wastebasket. I noticed the waiting nurses chuckling as I left the room.

I was impressed that there was no hysteria, no trauma and no apoplexy – just a calm resignation to the realities of our existence. One of the many life lessons I learned from our geriatric patients was that, after a certain age, death is taken more or less in stride. Of course, there are always tears and mourning, but when death arrives late in life, without rancor or distress, it is viewed as something of a victory. This gentleman made it to the age of ninety-two and died with his wits intact, peacefully and comfortably. He had conquered life; it did not conquer him. How many of us will be able to do the same?

At about this time, I learned another valuable lesson concerning mortality among the elderly. This incident was so instructive that I recounted it for many years as part of our regular training and orientation program for newly hired nurses.

Mrs. Huston was the mother of a prominent local attorney. Charlie Huston was serving in the Nixon White House, and he had approached me about accepting his young mother as a patient in our Indianapolis center. She was a fifty-six year old stroke victim and was, admittedly, a very difficult patient. Her condition had perhaps altered her personality, rendering her so hard to deal with that several other homes had asked her to take up residence elsewhere. In situations such as this, I would always sit down with the family and with the Director of Nursing to discuss the case before reaching a decision. In most instances, the head nurse would agree to take on the challenge, and that's exactly what happened in this case. But we did not accept her blindly. We developed a detailed game plan on how we were going to deal with Mrs. Huston, and we stuck to it. The plan involved providing extra care, extra nurses' aides, and generally more attention by the entire staff.

The family had been accurate and honest about Mrs. Huston. She was tough. She refused to get out of bed. She refused to eat in the dining room. She was abusive and belligerent to everyone, including her three sons. She was extremely demanding, and her nurse's call light was on constantly. It was rough going, but much to the credit of my staff, we were dealing with her successfully.

It was my practice to be on duty by 7 AM so I could listen in on the night shift's report to the arriving day shift. By making myself acquainted with the details of each patient's condition, I was able to act as an effective administrator. One day, something in the night nurse's report struck me as unusual.

"Just a little while ago, right before 6 AM, Mrs. Huston pushed her call button and I went to her room. She ordered me to call all of her children right away. When I asked what was wrong, she said she didn't feel well and that I must call her kids and tell them to come right away. I took her blood pressure, pulse and temperature. Everything was normal. I checked all of her vitals and there was no change. She buzzed me a few more times after that, and each time she screamed at me to call her children. I told her 'Mrs. Huston, there's nothing wrong with you. You're just fine,' but you know how she is."

At this point, I chimed in: "Well, did you call her children, then?"

"No, I didn't, Mr. Hasten," she replied, "because I couldn't find a thing wrong with her."

I decided to go see Mrs. Huston personally. I found her in her normal state of agitation and distress.

"Mr. Hasten," she said anxiously, "I told that nurse to call my children right away. I don't feel well and I want all three of my kids here right now!"

I tried to calm her down, although I knew it was probably not going to work.

"But, Mrs. Huston," I said soothingly, "the nurse said she checked all your vital signs and couldn't find anything wrong."

"I don't give a damn what she said," she shot back. "I want my kids here *now*!"

I went back to confer with the Director of Nursing and asked her to have another look at Mrs. Huston.

A few moments later, the head nurse reported back confirming the earlier findings. "Mr. Hasten, she seems okay. I can't find anything irregular," she said. There was something in Mrs. Huston's voice and demeanor, however, that stuck with me. I decided to comply with her wishes and instructed the nurse to go ahead and phone her children. They were all given the same information: "We don't see any medical problem, but your mother says she doesn't feel well and is asking that you and your brothers come over right away." All three children arrived within the hour, but they were too late. Their mother was dead by the time they got there. Shortly before they arrived, Mrs. Huston was struck by a massive stroke and passed away. Evidently, this poor, tortured woman understood better than those caring for her that her end was at hand. And, in her own way, she was crying out for help. This case illustrated a phenomenon that I observed repeatedly in my contact with those on their last leg of life. It was one I wanted my staff to comprehend – particularly those freshly hospital-trained nurses who understood pills better than people.

"Always listen to the patient," I would instruct time after time. "Always listen to what the patient is telling you and give it credence. This is not a hospital. This is a nursing home. Things are different in a hospital. Here, we listen to what the patient has to say and try to fulfill their wishes. Here, we look at things from a human point of view...not only from a medical point of view." And then I would recount the tale of the lonesome death of Mrs. Huston.

Years later, people who knew my story would ask me, "Hart, you were never educated in geriatric care. You had no experience. How did you know what to do? How did you know how to instruct your staff?" It's a good question. Sure, I knew about general business practices, but how did I learn the nitty-gritty of the nursing home business? The answer lies in a Russian idiom, *"B'yeh-dah nah-oot-cheet,"* which translates to: "You will be taught by your troubles."

We had gambled everything we had and more on this venture, and my determination to succeed was forged in cold steel. Nothing was going to bend it. And even though we faced numerous threats during those early years, any one of which could have wiped us out, I somehow always found the will to convince myself, as I had done before, that "I shall not die!"

Interestingly, my first exposure to an American nursing home took place years before, and it was also my first experience at something else I would become very involved with later in life: fundraising. It was during our first few years in Minneapolis that my father received a frequent visitor to our home, our good friend and spiritual leader, Rabbi Ginzberg. The Rabbi explained that he was in a terrible bind because one of his congregants, a Mr. Kitsis, was unable to fulfill a large pledge he had made to the synagogue's operating fund.

"Without that $1,000 gift, Berish," he said plaintively, "we won't be able to make the mortgage payments on the building. I don't know what we're going to do."

"Why did he back out?" asked my father.

"Actually, he didn't back out. His family put him in a nursing home in St. Paul and now they say he won't be able to keep the pledge."

I overheard the conversation and decided that maybe I could help.

"Come on, Rabbi," I offered. "I'm going to drive you to St. Paul to pay a visit to Mr. Kitsis. I'm sure we can talk to him."

Rabbi Ginzberg was what might be called a "shtetl rabbi." During his entire sixty years he had never wandered far from his neighborhood. The thought of tracking down a donor in the far reaches of St. Paul was something he never would have done on his own. I knew that this is what needed to be done.

"I don't know even how to find the nursing home, Hart," he moaned.

"Don't worry, Rabbi," I assured him, "we'll find the place okay." And, without too much trouble, we did locate the Sholem Home in St. Paul. I recall walking down the halls of an American nursing home for the first time and being quite impressed. It was supported by the Jewish Federation and was filled with Jewish elderly from the Twin Cities area. It appeared clean and well-maintained, and when I met Mr. Kitsis, he seemed quite frail, but well-cared for.

I explained how important his gift was to prevent the bank from foreclosing on the synagogue, and that the shul was having trouble getting the money from his family. He listened carefully, went directly to his nightstand, took out a checkbook, and wrote out the check for $1,000 on the spot. I delivered the check to Rabbi Ginzberg and I became an instant hero in his eyes. He shook my hand vigorously and paid me a great compliment in Yiddish.

"You're a fine young man, Hetche, and I can tell from this that you will be a big success in America."

I'm not sure if he was referring to fundraising or to nursing homes, but as it turned out, I managed to achieve some success at both.

Sadly, I was soon to learn that Mr. Kitsis died two weeks after our visit.

Chapter Ten

Grappling With Growth

Within six months of taking over the nursing home operation, we found ourselves filled to capacity. Every one of our forty-four beds was filled, and we had a long waiting list. While this situation was a gratifying vindication of my business plan, it nevertheless created some compelling challenges. The doctors who had been originally sending me their elderly patients were now putting enormous pressure on me to continue finding beds for more of them, even though I explained repeatedly that I did not have any more beds available. Expansion appeared to be the only solution. Was I ready for it? While I had, by this point, assembled an effective management team, Simona and I were still putting in long shifts, with no days off, taking care of our current patients. How could we dare add more beds?

I decided I needed to see things on paper, so I contracted with a local architectural design firm, Ostrom & Chance, to come up with an expansion plan. I looked it over and liked it immediately. It called for a quantum increase from forty-four to one hundred and forty-four beds, and it involved acquiring the neighboring property – a small house owned by a widow who was not particularly inclined to sell. After some strenuous negotiations, she relented and we reached agreement on a price that was about three times the fair market value of the house. Now, I had to locate the funding sources for my expansion project. This feat turned out to be much easier than it had been the last time around.

Doctors seeking beds for their patients were not the only ones beating down my door. The same bankers, in particular a certain fellow named Duke, who had deemed the nursing home business too risky for them to finance, were now jumping over each other to put money into my hands. They say that "nothing succeeds like success," and I was amazed at how true this turned out to be.

The same economics that had impressed me early on were now finally impressing my financiers. They could see that if I tripled my capacity, my revenues would also triple, but that my expenses would not. This meant that I would achieve higher profit margins, making it possible for me to easily repay any loans they would extend. It all hinged on my ability to fill up those hundred new beds. Their confidence in me was buoyed when they saw how quickly I had filled the original forty-four beds, and then I showed them the waiting list which would fill over half of the new beds immediately.

Once I saw the ease with which expansion could be funded, I began to think in even larger terms. Our facility, in very short order, had become an industry showplace and the darling of the government agencies that regulated us. The State Board of Health, for example, would often direct prospective nursing home operators from around the state to visit us in order to observe what a model facility looked like. This strong relationship with local government would become very important as the coming winds of change swept through our industry.

As mentioned, my in-laws in Los Angeles operated a private residential nursing home, and they kept on top of industry trends. They would regularly communicate them to me, and I found that there was something new happening in California in response to President Johnson's War on Poverty – something called Medi-Cal. This state-subsidized medical insurance program for the elderly was having an enormous impact, as families discovered that quality institutional care for their aging loved ones now fell within their financial grasp. I was proven correct in my hunch that Medi-Cal would soon be implemented nationwide when Medicare arrived on the scene a few years later.

It became more and more clear that I had tapped into a national social phenomenon and that I was looking at the tip of the proverbial iceberg. The aging of America was an enormous demographic force that was to be harnessed by several key industries. But aside from pharmaceuticals, geriatric care was to experience the most dramatic growth. As these realities began to hit home, I was torn between pride and panic. I was proud to have gotten into this business at the right time, but I was in a panic over how to manage the enormous growth opportunities that now confronted me.

If I held out any hope of exploiting the massive prospects I now faced, I quickly realized that I could not do it alone. I had to find someone to help shoulder the load. But it couldn't be just any someone – it had to be the *right* someone.

My brother was in the midst of a very promising career with General Mills. He knew about, and was sympathetic toward my motives for getting into my own business. Mark faced many of the same issues I had dealt with at Bemis, and he also shared my ingrained independent nature. I decided to make the call and invite Mark to visit. After a thorough tour and a review of my expansion plans, we sat down and had a heart-to-heart...or rather, a Hart-to-Mark...talk. He told me how impressed he was with what I had put together, but that he really did not have a desire to leave General Mills. I offered the opening gambit.

"Look down the road, Mark," I said. "What do you see for yourself in five years?"

"Right now, I'm a chief engineer," he responded.

Among other tasks, Mark was responsible for devising the technology for producing the latest varieties of Cheerios and other breakfast cereals.

"They treat me pretty darn good, Hart. I'm looking at becoming a VP in a few years."

"But you'll still be on a salary. You'll still be exposed to lay-offs, and you're not building up any equity."

I made the usual pitch and did not encounter much resistance, nor much interest either way. But when I pulled out our financial statements and Mark got a look at the numbers involved, he was amazed.

"This is the *emmes* (truth)?" he asked.

"These statements are certified. I had to show them to the bank to get the loan approval." I told him. "Mark, look, this is just what we're able to do with me and Simona working. This amount would multiply by three or four or even ten times if you join up with me."

I could see that I had finally succeeded in creating a paradigm shift in Mark's mind. I definitely had his attention. I then addressed the family angle.

"I want you to move here, Mark. Bring Anna Ruth and the kids, and bring Mother to live with us, too."

Simona was pregnant with our second child, and Mark and Anna Ruth had a growing family of two boys and two girls. It would be wonderful for my mother to be close to all of her grandchildren. The concept was also in keeping with my father's legacy of strong family cohesion. He taught us that we were all survivors, and that we had to stick together to maintain our strength.

"Mark, I want you here also, so you can be in charge of new construction," I told him, appealing to his love of engineering. "We're going to be doing a lot of building, and I need someone I can trust to make sure things get built right, and for the right price. You can do this much better that I can."

Finally, I laid all my cards on the table. I knew that going into business with a family member held its share of risk. I had seen cases where neither the business nor the family managed to survive as a result. Friction usually flared up because one family member wished to exercise a disproportionate amount of control. I knew that if we were to avoid those pitfalls, I had to place my confidence in Mark unconditionally. I understood fully that I was taking a chance, but in hindsight, it was the best decision I ever made to offer Mark a fifty percent stake in the business.

"This means that both of us have to approve whatever we do," I explained. "If either of us says no, it's no," I explained. I knew that granting this veto power to another person was a huge risk. What if we couldn't agree? Nothing would ever get done. We'd be in permanent gridlock. But I felt that this was not going to happen…and happily, I was correct.

I deliberated this move for a very long time. After all, I had founded the enterprise. I had several years of experience under my belt. Wasn't I entitled to a larger share? In addition, as a fifty percent owner, Mark was entitled to half the profits. In other words, I was cutting my family's income in half and giving the other half to my brother. Expansion costs and debt service expense, until the place filled up, would also cut into our cash flow. I, of course, had to discuss all of this with Simona.

"How much is Mark going to pay you for half the business?" she asked.

"Nothing," I replied. "I'm giving it to him free. He comes in as a full partner owing nothing. We'll both be on the same level that way."

This turned out to be a wise decision. Over the years, Mark and I have not agreed on every issue, but whenever we did face disagreement, it was never complicated by questions of which of us had more at stake. While it was never articulated, we both knew that we would be equally affected by any decision that was reached. If we were right, we would both benefit equally, and if we were wrong, we would both suffer to the same extent. I went on to tell Simona about another provision we had agreed to: "We also decided not to go into other businesses independently," I explained. "Whatever we do business-wise from now on, we do it together." Simona understood my thinking and, as usual, gave me her full support.

While Mark and I certainly did not agree on every aspect of the operation of the nursing home business, or in any of the other businesses we jointly built over the years, I am proud to report that my confidence at that time was very well placed. Mark and I established a highly successful working alliance that has endured over thirty years and has spanned several industries.

Mark turned in his notice at General Mills and began commuting from

Minneapolis to Indianapolis to oversee the expansion project. It took over a year for him to completely move his family and our mother. By the end of 1967, he had completed the transition.

As I looked around the Passover Seder table in the spring of 1968 and surveyed our extended family, I was overcome with a sense of gratitude to the Almighty who had permitted such a day to arrive. While my father was with us only in spirit, his namesake, our new baby boy, Bernard, giggled happily on Simona's lap. My mother, Hannah, sat at the end of the table and lit the candles. To her right sat Mark and Anna Ruth and their four children: Eddie, Michael, Monica and Judy. We sat on her left side with Renée and Bernard.

After we blessed the first cup of wine, I recall commenting to Mother that this would indeed be a Seder to remember. We were all together, in spite of the best efforts of our enemies. We were under our own roof, operating our own business, surrounded by our "kinder" who would never face the kind of terrors that marked our childhood. Welcome to America, Mama, I said as I planted a kiss on her smiling lips.

Mark and I, working side-by-side, were able to pull off the one hundred-bed expansion project on budget and ahead of schedule. We filled up the beds almost overnight. In fact, once the space for the first fifty beds was ready, we received a rare authorization from the State Board to open our doors. There was a strong demand, and we had already established such a sterling reputation that we were permitted to begin operating with the place only half built. Once the project was completed, we had, in essence, tripled the size of our business. And we came away determined that our geometric growth would be sustained.

The pattern established with this remodeling was to serve as a template for our coming business growth. At every new construction project, from that point on, we were permitted to begin accepting patients well before the construction crews were finished. We were never bothered by the fear that the "pioneers get all the arrows." Innovation was our watchword. Ours were the first nursing homes, for example, to install sprinkler systems, long before being required to do so by law. I was amazed to discover how much downward impact the sprinklers had on our casualty insurance rates. But even more dramatic was the response from our customers. Family members deliberating between placing a loved one into one of our facilities versus a competing one would invariably be swayed by the fact that we had modern smoke and fire detectors, as well as a sprinkler system, in place.

We also pioneered the one-story, fully-ramped building design which was soon to be copied by all of our competitors. Every facility we constructed was free of steps or stairways. Each was also fitted with wide corridors able to accommodate a 180 degree bed turn. In case of an emergency, evacuating one of our buildings would be efficient and safe, even for our handicapped patients.

Our second location was east of Indianapolis in the town of Greenfield, Indiana. We had been approached by one of our referring physicians who had been sending patients to us. He was familiar with our operation and thought very highly of it. The doctor owned a parcel of land adjacent to the local hospital and told us: "We need a nursing home like this one in Greenfield." We agreed, and within one year, we had designed, constructed and begun operations at our second location.

With each new project, we were laying claim to the high ground and gaining the attention of the government, of the industry, and of our competitors. We were mystifying our competition by raising the bar on industry construction costs. By limiting ourselves to one-story buildings, and by offering such amenities as extra-wide hallways, beauty parlors, chapels, expansive nurses' stations, therapy centers and the like, we were driving up our operating cost per square foot considerably. How could we get away with this, given the economics of our industry? The key was occupancy. We discovered that we could build a facility up to the standards we had set forth for roughly $5,000 per bed. The value of that bed, on the open market, doubled or tripled on the day we opened our doors. Of course, for this economic magic to happen, one more thing had to be added to each bed: a patient. In other words, by building top-of-the-line facilities, we were creating strong demand, and this in turn created value – value that far exceeded the initial investment.

This policy did not mean we could afford to be frivolous or extravagant. With Mark at the controls, all building materials were closely budgeted and scrutinized. Our nursing homes were not lavish palaces, but sensible, efficient residences that were soon evolving into full-blown convalescent centers. Aside from a newspaper ad announcing an open house each time we opened a new facility, we never spent a dollar on conventional advertising. We recruited customers for years strictly via doctor referrals and word-of-mouth.

One individual who took particular notice of our success was Bill Wells. He observed what we were doing and, whether out of envy or stubbornness, decided to try it again himself. Just as he had done before, he built a new, rather small nursing home in Indianapolis and attempted to manage it himself. And of course, he got into the same trouble as before. Not long afterwards, Bill turned around and offered to sell it to me.

"Buy this one from me, Hart," he asked. "You know I build high qual-ity homes."

"Bill, I won't even consider it because it's only got forty beds," I explained. "We give top-dollar care, and we need a certain minimum number of beds to make the numbers work. You're about ten beds short."

I don't think Bill understood the economics, but he did gather that in order to sell us this place, he would need to expand. He promptly developed the neighboring property and added ten more beds, after which we made our deal and we had our third nursing home.

A pattern was developing with Mr. Wells. He next ventured to Terre Haute, about eighty miles due west of Indianapolis. This time, he had learned. He had obtained a large parcel of land and built a one hundred-bed facility. He once again attempted to run it single-handedly. One would think that by this time he would have come to the understanding that he was not cut out to work as a nursing home administrator, but Bill was a stubborn sort of guy and was guided by his pride. "If a guy like Hart can figure out how to make money in this business, why can't I?" was his attitude. For the third time, Bill came to me with an offer to sell because he was unable to manage the operation effectively. And for the third time, we reached agreement, took over the Terre Haute home, and enjoyed almost immediate success.

That was our last deal with Bill Wells. He went on to open and operate several more homes in the Indianapolis area. He never offered to sell us any more of them. Once Medicare came into the picture, the economics of our business were altered to the point that even someone like Bill could make a viable go of it.

Throughout this period, we never deviated from the fundamentals of TLC and devout patient care. The example of Mr. O'Neil illustrates this point.

Mr. Ed O'Neil enrolled his sister, a bed-ridden stroke victim, into one of our centers for housing and treatment. We began a course of therapies designed to get her on her feet and make her ambulatory. Slowly at first, and then with the help of a walker, we were successful in getting her to walk on her own. As the therapy progressed, her overall disposition and general health improved dramatically. I knew that Mr. O'Neil was pleased with his sister's progress, so I was surprised when, after about six months, he came into my office on a Sunday afternoon with an announcement.

"Mr. Hasten, I'm pleased to see how well my sister's improving," he began. "but it looks like she still needs to be in a home for a while longer. I've looked into that new modern nursing home that just opened over in Carmel. They look pretty good and they don't charge as much, either. I've decided to take her out of here and sign her up over there."

Ed was right in one sense. Because we offered a full range of rehab services, and because we focused more intensely on quality patient care, we were able to charge a bit more than the standard market rate at the time. Nevertheless, we always had a long waiting list. So, from a business standpoint, I wasn't too bothered about losing Ed's sister as a patient. I was, however, genuinely concerned about his sister's ongoing care.

"Ed, that's no problem," I told him sincerely. "But let me tell you something as a friend. We've gotten to know each other these last six months, and I think you know that we've made quite an investment in getting your sister back on her feet. We're in the midst of several different therapy tracks, and I think it would be best if you let us work with her a bit longer."

"Well, I've already given them a deposit over there," he admitted. "I'm sorry, but I'm taking her out."

"Okay, Ed. But I feel you're making a mistake. I just want you to know that."

Ed removed his sister that day, and I had the bed filled with another patient by sundown.

Exactly one week later, on the following Sunday, Ed came rushing in to see me. He stood in front of my desk, turned around, bent over and picked up his coattails and implored me:

"Hart, I want you to kick me as hard as you can!" When he turned back around, I could see that he had misty tears in his eyes.

"Why? What's wrong, Ed?" I demanded.

"She's gonna die, Hart. My sister. She's undergone a complete relapse. The day I took her over there last week, they stuck her in a bed and no one so much as looked at her till the next night. She is in worse shape now than when I first brought her to you six months ago," he sobbed. "You told me not to take her out, but like a fool, I did, and now she's going to die. It's going to be my fault and I don't want this on my conscience." He was bordering on hysteria. "Please, Hart. Take her back, I'm begging you!"

"That's awful, Ed," I sympathized. "I'm terribly sorry but I'm full. I gave her bed away the same day you left."

"You don't understand, Hart. I must have it back or she's dead. I'll do whatever it takes."

"I'll see what I can do, Ed." I said finally.

I checked and found that a patient was scheduled to move out that day. I was able to contact the family of the patient scheduled to move into the vacated room and, after some juggling between locations, I managed to free up a bed. I found Ed waiting in the lobby and gave him the news.

"We can take her back today, Ed. Bring her over," I told him. "I even managed to get her back into her old room."

This turned out to be a lucky break, and it made me a real hero in Ed's eyes. They brought Ed's sister over to us that afternoon by ambulance, and I greeted her as she lay in the stretcher. I was shocked. After only one week's absence, I could not recognize her as the same patient! She was emaciated, disheveled and moaning with discomfort. Her facial hair had not been dealt with, and she sported a distinct beard. After she was checked in, I sent my nursing director to look after her immediately. I instructed her to conduct a thorough evaluation and to report her condition to me and Ed right away. After some thirty minutes, the nurse joined us, and I could see she was wearing a big smile.

"Is she going to be okay?" asked Ed anxiously.

"She's going to be fine, Mr. O'Neil," assured the nurse. "She simply has not been receiving any care. First of all, she's stuffed up to her eyeballs. I don't think she's had a bowel movement for a week. I gave her an enema and she's feeling greatly relieved already."

By the next day, the patient was sitting up in bed, and we had already started her therapy to get her up and walking again. Luckily, she had not undergone any type of medical setback. She was simply suffering from neglect. Like many of our competitors, this facility evidently did not stress personal hygiene or many of the other extra-medical issues that contribute so greatly to a patient's total well-being. After a few weeks, we had a prodigal patient back on track and one very enthusiastic supporter: her brother.

For months after that, Ed would visit my office daily for no other reason than to shake my hand and say thanks. "You saved my sister's life, Hart, and I'm never going to forget it," he told me repeatedly. At times, he would be forced to wait for me in the lobby area, and he would invariably bend the ear of any prospective family members he would come across.

"Are you thinking about checking someone in here?" he would ask. "Well, let me tell you about the owner. He saved my sister's life. No kidding." He would then go on to recount the whole story, ancient mariner-style, to anyone willing to listen. For a long time, Ed was my unpaid PR director, and I know he felt that, by encouraging others to enroll in our facility, he was repaying the debt he felt he owed me. I did not have the heart to tell him that, with a waiting list a mile long, I did not really need the endorsements he was issuing. In fact, in the case of his sister, I never felt as though I did anything out of the ordinary. With this patient, as with all patients, I did whatever I could to dispense proper care. I saw this as my job and my obligation. And, to put it mildly, I loved my job!

By the mid-seventies, we had established ourselves as the premier provider of nursing home services in the state. We were subjected to a non-stop barrage of inquiries from competing businesses interested in selling off locations. Most of these opportunities were of poor quality and held little interest, but occasionally one would come along that caught our attention. Such a location was the Rolling Hills Nursing Home located in the flat lands of Anderson, Indiana, some sixty miles northeast of Indianapolis.

Rolling Hills was a showplace. It was built by a consortium of doctors who recognized the boom taking place in our industry and wanted to cash in on it. They constructed a modern, full-featured facility and spared no expense when it came to amenities. Unfortunately (for them) they hadn't the faintest clue about how to properly manage a nursing home. They somewhat arrogantly presumed that their medical knowledge would entitle them to success in the business. However, they soon discovered that they were losing their monogrammed shirts and decided they had better bail out. They contacted us through an agent and asked that we look the place over.

After a few visits, I quickly understood the situation. By this time, I could walk into any nursing home and tell within five minutes whether the patients were receiving proper care. In this place, they clearly were not. I was, however, impressed with the physical facility and concluded that if we could take it over for the right price, it would become a terrific opportunity for us. But it would take some serious work, because we would need to overhaul the entire operation from top to bottom and re-train the staff to do business the right way – our way.

Absolutely nothing was being run correctly. First of all, the place looked and felt like a hospital ward. For example, all the walls were painted in olive drab. Didn't these doctors understand that this was a nursing "home"? There was nothing "homey" about it. *Would it have been too much trouble to decorate the place with some bright colors or patterned wallpaper?* I thought as I surveyed the site.

During another evaluation visit, I noted that the overly abundant staff was entirely misallocated. The home had male as well as female patients, and it therefore required the services of orderlies. But on this particular afternoon, I had shown up unannounced and observed that the entire facility was under the supervision of a single, unimposing LPN. Where were the RN's? Where were the orderlies? Where was the highly paid PhD director?

As I was pondering all this, I observed that one of the male patients was making his way toward the front door. Suddenly, the nurse on duty stepped in front of him and attempted to stop his advance. As I watched this drama unfold, I could see that the patient was rather cantankerous and suffering from some mild dementia. He got around the small nurse easily, opened the front door, and started to exit. At this point, she attempted to physically restrain the patient, but to no avail. She would need an orderly, or at the least some nurses' aides to keep the patient from walking off; but there was no one else in sight. I decided I had best intervene. I approached the patient and took his upper arm as he attempted to leave the front vestibule.

"You're coming with me, okay?" I said.

"Okay," he said mildly.

I was easily able to escort him back to his room as the nurse gushed with appreciation. She had no idea who I was – which was in itself another problem – and must have assumed I was a visitor. I got the fellow back into his room and seated in his chair. After accepting the nurse's thanks once again, I stepped out into the hallway and waited for a moment to make sure that the nurse had things under control. She did not. It was clear from his behavior that the patient needed to be restrained, in order to keep him from walking out the door again. This home, like most, used leather padded chair restraints that fit around the lap of a seated patient and fastened securely in the back. As long as the chair was sufficiently heavy, the patient was effectively immobilized. I peeked back into the room and observed the young nurse attempting to fasten one such restraint belt around the wayward patient's lap, with little success. I walked back into the room.

"It looks like you might need some more help," I offered.

"I sure do," she puffed. "Thanks, again, mister. He keeps grabbing the belt out of my hand."

I took the restraint from her and said to the patient: "Okay, now you're going to help me with this, right?"

"Sure thing," came the cooperative reply.

I deftly secured the belt around chair and patient with a few swift moves. The nurse was amazed, puzzled and impressed with my expertise in handling both the restraint and her patient. She once again lauded me for my assistance: "Boy, if you hadn't been around," she confessed, "this guy would have been long gone by now." The nurse eventually came to understand the reasons behind my proficiency when my identity was revealed to her some weeks later as we took over operation of the home. But first, we needed to strike a deal with the docs.

On the day following this incident, we had a meeting scheduled with the owners. The only item on the agenda was the negotiation of a price for the property. The attitude of the owners was one of utter condescension. How could we, two immigrant brothers with limited education, know as much about patient care as this lofty crew of medical practitioners? They were attempting to embellish the asking price based upon their alleged reputation as quality caregivers. One of the physician/partners was the first to speak.

"Rolling Hills enjoys an unparalleled reputation when it comes to quality patient care," he asserted haughtily. "You're not only buying a building, Mr. Hasten. You're also buying the goodwill associated with the excellent reputation we have built up."

At this, I had had enough. I stood up and gave it to them straight: "Let me tell you something. You give lousy care at this nursing home," I proclaimed. "I was there yesterday afternoon and saw exactly the way you care for your patients." I proceeded to tell them about the incident and how I was able to help avert a disaster. "Why was there only one LPN on duty? Where was the RN? Where were the nurses' aides? Where were the orderlies? Where was the director? I saw them all hanging around and socializing in the morning during shift change, while dozens of patient call buttons went unanswered. If this is what you call quality patient care, then, gentlemen, I'm afraid it's not worth very much."

Despite my outbursts, or perhaps because of them, we managed to reach agreement that day on the price and the terms, and we wound up adding Rolling Hills to our portfolio. I had made up my mind that turning this place around financially was going to require my full dedication. For the next six months I arose at 4 AM and made the drive to Anderson, in order to arrive at 6 AM every day of the week. The biggest problem wasn't training the staff to our way of doing things, it was "un-training" them, so they would discontinue all the misguided practices the previous owners had allowed.

For example, I noticed, a few days after we took over that every morning, around 10 AM, the receptionist disappeared for about an hour. When I inquired about this, I was told she had gone to the Post Office to pick up our mail.

"Why can't the post office deliver it?" I questioned.

"Because all of our stationery and envelopes list only the PO number; nothing carries our street address," said the director. "They would never deliver it here. We have to go pick it up."

This made no sense to me. A short time later, looking out my window, I spotted the neighborhood postal carrier making his rounds, and I decided to find out more about this mail delivery situation. I ran outside and caught up with him quickly.

"Excuse me, but would you like to come inside for some coffee?"

He accepted my offer at once. While we were sitting around the table having doughnuts, I asked if he would have a problem delivering the mail directly to us each day.

"No problem," came the reply. "I've been walking by this place for years and always wondered why you guys picked up your own mail."

We began to have our mail delivered to us directly on the very next day. Of course, the secretary, who had grown to enjoy her daily excursions to the post office – and other points – did not appreciate the change.

I recognized that it was going to take more than minor administrative changes to correct the course of this facility. I had to address the major fundamental issue of patient care in order to place it on the proper track. I used our daily staff meetings to communicate the changes that needed to be carried out.

"We all have to understand that at Rolling Hills, the patient comes first," I announced early on. "Every morning, at shift change-over, I see everyone sitting around chatting and drinking coffee, while dozens of patient call lights are ignored. This is going to stop. When a patient presses a call button, you are to respond immediately, regardless of whether you're on the phone, in a meeting, or whatever."

I soon addressed the question of patient therapy, as well. The home had high-paid therapists on the payroll, but from what I could tell, they were there in name only. There was absolutely no therapy whatsoever being given. I looked around and saw that all the patients were confined to their beds. The home also had a large, beautiful dining room that was completely unused. All patients received their meals in bed, just like in a hospital. Food preparation was carried out in assembly line fashion, with trays being prepared in the same manner as in a hospital kitchen. All of this had to change. I had to get across to our staff that we were in the business of improving the quality of life for our patients, not merely "stockpiling" them.

"As much as possible, we want our patients to get better," I informed the staff. "Every patient is to be evaluated at the time of admission, and unless otherwise instructed by their physician, they will be signed up for appropriate therapy. Physical, occupational and other forms of therapy will become a regular part of our patients' weekly routine. Unless confinement is ordered, every patient will get out of bed every day. Starting next week, all meals will be served, family-style, in the dining room, where patients can socialize and get to know one another. Meals will only be delivered on trays upon special request."

Not surprisingly, these sweeping changes did not go over too well with our newly-acquired staff. We also encountered problems with family members who had been brainwashed by the staff into thinking that their loved ones were being properly cared for. We had no choice but to confront these situations head-on. The story of a patient named Mrs. Winters provides a case in point.

In making my regular rounds one morning a few weeks after we had taken over, I learned from Mrs. Winters' chart that she was a stroke victim suffering from aphasia, and that she had been with us for several months. Even though her doctor had not ordered her confined, she had remained in bed since her arrival. In studying her history, I could easily see that her condition was deteriorating steadily. I approached the RN on duty to discuss her case.

"Why don't we prescribe some therapy for Mrs. Winters," I said.

"Yes, that's a good idea, Mr. Hasten," she replied. "I'll call the doctor and get the order right away."

"Great. And also make sure that she gets out of bed every day. Okay?"

At this, I could see the nurse bristle slightly. Mrs. Winters would initially require considerable assistance in getting out of bed. The physical exertion required to render a bed-ridden patient ambulatory was not trivial. It was definitely more work than simply dispensing medication. The nurse nodded her understanding and walked off. Shortly before noon, I received an angry phone call.

"Are you the new guy that's running Rolling Hills?" barked a male voice.

"Yes, I am. May I help you?"

"My mother is Mrs. Winters, and I understand that you want to get her out of bed. Is that right?"

"Yes, I believe that would be best for her," I replied.

"I want to tell you something, Mr. Hasten," he said in a menacing tone "I love my mother very much, and I visit her daily. If I come by there and observe that she is out of bed, I'm going to find you and punch you in the nose!"

"Well, I don't know if you're big enough to do that or not, Mr. Winters," I responded without missing a beat, "but I'd like to speak with you seriously about your mother's care. We have been at this for some time. We have hundreds of patients in our system and we do know a thing or two about proper patient care. Your mother has not been getting it. It is our policy that, unless there's a doctor's order on file to the contrary, every patient gets out of bed every day."

"I don't care about your policy," he said belligerently, "I want her to be comfortable. I'm going to be over there at two o'clock this afternoon, and she had better be in bed or I'm going to find you and punch you out. Understand?"

He hung up before I could respond. I located the nurse, who admitted that she had placed a call to the patient's son, alerting him about my instructions.

"Your phone call to Mr. Winters got him pretty shook up," I explained to the nurse. "Your actions are unacceptable. If you ever do something like that again, you will be fired. If you don't like something around here, you take it up directly with me. You do not go behind my back complaining to a patient's family. Is that understood?"

She once again nodded agreement and walked off.

At 2 PM I was at the front door awaiting Mr. Winters' arrival. As soon as he came in the door, I introduced myself to him. He appeared to be a little man in a big hurry. Built like a fire hydrant, he held up his palm as I offered my hand.

"I still feel the same way," he announced.

I was hoping to discuss the situation with him face to face, but I could see that he was still very upset.

"I'd like to talk to you about your mother's care when you stop by tomorrow," I said, and he agreed to do so.

The next day in my office, I reviewed the situation. "Mr. Winters, I have discussed your mother's case with her doctor, and there is absolutely no reason why she cannot begin a course of therapy. Therapy is what she needs, and if you love her half as much as you claim, you will not stand in her way."

I could see that Mr. Winters was impressed with the fact that someone at this home had taken a personal interest in the welfare of his mother. He agreed not to object to the therapy as long as his mother was kept "comfortable." I arranged for him to speak to his mother's physician, who concurred that therapy was a good idea. I continued discussing his mother's care with him on a daily basis until, little by little, he began to come around. What really convinced him, of course, was his mother's marked improvement.

We began to get Mrs. Winters out of bed regularly – although it was during times when we did not expect a visit from her son. The course of therapy had a rapid and dramatic effect on her condition. It took several weeks, but eventually it became obvious to her son that his mother was, in fact, getting better. Initially, she used a walker to get around, but within a few months, she had become fully ambulatory. As her condition improved, so did her son's attitude, until finally, after two months, he approached me.

"Mr. Hasten, I'd like to offer my apologies for what I said to you," he stated sincerely. "I never should have talked to you that way. You were right. Mother *is* getting better, both physically and psychologically. And it's because she's not stuck in bed any longer. She's full of life and much happier. Thank you."

In addition to vindicating our "out-of-bed" policy, this episode succeeded in convincing the entire staff that I was serious when it came to patient care. They could see that I was there every morning at 6 AM and that I wasn't on hand merely to issue orders and pontificate. My style was very "hands-on," and the nurses could tell that I was prone toward action rather than mere talk. My behavior was in direct contrast to that of the administrator under whom they had been working. And, not surprisingly, this disparity of management styles placed us on a collision course.

Dr. Robinson, the nursing home administrator, was an amiable, professorial type who had little stomach or temperament for the pressures of business management. He was never available on Sundays or holidays, even after I explained the importance of his presence during those high visitor traffic periods. He had set up the hospital-style food service that required a massive crew on duty in the kitchen in order to pull it off. One fellow's job description, for example, was to stand at the assembly line each morning and place a single slice of bread on each passing food tray. That's it. That's all this slice-meister did, and yet he drew a full salary with benefits. Despite the huge kitchen workforce, very little was getting done. I recall walking into the kitchen before lunch one morning and observing that the dishes from breakfast had not yet been washed. I stopped in to see Dr. Robinson about it.

"You need to see what's going on in the kitchen," I told him. "They're preparing lunch while the breakfast dishes are still dirty. You need to look into it and get this corrected."

A few hours later, Dr. Robinson got back to me and reported that he could get the dirty dishes problem fixed, but he would need to hire yet another person for the kitchen. I could not believe my ears. I concluded that I was facing a lost cause with Dr. Robinson.

"I don't think you quite understand the situation," I told him. "We have too many people working in the kitchen already. I feel that the right thing is not to hire another person, but to have one less person working here, and I'm afraid that one person is you."

I immediately requested his resignation and took over the administrator's position myself. After just six months of our common-sense management techniques, Rolling Hills had turned into a dream home. Nurses knew what they were supposed to do. Patient call lights were being answered promptly. Mealtime in the dining hall was a high point of the day. The place took on a bright, friendly appearance as we redecorated and dispelled the dismal institutional ambience. Most importantly, patients, freed from their beds, were getting better with each passing day. The word was spreading, as Rolling Hills became one of our most successful projects.

This success gave us the confidence to plan and execute an expansion that increased the capacity at this facility from 100 to 169 beds. Our company's growth spurt was to last ten years. During that decade, we grew from a single nursing home with forty-four beds to a ten-unit chain of premier convalescent centers housing 1,500 beds in all. Success brought new challenges as well as rewards. The sweetest benefit was in terms of my work schedule. By the early 1970s, my brother and I had developed a successful management structure that permitted us to devote a little more time to family and community.

Simona and I soon discovered that the relatively small Indianapolis Jewish community was vastly different from the much larger one we had known in Minneapolis. The Indianapolis community was founded by German Jews in the late 19ᵗʰ century who were aligned with the Reform movement. The Jewish establishment was still in the hands of their descendents, whose views about Judaism were considerably different from our own. I was to run into this disparity of Jewish values time and again in my dealings with the established community leadership, but my first taste of it came about through our own children.

Our two youngsters were attending a pre-school run by the local JEA (Jewish Educational Association). There they received a smattering of Jewish culture and were exposed a little to the Hebrew language, but from what we could see, there was no religious training whatsoever being offered. We were quietly told by one of the teachers that she had gotten chewed out by the school's administration for using a Hebrew prayer book (*Siddur*) in her classroom. At this institution, she was admonished, only modern conversational Hebrew was to be taught. And it was taught not as the language of our scriptures, but as one would teach French or Spanish. This eschewing of anything religious seemed to be at odds with our concept of Judaism. We were unhappy with this orientation, but since the JEA was the only source of Jewish education in our town, we had no other option.

Given our dissatisfaction, I was quite receptive when I received a phone call one evening from the new Rabbi at B'nai Torah, the Orthodox synagogue we had recently joined.

"Hello, Hart," said a pleasant young voice with a slight New York accent. "This is Rabbi Gray from B'nai Torah. I'm calling to ask you to attend a meeting next week."

"What sort of meeting?" I asked.

"It's about education for your children. I'm calling all the parents of young children in the congregation. We want to get together and talk about starting a day school in this town. I've invited an expert from New York to answer questions. We're trying to figure out if it's a good idea or not, and I'd like to hear from you. Can you be there?" and he recited the date and time.

"Okay, sure." I replied. "I'll be there."

To say that this conversation changed my life would not begin to tell the story. It marked the beginning of a process that changed the lives of every person in our family and, I'm proud to say, resulted in profound and positive changes in our community as well. I had no suspicion at the time, however, that this innocuous phone call would set into motion an extraordinary series of events that would catapult me toward the major philanthropic endeavor of my life: the quest for quality Jewish education.

Chapter Eleven

A New Calling

RABBI RONALD GRAY, a bookish young man of twenty-six with a strik-
ing resemblance to songwriter Marvin Hamlisch, came to Indianapolis in
August of 1970. He was hired by Congregation B'nai Torah, the city's major
Orthodox synagogue, to assume the pulpit of retiring Rabbi Nandor Fruchter,
an old-world, authoritarian figure whose piercing visage had been counte-
nanced by this small congregation for decades. By contrast, Rabbi Gray was
a cheery, enthusiastic fellow with a droll wit and a warm smile – a smile
that concealed the fact that he was in anguish over how he could possibly
succeed in leading a traditional congregation here, in this remote outpost
named Indianapolis.

From a traditional Judaic standpoint, our community was viewed as
being on the border of civilization. Observant Jews were mostly elderly and
dying off rapidly – a fact that eventually led to the demise of the only kosher
butcher shop in the city. Other traditional Jewish support structures were
non-existent or in decline. As young Rabbi Gray stepped into this *"Galut*
of the *Galut"* (exile of the exile), he was immediately struck by the glaring
absence of a Jewish elementary day school. Contacting Torah Umesorah, the
National Society for Hebrew Day Schools, he learned that his reaction was
indeed well placed. Indianapolis, they informed him, was the only community in America with a Jewish population of over 7,500 devoid of a Jewish
day school.

Rabbi Gray received encouragement from Rabbi Bernard Goldenberg
of Torah Umesorah, who not only urged him on, but offered to assist him
in the important task of establishing a new day school. Gray immediately
made this task his highest priority, and it soon became the central mission
of his rabbinate. He contacted noted Jewish day schools around the country, such as the Ramaz School in New York City. His efforts were strongly
praised by the school's administrator, Noam Shudofsky, who wrote several

months later: "If you are to leave your mark on this barren waste land (sic) called Indianapolis, it will certainly be through a Jewish Day School."

On the appointed evening of the meeting, February 22, 1971, I arrived at the synagogue and entered the small chapel. I spoke to none of the roughly 30 or so other parents and took my seat in the very last pew. I also spotted some of the synagogue's *"ba'alebatim"* (lay leaders) in attendance.

Rabbi Goldenberg was introduced and spoke about the importance of passing our traditions on to the next generation. He explained that only through intensive Jewish education can we hope to forestall the rampant tide of intermarriage among American Jews, which was decimating our numbers. Rabbi Gray made his pitch in favor of establishing a school. He then threw the matter open for discussion.

Naturally, the question of funding was the first issue to be brought up. Goldenberg explained that the start-up costs would not be too burdensome, since the school could be housed in the classroom section of the synagogue. Initially, a part-time administrator and a single teacher could handle the first year's class, with additional grades and staff being added each year as the school grew. Goldenberg estimated the total cost needed to get under-way at $13,000.

"I understand your congregation is in need of a cantor," said Golden-berg.

He was correct. The shul's beloved *hazzan*, Cantor Jade, had recently passed away.

"You could hire a cantor that is also a school administrator, so you wouldn't have double salaries to pay. In this way, you could get started enrolling the kids as soon as you have around $13,000 in the bank."

I kept silent and listened to the discussion volley around the room. Most parents initially seemed very positive and enthusiastic. They were prepared to enroll their children if the school could be successfully launched. One of the aforementioned congregational leaders, however, was anything but encouraging. Whenever the discussion would turn too positive, he would rise and, with a condescending air, as if he were lecturing a group of unruly school children, would say: "But where will you get the money?" I later learned that the gentleman's name was Shoolem Ettinger, and he was one of the synagogue's founders.

"Listen to me," he chastised, "I'm warning you right now, unless you've got the $13,000 in the bank, don't even think about opening a day school!"

As the meeting wore on, I found this fellow more and more irritating.

But I held my tongue. His words seemed to be having the desired effect on the crowd.

"People just like you," he exhorted pointing at Rabbi Goldenberg, "have been traipsing into this community for twenty years telling us we should start a day school. Well, I'm telling you the same thing I told all of them: unless you've got the money, don't even think about it."

After several hours, the meeting was about to break up under a negative cloud. Ettinger had everyone convinced that we couldn't make a move until the money was found. People seemed to be resigned to the fact that this was too big an undertaking and that they had better forget about it for now. This community leader, this "*macher*," had succeeded in paralyzing the group by generating an atmosphere of failure. He stood up one more time, unable to resist underscoring his own wisdom.

"I'd like you all to know that we almost started a day school here twelve years ago. I spoke up then and they listened to me. The synagogue leadership decided not to do it. If they had gone ahead with opening a school then, they would have gone right down the drain financially. Our history has taught us that we're doing the right thing by waiting until we have the money in hand."

Hearing this, I could not restrain myself a moment longer. I leapt to my feet and addressed the group.

"Wait a minute. Could I say something before we break up?" I asked. "My name is Hart Hasten, and, like most of you, I have small children in need of education. That's why I'm here tonight. I've been listening to the discussion, and I must say that I'm getting a little tired of listening to this fellow (pointing to Ettinger) go on and on about the $13,000 in the bank." I took a deep breath and continued. "I thought the purpose of this meeting was to find out if it was a good idea or not to start a day school – not to discuss whether or not we have any money in the bank," I announced with a bit more passion in my voice. "If it's a good idea, we'll find the money. They found the money in other communities, didn't they? That's not the problem. Finding enough parents who are committed to passing on their Jewish heritage to their children…that's the important thing."

I was getting rather wound up by this point. "I'm the father of two children and personally, I think starting a day school is a very good idea. We need intensive Jewish education in this community and I'm prepared to do whatever it takes to bring it about. This whole situation reminds me of the establishment of Israel. They didn't found the nation of Israel by waiting until they had all the money they needed in the bank before bringing in Jews to settle the land. The *idea* of a Jewish state, that was the important thing."

I then offered the oft-quoted Theodore Herzl remark: *"Im tirtzu, ayn zoo agadah"* – if you will it, it is no dream. If we all agreed that this was an idea whose time had come, then I knew we could get it done. And I knew we could raise the money. For us to give up on what we all seemed to agree was an important idea simply because we didn't happen to have $13,000 in the bank at the time struck me as foolish. After stating as much, I sat down and was completely surprised to hear loud and lengthy applause erupt throughout the room.

As the applause subsided, Rabbi Gray took the floor and proclaimed: "I nominate Hart Hasten to serve as chairman of an ad hoc committee to establish a new Jewish day school in our community."

The crowd responded with more applause. But I was not applauding. I jumped back to my feet and shook my head emphatically.

"No way. No way. I'm not your man," I protested. "I know nothing about day schools or education. I did not attend a day school. You need someone knowledgeable, and I'm totally ignorant on this subject. I do not accept. Period."

No one seemed to be listening to me. They were ignoring my protests as Gray quickly adjourned the meeting and thanked everyone for their input. I was confused and approached Gray and Goldenberg privately.

"Listen, I'm not a product of a day school. I have no conception of what a day school should look like. You've got the wrong guy here," I continued, protesting.

"Oh, but Hart," implored Gray, "you said the right thing just now. You heard the response. You were saying what was in everyone's hearts and minds. You've got to lead this thing."

"No way. I cannot accept," I said firmly.

"Look, Hart, will you agree to talk to us about this calmly tomorrow?" asked Goldenberg.

I reluctantly agreed to meet them both the following day. At our private meeting, I again explained why I was totally unqualified to head the initiative.

"The only way I would even consider doing something like this is if I had some concept of what a day school was all about," I said.

"I can arrange for that," said Goldenberg. "If I ask Rabbi Gross to give you an in-depth tour of the Miami day school, would you go there just to look around?"

"Yes, I would," I replied. Rabbi Goldenberg promptly contacted his friend Rabbi Alex Gross, the principal of the Miami Beach day school, and two weeks later I traveled to Miami at my own expense. I spent several days visiting the school and learning about all aspects of its operation. Rabbi Goldenberg was right. The sight of these sweet children studying Torah and learning about our heritage could not help but melt my heart. I was deeply impressed by what I saw and came away convinced that yes, this is the type of education I want for my children. I became awash in memories of the *cheder* I attended as a child in Bohorodczany so many lifetimes ago.

The building was new and modern, and as I sat in on one of the classroom sessions, I could almost taste the *"yiddishkeit"* (Jewish flavor) in the air. I admired the way the Hebrew and secular studies were interwoven and tightly integrated. Sitting in that classroom in Miami Beach, I reached a decision, which I announced to Rabbi Gray upon my return.

"Okay," I said. "You win. I'll do it. I'll give it my best shot."

Gray shook my hand and grinned from ear to ear. *"Baruch HaShem* (with praise to G-d), Hart. Let's get to work."

My motivation at this time, I must admit, was a self-serving one. I understood that Simona and I would not be able to adequately transmit our Jewish teachings and traditions to our children on our own. There was no Zayde available, as there had been during my childhood, to walk me to the Hebrew school each day and oversee my learning. We needed professional help.

Had my own schooling not been interrupted, perhaps I would have been in a better position to serve as my children's tutor. Thinking back, I realized that my own Jewish identity was absorbed mostly from my mother through osmosis. As mentioned, she was very learned and would dispense wisdom from the Torah and Talmud with almost every breath. This type of "through the flesh" inculcation was not going to happen here in America with our kids. I knew we needed some sort of delivery medium that would implant Jewish education with the same intensity as English, mathematics and other subjects. I recognized that a Jewish day school was that medium.

I didn't realize it at the time, but a day school also filled an important void in the lives of American-born Jews in our community. Through their assimilation into mainstream American life, many Jewish families had lost touch with their heritage and become more or less Judaically illiterate. They observed the major holidays and knew a few words in Yiddish, but by and large, their understanding, and hence their appreciation, of Judaism was extremely limited. And of course, with each passing generation, this phenomenon was accelerated. Many were concerned that if such powerful trends as assimilation and intermarriage were to go unchecked, the American Jewish community would soon vanish. A Jewish day school was viewed as a bastion against this tide. Parents, unable to pass on Jewish traditions because of their own lack of knowledge, would now be able to enroll their children in a school where Jewish education would be transmitted properly.

We shared the concern of many parents who worried that their children would become more knowledgeable about Judaism than they were themselves. I must say that this never materialized into a real problem in our family, or in any others, as far as I know. On the contrary, as the children learned, so did the parents. In this way, the Jewish knowledge base of our entire community was expanded and enhanced.

When word got back to Rabbi Goldenberg that I had agreed to accept the chairmanship, he contacted me and was very supportive. He wrote to me on March 1, 1971: "You impressed me with your sincerity...When we succeed, with G-d's help, you will have contributed to the Indianapolis Jewish community more than just another institution; perhaps even its very future."

After my return from Miami, I shared my enthusiasm with my brother, Mark, who pledged his full support and agreed to enroll his own four children as soon as it was feasible. I recognized that we had to locate funding sources quickly or else face the wrath of Mr. Ettinger and his followers. On March 15, we assembled a financial committee to raise funds for the new "Hebrew Academy of Indianapolis." There was no deliberation about the new school's name. Rabbi Gray suggested it and we all thought it sounded impressive (although Rabbi Gray was later to joke that he regretted not naming the school The Hebrew Academy for *Gifted* Children, since this name would probably have boosted enrollment).

Rabbi Gray and I made the rounds of those in our community who we felt might have the ability and desire to kick in some seed money. This process is sometimes known, in Jewish circles, as "*schnorring*," and I must say that we were rather effective *schnorrers*. Gray himself was a product of a day school education, and he spoke eloquently from the heart about what a difference the experience had made in his own life. I did the arm-twisting and served as the deal-closer.

Our first stop was at the office of another successful immigrant Jewish businessman, Zoltan (Zoli) Weisz. Weisz was a Hungarian Holocaust survivor who had built up a chain of neighborhood supermarkets. As Rabbi Gray and I explained our concept of a new day school, Zoli stopped us and summoned his twenty-three year old son, Peter, into his office. Peter had recently joined the business, and his father wished for him to become familiar with the company's philanthropic activities. I explained that we were trying to raise the $13,000 we were told it would take to start the school.

"How much have you raised so far?" asked Zoli.

"Actually, nothing. You're our first customer," I admitted a bit nervously. "We're looking to you to make a leadership gift."

"You know, I wish you guys would have done this when Peter was a kid. He didn't get much of a Jewish education growing up in this town. Maybe if you get this new school started, my grandchildren will be better educated. Would $1,000 help you get going?" he asked.

"It sure would," said Rabbi Gray. "Thank you."

We had received our first contribution and we did not yet have a bank account to put it in! I felt we were on our way and I was right.

After a few more successful stops, we began to pick up momentum. In a matter of days, we had commitments for the entire $13,000. The names of those donors, including Mark and myself, were recorded as the founders of the Hebrew Academy, as is stated on the Founder's Plaque that hangs in the front lobby of the school:

Our Founders

Early in 1971, a group of visionary members of the Indianapolis Jewish community gathered to plan, and underwrite, a dream. From their dream rose the beginnings of a new center for Jewish and secular learning.

The school in which you are standing is the direct result of their vision, their courage and their fundamental belief in the value of Jewish education. It is for these reasons that we do hereby honor and salute these esteemed founders of

THE HEBREW ACADEMY OF INDIANAPOLIS
Mr. and Mrs. Herbert Davidson
Mr. and Mrs. Eli Ettinger
Mr. and Mrs. Shoolem Ettinger
Mr. and Mrs. David Fogle
Mr. and Mrs. Lipot Frankovitz
Mr. and Mrs. Hart N. Hasten
Mr. and Mrs. Mark Hasten
Mr. Ruben Lipman
Mr. and Mrs. Ben Prince
Mr. and Mrs. Zoltan Weisz

Encouraged by this early show of support (including a gift from Mr. Ettinger),

I decided to start putting the functional pieces together. I contacted a member of the congregation, who was known to have extensive educational experience, and asked him to put together a personnel committee. Dr. Maurice (Moe) Schankerman had served as a principal in the public school system and was a well-respected figure among local educators. Moe was very enthusiastic and pledged his full support. He immediately set to work assembling the school's initial faculty. I'm happy to report that thirty years later, he, along with his wife Marilyn, is still fulfilling this pledge and is continuing to oversee the staffing needs of our school.

Next, I set up another committee to look after the other side of the equation. Without a critical number of students, we could not launch our school. We had set a date of a year and half hence, September 1972, as our target for opening. The recruitment committee's assignment was to locate a sufficient number of families willing to enroll their children into kindergarten and first grade classes beginning on that date.

On March 30, 1971, the Hebrew Academy of Indianapolis was incorporated as a not-for-profit corporation. I signed the incorporation charter along with Rabbi Gray and Irwin Prince, son of Academy founder, Ben Prince, and the attorney who had drawn up the document. Prince and his wife, Eileen, were the parents of two young sons, and they were both strong supporters of the day school initiative.

The charter called for the creation of a Board of Directors and the election of officers. I called a meeting at the synagogue for this purpose and invited parents, donors and others whom we had identified as having the skills to help guide our embryonic venture through its birth throes and beyond. I asked each of them if they would be willing to serve on the Board of our newly-formed school. I attempted to put together an assemblage representative of the entire spectrum of Jewish life in our community. It was our intention from the beginning that this school appeal to families from all walks of Jewish life. While I recognized that the school being housed in a wing of the Orthodox synagogue would cause some to conclude mistakenly that it was affiliated with the shul, this was never the case. The Academy, from its very inception, was governed by an autonomous, highly independent Board made up of dedicated individuals from across the denominational spectrum. And, of course, our school would be open to children from all sectors of the Jewish community.

At our first Board meeting, Rabbi Gray articulated our vision for the new school. Both the personnel and recruitment committees issued their reports, and an election of officers took place. I was elected as chairman (a post that was changed to president one month later), Irwin Prince was elected vice-chairman, Gilbert Cohen became our first treasurer and Aaron J. Jade served as secretary.

As Rabbi Gray handed me the gavel, I realized I was facing a new and very formidable challenge. Not only was I a complete neophyte when it came to running a day school, I knew absolutely nothing about chairing a formal parliamentary meeting. The business meetings I was familiar with were always informal affairs without such niceties as motions, seconds, points of order, new business, etc. I did not have the first clue about what I should do. Somehow, I got through that first meeting, and I was so thankful when someone suggested that we adjourn. One of the new Board members, Dorothy Friedman, recognized my distress, took me aside, and patiently explained the basics of parliamentary procedure to me.

I listened intently and then asked: "Where do you get all this stuff about abstentions and calls for the question and so forth?" It all sounded so alien to my ears.

"There's a book called *Robert's Rules of Order*, and everything is laid out there," she explained.

Irwin Prince said he had a copy at his law office and agreed to get it to me the next day. I devoured it cover to cover and was soon up to speed, brandishing my gavel with expertise and élan. Sometimes, my executive style during meetings can be rather despotic, and I've been guilty of occasionally dispensing with parliamentary niceties when the welfare of the school was at stake. However, thanks to my study of *Robert's Rules of Order*, I can honestly say that I am fully aware of the democratic processes that I'm occasionally ignoring.

Our next step was recruiting a director. Rabbi Gray did not have the time to serve as principal, and, of course, I was not even considered for the role. I was occupied with my business affairs, plus I had no credentials as an educator. We decided to heed Rabbi Goldenberg's suggestion and advertise for a part-time director who could also serve as a part-time cantor at the synagogue. We hoped that the two part-time salaries would be sufficient to attract a person of suitable quality. Fortunately, they did.

Edwin Epstein was a young man with three years' experience as a Jewish educational director. He was working on an advanced degree in educational administration, and to top it off, he was an experienced cantor. In addition, he had two children who were the right age for enrollment in the school. The personnel committee was unanimous in its endorsement of Epstein as the perfect fit, and I'm happy to say that their choice proved to be a great one.

Epstein guided the school with skill and dedication for seven years, from its birth throes through all of its early growing pains.

As it turned out, on the same day that we interviewed Eddie Epstein, I had another very important meeting scheduled. I had arranged to meet with the president of the local Jewish Welfare Federation, Martin Larner, about obtaining support for our new school. Larner had invited the Federation's executive director, Frank Newman, to the meeting as well.

I recall being impressed with Epstein to the point that I decided, on the spot, to invite him to join me at this meeting with Larner. I felt that presenting him as the school's newly-hired director would demonstrate to Larner that we were serious about the school. Epstein was also eloquent and highly knowledgeable, and I felt that he could field any specific questions about day schools that Larner might throw my way.

Sitting in Larner's office, I laid out my vision for the Academy and the positive impact I knew it would have on the quality of Jewish life in Indianapolis. I briefed him and Newman about our current status and explained that we were working toward opening our doors for the 1972–73 school year. Eddie Epstein, assuming the role of principal, a job that he had not yet secured, answered Larner's questions with precision and aplomb. After laying the foundation, I made my pitch.

"Marty, you represent the Jewish leadership of our community," I stated. "In order to make this a community-based school, servicing all its segments, we need Federation support – and not just because of the money. We feel the Federation's imprimatur will provide us with the legitimacy we need to attract parents from all of the synagogues in town."

"I don't know, Hart," he said shaking his head. "We've got a pretty good Jewish school here already."

"Of course, we do," I replied, "and the JEA is needed to provide after-school education for those parents who want it. But we also need to offer the day school option for parents who are looking for something more intensive. The two schools will serve to compliment each other." Then Epstein spoke up and made an important point.

"Day schools exist in every Jewish community of this size across America, and they all receive some level of Federation subvention," he said. Hearing this, Larner reacted strongly.

"Look, I don't give a damn what they do in other towns," Larner grumbled. "In Indianapolis, we do things our own way. Most Jews in this town support public – not parochial – education. Public education is one of the great things about America. It's designed to give everyone the same shot at advancement, regardless of their religion or race. I cannot imagine this Federation giving any money to a parochial school. Not only will we not support you, but I would feel compelled to oppose you."

He saw from my expression that I was disappointed. What he said next took me from disappointment into shock.

"Hart, I can see you're disappointed," he said a bit more warmly. "Please don't be. You may even be correct on this. Maybe we'll change our outlook about day schools at some point down the road. And if we do, it wouldn't be the first time."

I believed he was trying to ease me out the door by holding out some false hope in my direction. He explained further.

"Back in 1948, I was dead set against the establishment of a Jewish state. This community was strongly anti-Israel. I've changed my outlook over the years, and you know that today I'm a devout Zionist. These things take time. I suggest you be patient and put this whole thing off for a while."

His statement that he was against a Jewish state in 1948 shook me deeply. As we – the pitiful remnants of Europe's Jews languished in DP camps, praying daily for the emergence of a land we could call our home – these wealthy, well-fed American Jews were sitting comfortably in Indiana speaking out against the Jewish state. I was livid with rage and did my best to contain it...without total success.

"Marty, we don't have the time to wait for years to go by, or for your attitudes to change." I said. "Our children need schooling today, and we plan to give it to them. And let me say just one more thing to you: You were wrong about Israel in 1948 and you're wrong about our day school today. The only difference is that we're not going to wait twenty-five years for you to figure out how wrong you are. We are going to establish this school with Federation support or without it because we are totally committed to the need for it. And because of what you just said, I intend to go back to my Board and strongly recommend that we start the school this year, rather than wait until next year." I stood up, grabbed Epstein by the arm, and said, "Let's get out of here."

After I had cooled down, I realized what I had just done. I had suggested to Larner that our school could be ready and in full operation within thirteen weeks. At this point we had no teachers and we had not yet enrolled the first student. We had conducted only one interview, and we had no curriculum, books or other teaching tools. What had I done? After conferring with Rabbi Gray and with my executive board, I asked if they thought we could do it. They pledged their full support. The opening date was moved up to September, 1971. We agreed that it would not be easy, but it could be done if we all worked like crazy to make it happen.

With the timetable for opening the school moved up by one full year, we desperately needed to quickly attract the interest of parents to our new venture. We felt we had to conduct some marketing. The first thing we needed was an attractive brochure. Typically, brochures advertising private schools contain photos of happy, smiling children. We wanted some of those photos in our brochure, but the problem was, we didn't have any children at all, since we had not yet opened our doors. We did not have the budget to hire models or purchase stock photos. Fortunately, the problem was solved when Rabbi Gray offered to allow the photographing of some of his Sunday School students in a classroom setting at his synagogue. The photos made our first brochure look very professional and helped to define a positive image for our start-up venture.

It was during those early, formative days that I established a practice that is still maintained more than thirty years later. I made it a policy to invite all community Rabbis to attend our Board of Directors meetings. I felt this would be important to demonstrate that our new school was not under the control of any one Jewish branch or denomination. Over the years, the Rabbis have responded to our invitations, and one has even served as a Board member. Today, I'm pleased that the current Rabbi at Congregation B'nai Torah, Shlomo Crandall, has taken a strong interest in the school and never misses a Board meeting.

I also instituted the practice of starting each monthly Board meeting with a *D'var Torah* (a brief sermon dealing with the current week's Torah portion or *Parsha*) delivered by one of the attending Rabbis. This has always served to set the right tone and keep our Board members mindful of our primary mission.

On April 23, 1971, a full-page ad appeared in the local Jewish newspaper, *The Indiana Jewish Post and Opinion,* announcing registration for the 1971–72 school year. Two classes were being formed, a kindergarten and a combined primary division consisting of grades 1 and 2. When the school opened its doors in September with eighteen students, it was a sufficient number for the establishment of a third grade. A fourth grade was added the following year, and this pattern was continued, with one more class being added each year, concluding with an eighth grade in 1978. A pre-school division was added in 1976.

More important than ads and brochures, we understood that what was going to attract students through our doors was the school's curriculum and its core philosophy regarding education. I asked the Board to prepare statements outlining both the school's religious and secular educational philosophy, in order to make it clear to prospective parents what our school stood for. After some deliberation, the Board came up with a clearly worded statement that has served the school for over thirty years.

The secular philosophy emphasized open classrooms with low student-teacher ratios and much personalized attention, which allowed students to progress at their own pace. To quote from the statement: "...the adoption of progressive methodology can be implemented without sacrificing intellectual rigor...In a society where change is the only constant, it is the task of the educator...to provide a moral idealism which can mature without cynicism..."

While the secular portion of the school's philosophy betrays some of the "sixties" sensibilities of that era, the Judaic portion remains timeless in its commitment to *Halacha* (Jewish law) as the governing authority concerning religious issues at the school. From the first day of operation and ever since, the first half-hour of every school day has been devoted to traditional morning prayers, with boys wearing *tzitzit* (fringed garments) in accordance with Jewish law. Blessings were, and still are, recited as appropriate during the day, and the *Birkhat HaMazon* (Grace after Meals) is chanted after the daily kosher lunch. The curriculum, as developed by Epstein and others, was evenly divided between Judaic and general studies, with a good deal of overlap. The overall religious orientation is what has come to be known as "traditional," with boys and girls studying together.

Laying out the school's philosophy was helpful in defining our place in the community and in attracting those parents who found it to their liking. But in order to succeed, we had to draw from a much broader pool. I recognized that we would have a better shot at attracting non-Orthodox families if the school were housed somewhere other than in the Orthodox synagogue. Hence, I paid a visit to Rabbi Sidney Steiman at the conservative Beth-El Zedeck shul, as well as Rabbi Maurice Saltzman at the reform synagogue, the Indianapolis Hebrew Congregation. I wanted to know if either would agree to host our school until we were large enough to build our own facility. Steiman rejected the idea immediately while IHC studied the idea for a while before saying no. They claimed they were afraid that the school would compete with their own in-house religious education programs and create a burden for them.

Steiman, after just having turned me down, surprised me when he suggested that I become a member of his congregation. Congregation Beth-El was aligned with the Conservative movement and Steiman was a dedicated devotee of one of Conservative Judaism's eminent ideologues, Rabbi Mordechai Kaplan. Kaplan had developed a philosophy known as "Reconstructionism," which, at that point, I knew nothing about, and I said as much to Rabbi Steiman. He explained that it was a new "fourth branch" of Judaism. I later learned that Kaplan had actually opposed the creation of such a "fourth branch." He favored keeping Reconstructionism under the Conservative tent and felt that creating another splinter denomination would only serve to further polarize, and hence weaken, the American Jewish community. It was only a few years before this conversation with Rabbi Steiman, and at a point when Kaplan was too old to block the move, that a Reconstructionist seminary was founded and its first graduates, Rabbis Dennis and Sandy Eisenberg Sasso, were ordained.

I again explained to Steiman that I knew nothing of Kaplan's teachings or the principles of Reconstructionist thought.

"In that case, Hart, I am recommending that you obtain a copy of Rabbi Kaplan's seminal book, *Judaism as a Civilization,* and look it over."

I agreed to do so, located a copy of Kaplan's book, and read it from cover to cover. It was soon afterwards that I became aware of a problem involving Rabbi Steiman. The well-known publication, *Encyclopaedia Judaica*, contains descriptions about every major Jewish community in the world, including Indianapolis. The photo accompanying the article in the 1971 edition was an exterior shot of Steiman's shul, Beth-El Zedeck. Conspicuous in its absence was any mention in the piece about the Orthodox synagogue, Congregation B'nai Torah. When I noticed that the article had been written by Rabbi Sidney Steiman, I made up my mind to confront him about it as soon as the opportunity arose.

A few weeks later, Rabbi Steiman was a guest in our home during a fundraising reception. I took him aside and pointed out this obviously intentional oversight. He tried to justify the omission by claiming that the synagogue was not in its current location at the time the article was written and that, besides, B'nai Torah was really an amalgam of two other older congregations. He went on with more of this sort of double-talk, until I stopped him and asked if he would correct the omission in future articles. He agreed to do so.

Once this matter was out of the way, he again began his badgering. "Are you ready to join our congregation? Have you read Kaplan's book? What did you think of it?" And so on. I decided to lay it on the line.

"Look, Rabbi Steiman, with all due respect," I said as plainly as I could.

"I am just an *amcha*, a simple Jew. And after reading this book, I found that it really had very little to do with the Jewish religion. That's the noun, *religion*. I read about a lot of things that were 'religious.' There's Religious Zionism, Religious Civilization, Religious Culture. Everything is 'reliGIOUS.' What happened to the 'reliGION?'"

"You know, Hart," he replied, "you seem to understand Kaplan pretty well."

He was correct. Despite my posing, I understood Kaplan all too well. His premise postulated that much of the anti-Semitism and hatred that had been heaped upon Jews over the ages was brought on by the Jews themselves. He pointed to the concept of divine revelation and "chosen-ness" as evidence of the type of arrogance that causes other peoples to scorn and revile the Jew. He would "reconstruct" the relationship between G-d and the Jew. Instead of G-d selecting the B'nai Yisroel as recipients of his divine law, Kaplan reversed fields and posited that it was the Jews that selected G-d. By modifying this fundamental premise of Judaism, Kaplan was able to build a theology which placed G-d into a greatly diminished role. G-d was relegated to a point of personal preference. Under Reconstructionism, a Jew did not need to adhere to ancient, and often outmoded, ritual to become righteous.

I laid out my reservations to Steiman, explaining that I could not be a part of a Judaism that did not recognize G-d as the highest authority. Furthermore, I disagreed with the basic premise. I believed that the Jewish people were, in fact, "chosen" from among the nations. Chosen not for some exalted status, but to serve as an example to all the peoples of the world about how to live under a system of laws. But most importantly, I was in complete disagreement with Kaplan regarding his view that the proper response in facing anti-Semitism was to weaken, or water down, traditional Judaism. The antidote for anti-Jewish hatred is Jewish strength, not Jewish weakness! From that point on, until his death a few years later, Rabbi Steiman never again asked me to join his congregation.

I next approached Frank Newman again about housing the school at the JEA. The afternoon school had just moved into a large modern facility that sat vacant most of the day. We could easily set up shop in a few of the classrooms during the school day and be out of the way by 3 PM, when the afternoon school students began to arrive. This concept was rejected immediately. By this time, our activities had aroused the attention of the Federation leadership, and we were collecting a substantial number of enemies opposed to our efforts. As a result, we received no cooperation from Frank or from the Federation whatsoever.

Each time a door was slammed in my face, however, my resolve to succeed was only strengthened. In a way, I was glad that we did not receive any support from the mainstream Jewish community. Establishing this school became a matter of personal pride. I wanted to prove that we could create a major Jewish institution in this town even without any assistance from the Federation. And that's exactly what we did.

With some super-human effort on the part of a cadre of very dedicated individuals, we did meet our deadline. By the start of the school year, we had assembled a sufficient number of students, teachers, administrators and school supplies. We had also obtained our accreditation from the state authorities. The new school was very warmly welcomed by the small Orthodox community, but I wanted it to achieve a wider acceptance.

When Mark and I would talk about the future of the school, we would come up with some rather grand designs...many of which have come to pass over the years. But to accomplish these goals we had to achieve something else first – legitimacy. We could not presume to be a major force in the Jewish community by serving only one small segment of it. We needed validation in order to grow into the institution we had in mind. Not all at once, but step by step, validation and community acceptance were – at times grudgingly, but nevertheless emphatically – achieved.

Enrollment grew steadily as a new class was added each year. Starting with eighteen students in 1971, there were fifty-six by 1973, one hundred and eleven by 1977 and one hundred and fifty-five by 1979. By this time the children of every single congregational Rabbi in our community were enrolled at our school. This was beginning to feel like the validation we were seeking.

By 1975, the school could no longer be housed in the educational wing of the synagogue. A new home was needed, and the Board decided it was time to erect a new building. Mark and I had recently purchased a five acre tract of land near the synagogue from the estate of a certain John Bauer. Once approval was granted for a new building, we donated the land to the Academy and set to work designing a modern, inviting facility to house what had, by this time, become our pet project.

We hired the same architects and engineers we had used to construct our nursing homes to draw up the construction plans for our new building. They did a good job, although some cynics claimed that the building looked more like a nursing home than an elementary school.

Ground was broken on June 20, 1976, at a community-wide ceremony. One of the guests, a wealthy gentleman in his eighties, Mr. Lipot Frankovitz, was seated next to me during the ceremony. Frankovitz was friends with

Shoolem Ettinger and was impressed by the fact that Ettinger was now convinced of our school's viability. Frankovitz was aware that Ettinger had made
what he described as the largest charitable gift of his life: $25,000 earmarked
for the construction of a chapel in the new facility.

I could tell that Frankovitz had become quite moved by what he saw at
the ground-breaking ceremony. As the program concluded, he leaned over
to me and whispered in my ear:

"This is really happening. I want to give you a lot of money." I looked
at him and saw tears welling up in the old man's eyes.

"You're really going to do it. I want to give you a big gift to help you
build this school," he said in a hushed voice.

My heart jumped, and I became so excited that I shouted it out for
everyone to hear:

"Don't whisper that just to me! Get up there on the microphone and tell
all the people!" He slowly approached the microphone and announced that
he was making a $200,000 gift to the school's building fund. Lipot Frankov-
itz was an immigrant who had enjoyed enormous success in the supermarket
business. He had no heirs, and I know he felt that this extraordinary gift would
stand as his permanent legacy here in his adopted Jewish community.

The gift enabled us to construct the building and operate it with no
outstanding mortgage. It made a huge difference and enabled the school to
move out of the Orthodox synagogue and into a modern facility, where it
could begin attracting a much wider range of students.

The new 15,000 square foot building was completed in time for the
1977/78 school year. Mark's experience in constructing new facilities for our
business proved to be a real asset. Once we were moved in, I was able to
employ many of the professional management skills I had developed in setting up the operation of the school. We were never reluctant to share whatever resources we could between our business and the school. This proved
true in the kitchen operation, which was serviced by many of the same institutional vendors we were using at the nursing homes. The overlap between
the two entities enabled us to help the school get up and running through
the use of shared resources. I'm happy to say that this practice has continued through today.

As I indicated, the children of all of the congregational Rabbis in our
community were, by 1978, enrolled at the Academy. These included the
children of the newly arrived Rabbinic couple, Dennis and Sandy Sasso,
who took over the spiritual leadership of Congregation Beth-El Zedeck after
the untimely death of Rabbi Steiman. Despite the fact that the Sassos were

leading exponents of Reconstructionist Judaism, we enjoyed a very warm and cordial relationship, and I counted them among the school's vocal supporters. Only once or twice did an issue arise that might be considered something of a dispute.

A good friend of mine, who happened to be a member of the Sassos' congregation, met and fell in love with a non-Jewish woman. He informed her that before they could marry, he wished for her to convert to Judaism, to which she readily agreed. She enrolled in a series of Judaism courses conducted by the Sassos and, within a few months, underwent a conversion ceremony. I recall how she excitedly approached me with the good news.

"Hart, guess what? I'm Jewish!" she announced with obvious glee.

"That's great," I responded, "but, tell me, do you feel Jewish?"

"Uh…no. No, I guess I really don't."

"You know, I don't want to be a wet blanket," I said, "but I presume they told you that this type of a conversion would not hold up in Israel. I know you have no intention of moving there, but, just in case, you should know that such a conversion would be questioned there."

I soon regretted passing on this bit of information. She immediately contacted Rabbi Dennis Sasso and reported that Hart Hasten had told her that her conversion was not valid in Israel. The inevitable phone call arrived the following day. I recognized Dennis' terse voice on the phone.

"Hart, stay out of my business," he warned.

"Of course, Rabbi," I replied courteously. "I have no desire to interfere in your business. But it so happens that this woman is a friend, and I do feel it would have been nice if you'd have explained to her why she would not be considered Jewish in Israel."

Evidently, this issue touched a nerve. It was during this period that the whole fractious question of "Who Is A Jew" was being debated both in Israel and America. Apparently, while I viewed my words as a simple "FYI" conveyed to a friend, Sasso regarded them as a challenge to his rabbinic authority. I decided not to make an issue of it and, backing off, I agreed not to offer any further comments about his conversions in the future. For the sake of the school, I did not wish to alienate a key leadership figure in our community.

I never gave up in my efforts to win Federation support for the Academy, however. At times, I even tried some creative ideas to channel the needed funds to our school. One such idea involved an area where the Federation's role overlapped with our business. In their capacity as the provider of social services to the Jewish community of Indianapolis, the Federation supported the operation of a community old age home known as Hooverwood. Despite the fact that they charged higher rates than we did, Hooverwood operated at a huge deficit. The Federation was required to funnel hundreds of thousands of dollars into the home's operating budget each year to keep it afloat. This fact always struck me as puzzling. I was essentially in the same business, charging lower rates, yet generating significant profits. I could not understand why they consistently continued to lose money. I came up with an idea that I thought could remedy this situation while at the same time breaking the logjam of opposition to Federation support of the school. I scheduled a meeting with Federation executive director, Frank Newman. After being greeted by him in his office, I laid out my plan.

"Frank, it has always amazed me that Hooverwood operates at such a big loss. You know that, despite your advice to the contrary, I decided to go into the nursing home business, and we've been managing to turn a profit."

"Well, you know how it is, Hart," he replied. "We offer kosher food and have other expenses that really add up."

"I'll bet I could run the place without losing a dime," I said, "and without sacrificing the quality of service or skimping on patient care."

"Are you serious?" he asked. "You're interested in running Hooverwood?"

His eyes lit up, and I could see that the idea held enormous appeal.

"Absolutely," I said leaning forward. "And not only that. If I take it over, we'll run it completely, and I'll give you a written guarantee that the Federation will never have to put any more money into the place. No more subsidization whatsoever. We'll cover our expenses without raising the rates, and if we don't, we'll eat the losses. What have you got to lose?" Frank was taking all this in as I laid the kicker on the table. "And, if by some chance, we manage to make a profit," I explained, "I want it all directed toward the Hebrew Academy. That's my proposal. What do you think?"

"I don't know, Hart," he hedged. "There are a lot of bookkeeping issues involved with a scheme like that. It would require some serious study."

Needless to say, the study was never conducted and the proposal was completely ignored, even though it would have put millions into the Federation coffers over time. So great was the Federation leadership's antipathy toward the school that any proposal, no matter how attractive, that would result in support for the Academy was doomed at the outset.

Our stunning growth and acceptance continued to cause consternation among the established Jewish hierarchy, many of whom found our very presence in the community totally offensive. The most vociferous of these leaders was a gentleman named Robert Efroymson.

The Efroymson family was considered "old money," having made their fortune in the 1930s when Bob's father, Gustave, took control of the Real Silk Hosiery company in Indianapolis. When Bob took over control of the company after his father's death in 1955, it was a national operation with production facilities in three states. Bob eliminated most of the manufacturing and converted the company into a highly successful investment house. As head of the family, Bob had become active in both general and Jewish community affairs, and, being its largest single contributor, he, not surprisingly, held a seat on the Board of the Jewish Federation.

The protocol at that time was for local Jewish agencies to make an annual funding pitch to the Federation's Executive Committee. The committee would review the needs of each agency and then divvy up the monies collected during the previous fundraising campaign. Bob Efroymson was serving on the Executive Committee the first time we sent a delegation to request funding for our newly-established day school.

After we had presented our case, during which we pointed out that Indianapolis was the only city in America whose Jewish Federation did not support the local community day school, we made our modest request for financial support. The discussion afterwards was lively. We debated issues of church and state, of parochial versus public education, and we came prepared with compelling responses for each of these concerns.

Finally, Bob Efroymson stood up and made a stark pronouncement: "I've heard enough. You all need to know that I am opposed to this school. I have spent my life supporting public education, and I will not stand by while this Board doles out money to agencies bent on destroying it." He then offered the coup de grace: "If the Federation Board allocates a single dime to this parochial school, I will have no choice but to withdraw my family's entire financial support to the Federation."

Although threatening to withhold a gift is not exactly extortion, it sure smelled like blackmail to me. The Efroymson family was the largest contributor to the annual campaign. Their gift amounted to over one third of the roughly one million dollars raised each year. Withdrawal of that revenue stream, upon which local agencies had been feeding for years, would cripple the Federation. The whole concept of communal giving was being violated, it appeared to me. Federations were supposed to act as umbrella fundraising arms for a host of social service agencies. Donors were asked to put their contributions into a community pot where they were made fungible and available to local causes, based upon their respective needs. For a single individual to feel he had the right to dictate how the funds were to be allocated, simply because of his status as the largest donor, was contrary to the whole concept.

I attempted to privately address Efroymson's concerns during a lunch atop the Indiana National Bank tower, a building in which he owned a sizable stake. I gave it my best shot and Bob listened politely.

Finally he summed things up: "Hart, I'm not sure you understand how strongly I feel about this. I am violently opposed to funding this school!"

At this, I realized we had nothing further to discuss and I bid him goodbye. A few days later, he phoned to apologize for his hasty comment and explained that he was trying to emphasize a point and was not actually disposed towards violence.

In fairness, Bob was not alone in his thinking. Efroymson's attitude was shared by many other, lesser hosts within the Federation hierarchy. Even without his "violent" opposition, it is unlikely that the Federation would have given us much support, if any at all.

The acrimony, and at times, outright hatred, that the existence of our school engendered among the Jewish establishment in our community mystified me for quite a while. Why did they oppose us so passionately? Were we the Ku Klux Klan? The Nazi Party? What were we doing to merit their "violent opposition"? It took me a little while to figure this out, but I finally came to the realization that our school represented everything that the lives of these folks had been moving away from for generations.

According to the local power structure, Jewish tradition was something you watched on a Broadway stage performance of Fiddler on the Roof. In their eyes, we were regarded as an embarrassing anachronism, a throwback to an era long since left behind. Our adherence to the sanctity of the Sabbath and to kosher dietary laws, for instance, generated an awkward guilt among the Federation leadership, who would typically spend their Saturdays munching shrimp cocktails after golfing at the "Jewish" country club. Oftentimes, we were painted as "shtetl Jews" and as right-wing fundamentalist fanatics bent on brainwashing the youth of our community. Our presence could be tolerated as long as we were marginalized as merely "that Orthodox school." But whenever we attempted to break out of that mold, we met fierce resistance.

I recall how my pleadings on behalf of Jewish education were summarily dismissed by Federation leaders who pointed out that I was suffering from a "Holocaust mentality." My statements about Jewish survival were looked at as the rantings of some pitiful war victim and not to be taken seriously.

Most puzzling was the argument that our school was undermining the public school system. The same folks making this point had no problem with the Catholic Archdiocese that had been operating parochial schools in our community for decades. But for Jews to do the same thing – this was unacceptable to them!

Finding closed doors and closed minds at the Jewish Federation, the school looked elsewhere for financial support. During the second year of its existence, a group of us made a funding request presentation before the Lilly Endowment, a large philanthropic foundation headquartered in Indianapolis. We introduced them to our new school and explained that we needed money to underwrite our start-up costs until tuition revenues could grow and we could become self-sustaining. The Lilly folks were attentive, and I felt that their chairman, Bob Lynn, was particularly tuned in. As we concluded our prepared presentation, I publicly invited Mr. Lynn to visit our school for a first-hand look, and he accepted my invitation.

I made sure I was on hand for Mr. Lynn's visit a few days later. I showed him our classrooms, and he observed students involved in both general and Judaic studies.

"You're teaching these little kids Hebrew?" he asked in astonishment.

"Yes, that's right," I answered.

"And this is the same Hebrew that the Bible was originally written in?" he asked.

I assured him that it was, and I could tell that he was totally fascinated and impressed.

"So when these children complete their education, they'll be able to read the Bible in its original form?" he questioned.

"Oh, they'll be able to do that by the time they reach the sixth grade," I informed him.

I could tell that something clicked in his mind, and a few days after Mr. Lynn's visit, we received a letter advising us that our request had been granted. We would be receiving $80,000 in support over the next three years.

The irony of the situation was powerful. The Jewish Federation, an agency supposedly dedicated to maintaining and improving the quality of Jewish life in our community, would not give us a nickel because we were perceived as being "too Jewish." Yet a major non-Jewish charity was granting us financial support for exactly the same reason.

While my brother, Mark, felt differently, I never withheld my financial support for the Jewish Federation. Year after year, I would donate substantial gifts that placed me in the ranks of their largest donors and earned me seats on various Boards and committees. I did this in the full knowledge that not one penny of the money I was contributing would ever be used to support the Academy. My frustration at this situation was tempered by my optimistic belief that the Federation would eventually recognize the error of its ways and come around. It would be the mid-1980s before my optimism was justified.

The Lilly Endowment's support at this critical time made the difference between success and failure. They have extended support several more times over the past thirty years, pumping close to three million dollars into various capital and operational projects. Our school owes its survival and ongoing success to this amazing philanthropy. Thanks to the generosity of the Lilly Endowment, thousands of students over the years have received not only a first-rate education, but also a sense of moral and ethical direction, thereby making them better Jews and better citizens. We are forever in their debt.

Rabbi Goldenberg's projection of a $13,000 first year operation budget turned out to be completely off the mark. It wound up being over $50,000 and has grown steadily over the years. The approved operating budget for the 2002–2003 school year stands at $2.4 million.

In terms of Federation support, the Academy continued making annual pleas for funding from 1973 through 1985. Every single request was turned down cold. This situation naturally created friction, as strong feelings were expressed on both sides of the issue. At times, these feelings would erupt into public squabbling, as it did in 1979, when the Academy was again turned down in its request for a $60,000 operating grant. Public debates were held and the matter was addressed from all the synagogue pulpits and debated on the pages of *The Jewish Post & Opinion*. A nine-page letter from Federation president, Phillip Pecar, defending the Federation's justification for non-support of the Academy, was mailed to every Jewish household in the city. In it he stated: "…that traditionally, the Jewish community has found great strength in the existence of the public school system."

While the public airing of this highly divisive issue served to harden attitudes on both sides and to create an "us vs. them" mentality, it also brought the matter out of the closet. I knew that the Federation's position was untenable and that, once it was exposed openly, it was only a matter of time before it would be abandoned. I was correct in my assessment, and by the mid-eighties, things had begun to change. The key to this change, surprisingly, came from Russia.

From its earliest days, the Academy's doors were open to any Jewish student wishing to learn. An active scholarship program was constructed early on, and, every year, the school has issued tuition grants to students based upon financial need. No child has ever been turned away because of financial inability to pay the tuition cost. This open-door policy became crucial as other doors began to open for the first time on the other side of the world. In the mid-eighties Jewish immigration from the Soviet Union began to swell. As Jewish families were settled into communities such as ours, it became the role of the Jewish Federation to provide needed resettlement services, just as they had done with our family back in the 1950s.

Providing for the educational needs of newly arrived immigrant families was a key component of the resettlement process. It soon became obvious to the social workers at the Federation that a Russian child enrolled at our school would fare much better than if he or she were enrolled at a public school. Even though they would be required to learn not one, but two new languages (English and Hebrew), the personalized attention made a world of difference. The fact that they were, for the first time, learning about their Jewish heritage – something that was denied to them in their former homeland, was an added benefit.

As immigration increased during the Perestroika/Glasnost/Gorbachev period, the Federation allocated a growing sum to Russian resettlement. The school was offered a per head scholarship grant for each Russian student it permitted in its doors. A total of $42,500 in Federation scholarships was granted in 1985. These funds did not begin to offset the true cost of servicing these students, but it was helpful – and it represented the first time even a single dollar had flowed from the Federation to the school.

By this time, some of the old guard had passed on and the Federation leadership was being replaced with a younger generation, many of whom were parents with children enrolled at the school. Frank Newman's successor as Federation executive director, Harry Nadler, had two children studying at the school, and his wife, Ellen, served as a member of the middle school faculty and as guidance counselor.

Russian resettlement helped to swell the ranks of our student body, peaking at a total of 309 in 1990. During these years, the allocation from the Federation continued to rise. By 1994, it became obvious that the continued labeling of the Federation allocation as "Russian scholarships" was a pointless charade. Once these "scholarship" funds were received by the school, they were fungible and could be used to defray any of its general operating costs. In 1995, the Academy received an allocation from the Federation of over $125,000, directed to the school's general operating fund. This annual subvention grant has more than trebled since then, as needs have grown and attitudes have continued to change for the better.

It appears that the battles of the past are behind us. Today the school enjoys the legitimacy we had hoped for, and it draws its students from all segments of the community. Sending a child to the Hebrew Academy nowadays is considered somewhat fashionable and even a bit prestigious. The Hebrew Academy is a respected and integral part of the Federation family. No longer a step-child, it is a proud and recognized institution of Jewish learning. The current president of the Jewish Federation has a seat on the Academy's Board of Directors, and the two entities enjoy a strong and mutually beneficial relationship.

The Academy has played host to numerous VIPs and dignitaries over the years, including Menachem Begin and Elie Wiesel. In terms of academic excellence, the school enjoys an unparalleled reputation. It is the only school in the state to have twice received the US Department of Education's coveted Blue Ribbon of Excellence award. In 1993, the Academy also received Israel's highest civilian honor: the Jerusalem Award. It consistently turns in the highest standardized test score averages (ISTEP) of any school, either public or private, in the state of Indiana.

In 1996, the school celebrated its 25th anniversary with a series of special projects and community events. These included the commissioning of an authentic handmade 25th Anniversary Torah scroll that took a full year to produce. The anniversary culminated in a gala celebration banquet featuring Nobel Laureate Elie Wiesel, who was invited to inscribe the final letters into the new Torah. In addition, it was announced that evening that the Board of Directors, in recognition of our family's lifetime support of the school, had voted to change its name to The Hasten Hebrew Academy of Indianapolis. Mark and I were overwhelmed by this honor, as were our families. Originally, we shunned this distinction, since enhancing our personal glory was never our objective in founding and supporting the school. I recall a conversation with the school's Development Director, Peter Weisz, on this subject.

"Peter, I don't think putting our name on the school is the right thing to do," I stated.

"But, Hart, the Board feels otherwise. Most of them believe that this is long overdue. You built this school from the ground up and deserve the honor," he protested.

"But we didn't do it to see our name on the door," I said.

"Everyone knows that. But don't you think this would be a nice way to honor your mother's memory?" Peter pointed out.

That was indeed an attractive thought. Our dear mother, Hannah, had died a few months earlier at the age of 102. She was a familiar figure at the school and was beloved by all the teachers and staff. He was right. I decided to accept the honor in Mother's memory and continue to think of it in this way. Although the school is today known as the Hasten Hebrew Academy, in my mind, it is actually the Hannah Hasten Hebrew Academy.

As mentioned, the Academy has played host to a number of noteworthy individuals. Luminaries such as Menachem Begin, Moshe Dayan, Yigael Yadin, Elie Tavin, Benny Begin, Haim Landau and Yakov Ne'eman have toured our corridors and classrooms. We have also been honored by visits from Nobel Peace Prize Laureate Elie Wiesel and by entertainers such as Jan Pierce and Monty Hall, astronaut David Wolf and countless political and civic leaders. But from among this list of luminaries, one visitor stands out in my mind as unforgettable.

It was in 1978 that famed Austrian Nazi hunter and Holocaust survivor, Simon Wiesenthal, was touring the US, raising money to establish the Simon Wiesenthal Center and Museum of Tolerance in Los Angeles. During his stop in Indianapolis, he accepted my last-minute invitation to visit our newly constructed Jewish day school. Wiesenthal, along with his entourage, which included Sam Belzberg and Rabbi Marvin Hier, toured the building and sat in on classes. Finally he was escorted into the auditorium, where I introduced him before an all-school assembly. After the children were informed about Mr. Wiesenthal's accomplishments in bringing Nazi criminals to justice, I turned the microphone over to him. Wiesenthal immediately passed the microphone over to Rabbi Hier, who then went on to address the assembly.

After the school day was over, I received countless phone calls from upset parents who wanted to know why they weren't informed in advance that such a well-known visitor would be at the school. I explained repeatedly that the decision to visit was a spontaneous one and the lack of notice was unavoidable. Many parents also voiced an objection to the fact that I "didn't let Mr. Wiesenthal speak to the kids!" This really upset me. Out of deference at the time, I held my tongue and did not reveal the true reason for his silence. I did not wish to tell parents about the tears I saw emerging from Wiesenthal's eyes.

Wiesenthal, after having seen so much cruel suffering endured by children, so many babies marked for death, so many young innocents wiped out, was deeply moved by the sight of our bright faced students studying

Hebrew in freedom, filled with obvious Jewish pride. In fact, he was moved to tears. Wiesenthal was so overcome with emotion that he found himself unable to speak. His eyes…eyes that had witnessed mankind's worst depravities, now provided him with a clear image of man's best potential. His experiences had shaped and broadened his world view and placed matters into proper perspective.

On that day, I also gained a new perspective on what we were doing in creating a home for Jewish academics in Indianapolis. It is this perspective that has helped guide me in my leadership capacity at the school.

I often wish I could impart this same perspective to parents as they strive to do what they consider best for their children. So often, parents become wrapped up in issues that appear important at the moment, but which are actually inconsequential when compared to the school's main mission of teaching love of Jewish heritage and learning. So many times, petty disagreements arising from disciplinary policies, teaching styles, student dress codes, food quality and so on cause parents to become distracted from the Academy's true purpose. As I often explain to parents and grandparents, we must never allow these larger considerations to become sidelined. We must not allow ourselves to become mired in the mundane. Instead, we must always strive to remain focused on our future.

As we did then, we continue to offer our students a well-rounded and balanced educational experience. In this regard, I can't help but recall a conversation I had with my old friend, Jerry Rubin, who had accompanied me on that fateful trip to Los Angeles back in 1961 when I met my future wife. Jerry, a professor of psychiatric social work (as described in Chapter 7), was visiting Indianapolis in the early 1980s, and when he returned to Las Vegas, he was inspired to write a paper which sought to instruct teachers at Jewish schools on how their students should respond when faced with anti-Semitic incidents. I called to thank him for sending me a copy of the paper.

"This is excellent work, Jerry," I said. "And I will pass it on to our teachers."

"Do you currently have any type of program in place that teaches the kids how to deal with anti-Semitism, Hart?" he inquired.

"As a matter of fact, we do." I responded. "We teach the kids karate!"

I heard him chuckling on the phone, and I'm sure he could tell that my attitudes about Jewish defense had remained constant.

With the exception of a few years during the early 1980s when my brother, Mark, served as president, and a few years during the late 1990s when my son, Bernard, did the same, I have had the privilege of working as the Academy's lay leader since the school's inception. While I am looking forward to permanently passing the mantle of leadership on to other capable shoulders, I am today just as involved in the day-to-day operation of the school as I was at its founding.

The Academy has stood at the central core of my life for more than thirty years, and my heart still swells as I walk the hallways and peek into classrooms to observe the little ones learning about their proud heritage. It is indeed comforting to contemplate that this school will still be carrying out its important work long after I have departed the scene. It is this school, more than anything I can name, that I hope will serve as our family's legacy to our children, our community and our people for generations to come.

Chapter Twelve

Building, Banking & Cable TV

Our early success with our first nursing home provided Mark and me with the confidence to take on bigger challenges. This confidence enabled us not only to expand our core business through acquisition and new construction of more nursing homes, but it also gave us the impetus to look into other businesses that we found appealing. We came to understand that sound business principles were more or less universal. We believed that if we possessed the leadership skills to recruit and motivate a skilled management team, we could conquer any business. Our first venture outside of nursing homes took us into the frenetic world of residential real estate development.

Our introduction to multifamily housing was the result of our desire to attract top people to staff our first nursing home. While managing that first facility, I had noted that several of our nurses lived in a suburban apartment complex, Shadeland Squire, located next door to our building. There were only thirty-six units, but I recall thinking to myself, "If we owned those apartments, we could provide housing for our staff next door and they could walk to work. This would save them money and keep them nearby in case of emergency."

In mid-1968 we contacted the owners and asked if they were interested in selling. As it turned out they were, and we quickly arrived at a price. Of course purchasing an apartment complex is one thing, but managing it successfully is quite another. We hired an onsite apartment manager to collect the rents and show the units to prospective tenants. For maintenance, we were able to employ the crew from the nursing home. We were also able to share vendors and service providers, such as landscaping and snow removal.

While the apartments enjoyed a respectable occupancy rate and managed to turn a modest profit right from the start, they never became a huge financial success. But they did serve the purpose I envisioned. The fact that we held available housing adjacent to the workplace was a compelling incentive for a number of our nursing home employees. We were also able occasionally to provide housing for a patient's family member who wished to live near an institutionalized relative. The apartments acted as an enhancement of what we regarded as our primary mission: providing top quality patient care.

Over the next few years we discovered the bitter and the sweet of multifamily property management. Evictions, burst water pipes, lease skippers, liability claims – we learned about all these and more. While I viewed the apartments as simply an adjunct to our core business, I could see that Mark was taking a real liking to it. He began looking at other apartment buildings on the market and started putting together financial projections.

"You know, if we could finance this complex at 90 percent of the purchase price," he told me, "at today's interest rates we could be in the black within one year. Of course, we'd have to increase occupancy by five percent." Mark also understood the sizable tax benefits associated with real estate development in those days.

"Because the interest on the note and the accelerated depreciation are deductible business expenses, we'd be operating at a loss on paper, even though we'll have a positive cash flow. We can use that loss to reduce the taxes on our nursing home income."

I was from the old school. You work hard. You make money. You pay your taxes. But Mark had the sophistication to understand what would soon become known as "tax shelter" investments. He also had an engineering background and was very adept at construction cost analysis. In addition, he was also quite talented at negotiating attractive financing deals. I didn't need a lot of convincing to agree that real estate development had some most attractive benefits. As a result, we decided to expand our apartment business through both acquisition and new construction.

We established a property management company, Harcourt Management, and followed a steady growth path over the next twenty years. At our peak, we owned and managed eleven apartment communities around the Midwest, comprising over four thousand units. Most were A and B grade garden apartment complexes containing one, two and three bedroom one-story flats, as well as two-story town houses. In the late 1980s we designed and erected Lion's Gate, Indianapolis' finest luxury apartment community. These units were appointed with every conceivable amenity, including airport limo transport and housekeeping service.

Unquestionably, our most ambitious real estate project was a development known as Deer Creek in Deerfield Beach, Florida. It came about through our banking relationship with what was then known as the American Fletcher

National Bank. AFNB had provided the financing for a number of our nursing home and apartment projects and had ably supported our growth in both businesses. One day in 1982, Mark and I were invited by Larry Kennedy, an AFNB senior vice president, to join him and some of the bank officers for lunch. Larry explained that the bank had foreclosed on an attractive real estate project in Florida and had been successfully operating it for the past several years. A recent turn of events had created a conflict of interest, and the bank was advised by its examiners that it could no longer maintain ownership. The bank wished to find a buyer and was willing to finance the deal on some very attractive terms. Mark and I agreed to review the offering packet that had been put together.

After studying the material we decided that the deal held sufficient appeal for us to take the next step. I had not been to Florida since my visit to the Miami day school, and I decided to go have a look. Upon my arrival at the site, I was given a tour of the 200 plus acre community that featured a country club with an adjoining 18 clay court tennis center. The country club grounds were lush and expansive. They were surrounded by some upscale resort condominiums that were owned mostly by "snowflakes" – northerners who spent their winters in the Florida sunshine. It was during those years that I was beginning to become more serious about my own tennis game, and this property appeared to be nothing short of tennis heaven. I quite simply fell in love with the place.

I rushed home and set up another meeting with Larry. I did not wish to appear too eager, so I simply said that yes, I had inspected the property and we were ready to take the next step, but that I first wanted Mark to take a look. Larry offered us one of the bank's luxury condominiums at the complex and we were soon back for another tour. After looking over both the grounds and the financial statements, Mark agreed that this could be a terrific deal if certain conditions were met. Mark envisioned the erection of permanent single and multifamily housing at Deer Creek, not merely vacation homes. Rather than developing this residential housing for such a large tract ourselves, we would be better off providing the infrastructure and then parceling it off to local developers. Our plan called for the grounds to be subdivided into eleven parcels that could then be offered to luxury residential housing developers.

Our next meeting with the bank was with their top executives including bank president, Frank E. McKinney. Mr. McKinney was extremely gracious and referred to us as one of AFNB's prime customers. After accepting the flattery, I described our thinking and informed the bankers that we were indeed interested in the acquisition, if certain zoning issues could be resolved. It was at this point that Mr. McKinney revealed something shocking.

"You know, I just remembered something," he said off-handedly. "I believe that Deer Creek Country Club is restricted." I was familiar with the term. It meant "no Jews." I couldn't believe my ears. This was America in 1982, not 1947. Such "gentlemen's agreements" were a thing of the past. I must have misunderstood him, I thought.

"What do you mean?" I asked, incredulously.

"As I recall, they have a policy that restricts their membership to non-Jews," he said plainly. "That could be a problem here." If his intention was to get me heated up, he had pushed the right button.

"If that's true, I can tell you one thing, Mr. McKinney," I retorted, "if we were interested before hearing this news, we're twice as interested now!" I was never sure if McKinney was playing a psychological game here, passing on this tidbit in the hopes that it would prod us into closing the deal.

Upon investigation we discovered that there was actually no such policy in place. In fact there were a number of Jewish families living at Deer Creek and they all enjoyed full membership rights at the country club. Presumably, what McKinney had been thinking of was something that harked back to the initial founding of the project. The original developers had intended to create a restricted community when the country club was still in its planning stages. It had never materialized as such, but the reputation still lingered on.

After completing our due diligence process and resolving the zoning issues, we made a deal for the purchase of Deer Creek in the fall of 1982. Mark and I traveled to the project and arranged for an introductory meeting with the entire staff. I rose first and addressed our new employees:

"I want to tell you all how pleased we are to be working with you. In a minute my brother, Mark, will explain some of the very exciting plans we have in store for Deer Creek. But first, I want to clear the air about something. I understand that once upon a time, this place started out as a restricted community. I know there's been some concern about this since Mark and I became the new owners. What will our policy be regarding employment and membership? Well, I just want to assure you all right here and now, as Jews, we will never discriminate against any non-Jews in any way, shape or form." This got a big laugh and helped to break the ice by defusing a touchy issue.

Over the next thirteen years we proceeded with our game plan and, with one notable exception, successfully sold off the parcels to developers at attractive prices. We eventually sold off the country club and tennis center that had never been able to generate very much of a profit. But it wasn't all smooth sailing, I'm afraid. We encountered resistance from the homeowners' association, when we attempted to sell a parcel to an apartment developer. They were afraid that multifamily housing would damage their property values. We were able to demonstrate, however, that this was not the pattern in this part of Florida and succeeded in obtaining the necessary zoning permits.

Our ongoing success in the nursing home and real estate businesses caused Mark and me to face a new question. How should we invest our earnings? Up until now we had plowed our nursing home profits back into the business, fueling our rapid growth. We agreed that further growth would limit our ability to maintain "hands-on" management control, so we began to look around for attractive investment opportunities. Our primary objective was long-term appreciation. We were not interested in gambling on the stock market or, aside from our own developments, getting involved in any of the ubiquitous and exotic tax shelter schemes floating around at that time. We wanted to put our money into businesses with good past performances and even better future potential.

We had been successful in building a streamlined business structure in our nursing home business. There was a Supervisor of Nursing, a Chief Therapist, a Director of Operations and a whole chain of command in place. As owners, we were mostly involved in oversight and making sure that everyone was doing his or her job properly. Although Mark and I were still on call 24 hours a day and we had purchased a helicopter to facilitate our around-the-state travel, the business had become more or less self-sustaining and was making fewer demands upon our time. This fact enabled us to look for businesses where we would be able to take an active role. We wished to become vocal, not silent, partners and began seeking out business investments that would permit us to leverage our management skills.

Once we put out the word that we were in the market, it didn't take long before a pile of offering circulars and business plans began to accumulate on my desk. Most held no real appeal and carried either too much risk or too little upside potential. Finally we were informed about a small bank in Kokomo, Indiana, that was up for sale. It was the First National Bank of Kokomo and had only about $69 million in assets. The financial statements looked strong and their loan portfolio looked very solid. And there was another factor. After the grueling hours required by our current enterprise, the nine to five schedule of the banking business held a good deal of appeal. We decided to look into it.

We set up a meeting with the bank's majority stockholders, Larry

Hannah and Jack Fell. Larry explained that he was involved in numerous other business activities. In order to devote his time to them, he felt he needed to divest himself of his interest in the bank. We met with the bank's president and its Board of Directors.

The more we talked, and the more we investigated, the more attractive this opportunity became. We placed an offer on the table and began a six-month round of negotiations that culminated in a final sales agreement. Although the bank was profitable, it was not performing at the level it was capable of. If the bank continued performing at its current level it would provide us with an acceptable return on our investment. But we were looking for something more. Our strategy was to stimulate the bank into higher levels of profitability through innovation and by bringing our proven management techniques into play.

Although Mark and I understood enough about the banking business to be able to analyze a bank's balance sheet, we knew little about the nuts and bolts of banking. We were relying upon most of the existing staff to remain in place after the acquisition. In particular, the bank's president was extremely supportive and positive during the negotiations. He continually provided us with inside information about the bank's operations that proved very helpful in our evaluations. He also impressed us with his deep and detailed understanding of the bank's business activities. We felt comfortable that, with the president staying on to run bank operations, we would experience a very smooth transition. After listening to him talk about expanding the bank and other bright plans for the future, we trusted him to hold our hands as we jumped feet first into this new and unfamiliar industry.

On the very day we took over operation of the bank, Mark phoned to advise me that we had a problem and that the bank president needed to speak with me right away. I told Mark to bring him over to the house without delay. We sat in the living room and, as the bank president took a chair, he dropped a bombshell right into our laps.

"I know this is not good timing," he told us, "but I need to turn in my notice. I know you guys don't know much about banking, so I'm willing to stick around for six months to help you get established, but then I've got to move on." The fellow declined to tell us what he had lined up, and it really was irrelevant at this point.

Mark and I were both stunned and didn't know what to say. We had just made a huge investment based, in large part, upon information gathered through this man. While we had no formal employment contract in place, he had always spoken as though he would continue to run things after we took over. Finally, I spoke up.

"Can we convince you to change your mind?" I asked. "You know we were depending on your continued service when we made this deal."

"There's something else," Mark pointed out. "We've heard some nasty rumors about possible panic. The bank changing hands might make depositors nervous. Once word gets out that you're also resigning, it might trigger a run on the bank. Overnight, we could wind up with nothing."

"Can you reconsider your decision?" I asked again.

"I'm sorry," he said forthrightly, "but my decision is irrevocable." As soon as I heard this, I immediately made up my mind about this fellow and about what I had to do next.

We looked at each other and Mark nodded his agreement. "In that case, you're leaving today," I told him. The bank president was stunned.

"We're not going to have a guy running things who we know is leaving in six months," I said to Mark. "You're absolutely right," he replied. The bank president recovered from his shock and spoke up.

"I don't believe this," he managed to get out, eyes wide, head shaking. "You fellows know nothing about banking!"

"Perhaps we don't know much about the banking business at this point," I responded, "but we've spent our entire careers in management, and we know that this is the right decision." I instructed him to return to Kokomo immediately and clean out his desk.

Mark and I called an emergency meeting of the Board of Directors the following day and explained the situation. They gave us their full support and agreed that we had done the right thing. Jack Fell, the Chairman of the Board, was the largest stockholder after us. He was an attorney and had long been involved in small-town banking. At the Board's request, Jack agreed to take the post of acting president until we were able to recruit a replacement.

We decided to take our time and be very selective in our search for a new president. Mark and I both personally interviewed every candidate for the position. The obvious choice was a man named Charlie Cameron. Charlie had been with the bank for over 35 years and was the most senior member of the management team. He had made it clear that he was available and interested in the position. In fact, his attitude was that he was owed the promotion, in consideration of his lengthy service.

A bank employee, Conrad (Connie) Uitts (pronounced: *YOU-its*), who had been with the bank about 15 years at the time, was also a candidate. He had started as a teller and had worked his way up through the ranks. We conducted a number of interviews with Connie and the more we talked, the more impressed we became. Mark and I both agreed that Connie had the right set of qualifications and seemed ready and eager for the challenges that lay ahead. After several months of deliberation, we recommended to the Board that Connie be named the new bank president, and they unanimously agreed. Connie turned out to be a great choice. He served as president for the next twenty years, until his retirement, and successfully shepherded the bank through rapid and enormous growth. Today, Connie sits on the bank's Board of Directors.

Looking back, it is clear that the original bank president's resignation – which seemed like a major disaster at the time – turned out to be a huge blessing. Had he not departed when he did, we would have missed the opportunity of working with Connie at that critical early stage of the game. I am convinced that we would never have achieved the level of success we did without the benefit of Connie's highly effective leadership.

Not surprisingly, we encountered a number of raised eyebrows as we made our entry into the world of finance. "Who are these two Jewish brothers, with no training or background in banking, coming into our community and running our bank?" But I had faced this sort of situation before in the nursing home business. I realized that, to gain the respect of our Board and our staff, we needed to employ common sense management methods and be prepared to work very hard. We soon became familiar with the dynamics of the banking business and found it fascinating. Mark, in particular, enjoyed serving on the loan committee, reviewing prospective financial deals and becoming adept at risk management. I became more focused on the operational issues such as training, customer service and marketing. Within a matter of months we had dispelled any doubts about our abilities.

Once our initial orientation was over with, we set out to make improvements in order to gain a higher level of profitability. We embarked on a program of modernization and took full advantage of the new technologies that were making their impact felt on our industry. Success in the banking business is measured by return on assets (ROA) and return on equity (ROE). As we reviewed operations, we began to develop and introduce efficiencies that served to increase the bank's ROA We watched as our deposits grew every month while our innovations helped to keep overhead expenses level. Little by little we witnessed the bank's ROA climb steadily over the coming months.

We worked closely with Connie, who did an excellent job of educating me about the nuts and bolts of our business. He turned out to be a very thoughtful and methodical executive who was enthusiastic about implementing the improvements we were developing. As it turned out, the fact that we came into the picture with no preconceived notions – with fresh eyes, if you will – turned out to be an advantage. We were not afraid to ask: "Isn't there a better way of doing things?" and we did not accept: "That's the way we've always done it" as a legitimate reason for anything.

I recognized that, in order to succeed in the highly competitive banking environment, we had to train our staff to be totally "people-oriented." This emphasis began right at the top, with the president. I encouraged Connie to join civic and service organizations, such as the Rotary Club and the local Chamber of Commerce, in order to become a more visible figure in the business community. Connie was eventually elected president of the Kokomo Chamber of Commerce and became an active civic leader. He enjoys the distinction of being the first non-Catholic chairman of the board of the local Catholic hospital, St. Joseph's. In this way Connie, and other bank executives, began networking with the town's business leaders and establishing vital community contacts. As a result, these contacts, established through civic affiliations, would increasingly turn to our bank when the time came to fulfill the financing needs of their businesses. I encouraged the bank's top management to get to know the town's political movers and shakers as well, including the mayor and public school commissioner.

Mark and I have always believed in the importance of charitable giving. For this reason, and because it would help to enhance our community standing, we authorized a more aggressive philanthropic program, directing donations to such visible agencies as the YMCA and Boy Scouts. We okayed a major contribution to the Kokomo hospital's expansion project, for example. The goodwill generated by such gestures helped to elevate the bank's reputation in the eyes of the community. In this regard, we stressed that all aspects of the bank's operation be conducted in an ethical and honest manner. We understood that a bank's reputation is based upon its perceived integrity. Therefore, we insisted that the bank steer clear of any dealings that might appear to compromise that integrity.

Steadily, our bank's profitability and community standing both began to improve. Likewise, we began to gain the confidence and trust of our associates and employees. As our methods proved successful, we were no longer regarded as outsiders, and we began to enjoy the full respect and cooperation of our Board members, our management team and the business community.

Soon a year had gone by and both Mark and I were very pleased with the results of our venture into the banking world. We found it challenging, profitable and, most of all, respectable. The civility found in banking circles was such a contrast to the brutal rough and tumble of the nursing home business that it's no wonder we were drawn to it. We learned that another bank was on the market in Martinsville, a small community south of Indianapolis. It was being offered by the same fellows, Hannah and Fell, with whom we had dealt during our purchase of the Kokomo bank. We acquired the Martinsville bank, and this time, things were a bit easier. We already had a track record and quickly began to implement some of the same measures that had worked well for us in Kokomo. The president of the Martinsville bank, Don Winters, stayed aboard and gave us his full cooperation.

Our next move was to embark on a plan for growth that involved the building of new branch banking centers and remodeling of existing facilities. This growth paid off in increased earnings that more than offset the capital expended to underwrite it. We realized that we had developed a formula for success that could be transplanted from one community to another and began seeking out new acquisitions. Our next bank was in Tipton, Indiana, and within two more years we had expanded our holdings to six banks, all located in medium to small Indiana communities such as Sullivan, Brazil and Farmersburg.

Initially each bank operated as a separate business entity, with its own Board of Directors. A few were national banks, while the rest were chartered by the state. Once we had reached a critical size, it became clear that we could enjoy tremendous efficiencies through consolidation. One by one, we began merging the banks under the First National Bank & Trust name and blending their respective management teams. We created an umbrella corporation, Hasten Bancshares, to serve as a holding company and began to emerge as a force in the regional banking industry. In 1994, Mark was appointed by Governor Evan Bayh to serve as chairman of the Indiana Department of Financial Institutions. Our growth over the ensuing years has been sure and steady and culminated in the acquisition in 2001 of a competing bank chain, the Harrington Bank.

With the Harrington Bank acquisition, First National Bank has grown to encompass $1.6 billion in assets and employs roughly 450 employees at 22 branches throughout the state. Working with the bank's current president, Walter Wolff, as he steers the company to higher levels of success, is a rewarding and very exciting pleasure. The fact of the matter is that the longer I remain active in the banking business the more I love it.

Throughout our banking venture, Mark and I maintained our close working partnership that I believe contributed greatly to our success. We didn't mind, and still don't, when people would refer to us jointly as "The Hastens" or often as a single entity named "MarkandHart."

We have even managed to work with a single administrative assistant over the past twenty-five years. Martha (Marty) Havely joined our organization as a secretary in the 1970s and has been our trusted and extremely efficient right hand to this day. Mrs. Havely, as I prefer to call her, enjoys a scope of responsibility that encompasses all aspects of our business, civic and volunteer activities. From setting up international conference calls to managing the tidal wave of mail, we look to Mrs. Havely to be our link to the world.

In 1987, on the occasion of my daughter, Renée's, wedding, I invited Mrs. Havely and her husband, Rod, to join our family celebration in Israel. We had also invited and arranged for all of the various bank presidents to attend. Their presence at this *simcha* (joyous occasion) turned it into an unforgettable event – both for them and for us.

As our success in real estate development and banking began to take off, I was starting to become more and more disenchanted with the nursing home business. With the advent of Medicare and similar government programs, I could see the emphasis shifting from patient care to bureaucratic paperwork. In order to remain in compliance, the nursing home operator had become buried under a mountain of reporting forms while being under the perpetual scrutiny of an army of government inspectors.

We soon learned what it means to be under the yoke of a government bureaucracy. Whereas, in the past, our facilities were inspected by seasoned professionals who were knowledgeable in geriatric care, we now found ourselves regularly being invaded by up to a dozen inspectors at a time, all bent on earning their salaries by uncovering petty violations. The unending stream of report filings became a huge burden for our administrative staff. I recall walking into one of our administrators' offices and noticing that a new bookshelf had been erected along the length of his wall, stacked full with bound notebooks.

"What's all that?" I inquired.

"Those are all the reporting forms we need to complete each day," he replied shaking his head wearily. I was incredulous. How did he have the time to look after patient care if he was forced to spend his day shuffling papers? We were continually being evaluated for our level of utilization upon which our reimbursements were based. This created an inverted incentive system that rewarded inefficiencies. We soon found ourselves working under a socialized medicine system that Mark and I both found abhorrent.

Ever since we first became established in the nursing home industry, we had been receiving a steady flow of acquisition inquiries from competitors, business brokers and the like. For the most part we discarded these offers, since we had no interest in selling any part of the business we had built up with so much care and effort. But as the burden of government regulation began to weigh us down more and more, these offers began to appear increasingly attractive to us.

In 1982, after reviewing proposals from a number of prospective suitors, we finally reached an agreement with an investment syndicate offered a very generous purchase price. The new owners contracted with a management company, Beverly Enterprises, to carry out day-to-day operations. The syndicate has retained ownership for the past twenty years and continues to prosper. We left the nursing home business with the satisfaction of having raised the standards of care for our industry, while at the same time building a highly successful and enduring organization.

Our next business opportunity came our way because of our close ties with the Israeli government. It was those ties that prompted local entrepreneur, Bob Schloss, to contact us. I had known Bob's late father, Bill Schloss, since first becoming involved in community affairs in Indianapolis. He was a pioneer in the banking business and had amassed a personal fortune in the Savings & Loan industry. Bill, a generous philanthropist, was also very active with the Jewish Federation and was held in high regard as a stalwart and dedicated community leader. After Bill's death, his son Bob carried on his tradition of entrepreneurship, founding and managing a varied string of successful companies. He was primarily focused in mass media and had founded a cable TV service, just as that industry was taking off. He had built up a substantial number of subscribers throughout the Midwest and was looking for new growth opportunities when, in 1985, he learned from a Washington business brokerage that the Israeli government was about to issue exclusive franchise contracts for the cable TV service districts that they had recently established.

Bob felt that, with his expertise in the cable TV business and with our close political connections to the Israeli government, we stood a good chance of capturing one of the contracts. He approached me and suggested we form a new company and submit a bid. After some deliberation about the details, we decided to give it a try. We established a 50/50 ownership position in the new company, with Bob and his sisters owning one half of the equity and with Mark and I controlling the other half.

We soon went to work submitting applications, bids and projections to the multitude of governmental agencies involved in this new industry. It took about a year and a half, plus a good deal of effort, to assure that our bid made its way properly through the bureaucratic labyrinth. I am certain that, were it not for our government connections, we would certainly have drowned in a sea of red tape.

At the end of the day, our company was awarded one of only five exclusive cable TV franchise contracts issued by the Israeli government. Our primary district was to be in the south, covering Be'ersheva and other Negev communities such as Arad, Yerucham and Dimona. Each cable TV franchise holder also had to agree to operate in certain assigned areas that were considered to be under-serviced. So we were given the towns of Rehovot, and Nes Tziona in the central area of the country as well as Naharia and Akko in the north.

Operations soon got underway, with Bob traveling regularly back and forth to Israel. We called the company ICS Ltd. (Israeli Cable Service), and we soon assembled a first rate management team, several engineers, and began the training of our installation crews. I recall our first staff meeting, when we were just getting things started at our headquarters. I was asked to say a few words:

"I want to welcome you all onboard at ICS. We are about to start on an exciting adventure that will bring cable TV to Israel and bring us challenges, achievements and hopefully, profits. I want you all to know something. This company is going to be run 'American-style.' What I mean is that we are going to emphasize customer service. We are going to make sure that the phone is picked up by the third ring. When you answer the phone, you will identify yourself and say 'May I help you.' We are going to be polite and courteous to every customer – even if they are rude to us. Before we hook-up a new account, we will tell the customer that a service technician will be at his or her home between, say, 1 and 3 PM next Tuesday – and we see to it that these appointments are kept faithfully. There will be no smoking on the premises, except in specially designated areas. It is in this way, and it is in *only* this way, that we will build our business and achieve success. Anyone who does not understand this, or is unwilling to comply, should turn in his resignation right away. To the rest of you I say, let's get started. There's a lot of work to be done."

Bob did an outstanding job in managing the technical end and building the needed infrastructure. I saw my role as educating our Israeli employees about American-style business practices. This was a formidable task, since most Israelis were not used to customer courtesy and other such niceties. The idea that a customer should be met with a smile and a greeting of "May

I help you?" or "Please take a seat" was completely alien to most Israelis. How many times had I observed a clerk lazily finishing her coffee and phone conversation with her boyfriend, as I waited for service and cursed Israel's socialist economy?

Some were moved to question my over-arching emphasis on quality customer service. "Why bother?" they would ask. "We have an exclusive franchise with no competition. We're the only game in town. If the customer isn't entirely happy, where else is he going to go?" I pointed out again and again that this cynical and cavalier attitude was a mistake and would result in our eventual failure if not checked. Our company experienced growth by continually adding subscribers. The idea was to add more than we lost. Broadcast TV was available for free, and cable TV was viewed as something of a luxury item by the public. The only way we could hope to increase our subscriber base was if we enjoyed a first rate reputation for service. Our most powerful marketing tool was word of mouth. One satisfied customer telling his neighbor how happy he or she was with the service and reliability of the cable provider is how we intended to grow our company. It was basically the same formula for success that we had used in the nursing home and banking businesses.

Israel's general deficiency in the area of customer service was indelibly marked in my memory, thanks to some rather unpleasant experiences years before when I first brought my family to Israel for a visit. Back in the early 1970s, attitudes towards Westerners, and especially towards Americans, were far different from today's. The prevailing mindset during those years after Israel's stunning victory in the Six Day War was, "We're Israeli and we don't answer to anybody – especially fat cat American Jews who sit comfortably back in the US while we risk our lives for a Jewish homeland." Such niceties as customer care were non-existent, even in the hospitality industry which sought to attract hard currency through tourism.

I was eager to experience Israel with Simona, who had lived there years before, and with my two children at the time, Renée, aged 7, and Bernard, aged 5. After an all night transatlantic crossing, we arrived at our Tel Aviv hotel at dawn. As we checked in, the desk clerk advised us that our rooms were not yet made up and urged us to visit the dining room where we could enjoy a complimentary breakfast. The kids were exhausted and needed sleep, but since the clerk assured us that the rooms would be ready promptly, we accepted his invitation and made our way to the second floor dining room. Since no hostess greeted us, and since only a few patrons were on hand, we selected a table and sat down. Fifteen minutes later, no one had yet approached us and we began to get a bit restless.

"I see why they call them 'waiters,'" I quipped. "They sure do make you wait." But the kids were not amused and I was becoming slightly annoyed as well. After repeated attempts to flag down one of the waiters, I gave up and walked in to the kitchen to ask if anyone would be taking our order. I was urged to be patient and told that someone would be with us soon.

Once the somewhat truculent waiter finally ambled over to take our order, we asked him to bring some breakfast cereal for our children. "Cereal is not included in the complimentary breakfast. You will need to pay extra." That's fine, we assured him, just hurry since the kids are very tired and hungry.

When the order arrived, we were presented with the standard continental breakfast – no cereal. When I protested, I was again told that cereal was not included. "Just bring the cereal," I begged in exasperation. Finally, after repeated urgings, the waiter delivered two packages of cereal. That was it, cereal, but no milk. After again being advised that the milk was not included, I authorized two glasses of cold milk. The milk finally arrived and it was steaming – and, by this time, so was I. The kids began whining because each glass of hot milk had a "yukky" film of skin that they refused to touch. So I ducked in to the kitchen and secured two glasses of unheated, skin-free milk. This seemed to calm the children down, and so, feeling somewhat confident, Simona requested a glass of ice water. This opened a whole new controversy. Two more waiters now descended upon our table to advise Simona about the evils of drinking liquids over ice. In Israel, as in many countries where ice-makers are not common, this sour grapes myth about drinking chilled beverages had emerged. "If you drink water with ice, you will suffer a terrible sore throat," Simona was advised repeatedly. Simona finally convinced the hotel staff that she liked to live dangerously and would not hold them responsible if she did suffer any harm from the glass of ice water.

After about four hours of this jousting, Renée and Bernard were sleeping at their seats and I had made repeated trips to the front desk to inquire when we would be able to enter our hotel rooms. "Very soon," I was assured each time. Finally, Simona joined me at the desk as I once again explained our plight to the uncaring desk clerk. When I began to get a bit boisterous, the manager rushed out to investigate. "What's the trouble?" he asked the clerk in Hebrew. "No trouble," he replied dismissively. "just some Americans in a big hurry. Don't worry, they'll wait." While my Hebrew was not adequate for me to understand this exchange, that was not true for Simona who understood every word. She let them have it!

"How dare you?" she stormed in Hebrew. "How dare you talk about a guest at your hotel that way. Don't you know that we came all the way from America and brought our children to spend our money in your hotel? We could have gone to Italy or Spain, where we would not have to be treated like dogs. You should all be ashamed of yourselves!" Needless to say, our rooms were ready for us five minutes later.

After getting some rest, I contacted some of my DP camp friends from Ebelsberg who now made their home in Israel. I invited them to our hotel at 6 PM and was looking forward to reminiscing about old times over dinner. As we entered the dining room, I asked the maître d' to provide us with a table for eight. He showed us to two four-top tables next to each other.

"No, we need to sit together," I explained patiently. "We're old friends who haven't seen one another for many years, and we want to talk to each other during dinner. Why don't we just push these two smaller tables together and then we'll be fine." When I was told that this was not permitted, I became aroused. Perhaps because I wished to appear bold before my old buddies, I demanded that the tables be pushed together and, with the help of my friends, we rearranged them to suit us.

I was beginning to develop a reputation among the hotel staff as a hard case, although this perception did not cause the level of service to improve and we were still forced to endure one indignity after another. The hotel was ruining what I had hoped would be a wonderful family vacation. By our third day, I had had enough. As we entered the dining room for breakfast, I asked to see the *menahel* (manager). He was a weasel-faced little fellow whose eyes flicked quickly in all directions as he spoke. As soon as he arrived, I read him the riot act right there, in front of his staff and the other hotel guests.

"Staying in this hotel has been my worst experience since I left the DP camps," I exclaimed. "It has been awful. Every morning we are put through the same breakfast ordeal, and I've had enough. I want to be seated when we arrive and provided with chilled orange juice and hot coffee. I do not wish to hear any more lectures about the dangers of ice water or about how the cereal costs extra. I want to have cold, skin-free milk available for my kids' cereal every morning, and when I show up here with a group of friends for dinner, I want us all to be seated together. If you cannot accommodate us properly, we intend to pack up and leave this hotel, and maybe we'll just leave the country as well. Do you understand me?!" The manager nodded rapidly and then scurried off.

By the next morning, a metamorphosis had taken place. Evidently the manager had held a meeting with his staff and had ordered them to provide us with "American-style" service. We were greeted at the dining room as we entered and immediately seated. Orange juice and coffee were provided at once, and cereal, with cold, clear milk, materialized on the table magically. As we were enjoying our breakfast for the first time, my eyes fell upon a solitary fellow sitting at a nearby table. From his sorrowful demeanor and his hands covering his eyes, I could tell that he was in some sort of difficulty. I pointed him out to Simona. "Don't get involved," she advised. "But something's wrong, Mama," I said and got up to investigate.

"Is everything alright?" I asked cordially.

"Are you kidding? I've been sitting here waiting for a cup of coffee for the last hour," he moaned, "and I see you folks sit down and get waited on immediately. I am so sick and tired of this place that I just want to go back home."

"Well, my friend," I advised him, "we were in the same situation as you for several days, but then I decided to speak up. I took it up with the manager yesterday and I got kind of hot with the little fellow. But it paid off. Ever since, we've been getting great service."

"I figured I had to do something," he went on, "so I tried offering everyone tips. Well, that didn't work at all. They got upset that I was trying to bribe them, and I wound up getting even worse service because they were all mad at me. What's wrong with these people?"

The fellow explained that he was an accountant from Los Angeles traveling with his wife and that he had spent most of his trip in his hotel room.

"Look," I offered, "I'll fix things up here with the hotel staff, but you've got to get out more and see something of Israel. It really is a wonderful place, and you're getting the wrong impression if the only Israelis you're meeting are the rude hotel staff." He started to cheer up a bit when I called the waiter over and told him, "This gentleman is a friend of mine. I want you to give him the same type of service you give me. Okay?" And it was done. The fellow's coffee arrived instantly, and he was soon enjoying a hot breakfast.

"What sort of things are you interested in?" I asked. After he responded, I suggested he visit the Tel Aviv Museum where I had read that a new exhibit was opening that day. I thought that he would find the exhibit extremely interesting and advised him to take a cab that morning. He said he would do it. After breakfast, Simona and I lingered outside the hotel entrance waiting to see if our new friend would, in fact, make the trip to the museum. After a few moments, he emerged from the lobby, wearing a trench coat and sporting an umbrella, although there wasn't a cloud in the sky. He arrived at the curb just as a taxi was pulling away.

"Don't worry," I assured him. "another taxi will be along soon." After about five minutes, another taxi did, in fact, pull up. Our friend opened the backseat door, stopped himself and then looked towards me. "Oh, you were here first. You should take this one."

"That's fine," I assured him. "You go ahead. We're waiting for a friend." And just as I said that, a little Israeli lady snuck into the back of the cab, slammed the door shut and instructed the driver to take off quickly.

"Did you see that?!" he exclaimed in astonishment. "That does it. I'm going back to my room, and tomorrow we're getting out of this place." I just shook my head in frustration.

After experiences such as these, first-time travelers to Israel would often become disenchanted with the place and its boorish, arrogant citizenry. "I'm never going to come back here again," was a phrase I heard repeatedly in those days from Jewish Americans who had just gotten a bitter taste of Hebrew hospitality. I was sympathetic to their reaction. This "don't give a damn" attitude among Israelis seemed short-sighted and foolish to me – even though I fully understood the forces that had shaped this national mentality. Over the years, however, I observed that things began changing for the better. Israelis involved in the travel industry were the first to understand the importance of quality customer service. I felt that this change in attitude had to become pervasive among all of Israel's service-based industries – including the newest one, cable TV. I explained to our new employees that they must treat our customers with the same deference they might expect in a fine New York restaurant. To this day, I firmly believe that this policy helped to fuel our success and helped us gain wide market acceptance in every community we serviced.

In order to comply with the Israeli government's requirement that any foreign-owned company operating in Israel be partially owned by native Israelis, we transferred equity in the cable TV company to my daughter, Renée, who was now living full-time in Israel. Some equity was also transferred to my niece, Judy Kaye, who had also made *aliyah* a few years earlier.

Sometimes our celebrated government connections did not work out as well as we might have hoped. For example, in Be'ersheva we were good friends with the mayor, Ijo Rager, and had hoped for his cooperation as our crews strung coaxial cable throughout the community. Instead Rager placed unnecessarily burdensome requirements that created long delays and added to our costs. For example, we normally cut a slit in the street about 12 inches from the curb, laid the cable and patched the slit. Rager told us "You're not going to mess up my streets like that," and forced us to cut trenches in the sidewalk where the patches would be less visible. We were required to carefully remove a layer of pavers instead of four inches of asphalt, effectively doubling our costs and installation time.

Despite this problem, I still maintained a good relationship with Rager. This proved prudent as Rager was able to help with another project. Rager helped me to secure employment for members of the Friedman family. Two of the four brothers whom we had rescued from Bohorodczany had settled in Be'ersheva, and I was able to use my influence with Rager to find employment for several of their family members (see Chapter 17).

Once we had our infrastructure in place, we were ready to launch our first cable TV community in Be'ersheva. In 1988, we organized a large celebration and ribbon-cutting ceremony to mark the occasion. The company had contracted with Bedouin tribesmen who traveled the Negev to set up some large tents and prepare authentic Bedouin fare for the guests. The stark contrast between these primitive tents and the huge satellite dishes in juxtaposition nearby, created a vivid image in the settling dusk of the desert sunset. Among the many dignitaries in attendance that night was Gad Yakobi, Israeli Minister of Communications. We toasted the success of our new venture, along with the future of technological development in Israel.

I'm pleased to report that we did achieve rapid and substantial success. We were soon signing up subscribers at a record pace and became the fastest growing cable franchise in Israel. Like most cable operators, we were plagued with cable theft and piracy. We had heard that these practices were rampant in Israel, but we actually discovered that our losses due to cable theft were not great and the problem was easily manageable.

Our projections indicated an upside market potential of 200,000 subscribers in our districts. After building the business year after year, by 1992 we had gone from zero to about 125,000 billable accounts. We used traditional marketing methods to attract subscribers: TV advertising, billboards, print ads and special promotions. All of these were effective, but I believe what really accounted for our meteoric success was the positive reputation we managed to build up through high-level customer service.

At this juncture, Mark and I agreed that this would be the ideal point to sell our interest. Without much difficulty we identified a buyer, a large Israeli utility conglomerate, and we exited the Israeli cable TV business in 1993. Bob stayed on for four more very successful years before he sold out as well.

I came away from the experience gratified that we were able to establish a successful business in Israel. But in all honesty, I don't believe it would have been possible if we had not been able to exercise our influence and strong connections with the Israeli government. I believe that had we, as an American company doing business in Israel, attempted this venture without such *protekzia* we could not have achieved the success we did.

I am hopeful that, someday, circumstances will permit foreign investment to flourish in Israel without the need for special government connections. Obviously what is needed is an atmosphere of peace and an eradication of the shadow of terrorism. Secondly, a business environment that allows for capital formation unhampered by burdensome government bureaucracy is desperately called for. I hope to see this come to pass in my lifetime, so that my own children, as well as Jews and non-Jews from around the world, will look to Israel as a true source of economic opportunity. From my pen to G-d's ears.

Chapter Thirteen

Mar Begin

ONE of the first Jewish causes I became involved with as soon as I was in a position to do so, was Israel Bonds. Israel Bonds was started in 1951 by David Ben-Gurion, among others, as a means of raising revenues badly needed by the young Israeli government. The idea was to build a "bond" between Israel and its supporters around the world through the creation of a financial instrument. Investors, in addition to earning a market rate of return, would have a stake in the future of Israel. If enough bond holders could be created, the effort would yield far-reaching political, as well as financial, objectives. Money raised through the sale of Israel Bonds is typically used to finance the many non-military projects carried out by the Israeli government such as highways, bridges, canals, power plants and the like. But unlike other types of foreign securities, Israel Bonds are not sold through brokerage houses. Instead they are marketed using a fund-raising model. Bond dinners, where investors are encouraged to stand up and publicly announce their purchase of Israel Bonds are commonplace. Israel Bonds offices operate in major cities across America, handling transactions and working with lay volunteers to organize Bond drives. It was in my capacity as an Israel Bonds leader that I was afforded the opportunity to meet, in person, the man who had been my lifelong hero, Menachem Begin.

Since Israeli independence in 1948, Begin had served as the leader of the largest non-Labor political party in Israel. As discussed earlier, Begin's Irgun Zvai Leumi Jewish underground was a key factor in the establishment of the State of Israel. During the revolt against the British mandate, Begin had ordered the Akko prison breakout and the destruction of the central British administrative offices at the King David Hotel.

After Israeli independence, Begin, as leader of the Herut Party, served as head of the loyal opposition during the long tenure of the prevailing Ben-Gurion Mapai Party. It was in this capacity that he led the movement against the acceptance of German reparations for the Nazi Holocaust. In 1965 Begin merged the Herut Party with the Liberals to form Gahal, which would later serve as the foundation for the Likud Party. The crisis atmosphere of 1967 saw the creation of a National Unity Government that brought Begin to the cabinet table. It was in this role that he visited Chicago in 1969 as the keynote speaker on behalf of Israel Bonds.

When I got word that Begin would be speaking at the Chicago Bond Dinner, I immediately made plans to attend. I was hoping to listen to the hero of my youth and perhaps shake his hand. As I moved through the reception line, I introduced myself and offered a few words in Yiddish:

"I've waited all my life to shake your hand, Mar Begin. You were a hero to all of us in Betar when we were stuck in the DP camps," I said eagerly.

"You? You were in Betar?" He looked a bit confused. Finding an *Etzelnik* here among these American Jews appeared to catch him off guard. "Where are you from? Where were you during the war?"

"I'm from Galicia and we survived the war in Kazakhstan." I didn't want to hold up the line so I answered hurriedly and made to move on. "Wait! Let's have a word afterwards," he called as I nodded gladly.

Begin's remarks that night were stirring and succeeded in motivating the assemblage to new heights of Israel Bonds investment. Sometimes, when a person meets a hero in the flesh, there is a sense of disappointment as the legend becomes humanized. There was none of that with Begin. I was enthralled by his powerful message. He spoke in English with heartfelt passion about the recent unification of Jerusalem and its impact on the future of Israel. He was still something of the firebrand, but his current role as cabinet minister had seemed to mellow his rhetoric a bit. True to his word, he graciously approached our table afterwards and engaged me in an extraordinary chat.

Begin was curious about my family, and when I told him that my brother was aboard the Altalena, he seemed very pleased. I shared stories with Begin about how we distributed his words in the camps and how they provided hope and pride to our shattered numbers. I recounted my personal history to Begin, and he was quite moved. I recall a couple of Israeli VIPs coming over to our table to greet Begin, who immediately introduced me and said:

"You must meet my friend, Mr. Hasten. Do you know what this kid went through during the Shoah? He had next to no chance of survival and yet he made it!" Over the years Begin would re-tell my story repeatedly whenever he introduced me to someone new. I was amazed at how he always got the details exactly right, and I became convinced that he enjoyed a truly photographic memory.

The genuine warmth I felt from this man reminded me of my own father. The friendship we developed over the next twenty-five years, I can proudly say, was every bit a "father and son" relationship. We developed an immediate and lasting linkage that night in Chicago, and as the conversation wound down, Begin pressed my arm and leaned closer: "You must look me up the next time you're in Israel." He gave me his home address and phone number and bade me good night.

Although I had not mentioned it to Begin, at this point, I had yet to set foot on Israeli soil. I made up my mind that night, however, that I would travel there as soon as possible. I signed up for the next UJA (United Jewish Appeal) mission to Israel in January of 1970.

Of course, being in Israel for the first time was a transcendent experience. It felt strangely dreamlike, and yet charged with the electricity of the unknown. It was a homecoming, to be sure, but I was too excited to feel completely at home. The sight of thousands of Jews, strolling down boulevards, emerging from Jewish shops – simply living normal everyday lives – filled my heart to overflowing.

The moment that has stayed with me, as I'm sure it has for many Jews, was my first glimpse of the Kotel, the Western Wall, in Jerusalem. I rushed there as soon as I entered the city, and my emotions overcame me as I observed the ancient edifice. Gazing through my tears, I was permeated with a strange feeling of having somehow been here before. It wasn't simply a déjà vu, but rather a sense of wholeness or completion in the pit of my psyche. After over a hundred journeys to Jerusalem over the past thirty years, a visit to the Kotel is still my first stop.

I phoned Begin as soon as I arrived at my hotel in Jerusalem, and he suggested we meet for breakfast. When I asked where, his answer gave me pause. He suggested we meet at the King David Hotel. Begin, of course, had been a wanted man by the British when, as head of the Irgun, he had ordered the bombing of this hotel, which then housed the British administrative offices.

"Don't you feel odd coming here?" I inquired after we had taken our seats.

"Actually I like to come here…but not for the reason you think," he replied with a hint of a smile. "When I first arrived in Palestine as a private in the Polish army, I attempted to come into the front door of this hotel. I was stopped by a Polish officer, who informed me that enlisted men could not enter this way and that I was obliged to use the back door. The front door was only for officers. I kept trying, but I was always stopped. I think about

that every time I visit here and enter through the front door with no problem." He made no further reference to the bombing, and I left it at that.

Begin was absolutely fascinated with my story. He probed me and
devoured every detail. As we spoke, I could sense a kinship being forged.
This man had been my hero since my youth and now, here I was, relating
stories from that period to him face to face. "We admired you because you
fought back," I explained. I believe he could also sense that I had attempted
to pattern my life to encompass many of the same traits I had observed in
him. Tenacity, courage, direct action. These were values I learned from my
father and observed in Begin years ago. But our discussions also centered on
the here and now. As leader of the minority Herut party, Begin was in constant need of support, both political and financial. I sensed that he viewed
me as someone who could be groomed for leadership in advancing his current political agenda in the US. It was these forces that formed the foundation of our lasting friendship.

Over the next few years I would meet with Begin whenever I traveled
to Israel. We would also get together during his visits to the US. In 1973, I
succeeded in bringing him to Indianapolis for an Israel Bonds dinner and
showed him around our fledgling day school. He was deeply moved by the
experience and would always inquire about the school whenever we would
meet. I recall a discussion with Federation director Frank Newman before
the event:

"Who are you bringing in as a speaker for the Bond Dinner, Hart?" he
asked.

"I've invited Menachem Begin, the leader of the opposition party in
Israel, to speak," I replied.

"Oh, then you shouldn't expect a very big turnout," he advised.

"Why's that?" I asked.

"Well, everyone knows that Begin's a fascist."

Despite Newman's warning, we sold a record number of tickets to the
dinner, although there was one fellow to whom we did not sell one. Robert
Efroymson, my nemesis in our battle with the Federation over support for
the Hebrew Academy, did not wish to be seen attending an event featuring
such a right-wing "fanatic" as Begin. He, nevertheless, was very interested in
hearing what the man had to say. I recall catching a glimpse of Bob, standing in the corridor outside the dining hall, listening intently, throughout
Begin's speech.

At this time Mark and I had agreed to serve as Israel Bonds co-chairs
for our community. This role had secured me a seat on the National Execu-

tive Committee working under the leadership of Sam Rothberg. In this capacity I was involved in putting together Bond missions to Israel. Bondholders, and potential bondholders, were encouraged to visit Israel in order to witness how their investment dollars were being deployed, and also to generate inspiration and stimulate further purchases. These groups would be addressed by a running stream of Israeli dignitaries. Invariably I would note that the agendas only included *Mapainiks* or members of Ben-Gurion's party. I would frequently complain and always succeeded in getting a few Herut leaders, sometimes Begin himself, on the mission agenda. In this way, a more balanced and accurate picture of Israel's political diversity was presented to the visitors.

Initially, in response to my pressure, the Herut speaker would be given a spot on Friday night's agenda. Such events were very poorly attended, since most participants made private plans for the Sabbath. Also, because of the Sabbath sanctions, no microphone amplification was permitted and speechmaking was severely impaired. After a few such debacles, I learned my lesson. As the agendas were being formulated, I would insist: "I want Menachem Begin to speak to the group…and NOT on Friday night!" I even, at times, had to threaten to boycott the mission if my wishes were not carried out. I didn't like using such tactics, but I was fervent in my belief that Begin should get his story out to as large an audience as possible, particularly to affluent Americans who were in a position to offer financial support.

At this stage, Begin had been leading the political opposition to the prevailing Mapai party for roughly twenty-five years. He was labeled in the media as a "former Irgun terrorist" and was described as intransigent, radical, right-wing and worse. The common wisdom was that both Begin and his Herut party, would forever be a voice in the wilderness, never destined for Israeli political leadership. I, however, felt differently. I could see in Begin an intellectual capacity and firmness of character lacking among the members of Israel's ruling party. I came to believe that Begin could be, should be and would be the next Prime Minister of Israel, and it was in the following manner that I would introduce him to audiences both in the US and in Israel.

"Ladies and gentlemen, it gives me great pleasure to introduce to you the next prime minister of the State of Israel, the Honorable Menachem Begin." The changing demographics, along with internal Israeli political dynamics, would soon prove me correct.

In Begin I observed an almost Trumanesque rectitude and earthy collegiality that were such a departure from the traits of the seamy Mapai/Labor political hacks. Over the years, I had occasion to meet and to know nine of

Israel's eleven prime ministers (I never met Moshe Sharett or Levi Eshkol). The libertine excesses of some of them were legendary. I witnessed extended all-night drinking sessions with Rabin and Peres, as attractive young political groupies hung on them from every side. Their animosity toward anything religious, and particularly the religious right, would become more pronounced as the evening progressed and the liquor flowed. How could the future of the Jewish people be entrusted to those who held our heritage in such low esteem? Begin was different. He was fanatically faithful to his wife, Aliza (whom he called Alla), and while he was certainly no ascetic, I never observed him in an undignified posture. Furthermore, he was a traditional and educated Jew whose political underpinnings all emanated from the Torah.

After his election as prime minister in 1977, Begin would frequently make mention of my early support. "You believed I would become prime minister before I believed it myself," he would often say, and he was right. I wasn't merely blowing smoke when I introduced him in that way. I sincerely believed that he was the right man for the job. I had the chance to observe all of the players on Israel's political landscape, and I came away convinced that Begin's qualifications were the most impressive. If only he could somehow overcome all the old Irgun/Herut baggage that the press continued to burden him with. From the earliest days of statehood, when Ben Gurion would not even dare to utter Begin's name in public, preferring instead to refer to him as "the leader of the opposition" or "that man sitting next to Dr. Bader," Begin had borne the stigma of the extremist element. But I knew the man, and hence I could see him as he really was: a simple, deeply compassionate Israeli patriot with absolutely no interest in self-aggrandizement.

In 1975, Simona and I learned that we would once again become parents. Some might argue that, at age 45, I was too old to be fathering babies, but I disagreed. Having another baby energized both Simona and me and served to make our marriage an even happier one. On February 23, 1976, Joshua was born. Among the congratulatory messages we received, one originated from Begin, who was in the US for a visit. I immediately phoned him:

"Mar Begin," I said, "thank you for the good wishes. Is there any way for you to travel to Indianapolis next week for the Bris? You would honor us greatly if you could serve as the *sandek* (godfather) for our new son." I was, of course, delighted when he agreed.

On the morning of the *Bris*, I greeted Begin at the airport. He had arrived with his aide, Dr. Eliyahu Ben-Elissar, who would serve as Israel's first ambassador to Egypt and later as ambassador to the US and France. Driving back from the airport in my car, I put on a cassette tape of Israeli music to make everyone feel at home. Begin, assuming it was the radio, acted impressed:

"They play this *klezmer* music on the radio in Indiana?" he mused. I explained that he was listening to a cassette, removed it, and then treated him to a few seconds of real Hoosier country and western music from the actual radio. "Now I see why you listen to tape recordings."

His wit was mischievous and clever. Peering out the window at the fleeting highway signs, he commented:

"I see you had the city put up some road signs in my honor," he deadpanned. "Begin 55 mph. Begin 60 mph. Very nice of them. Thank you, Hart."

I could see that Begin's wit had not been dulled by the last several weeks of constant travel. I asked him:

"Mar Begin, how long has it been since you spoke with your wife?"

"Oh, a couple of weeks. Why?" he said.

"Do you want to speak to her now?"

"Of course. What do you mean?" I reached for my mobile phone, which, in 1976, was a true novelty, and asked him for the phone number. I got through immediately and handed him the receiver. He was touched by the gesture and shared his feelings with Aliza:

"I'm in Indiana with this good man. Such a good man," he confided in Hebrew.

We arrived at our home, and I escorted him upstairs to the guest room where he would be staying. He took the suitcase from me and immediately pulled out a very well-worn copy of the *Tanakh*, the Hebrew Bible, and placed it on the nightstand. I commented on this, and he picked it up to show me. He explained that this was the *Tanakh* that he had kept with him during his years of imprisonment in the Siberian Gulag. He carried it with him wherever he traveled.

After the ceremony, I stood before my fireplace and again introduced Begin as the next Prime Minister of Israel. He delivered a stirring, off-the-cuff speech that interwove Biblical teachings with the event at hand and with the political situation in Israel. After the *Bris*, I had organized a parlor meeting in my home for some solicitation. Begin needed money to retire outstanding notes dating back to 1948. At that time money was borrowed to fund pensions for the widows and orphans of fallen Irgun fighters. While families of slain Hagganah fighters were receiving government pensions, the Ben-Gurion administration saw fit to ignore the needs of the Irgun families.

Named for the burial place of Trumpeldor, the Tel-Hai Fund was established to raise money in the US for this worthy cause. Begin was concerned that failure to repay the loans would result in the loss of these pensions and impose a hardship on the families dependent upon them. He explained how he would awake during the night, unable to sleep, in turmoil over how to repay these loans. His impassioned pitch got through to the well-heeled crowd I had assembled, including the brother of Robert Efroymson.

Robert's older brother, Clarence, was a scholar and something of a black sheep of the family. He once told me that he had been "infected" with Zionism while living in Austria during the 1930s. Clarence contacted me when he heard that Begin would be in town and I arranged a private meeting between the two. After their visit, Clarence presented Begin with a copy of a book that he had recently translated from the original Hebrew into English: Yehezkel Kaufman's *History of the Religion of Israel* (1970, Union of American Hebrew Congregations). This encounter proved fortuitous years later after Begin was elected prime minister. He and I were in Los Angeles attending a private Tel-Hai fund-raising luncheon at the home of national Israel Bonds leader, Bill Weinberg. Begin inquired about the "fellow who translated the book." I explained that Clarence was back in Indianapolis, but I would be happy to phone him.

"Clarence, I have an old friend of yours here with me in LA," I told him once we got him on the line. "It's the Prime Minister of Israel and he would like to speak with you." They chatted for a few moments about Tel-Hai and Clarence agreed to help out.

After returning to Indianapolis, I visited with Clarence and he told me: "Hart, we need to have a prime minister in Israel that's focused on his job, not up all night worrying about some 30-year old debts. Here's a check for $25,000 and I hope that helps." It certainly did.

It was during the 1976 visit that I encountered Begin's wrath for the first time. As I introduced him to the Tel-Hai fund-raising group, I remember saying: "...and Menachem Begin has always been my personal hero and idol..." He said nothing at the time, but as soon as we were alone, he exploded:

"How dare you introduce me as your idol?" he said indignantly. "You worship idols? I'm not your idol! I don't believe in idols!" Judaism contains major sanctions against idolatry of any kind. I calmed him down by explaining that I was speaking figuratively, not literally, and that the audience fully understood it that way. I'm not sure he entirely accepted this explanation.

One incident from this visit served to clearly establish the character of this humble and highly committed man. When Begin came downstairs to join our guests for the *Bris* I could see that he had changed into a 1950s vintage suit. The suit was clean and freshly-pressed, but very worn and thread-bare. I guessed that, like many Israelis, he only owned one suit. It pained me to see my hero in such attire, so I quietly approached Ben-Elissar and asked about the suit.

"Eli," I said, "we can't have our leader running around the country in a threadbare suit like that."

"I know. I know. I've told him. But he literally cannot afford a new suit," he said convincingly.

"I want to do something about that," I offered. "How do I do it? Can I buy him a new suit?"

"I know my man, Hart," said Eli. "He's got his pride. He'll never accept such a gift from you."

"Then it shouldn't come from me," I countered. "Here's my idea. There's a gentleman in our town named Ettinger," I said referring to the fellow whose hard-headedness had provided the impetus for the founding of the Hebrew Academy five years earlier.

"Ettinger is a tailor who specializes in making beautiful custom hand-made suits. He also happens to be a big admirer of our leader. I'll set up a meeting with him at the tailor shop for you and for Begin to discuss the Tel-Hai Fund. While you're there, Ettinger will take Begin's measurements. He'll make the suit in a few days and we'll forward it on to Begin. He'll never know it came from me. What do you think?"

"It just might work," said Ben-Elissar, as I handed him an envelope con-taining enough cash to pay for the suit. I phoned Ettinger and arranged a meeting at the tailor shop for the next day.

The following morning, as they headed off to meet with Ettinger, Begin handed me a slip of paper. I looked and saw that it was a receipt for a con-tribution to the Tel-Hai fund in the exact same amount as the cash I had placed in the envelope. I looked up startled. "What's this?"

"Hart, I know what you were trying to do and I appreciate it very much," said Begin, as he cocked his head and spread his arms, "but honestly, what's wrong with *this* suit?"

I gazed at Ben-Elissar, who shook his head as if to say "he's hopeless." I was impressed and later old Simona: "He's unbelievable. He'd literally take the clothes off his own back to help the widows and orphans of the Irgun fighters. That's what it means to be a real leader."

Begin's election in 1977 caught the entire world by surprise. The entire world except for me. We had wanted to be in Israel for the election, but were unable to make it (Simona and I have been in Israel during every election

since that one). As we retired to our own beds with the outcome still unde-
termined, I said to Simona: "Tomorrow our friend will be the new Prime
Minister of Israel." My prediction was not based on anything more than my
own instincts and exuberance. I just felt that this was his time.

We rushed to Israel shortly after the election, and Begin greeted us for
the first time in the Prime Minister's Office. He made the comment that we
would hear over and over again during the coming years:

"Hart, you had more confidence in me than I had in myself," he said
generously. Everything was open to us. Regardless of whom he was meeting
with, we enjoyed full access to his office at any time. This access presented
several amazing opportunities for me to enjoy a ringside seat to history.

I recall how, a few months into his term, Begin had run into the Romanian ambassador, Imre Kovacs, at the Israeli president's official residence.
Shortly after this brief encounter, he summoned the ambassador to the Prime
Minister's Office for a conference. Kovacs was just walking out as I entered
the room. As I sat down, Begin explained:

"Do you see that man? He's the Romanian ambassador. I asked him to
deliver a letter to Ceauçescu (the Romanian head of state). Can you keep a
secret? This is all hush-hush." I assured him that I would keep mum.

"I'm asking Ceauçescu to meet with me so we can talk about Sadat. I want
to know if Sadat can be trusted. Can I negotiate with him? Does he keep
his promises? If I get a good report, then this will be the first step towards
making peace with Egypt."

Begin intended to remind Ceauçescu during their meeting that Israel had
years before agreed to pay him $10,000 for every Jewish man, woman and
child he released for immigration to Israel. From this arrangement Ceauçescu
knew that Israel could be trusted to keep its word. He also had conducted
direct dealings with Egypt and therefore seemed to be the ideal candidate
to serve as a conduit between the two nations which were, at this point, still
technically in a state of war.

Begin did travel to Romania shortly thereafter and succeeded in establishing a diplomatic back channel to Sadat through Ceauçescu. It was through
this channel that the first tentative peace feelers were transmitted. It would be
six months before the first hints of an Israeli/Egyptian rapprochement would
be reported in the media. As the process picked up steam and as Sadat's visit
to Jerusalem was announced, I was finally able to tell Mark and Simona: "I
was there when all this began."

I recall marveling at Begin's determination to improve the lot of Israel's most impoverished citizens. He spoke often about helping "those poor

needy families" and about rebuilding the blighted Hatikva Quarter in Tel Aviv, where many of them lived.

"Hart, I want to do everything we can to help those people," he confided in me. "And I'm going to appeal to American Jews to help me with this."

I brought up Lyndon Johnson's War on Poverty and pointed out that, despite all of his efforts, we still had lots of poor people in the United States.

"But I'm doing it differently. I've started a special project," he said. "I call it Project Renewal. A wealthy Jewish community in America adopts a poor Jewish community in Israel, and they help them out one-to-one." He went on to outline an ambitious plan that I frankly viewed with some skepticism as too simplistic and pie-in-the-sky. But the plan was adopted and successfully implemented by the Jewish Agency and the UJA, raising millions in the process. Soon every major Jewish community in the US had a "sister city" in Israel to which it channeled money and other forms of support. They even adopted Begin's name for the initiative, Project Renewal. Witnessing this process, I came to understand, for the first time, the sizable power wielded by a head of state.

Directly across from the Prime Minister's office stood the headquarters of Yechiel Kadishai. Kadishai's official title was Director of the Office of the Prime Minister, something akin to the White House Chief of Staff, but in reality his role was much more expansive. He served as Begin's closest confidant, his associate and, at times, his alter-ego. All traffic in and out of Begin's office flowed through Kadishai. Simona and I developed a deep personal friendship with Yechiel and his wife, Esther (affectionately known to her friends as Bambi) that has lasted to this day. Yechiel was known for his deep loyalty to the prime minister.

Just as a stop at the Prime Minister's Office was a regular event when Simona and I visited Israel during those years, Begin never failed to get in touch whenever he traveled to the US. We joined him during every visit to America during his term in office. Many times we would visit with Begin at Blair House when he was invited to the White House to meet with the president.

During the months leading up to the Camp David Accords, Begin participated in numerous one-on-one meetings with American president, Jimmy Carter. Oftentimes he would be invited to the White House residence for some late night arm-twisting. I recall how a dejected and frustrated Begin returned to Blair House after one of these marathon sessions with Carter that he had dubbed "nocturnal meetings." He fell into a chair looking drained and exhausted. We could see that things were not going well.

"Again he pressured me about Jerusalem," said Begin in a raspy voice. "'Let's talk about Jerusalem.' Over and over. That's all Carter can say." He took a sip from a water glass and continued.

"But I never hesitated. I told him a hundred times: 'Mr. President, Jerusalem is not negotiable. There is nothing to talk about.' And Carter would say to me: 'You don't have to give me an answer now. Take a few days to think about it and give me an answer later.' But I told him 'I don't have to think it over. I can give you the answer right now. The answer is the same. Jerusalem is not negotiable.'"

"So how did you make him understand, Mar Begin," I asked.

"I know he likes stories, so I told him the story of the Rabbi from Mainz." This was a Chassidic parable about a tenth century Rabbi Amnon from Mainz, Germany who was the author of the solemn *U'netaneh Tokef* prayer included in the Rosh HaShanah liturgy. Begin recounted the tale to us:

The Bishop of Mainz summoned Rabbi Amnon, a well-known Jewish leader, and offered him a job as a government minister, on the condition that the Rabbi undergo a conversion to Christianity. The Rabbi refused the offer, but the Bishop continued to insist and placed great pressure on him. The Rabbi was called back many times and each time he refused. One time, however, in order to placate him, he asked the Bishop for three days to consider the offer. As soon as he got home, the Rabbi became very upset at the terrible mistake he had made. How could he even appear to consider such an offer before G-d? He could not eat or sleep and prayed continuously to G-d for forgiveness. When the three days elapsed, the Bishop sent for the Rabbi but the Rabbi refused to come voluntarily. So the Bishop had him brought before court by force and demanded a response to his offer. "I should have my tongue cut out for not having refused you immediately." The enraged Bishop ordered the Rabbi's hands and feet cut off and sent him home. There the Rabbi asked to be brought to the synagogue where he uttered the words of the famous prayer with his dying breath.

After recounting the anecdote, a weary, yet prideful Begin looked at us and said: "'I am not like the Rabbi of Mainz,' I told Carter. 'I do not need three days to consider the matter. I tell you here and now that Jerusalem is the eternal capital of the Jewish people, and even cutting off my hands and feet will not make me change my position!' I think I made him understand."

Begin developed a deep resentment toward Carter as a result of the constant pressure being exerted on him. Years later, when both men were out of office and Begin was living in seclusion in Jerusalem, Carter would attempt to meet with him whenever he visited Israel. He would contact Kadishai and ask to see Begin, but Begin would always refuse. With a single exception, Begin would not even accept telephone calls from Carter because of the unpleasant memories from that period.

In 1978, what came to be known as the Camp David Accords were hammered out by Carter, Sadat and Begin during an historic 13-day negotiating session. Simona and I were in Washington when the three leaders departed for Camp David, and no one had any idea how long they would be there. We waited in Washington over the next two weeks and followed the sketchy news reports of their historic activities.

After he emerged, Begin referred to his time at the mountain retreat as "my incarceration." He would complain to Carter, asking him: "How long will we be imprisoned on this mountaintop?"

"I told him (meaning Carter) that I have a friend who was very good at breaking out of prisons," Begin went on. "This fellow became famous for escaping from British prison camps in Palestine, and I'm going to call him up to help me get out of here." He smiled and asked me: "Do you know who I was referring to?"

"Of course I do, Mar Begin," I responded in schoolboy fashion. "Yaakov Meridor, who else?" Meridor was a member of the Etzel high command and a follower of David Raziel. Meridor was arrested by the British in 1945. They had been directed to his house by the Hagganah in a shameful episode that came to be known as "the season." He was sent to Asmara Prison in Eritrea, from which he made seven unsuccessful escape attempts, finally succeeding on his eighth try. He remained in Europe until Israeli independence had been achieved. Eventually he was elected to the *Knesset* (Israeli parliament) and became a successful shipping tycoon and one of Israel's wealthiest men, before his death in 1985.

Briefing us about his experiences at Camp David, Begin went on to describe his numerous chess games against National Security Advisor, Zbigniew Brzeszinski.

"Who won?" I asked.

"It was a draw," he replied with characteristic diplomacy.

Begin revealed the factor that finally resulted in an agreement being reached. Sadat had threatened to walk out several times during the talks, as had Begin, who even had packed his bags and started loading them into the limo before he was called back for yet another meeting. When the discussions seemed to be at an impasse, Carter appeared with some photographs. Both Begin and Sadat had arrived at Camp David bearing pictures of their grandchildren. They each wanted them signed by the other to take home as souvenirs. Carter had rounded up the photos and laid them out before the two leaders. "It's for them that we're doing this," explained Carter. This emotional appeal evidently succeeded in getting the two sides back to the negotiating table, where an agreement was eventually worked out.

Unlike Egypt, Israel is a democracy and, therefore, the peace accords had to be ratified by the Knesset before Begin was free to sign them. The treaty did not enjoy universal support in Israel. Only 29 of the Likud's 43 representatives voted in favor of ratification. Nevertheless, it was finally approved, and a signing ceremony was scheduled to take place in the White House Rose Garden on March 26, 1979.

Simona and I were invited to attend the signing ceremony and were offered seating among the Israeli dignitaries. It was a chilly morning as we took our seats to the incessant sound of the Palestinian protestors being held at bay by the police.

I recall Begin's impassioned message when it was his turn to speak after the signing ceremony. Begin never relied upon speech writers, even when he knew that world attention would be focused upon his words. I can attest to this personally, since I was with him on the night before the ceremony as he drafted his speech by hand. I observed as he wrote the words: "No more war, no more bloodshed, no more bereavement. Peace unto you, Shalom, Salam." He delivered these words in English and then, placing a *kippa* (skullcap) on his head, directed his words to the people of Israel as he spoke in Hebrew, quoting from the Book of Psalms.

We rode on the bus that evening with Begin's Israeli entourage, and soon arrived at the official banquet held inside a huge tent set up on the White House lawn. Our table was adjacent to the one where Begin, Carter and Sadat, along with their wives, had been seated. We sat with the Speaker of the House, Tip O'Neil and his wife Millie. Entertainment was provided by soprano diva, Leontyne Price and Israeli violinists, Yitzchak Perlman and Pinchas Zuckerman.

Begin clearly realized at the time that he was participating in a great historic moment. He recognized the fact that this would be regarded by history as his greatest accomplishment as prime minister. And although we were not together in Oslo, Norway, in December of 1978, when Begin was awarded the Nobel Peace Prize, I am certain that his inspiring words on that occasion also flowed from his own pen, as well as from the depths of his heart:

"Peace is the beauty of life. It is sunshine. It is the smile of a child, the love of a mother, the joy of a father, the togetherness of a family. Peace is the advancement of man, the victory of a just cause, the triumph of truth. Peace is all of these and more, and more…"

Very few people realize what a price Begin paid for the concessions granted at Camp David. In agreeing to turn over the Sinai settlements, he was giving up his own future retirement community in Yamit, his favorite spot in the entire region. But beyond his personal considerations, he was forced to endure the vilification of the right wing faction of his own Likud party. Geulah Cohen, who later broke away from Likud to form the T'chiah Party, rose in the Knesset to denounce Begin as a traitor for signing the Camp David Accords. Begin never forgave her for this outrage.

As Begin's brilliance in foreign affairs became more fully appreciated both in Israel and abroad, his domestic initiatives did not attain the same level of achievement. His attempts to curtail Israel's spiraling inflation rate had minimal effect, and his efforts to reduce the hammer-hold that the national labor union, the *Histadrut*, had on Israel's economy were a complete failure. Sadly, economics was not Begin's forte. He relied upon finance ministers to develop a fiscal policy for his administration. His disdain for monetary issues carried over to his personal life. Unlike so many in public life, it never occurred to Begin to capitalize on his celebrity in any way. The notion that he could make money by writing books or going on the lecture circuit after leaving office never crossed his mind. Simona would commiserate with his wife, Aliza, when she said:

"I can't talk to him about money. He doesn't understand anything about paying the bills or managing a budget." Aliza maintained the family finances throughout the marriage, but after her death the task of paying Begin's monthly bills fell to Yechiel Kadishai.

The one exception to Begin's oblivious attitude towards money was the issue of paying off the old debts incurred by the Irgun after the War of Independence. He understood that to be effective in politics one needed money, and that he would not be in a position to raise funds for the party until all outstanding debts had been wiped out.

In 1981 Begin was reelected after a surprisingly close race. This time Simona and I were on hand to savor the victory. We watched the returns from our hotel room, along with our friends Harry and Freda Hurwitz and Nate and Lil Silver. About one hour after the polls closed, Nate telephoned the prime minister. After a moment, I took the phone and expressed my concern to Begin about the uncertain outcome of the election.

"No, no. You should not be worried at all," he said confidently. "In fact, go call your brother and tell him that I will definitely be forming the next government." His optimism proved warranted since at 2 AM we were on hand as Begin appeared at *Metzudat Ze'ev* (Likud party headquarters) and declared victory before a huge crowd of jubilant supporters. Many of the celebrants were Sephardic Jews who had become politically active for the first time in support of Begin's candidacy. *"Begin Melech Yisrael"* (Begin is the king of Israel) was their incessant chant as we pushed our way through the massive throngs of dancing, joyous Sephardic supporters.

Begin, an Ashkenazi Jew, earned the deep respect of Israel's burgeoning Sephardic community. He accomplished more on behalf of the Sephardim than any other leader in Israel's history, working hard for the elimination of bigotry and discrimination, and investing national resources in the development of Israel's poorer neighborhoods. In turn, the Sephardic community responded warmly to Begin. They loved him and voted for him en masse.

Simona and I decided to host a victory party to celebrate Begin's reelection a few days later. It was a marvelous affair at the Plaza Hotel in Jerusalem, and every major Israeli political figure was in attendance, including Ariel Sharon and the entire cabinet. We had our five-year old, Josh, with us and, with all the excitement, no one was paying much attention to him – this despite the fact that many people were aware that he was the prime minister's godson. The crowd was focused on the prime minister, who began his remarks by thanking all of his loyal supporters and then went on to expound on the Ten Commandments as the basis of all human law. Upon concluding, Begin took his seat at our table to resounding applause. Just then, our Josh climbed up onto his godfather's lap and whispered something into his ear. Begin smiled broadly and rose once again to the podium, quieting the crowd with his hands.

"My American godson, Yeshayahu Alexander, has just advised me that there should be an eleventh commandment: Thou shalt honor thy children. I agree that this would be a very good addition, don't you?" The crowd roared as Simona and I nearly burst with *nachas* and parental pride.

Earlier that day I had quite unexpectedly run into my friend, Rabbi Jonathan Stein, who headed the Reform synagogue in Indianapolis. He was leading a congregational mission and happened to be staying at the same hotel. I mentioned to him that we were hosting a little reception that evening and invited him to join us. I did not elaborate, but I did drop a hint by saying: "You won't regret it, if you decide to come."

"Thanks for the invitation, Hart," he demurred, "but I already have a commitment and won't be able to make it."

"That's too bad, Rabbi. You know, I'm putting this on for the prime minister and I just thought…"

"Prime minister?" he gasped. "Did you say prime minister?"

"Yeah, that's right," I said. "Menachem Begin. I'm putting on a little victory party tonight. Too bad you can't be there."

"Yeah, too bad," he said softly as he walked off. Thirty minutes later, I received a phone call from Rabbi Stein in my hotel room.

"Listen, Hart. I cancelled the other thing. I want to go to this party. Am I still welcome?"

"Of course, Rabbi," I said. "We'll see you and Susan around six in the banquet hall." Rabbi Stein and his wife joined us and enjoyed an unforgettable evening.

Begin underwent harsh international condemnation when, in 1981, he ordered the Israeli Air Force to bomb the Osirak nuclear reactor in Iraq. He relied upon solid intelligence clearly indicating that Iraq was using the reactor in the development of nuclear weapons. He did live long enough to see this decision vindicated during the 1991 Gulf War, when Israel's action was credited with hampering Baghdad's drive to acquire a nuclear capability.

It is no secret that, when it comes to affairs of state, world public opinion holds Israel to a different – some would say "double" – standard of behavior. This was recently demonstrated when, even after the events of September 11, 2001, world leaders were urging Prime Minister Sharon to engage in good faith negotiations with master terrorist, Yasser Arafat. At the same time no one was calling upon President Bush to sit down with Osama Bin Laden or Mohammed Omar to discuss the legitimate rights of the Islamic people.

Begin ran into this double standard during a state visit to Great Britain in 1981. He had been invited to attend a luncheon at 10 Downing Street, hosted by Prime Minister Margaret Thatcher. As an Irgun resistance fighter, Begin had been, to a large degree, responsible for driving the British from Palestine in 1948, often resorting to guerilla tactics and sabotage. He was labeled a terrorist by the British, who placed a price upon his head. It afforded Begin deep satisfaction now to be ushered into the highest halls of British power as the representative of a free and democratic Jewish state.

As Begin sat beside the British prime minister, neither brought up the subject of Begin's anti-British past exploits. The conversation was cordial and low-key. But then, out of the blue and in connection with nothing in particular, Thatcher dropped a bombshell that left Begin stunned and incredulous.

"You know, Mr. Prime Minister," she said earnestly, "Britain has endured a good deal of criticism over our lack of action to save Jewish lives during the Second World War. I must say, however, that had I been in office and in Churchill's shoes, I would have behaved exactly as he did and refused to bomb the rail lines into the Nazi death camps. You see, I believe that in wartime one must concentrate on a single objective. Every airplane, every bomb was needed for the war effort. First beat them militarily and then worry about rescue." Begin was shocked and struggled to form a response.

"Madame Prime Minister," Begin said, after recovering somewhat, "I very much resent what you just told me. You know that by 1944, at a time when the war was surely won and the notorious activities going on at the death camps, such as Auschwitz where 10,000 Jews were being slaughtered daily, were fully known to the Allies, the easiest thing in the world would have been for the RAF to bomb those rail lines. Disrupting the death machine for only one day would have saved the lives of thousands of our people."

Thatcher immediately dropped the subject as suddenly as she had brought it up and went back to making polite small talk, leaving Begin dismayed and incredulous.

During his lifetime Begin was roundly criticized for his decision to launch Operation Peace for Galilee in 1982. Many felt that his regret over this Lebanese military incursion is what sent Begin into seclusion and retirement. I don't agree with this view in any way. I do not believe that the Lebanese War was a mistake, and recent events clearly support my position. In 1982, Israel was being victimized by repeated acts of terror orchestrated from PLO installations in southern Lebanon. The Lebanese War succeeded in neutralizing this threat. The parallels between that scenario and Operation Enduring Freedom, currently being waged by the US against terrorist strongholds in Afghanistan in the wake of the September 11, 2001, attacks are unmistakable. Unfortunately it has taken America nearly twenty years to understand how to effectively deal with state-sponsored terrorism. History has clearly vindicated Begin's foresight and profound understanding of the true nature of terrorism. An understanding that was, once again, well ahead of its time.

Perhaps Begin's most overlooked achievement was his role in one of history's greatest rescue efforts known as Operation Moses. Working with then US Vice President, George Bush, Begin sought to provide safe passage to tens of thousands of Ethiopian Jews threatened with starvation and repression in their ancient homeland. I was with Begin during a key phase of this extraordinary airlift. "I am so proud of our boys," he confided with heart-felt emotion. "We sent our best pilots to Ethiopia for this mission. They know how to land our planes with no runways over there. They're landing on fields and dirt roads at night and picking up these poor people and bringing them home to us."

Although it became a matter of some controversy, there was never any equivocation in Begin's mind about whether Ethiopian *falashas* were true Jews or not. Their rescue and eventual integration into Israeli society, despite racial and extreme cultural obstacles, served as a shining example of the true mission and unquestionable need for the Jewish state as a safe haven for Jews in jeopardy anywhere on earth. Considering how Israel welcomed the dark-skinned Ethiopians with open arms, I am shocked when I hear charges today by our enemies that seek to brand Israel as a "racist state."

While Begin, at this time, was a head of state and a respected world leader, he never forgot his obligations to the widows and orphans of the Irgun fighters. During his terms in office, he continued to raise money for the Tel-Hai Fund in order to pay off the long-standing debts incurred by the Irgun pension fund. Begin would invariably take time out from his busy schedule, whenever he visited the US, to raise money for Tel-Hai.

At this point I was serving as president of Herut Zionists of America, and it was my job to identify and contact potential American donors with the means to contribute substantial financial support to our cause. I would schedule private meetings with each donor, and the prime minister would then solicit them for a contribution to Tel-Hai. I had asked my predecessor, Eryk Spektor, to contact some potential supporters in the New York area during one of Begin's visits in 1980. Eryk mentioned that he played cards with an elderly gentleman by the name of Milton Petrie whom Eryk knew to be a very wealthy Begin admirer. Eryk felt that a private meeting with Begin might result in a $100,000 contribution.

Petrie was delighted when I phoned and asked if he wished to meet the prime minister to talk about an important matter. He agreed to meet with us in Begin's hotel room. After the introductions had been made, Begin explained the need to pay off these long-standing debts in order to preserve the pensions for the Irgun heroes' families. Begin finished the pitch with a plea: "Can you help us with this, Mr. Petrie?" Petrie thought it over for less than ten seconds.

"Mr. Prime Minister," he said slowly. "I'd like to give you a million dollars. Is that okay?"

"Why, of course, Mr. Petrie," replied Begin without showing a hint of surprise.

They exchanged good-bye greetings as I escorted Petrie to the door. Judging from Petrie's bent posture and general appearance, I was none too confident that he would survive long enough to fulfill the generous pledge he had just made. I decided to follow him down the hall clutching a standard pledge form.

"Excuse me, Mr. Petrie," I said as I stopped him. "Would you mind completing this form to document your gift?"

"Young man," he said, "you fill it out and I'll sign it." With a quivering hand I wrote $1,000,000 in the box labeled "Amount" and presented it to him. As he signed, he realized that he had no idea who I was.

"There you are," he said. "By the way, who are you, anyway?" I identified myself as the person who had called him earlier to arrange this meeting. I mentioned that I was from Indianapolis.

"Indianapolis? Did you say Indianapolis?" he said extending a smile, "My father was a policeman in Indianapolis. Do you know the Efroymsons?"

"Of course, Mr. Petrie, I know them well, and Clarence Efroymson has met with the prime minister and has given us support in the past."

"Be sure to say hello to the Efroymsons and tell them I'm doing fine."

"I sure will, Mr. Petrie," I assured him. Petrie made good his pledge by giving us appreciated stock in his company. His gift, like that of many others, was not motivated by his support for Begin's party agenda, but rather by his abiding affection for Israel. This fact was demonstrated several years later when Shimon Peres was serving as prime minister. Petrie also gave him a gift of $1,000,000, telling a reporter at the time: "Well, I gave Begin a million, so I felt I should give Peres a million also."

Another wealthy individual we met with during this period was Bill Levitt, the housing developer who had created the noted "Levittown" tract house community in Long Island. Levitt wanted to meet the prime minister in order to express his displeasure over Begin's agreement to give up the Sinai as part of the Camp David Accords. Levitt had invested heavily into oil drilling operations in the Sinai and had lost everything when the area was turned over to Egypt. Levitt and Begin were discussing the situation, with the prime minister explaining the extreme pressure he faced from US officials such as Secretary of State Cyrus Vance. At this, Levitt, who spoke an excellent Yiddish, asked:

"Mr. Prime Minister, you speak Yiddish, don't you?"

"Yes, of course," Begin replied.

"Well, in my opinion, Cyrus Vance is *nisht kine übber geshpitzter* (he's not the sharpest knife in the drawer). Do you know that word, Mr. Prime Minister? *Übber geshpitzter?*"

"I certainly do, Mr. Levitt," drawled Begin. "In fact, those are two words." They shared a good laugh and the friction was set aside.

Sometimes large donors would contact me in order to gain an audience with the prime minister. It was during this period that I received a call from Abe Spiegel, whose family had created the Children's Pavilion at the Yad Vashem Israeli Holocaust memorial. He wanted to meet with Begin during his upcoming visit to New York.

"I can try to arrange that, Abe," I told him, "but you must understand that he will solicit you for Tel-Hai and he will expect you to be generous."

I felt that this warning was in order, because I recalled how years before I had solicited Spiegel in Los Angeles for the same cause and I had brought along a true hero of the Israeli revolt against the British, my friend Haim Landau. Landau, whose nom de guerre was Avraham, had been a member of the Etzel high command and served as its Chief of Staff.

Landau's visit took place prior to Begin's assuming the prime ministership, and while he was serving as head of the opposition party. In this capacity, he was able to dispatch a stream of Israeli VIPs to the US to accompany me on my fund-raising junkets on behalf of the Tel-Hai Fund. He had previously sent me General Ariel Sharon, Moshe Arens and others. When Landau and I arrived in LA, Haim suggested we contact his old friend, Abe Spiegel.

"Abe is a wealthy and generous fellow and my good friend," said Landau. "I know he'll help us out." Sure enough, when we arrived at Spiegel's office he greeted us warmly, directing our attention to a photo of himself and Menachem Begin mounted on his wall. After some small talk, I cut to the chase:

"Mr. Spiegel, you know we came here for a purpose," I explained bluntly. "Because of your position in the community, we have come to you first looking for a leadership gift. We have to pay off these debts, and we need to know if you're prepared to help us."

"Of course I am, gentlemen." Spiegel called in his secretary and instructed her:

"Please go to the safe and pull out a $1,000 Israel Bond so I can give it to Mr. Landau."

We sat stunned. Landau spoke first. "I traveled 10,000 miles from Israel to see you, so you can give me $1,000?! Why are you insulting me like this?"

"Take it or leave it," responded Spiegel. "That's all you're going to get." Landau turned white and then several shades of red. He was beyond anger. "I thought you were our friend," he managed to get out between clenched teeth.

"Take the thousand, Haim, and let's go," I said, standing up. After some further protests from Landau, I took the Bond, had Spiegel sign it over to us and followed Landau as he stormed out of the office in a rage. Once outside I tried to calm him down.

"Haim, take it easy and don't worry about it. We're going to meet some of my friends here in LA and I know they'll come through." I immediately phoned Bill Weinberg, who was then serving as the chairman of the Israel Bonds Million Dollar Note Society.

"Bill, we're here in LA and I'm with Haim Landau. We'd like to come see you about the Tel-Hai Fund and we're going to solicit you."

"Come right on over," he said warmly. Arriving at his luxurious Wilshire Boulevard offices, I got quickly to the point:

"Bill, I need some money from you for Tel-Hai."

"How much do you want?" he asked.

"I need $25,000," I shot back.

"If you say you need it, that's good enough for me," he said, pulling out a checkbook and making out the check on the spot. Landau was impressed and I could see his jaw drop. I could not help teasing Landau a bit afterwards. "You see, Haim. That's the difference between your friends and my friends."

Based on this experience with Spiegel, I was hesitant to schedule a meeting with the prime minister without first getting some assurance that it would be worth his time.

"Don't worry, Hart," Spiegel assured me, "I intend to be very generous indeed. You see, I have a special request for Menachem."

"Special request?" I said.

"Yes. I read that Menachem has been invited to travel to Cairo," Spiegel went on, opting to refer to the Prime Minister of Israel by his first name. "I would like to accompany him on that trip. And to show you how much this means to me, I'm going to give you guys $50,000." While this was not in the same league with the Petrie gift, it was still a substantial sum and certainly a big step up from the $1,000 gift he had extended the first time we met.

"Look, Abe," I said, "I can't promise you anything, but I will ask the prime minister and see what he says." I met with Begin in his hotel room later that day and told him about Spiegel.

"Abe wants to go to Cairo with you, Mar Begin."

"Oh, really?" said Begin.

"And he's prepared to give us $50,000 if you agree to take him," I explained. Begin's reply was quick and definite.

"No. Not for money," he said shaking his head. "This is not for sale."

"I understand, Mar Begin, but I have a question," I said. "What if Mr. Petrie had said he would only give us the million dollars if you allowed him to go to Cairo. Would you have agreed?"

"Absolutely not, Hart," he said with no hesitation. "If something is not for sale, that means it is priceless. I tried to explain this to Carter about Jerusalem. You should not try to buy something that is priceless." I smiled at the comparison and went to phone Spiegel to tell him that the deal was off.

Thanks to our work, and the work of others like Nate Silver, the Tel-Hai Fund was able to negotiate a settlement of all its outstanding debts before Begin left office. Nate was successful in working out payment deals with lenders for as little as fifty cents on the dollar. This accomplishment provided Begin with a great deal of satisfaction, and he never forgot to express his gratitude for my role in lifting this burden from his shoulders.

Whenever Begin visited the United States as prime minister, Simona and I would travel with him. Begin would introduce us as his close friends to such luminaries as Secretary of State Cyrus Vance, Alexander Haig and Henry Kissinger. But despite traveling in such rarefied circles, Begin was at all times a very down-to-earth fellow. For example, when we visited him at the prime minister's residence, he would usually invite us upstairs to the living quarters, where we sat around the kitchen table and just *schmoozed* (chatted) informally with him and Alla. I recall one such evening quite clearly.

"Another book came out last week about you, Mr. Prime Minister," I commented. "The author made a big deal about how you and Jabotinsky were always quarrelling. He says that Jabotinsky was so upset with you that he refused to attend your wedding."

"Ach, such stupidity," exclaimed Alla, "It so happens that Jabotinsky did attend our wedding. We lost the photos during the war, but of course he was there."

"It's too bad that authors don't check their facts before they write things like that," said Begin. "That's one thing I was always careful about. Every fact I put on paper had to be the truth."

"Speaking of your books, Mar Begin, I was extremely impressed with *White Nights*" – referring to his account of his interrogation and conviction at the hands of the Soviets in 1941 for his Zionist activities and of his being sentenced to eight years of hard labor in Siberia. He wound up serving only a year and a half.

"Your stories had a real ring of truth to me," I said. "I thought the book was an outstanding work. In fact, I felt it should be considered a work of literature." I wasn't offering hollow flattery. I truly believed that this book was written far better than anything I had read by Solzhenitsyn on the subject of the Russian Gulag.

"You know, it's funny," responded Begin. "My wife also thinks that book is really good literature. And every word in it is absolutely true."

Years later we learned how true this book really was. After the collapse of the Soviet Union in 1991, the contents of secret Kremlin archives became available for the first time to historians and scholars. Menachem Begin's son, Benny, succeeded in obtaining transcripts of the actual sessions during which his father was interrogated by the NKVD. These same interrogations were described, in word-for-word detail, by Begin in *White Nights*. But of course he had only his memory to rely upon when authoring the book more than ten years after the events being described. Benny showed me the transcripts and the corresponding accounts from *White Nights*. They matched precisely, attesting once again to Begin's amazing photographic memory. The transcripts have since been published as an addendum to a new Hebrew language edition of *White Nights* printed in Israel. They make for fascinating, and frightening, reading.

Sometimes my friendship with Menachem Begin got me into some difficult situations. One such moment occurred in 1982 during the Lebanese War shortly after the massacres at the Sabra and Shatillah refugee camps. Simona and I were guests at a Bar Mitzvah celebration in Indianapolis. The grandmother of the Bar Mitzvah boy approached me with a stern look on her face. I had met the woman before and knew that she was a Holocaust survivor.

"You're a friend of Menachem Begin's, aren't you?" she said angrily. I admitted that I was.

"Look what he and that General Sharon have done. Isn't it simply awful. Aren't you ashamed?" She was shouting at me at this point and a small crowd began to gather to see what was going on. I tried to calm her down, but it was impossible to stop her.

"How can you be friendly with such murderers? This is a disgrace and an outrage!" she ranted on without letup. I decided that the only way to deal with her was to give it to her straight.

"Lady, let me tell you something," I shot back, confronting her with my face just inches from hers. "I am *glad* about what happened over there."

"What?" She could not believe her ears.

"That's right, I'm glad," I repeated strenuously. "Do you know why I'm glad? I'm glad because this time the victims were not Jews. Finally, for the first time, we are not reading about Jewish victims. Usually it's the Jews that are being killed either by Christians or by Moslems. But this time, it's Christians killing Moslems."

She stood there with her mouth agape, at a loss for words.

"Don't get me wrong, lady," I said calmly. "I am not happy that innocent people were killed. That is a tragedy no matter who they are. But I am happy that this time they were not Jews." I decided to take the next step.

"As a Holocaust survivor you should understand my feelings," I told her. "What about you? Do you ever suffer from feelings of guilt because you survived and those around you were killed?" Her demeanor changed dramatically. A faraway look crossed her face and she spoke softly:

"That's right. I do have such feelings."

"Well, don't you see, that is your problem," I stated. "I know many survivors just like you who suffer from guilt complexes over what happened. Well, I don't have any such guilt, and I'm not going to permit you to place your feelings of guilt onto me." She stood silently and pondered my words.

"And so, you see, this is a happy day for me," I concluded. "First of all, Jews did not kill anybody. All the killing was done by Christian Phalangists. And, more important, the victims were not Jews and I am happy about it."

She gave me a resigned look and walked away quickly. I just shook my head, thinking that such Jews are not happy unless other Jews are the victims. If anyone else should happen to be the victim, they become guilt-ridden and uncomfortable.

I recall how Begin expressed puzzlement over this issue at the time. In response to a reporter's question about the massacres, he responded: "I actually don't understand it. The Christians are murdering the Moslems, and they're blaming it on the Jews."

An Israeli commission investigating the matter concluded that, although they never ordered the attacks, the Israeli military was guilty of indirect culpability for failing to properly control the Phalangist troops under their command. Sharon decided to resign, based on the results of their findings.

While Begin's popularity in the US suffered as a result of the Lebanese incursion, he still maintained wide support, oddly enough, from the Christian conservative movement. Fundamentalist Christians, like Jimmy Carter, respected Begin because of his dedication to Biblical teachings and because he behaved like a man devoted to his own faith. It was for this reason that the Christian Coalition, headed by Reverend Jerry Falwell announced that they had invited the prime minister to address their annual convention in Dallas during his next visit to America.

It was about two weeks before Begin was scheduled to arrive in the US for what was to be his final visit as prime minister that I received a phone call from, of all people, Norman Lear. Lear, at this time, was perhaps the most successful and celebrated television producer in the country, with such popular programs to his credit as "All In The Family," "Maude" and "The Jeffersons." As his fame grew, he, like other Jews in the entertainment industry, sought to use his celebrity as a platform to espouse his liberal political opinions. I was surprised by the call since, like most people, I was familiar with Norman Lear by reputation, but I had never met him face to face.

"Mr. Hasten," he began, "I was given your name and phone number by someone who says you are a close personal friend of Prime Minister Begin's. Is that right?"

"Yes," I replied, "I'm pleased to say that is correct."

"Well, I understand that during his upcoming visit to this country he is scheduled to address a large contingent of evangelical Christians in Dallas."

"Yes, I'm aware of that, Mr. Lear," I said.

"Well, I think it's a terrible idea," said Lear. "I'm sure you understand what these folks are trying to do. Their mission is to convert us Jews to Christianity. I'm sure that the prime minister doesn't understand who these people are or he never would have agreed to it in the first place. You simply must tell your friend to call off this trip right away. I'm sure that if you explained the situation to him, he would agree that he shouldn't go."

"Mr. Lear," I said after a short pause, "you don't know me, but as it turns out, I happen to agree with his decision on this matter. These are Christians that love Israel. They have a history of supporting Israel politically and financially. They lobby their congressmen on Israel's behalf. They invest in Israel in a major way through the purchase of Israel Bonds. Many of them travel to Israel and bring needed tourist dollars. Most importantly, they do not abandon Israel during times of crisis. In fact, it is when Israel has been threatened in the past, that the Christian community has shown its true solidarity by not canceling its missions even when Jewish groups did so. I happen to agree with Begin. These people have shown themselves to be friends, and Israel does not have that many friends that she can afford to turn her back on any of them."

"I can't believe you're saying that," responded Lear, somewhat stunned. "Surely you understand that the only reason they are interested in Jewish sovereignty of Jerusalem is for the fulfillment of a prophecy about the second coming of Jesus, when all Jews will be baptized as Christians, according to them."

"Who knows, Mr. Lear? Perhaps they're correct," I said good-naturedly. "I, for one, would be pleased if he showed up and turned out to be the Messiah. We could ask him the important question 'Have you been here before?' and get this Christian–Jewish thing settled once and for all."

We bantered back and forth like this for over an hour. I believe that I was finally beginning to convince him that the religious questions involved were secondary to the more important issue of Israeli security. I explained that Begin wisely felt that forming an alliance with the American Christian right would enhance that security. Once Israel was no longer threatened by its physical enemies, it could afford to worry about those who would do away with us through kindness and Christian conversion. Now was not the time for Israel to distance itself from its true friends, such as the Christian Coalition and the Moral Majority.

"When will you be seeing the prime minister next?" asked Lear.

"I'll be in Los Angeles to greet him when he arrives in two weeks." I said that we'd be staying with him at the Century Plaza Hotel.

"Really, Century Plaza? Well my office is right there in the next building over," said Lear. "I'd like to meet with you when you're in Los Angeles. Can you come and see me?"

"Certainly, I'd be glad to," I replied.

A few weeks later, after Begin's entourage had arrived and settled in at the hotel, I walked next door and went up to Lear's lavish office that occupied an entire floor of the modern high-rise structure. He offered me a seat, and we immediately began talking right where we had left off on the telephone. But, by now, I wanted to know a few things as well.

"So what about you, Norman?" We were on a first-name basis by now. "What is your connection to Israel?" I had assumed that, since he was interested in this matter, he was in some way involved with Israeli affairs. I learned, however, that he had never visited Israel and knew next to nothing about its history and politics. Not only that, he was not knowledgeable at all about basic Zionism. He had no conception that Israel is surrounded by huge enemy nations and that it had been forced to fight five wars to sustain its very survival. I was surprised by this apparent ignorance on the part of TV's "King" Lear. I had met a lot of assimilated American Jews, but for the most part, they had some interest in Israel. In Lear's case I felt that his key concern was being spared the embarrassment of having to explain to his non-Jewish friends what the prime minister of Israel was doing hobnobbing with the likes of Jerry Falwell. I patiently provided him with a basic Middle East history lesson and in the end felt that I had persuaded him.

"You know that makes a lot of sense, Hart," he admitted towards the end of our hour and a half meeting. Lear agreed to drop his public opposition to the Dallas trip. As it turned out, Begin never got the chance to go to Dallas because, a few days later, he was notified of his wife's death and immediately returned to Israel.

The following incident, concerning the death of our dear friend, Aliza Begin, was probably one of the most traumatic experiences of my life.

It was during his final visit to the US as prime minister that we found ourselves, on a Saturday afternoon, November 13, 1982, housed at the Century Plaza Hotel as part of the prime minister's entourage. He was scheduled to deliver a major address before a large audience at an Israel Bond event that evening. The Israeli contingent had taken over the entire 19th floor, where very tight security was maintained, while we, along with other Americans, were ensconced one floor below. I enjoyed free access through the security apparatus, thanks to my lapel pin pass. I walked up to the 19th floor, through the checkpoint and was making my way towards Begin's room, when I was nearly tackled by Yechiel Kadishai. He grabbed me and pushed me into an empty room.

"What's going on, Yechiel?!" I demanded.

"Where's Simona?" he said gravely.

"She went to visit her mother. What's the matter?"

"I just got off the phone with Benny in Jerusalem," he said, referring to Begin's son. "It's Alla. She's dead."

"Oh, no. What happened?" Yechiel quickly recounted what he knew about Aliza's death from a long-standing battle with emphysema and then turned to the matter at hand.

"We have to tell Menachem," he said, looking me in the eye. "Benny gave me strict instructions that you and Simona must be in the room when we give him the bad news."

"Are you going to tell him?" I asked.

"No, Dr. Gotsman will see to that," he replied, referring to the head cardiologist from Hadassah hospital, Dr. Mervyn Gotsman, who, because of Begin's heart condition, always traveled with the prime minister.

"Can you locate Simona quickly?" asked Yechiel.

"Yes, of course. I'll phone her right away." Simona returned to the hotel within thirty minutes, but locating Dr. Gotsman was not so easy. He was an observant Jew and had gone to pray at a small synagogue somewhere on Pico Boulevard. We were unable to reach him and had to wait nearly two hours for his return. Once he arrived, we were assembled and ready to deliver the news to the prime minister. The tragic scene that followed will be etched into my memory for the rest of my days.

By now it was 6:30 PM and Begin had finished getting dressed for the evening. He was seated on the sofa wearing a tuxedo. Kadishai, Dr. Gotsman, Simona and I filed into the room and closed the door behind us. Begin immediately sensed that something was wrong. Dr. Gotsman stood before him and in hushed tones delivered the news that his Alla was gone. The prime minister cried out as if wounded. As bitter tears welled up in his eyes, he kept repeating: *"Lamah Azavti Otah?"* Oh, why did I leave her? His lamentations were heart wrenching. "I should not have listened when she told me to go. She was in the hospital. I should have stayed beside her."

Simona tried to console him, "Don't blame yourself. The doctors told you that it was okay for you to go."

"Doctors! What do they know?" he cried.

Yechiel handed me the telephone. "It's Benny."

"Benny, I'm so sorry about your mother," I said. "She was a great woman. Please accept our condolences."

"Thank you, Hart." he said. "May I speak to my father?" I looked at the prime minister and could see that he was completely overcome and in no condition to talk. "Maybe later, Benny," I said.

"Well, please, you or Yechiel ask him where we should bury mother," he asked. "Let me know as soon as you can."

After a few moments, Yechiel broached the subject.

"Menachem, Benny wants to know where Alla should be buried," he asked gingerly.

"The same place as me," came the curt reply.

"I don't know where that is," admitted Yechiel.

"What do you mean, you don't know? Don't you remember? I gave you an envelope with all that sort of information in it."

"But, Menachem," explained Yechiel, "I never opened the envelope…"

"Of course, you're right," he said, realizing that he had always assumed that his own death would precede his wife's. "Bury her on the Mount of Olives, next to the graves of my heroes." He was referring to the two captured *Irgun* and *Lehi* martyrs, Moshe Barazani and Meir Feinstein, who elected to commit suicide rather than face hanging at the hands of the British.

At this point Begin caught a glimpse of himself in the mirror. "Look at me," he wailed. "I'm in a tuxedo. Why am I in a tuxedo? Oh, yes, I'm supposed to speak somewhere tonight," he recalled.

"We've canceled your speech, Menachem," said Kadishai taking charge of the situation, "and we're flying back home tonight. Simona and Hart will help you pack your suitcase, and you should change into something more comfortable."

At this point, Begin's daughter, Leah walked into the hotel room. She took one look at the activity and demanded to know what was going on. We all stopped what we were doing and stood mutely, just looking at each other for an awkward moment. Leah peered into one face and then the next and finally shouted: "*Ima*! It's *Ima*! Something's happened to my mother! What has happened? Someone please tell me."

I expected Dr. Gotsman to give her the news, but he remained silent. I couldn't take it anymore. I walked over, took Leah's hand and bid her sit down. I looked at her squarely and pulled no punches as I told her: "Correct. Your mother has died." I had faced this type of situation fairly frequently in the nursing home business, and I had learned that the direct approach is always the best way to deliver this type of news.

Leah was devastated, and now we had two distraught people to deal with and to pack for. After helping to assemble Begin's suitcases, we walked towards Leah's room to assist her. I ran into national Israel Bonds leader, Sam Rothberg, who had been waiting for some time to see Begin. I gave him the bad news and he asked that I pass on his condolences. By now the news was spreading quickly among the group that Aliza had died and that the prime minister was returning to Israel.

At this point, Kadishai walked into the room and announced to us: "The prime minister wants you and Simona to come back home with us." We quickly agreed and went off to pack our own bags and prepare for the flight. We soon realized that we did not have our passports with us. Kadishai assured us that this would be no problem since we would be aboard the prime minister's plane and would not need to pass through customs.

By 10:30 PM we were assembled on board as the prime minister's jet took off towards the east. Begin was stretched out on a cot behind a partition from which he would emerge from time to time. Simona prepared tea for him during the flight, but her major role was in consoling Leah. I believe that it was for this purpose that Begin and Benny had asked us to come on board. They understood that Leah would take the news of her mother's death very hard and that our presence would be a comfort to her. He was correct. Leah spent the entire flight clutching Simona's arm so tightly that her flesh was marked with black and blue bruises by the time we arrived in Israel.

Simona and Leah have developed a close friendship that has lasted to this day. Through her position with El Al Airlines, Leah always seems to be aware of our presence whenever we travel to Israel and never fails to drop by for a visit.

The flight touched down in New York where Israel's ambassador to the United Nations, Yehuda Blum, and his wife Moriah, came aboard the plane to extend their condolences to the prime minister. After taking on fuel, our plane took off again, arriving at Ben Gurion airport at 1 AM. The funeral was scheduled for later that day, and by that time word had spread throughout the country. What was to have been a private family funeral was soon swamped by thousands of Begin's admirers wishing to pay their respects.

Afterwards, Begin asked that we stay with him during the traditional seven-day mourning period. According to Jewish custom, during this time of *shiva* the mourner is to wear rent clothing and remain seated close to the floor. Simona and I sat next to the prime minister during this period as he accepted the condolences from an unending stream of well-wishers, including top Israeli officials, chief rabbis, celebrities and representatives from dozens of nations around the world.

In a form of ancient cathartic therapy, Jewish tradition encourages a mourner to talk during the initial mourning period. Accordingly, we refrained from initiating any conversations and permitted Begin to speak uninterrupted about any topic he wished. And talk he did. Sitting in a torn shirt, he reminisced freely about such topics as his relationship with Jabotinsky, his years in a Soviet prison and the birth of his children. But his recollections would always turn back towards his Alla. In this way, I believe he did manage to expiate his guilt over not being at her bedside at the end.

Each morning a crowd of men would fill the residence for the traditional prayers, donning the black leather phylacteries and chanting the call and response as Menachem and Benny Begin recited the *"Kaddish"* prayer in memory of their departed wife and mother.

I had contacted Mark and asked that he mail us our passports, which he did, enabling us to return to the States with no difficulty after the initial mourning period had concluded. Both Benny and Leah thanked us for staying and said that our presence was a comfort to their father. We, of course, considered it an honor and an unforgettable experience.

On August 14, 1983, I had the *zechut* (privilege) of being asked by Israel Bonds leader David Hermelin, to introduce Prime Minister Begin as he delivered what turned out to be his final public address before going into retirement. Of course we were unaware of this fact at the time. The occasion also happened to correspond with Begin's 70th birthday. The audience was made up of 400 Israel Bonds leaders assembled from around the world for a keynote address in the Chagall Hall of the Knesset in Jerusalem. In my remarks I mentioned how Begin had been my hero since I was 13 years old, during a time when Jews were homeless and helpless. I gave him credit for kicking the British out of Palestine and helping found the Israeli state. As Begin stood to speak after my intro, many were struck by his appearance. I could see that he was pale and looked suddenly frail for the first time. While his speech was labored, his message was a resounding one that Harry Hurwitz has dubbed his "political testament." His first words indicated that, despite his appearance, his wit remained intact. Some excerpts from this landmark address are included below:

"Hart, you overdid it with that introduction. But, since it came from the 'Hart,' I gladly accept your praise and kind words."

"…the Israel Defense Forces did not enter Lebanon in order to attack that country or because it wanted anything from it. The IDF used the most legitimate right of national self defense, facing for years permanent attacks, either through incursions or by long-range arms from that country by those who called themselves the PLO."

"…now also in the United States it is clear who took the decision to prevent a peaceful agreement from coming into being, a peaceful solution being reached. Israel wants peace with Lebanon and all its neighbors. For the sake of peace with Egypt, Israel made great sacrifices. We don't have to prove our love for peace. It is in our hearts. As we hate war, we love peace and vice versa. Whenever it is necessary to defend our people we shall fulfill our duty. Therefore, we still have this problem facing us. We are prepared to do our share to reach a peaceful solution."

"…for too long has the Jew been an exception to the rules applying to other peoples. Enough of it. The rules applying to other nations will apply to the Jewish state as well."

"Remember, my dear friends, our people suffered much, lost many, won the day; nobody gave us our freedom. We had to fight for it, to redeem it, to give for it sacrifices, to defend it. All of us, without exception of party affiliation, and we won. Why? Because our cause is just. So take note, my dear friends, and when you meet your friends, tell them so. There is a rule, unchangeable. The just cause will always win the day."

And with these words, Begin, soon after, resigned his office and withdrew from public view for the remaining nine years of his life. He did not reveal his plans to anyone, although looking back, I can discern a dropped hint of his intentions during our visit to his office on the following day. Simona and I were on our way to the airport and had stopped off to say good-bye.

"Hart," he said, "you did such a fine job last night. Thank you for introducing me in such a wonderful manner."

"It was my honor, Mar Begin," I replied. He also thanked us for the beautiful historic artifact, an ancient water jug, which was presented to him as a birthday gift during the previous night's event. What he said next surprised me a bit and should have tipped me off:

"But you know, Hart, I'm seventy years old today. I'm getting to be an old man."

"Mar Begin," I protested. "What are you talking about? Seventy is not old. President Reagen is now 74, and everyone knows he's getting ready to run for re-election."

"Well, Hart," he said dismissively, "Reagan is a *gezunter goy* (healthy gentile)." I laughed and came right back with:

"But you're a *shtarker Yid*! (a strong Jew)"

Begin laughed and said: "No, I'm seventy and I feel every bit of it."

Despite this friendly exchange, I left his office with no inkling of his intention to resign. Simona and I had noticed that he did appear more withdrawn and not as gregarious and outgoing as in the past, but we did not see what was coming. The announcement caught us, along with the rest of the world, by complete surprise. Thinking back after digesting the news, I recalled that Begin had spoken to me, on more than one occasion, of his intentions to retire when he reached age seventy.

I remember receiving a phone call from a reporter with the US Jewish press at the time:

"Hart, you just got back from Israel. Didn't your good friend Menachem Begin tell you he was going to resign?" I had to admit that he had not, although I mentioned the hints that he had dropped and our discussion about Reagan. I did not wish to quote him exactly, so I paraphrased Begin as responding with: "Your president is a 'robust individual'" replacing the actual term *gezunter goy* with something more politically correct.

Soon thereafter I placed a call to the prime minister and urged him to reconsider his decision. But by this time, it was too late and his mind was completely made up. Yechiel Kadishai, like the rest of his staff, was dismayed and disappointed by the decision. Despite all the criticism he had received recently, Begin still enjoyed a wide base of popular support and would have had no difficulty in retaining his leadership for many years to come.

After his resignation, Begin withdrew into a state of private seclusion. I was, at first, puzzled by this move and sought to discover the reasons for his decision to become something of a recluse.

I was not the only one speculating on the behavior of Menachem Begin in those days. The media were filled with stories of his chronic depression, of his encroaching Alzheimer's Disease and even assorted cancer diagnoses. Wolf Blitzer reported on CNN that Begin stayed in bed all day in a windowless cell. All of this was pure poppycock. He lived in a lovely apartment with an expansive view of *Ya'ar Yerushalayim* (the Jerusalem Forest) and, ironically, his apartment also overlooked Dir Yassin, the Arab village that Begin was accused of attacking during the War of Independence.

Many times I was asked by reporters and others who were aware of my friendship with Begin about the real reasons for his decision to go into seclusion. Was it because of the loss of his wife? Did he feel guilt over the casualties during the Lebanese war? My own opinion is that he was simply burned out. He had endured worldwide attention and fielded dozens of phone calls per day for decades. The weight of being Menachem Begin every day had become a monumental burden. He was exhausted and drained and decided to withdraw completely from the arena.

There were times, in the early months of his seclusion, when he even refused to see Simona and me. I recall that we had phoned Kadishai shortly after Begin left office and asked to see him. We were told to come right over. We entered the apartment and sat in the living room, waiting for Begin to emerge from the bedroom. But he did not come out. We waited for about thirty minutes, and he still failed to join us. I delivered a knock on the bedroom door and received no answer. Perhaps he's fallen asleep, I thought; so I told Simona, "Let's wait a little longer."

After about ten more minutes, I said to Simona: "I know he's in there. Why don't you give it a try?" She agreed and knocked on the door. No answer.

"You know what?" I said. "Just go on in. Open the door and walk in. You were a nurse. It's okay." Simona did as I asked and found Begin sitting up in bed, wearing a bathrobe and reading calmly.

"He's okay," Simona relayed, and I followed her into the bedroom. He looked pale and withdrawn, but otherwise appeared to be in good health.

"Have you been out of bed today?" Simona asked.

"No. Not yet today, Simonela," he replied.

"Okay, Mar Begin, today we're getting out of bed. Let's go," she said. Simona was never awed by the former prime minister. She spoke to him plainly, like a member of the family.

"Naw, I don't feel like it. Not today, Simonela," he whined.

"No, no, no. We're going to walk around a little. It's not good for you to stay in bed all day," she insisted. Simona assisted him out of bed and offered her support as he began walking out the door and back and forth around the apartment.

Whenever we were in town, Simona took charge of his care. She advised his cook not to serve his meals in bed. He should come to the table to eat. Begin would chide her:

"Simona. What do you want from me? Who are you? Napoleon?" he protested.

"Mar Begin," I responded. "You just promoted her. My mother calls Simona 'The General' and now you've made her the Emperor. You're promoting her and I have to live with her."

Our proactive style of care for Begin did not sit well with his family. His son, Benny, would tell me: "Just leave him alone. Don't bother him. He's a grown adult."

"That's the worst thing you can do," we told him. "You're wrong. You have to force him to get out of bed and to interact with people – even if it's just for short periods each day." Maybe we were overstepping our bounds, but I had seen this type of behavior among nursing home patients, and I knew that if they were simply left to themselves they would fall into deep depression and eventually wither and die. We did not wish to see this happen to our friend.

Over time and, I believe, thanks to our efforts, Begin did start to open up a bit more. He would meet with us in the living room, and he appeared to be his old self. He was always on top of the latest news developments and would comment to us about the events of the day. "Shamir handled that pretty well," or "Reagan should not have gone there." Finally, his son, Benny, had to admit that we were right in insisting that we force him out of bed.

While Begin always refused to meet with the media during his seclusion, certain special visitors were welcomed from time to time. I recall arriving at his apartment to find him all decked out in a blue suit and necktie. I asked Kadishai, "What gives? Why is he all dressed up?"

"His girlfriend is coming over," he replied.

"Who?" I exclaimed.

"Don't worry, it's Jeanne Kirkpatrick. She's on her way." I knew that Begin was very fond of the former US ambassador to the United Nations and held her in high esteem. I greeted her as she arrived and saw her enjoy a very warm welcome from Begin.

Over the years of seclusion, we became part of what may be viewed as a rather exclusive group, Begin's inner circle. Actually, there was no outer circle, so one could call it simply "the Circle." At the core of the Circle were Begin himself and his family, son Ze'ev Benjamin and his wife, Ruthie. Others included his biographer and current director of the Menachem Begin Heritage Foundation, Harry Hurwitz and his wife, Freda. The young Likud leader, Dan Meridor, would drop by every Friday at 2 PM to brief Begin on the week's affairs. Of course, Yechiel Kadishai was with him daily. Old friends, Nathan and Lil Silver, originally from Toronto, were regular Circle members. One more neighbor, a former cabinet minister, Chaim Corfu, who now lived in the same apartment building, rounded out the group. We would typically convene at Begin's apartment on Shabbat afternoon and discuss everything from the weekly Torah portion to the American presidential elections. The conversation was always sparkling, and Begin's engaging manner would put to the lie all rumors of his alleged mental impairment.

An occasional visitor was General Ariel Sharon, who had spearheaded Israel's incursion into Lebanon under Begin. I recall much speculation in the press about a rift between the two men over the conduct of the Lebanese war. Reporters liked to compare it to the relationship between Harry Truman and General Douglas McArthur during the Korean War. This might have made good copy, but I saw no evidence of any animosity between them. Begin always spoke of Sharon in the most glowing and respectful terms and, whenever they were together, I could see that a strong bond existed between them.

In the mid-eighties, Sharon was embroiled in a successful libel suit against the publishers of TIME Magazine. TIME had falsely reported that Sharon had received advance knowledge of the tragic massacres carried out by Israel's allies at the Sabra and Shatillah refugee camps during the Lebanese war, and that he had failed to intervene to stop them. Begin was following press accounts of the trial closely and would question Sharon about the case whenever he would stop by. I recall how Begin would press Sharon for details. After one response to his probing, Begin corrected his former general:

"No, that's not right," he said. "That's not what their lawyer said. He said he would not call that witness." Sharon was amazed by the depth of Begin's knowledge.

"Mar Begin," spouted Sharon. "Why are you asking me questions? You are more familiar with this case than I am!"

It was clear from my encounters with the prevailing Israeli leadership during the 1980s that Begin, despite his self-imposed exile, was still an eminent presence on the political landscape. I recall how his successor, Yitzchak Shamir, said privately to me: "I have some very big shoes to fill." Shamir, as well as Sharon, and others such as Moshe Arens, would often contact me after one of my visits with Begin to inquire about his current thinking. Did he say anything about me? What does he think about this matter? Does Begin approve of how I handled that situation? These were common questions I would encounter during those post-Begin debriefings.

During our many visits to his home during those last years of his life, not once did I observe any type of depression or any other signs of mental disorder. His personality was always warm, and his wit was sharp to the end. He would joke and laugh easily. An example:

Simona and I had just arrived in Israel and had come straight from the airport to Begin's apartment. As we entered, Begin stood up to greet us with open arms. He was always excited to see us, because we would bring him books that he devoured at the rate of one per day. After kissing Simona's hand in his courtly manner and hugging us both, he bid us sit down.

"So, Hart, how did you get to Israel this time?" he asked. "Did you fly El Al?" When I replied that I had, he asked:

"I'll bet you flew first class, right?" he ventured.

"Actually, Simona and I like to fly Business Class."

"You know when I used to travel by train around Europe before the war, I always went third class," he said and then paused.

"Well," he said finally, "aren't you going to ask me why I always rode third class?"

"Oh, yes, of course, Mar Begin," I obliged. "Tell me, why did you always travel third class?"

"Because there was no fourth class," he said with his characteristic, gap-toothed smile.

It was during the years of seclusion that Begin became very angry with me once again. In 1986, Likud Party leader Yitzchak Shamir was running for the premiership in a close race. Begin's endorsement, if issued, was seen as being a big enough factor to influence the outcome of the election. Nevertheless, Begin refused to issue such an endorsement or a statement of any kind. Shamir, Begin's son Benny and Kadishai had all pleaded with him to agree to an interview. All to no avail. On the day before the election, I was asked by the party leadership to speak to him and see if I could convince him to offer a last-minute public word of support for Shamir. As I sat in Begin's living room, I reviewed the importance of his endorsement for the future of the party and the country. The discussion became a bit heated after he turned me down flat. I decided to try a new approach.

"I think I know why you've gone into seclusion, Mar Begin," I stated.

"Oh, you do?" he questioned.

"Yes. I believe you've taken a vow. A *neder*," I said using the Hebrew word for oath. "I think you've made a vow to yourself to withdraw from the world. A vow that you cannot break. You have, for whatever reason, decided to go back into the state you found yourself in back at that Siberian prison. Completely alone and cut-off."

I could see his displeasure welling up inside him. But I wanted to shake him up, so I continued.

"Mar Begin, with all due respect, I see you regressing back to that time in your life. But instead of the Russians, this time you are your own jailer." His features made it plain that he was not at all impressed with my armchair psychoanalysis.

"You don't know what you're talking about," he said abruptly. "Do you have any idea what a *neder* is? Would I do such a thing? I would never make a *neder*. Don't ever say such a thing to me again!"

He completely rejected my conclusions. And yet, when a reporter phoned thirty minutes later, Begin, for the first time, agreed to take the call. He extended a solid endorsement of Shamir over the phone, but to make it effective it had to come from Begin's own lips. Begin's nephew and radio news bureau chief, Emmanuel Halpern, rushed over to the apartment with recording equipment. He succeeded in capturing Begin's endorsement on audiotape, but he was too late. By the time he returned to the studio to broadcast it, the moratorium on last-minute campaign advertising had gone into effect. Despite the fact that voters did not get to hear Begin's endorsement in his own voice, Shamir nevertheless won re-election.

I witnessed another memorable example of the Begin wit in 1988 during one of my visits to Jerusalem. As I was unpacking at the Jerusalem Hilton, the phone rang; it was Yechiel Kadishai.

"Hart," Yechiel said, "Menachem would rather see you this morning than in the afternoon; can you come over right away?"

"Of course, Yechiel," I said. I ran downstairs and grabbed the first available taxi.

"Take me to the *Yefe Nof* area, please," I said to the driver. "Once we're there, I'll show you where to drop me off." I did not want give him Begin's exact address. The driver was a smart, young Sephardic Jew who, I later learned, was born in Iraq and came to Israel as a child. The driver turned around to face me in the backseat and inquired:

"Are you by any chance going to see Menachem Begin?"

"As a matter of fact, I am," I admitted. He seemed incredulous.

"Are you really going to see Menachem Begin?" he asked again, turning all the way around as his voice wavered with excitement.

"Yes, I really am. Please keep your eyes on the road," I instructed. He complied and then asked:

"Could you deliver a message to Menachem Begin from me?" I said I would be glad to.

"Tell him that we miss him so very much. We haven't seen him for such a long time. Tell him that I personally love him so much. Do you realize how much I love him?"

"How much?" I asked.

"I love him more than my own wife!" It was obvious that Begin's support among Israel's Sephardic community was still very strong.

At this point I got out of the taxi and walked the short distance to Begin's apartment at Tzemach No. 1. After greeting and embracing each other, we sat down in the living room, and I immediately brought up the taxi driver.

"Mar Begin, the taxi driver who brought me here today asked me to relay a message to you. He said that he misses you and that he loves you. In fact, he said he loves you more than his own wife." Begin stared at me wide-eyed.

"I hope it's a different kind of love," he quipped.

From the moment Begin left the Prime Minister's Office, he observed a strict rule of silence when it came to issuing any evaluations of the performance of his successors. He understood that the prime minister had a difficult enough job without being continually second-guessed by his illustrious predecessor. I did succeed, on only one occasion, in convincing Begin to reluctantly forego this rule and offer an opinion on one of Shimon Peres' decisions.

In 1985 Israel was governed by a National Unity coalition that called for a 2-year rotation of the premiership between the Labor and the Likud parties. It was Peres' turn at bat, and he had authorized the release of over 1,000 Palestinian terrorists in exchange for a handful of Israeli hostages. It was a highly controversial decision and one that I personally disagreed with. I wanted to know how Begin felt about it. Naturally, when I posed the question, he declined to offer an opinion.

"Mar Begin, I want to ask you a very important question," I asked during one of our private visits. "If you had still been prime minister today, would you have agreed to the exchange?"

"What can I say, Hart?" he begged off. "I'm out of office. I don't have all the information. I really couldn't tell you." But I wasn't about to let him off the hook so easily. I persisted.

"I understand all that, but this is just a simple question," I said. "Had you been prime minister, would you have done the same thing as Peres?"

"Don't ask me questions like that," he pleaded. "I'm not in office and I really don't know." I wasn't going to let him sidestep the question. I had to have my answer.

"I want an answer from you," I insisted. "This is just between us. You know that I'm not going to repeat your answer to the press." He pondered for a minute, and I again formulated the question: "Had you been in office, would you have done the same thing?" He saw that he was not being allowed to slip away and finally relented.

"Okay, Hart. I will tell you what I would NOT have done, not what I would have done." I nodded and indicated he should go on. "If, after weighing all the facts, I had made the decision to make the exchange, I would never have allowed the released terrorists to remain in Judea and Samaria. I would insist that they be exiled to some other place in the Arab world and not be permitted to live freely in our midst. These are the real trouble-makers, and by letting them remain in Judea and Samaria, we are surely inviting more trouble."

I thanked Begin for his candor. I could not help recalling these highly prescient remarks when, a few years later, the so-called Palestinian uprising, known as the *Intifada*, erupted – led by the very same terrorists that Peres had freed and permitted to remain in the territories.

It was a few years later, in 1991, that I raised a question with Begin that had been on my mind for many years. I knew it would be a sensitive subject, so I asked Begin's permission before posing this difficult question. He bid me to proceed.

"Mar Begin," I began a bit hesitantly, "the Betar banner we waved back in Europe after the war contained the words: *Shtei Gedot LaYarden* (Both Sides of the Jordan). This was the motto of Jabotinsky. You made it the motto of the Irgun underground along with *Rak Kach* (Always Thus). The emblem shows Israel sitting on both sides of the Jordan. What happened? What happened to *Shtei Gedot LaYarden*? Why didn't you pursue that ideal when you had the chance as prime minister?" Begin shook his head slowly and gently placed his hand upon my shoulder. I could see that something had lit up behind his eyes as a crooked smile danced across his lips.

"Hart, did you want me to start a war with Jordan?" he asked quietly, with a bemused look on his face. "Let's just leave it at that. Okay?" But, as before, I persisted.

"I can't just leave it. I must know if all that business was just propaganda." At this he became indignant.

"Propaganda? What do you mean?" he retorted. "I believed it then and I believe it now. The Jewish people must never give up the Zionist endeavor. We must never abandon the dream of a Jewish nation on the land given to Abraham by G-d. No Jew should ever agree that this land, on both sides of the Jordan, is not ours. We don't know what history will bring. Today there's a country called Jordan. They leave us alone, we leave them alone. But things change. Jordan wasn't always there, and in another generation, in another time, who knows where we could find ourselves?" By way of example, he pointed to recent events in Eastern Europe and the former Soviet Union.

"Who could have predicted that things would collapse so quickly?" he commented. "I could tell it was all over when I saw Ceauçescu's face on television. I saw how he stepped backwards when he saw the crowds that had assembled in the streets against him. I realized then that he was finished and probably the rest of Eastern Europe as well."

Begin's statement that he would never have agreed to relinquish Jewish sovereignty over the territories underscored the core difference between his policies and those of his leftist successors, Rabin and Peres. Sign away Jewish land to a foreign power? Never!

Begin's plan, articulated in the Camp David Accords, was inspired by Jabotinsky's vision of Palestinian Arabs living under an autonomous administrative authority. Begin believed in full autonomy, but not sovereignty, for the Arab populated lands of ancient Israel. Sovereignty must be reserved for the Jewish state. Of course, he understood, as the *Intifada* raged on, that before a Palestinian Authority could be created, it must be rendered peaceful and non-threatening to Israel's security. The primary, and clearly fatal, flaw of the Oslo Accords, as implemented, was that a Palestinian Authority was established before those Arabs living under it agreed to Israel's right to exist.

Furthermore, once a Palestinian Authority had been established, I am certain that Begin would never have agreed to arm that entity with automatic weapons that could easily be turned against Israel. A Palestinian police force could be adequately armed with nightsticks and similar non-lethal weapons to carry out its domestic duties. I recall Begin articulating his vision of a peaceful Palestinian Administrative Authority.

"They can have everything they need. They can have their own currency, their own police force, their own parliament, and their own school system. Only two things they cannot have if they wish to continue living on Israeli land. No army and no foreign policy." But I could see the risks inherent in this vision and pointed them out.

"But Mar Begin," I protested, "what about the risk? What happens once this autonomous authority is in place and they decide to declare a Palestinian state? What do you do then?"

"I would arrest the leadership immediately," he shot back. "An independent Palestinian state means they would have their own army, which would pose a military threat to Israel. And that we could never tolerate."

It was actually Yitzchak Shamir, Begin's immediate successor, who had the clearest vision of how a peace in the region might best be manifested. Once a working and non-threatening Palestinian Authority was established, Shamir pictured an evolution towards what he labeled a "Confederation" composed of Israel, Jordan and the Palestinians. Each entity would enjoy various levels of independence, but would be conjoined in a strategic and economic union not unlike the European Community. In this slightly utopian vision, the diverse populations of the region would work towards living in harmony along the lines of a racially pluralistic nation such as the US. While Begin's and Shamir's vision of a peaceful Middle East seems farther off today than ever, I feel it still represents the most equitable and workable scenario for all the parties in the region.

Begin's reputation as a recluse was reinforced by the fact that, despite numerous entreaties, he never agreed to an authorized biography of himself. One author, Ned Temko, aware of my relationship with Begin, contacted me when I was in Israel and asked me to arrange for an interview. When I told him that this was impossible, he asked if he could speak with me about my friendship with the man. I agreed, and he conducted a series of interviews with me during my next few visits to Israel. Finally, he showed up at my hotel with his manuscript entitled *To Win Or To Die: A Personal Portrait of Menachem Begin*.

"Just one favor, Hart," he asked plaintively. "Take this to Begin and ask him to read it. Can you do that?"

"I suppose I can," I replied.

"Maybe if he likes it, he'll agree to an interview," said Temko. "And if he really likes it, he'll agree to let me call it the authorized biography." The next day I delivered the manuscript to Begin.

"This fellow Temko seems very serious about this biography, Mar Begin," I said as I handed him the manuscript. "He even traveled to your birthplace in Brest-Litovsk to do research. He'd like you to read this over."

"I can't do it, Hart," said Begin. I was surprised.

"You can't even read it? Why not?" I asked.

"Let me explain it like this," he said. "What if I read it and what if I find some mistake and I tell the author about it and he corrects it. Now the fellow can go around saying 'Menachem Begin read my book and approved every word as true, except for one thing which I fixed.' If I read it and don't go over every word with a magnifying glass, whatever I don't correct will be assumed to be approved by me. Tell Temko that I greatly appreciate his interest in my life, but I simply cannot agree to read the book before it is published."

It was in early March 1992, that I received a call from a somber Yechiel Kadishai.

"It's his heart," reported Yechiel. "He collapsed and was rushed to Ichilov Hospital. At first they thought it was a stroke, but it's his heart and it doesn't look too good. He was in a coma for a whole day, and now they've put a pacemaker in." At 3:30 AM the following Monday, March 9, with his children and Kadishai at his bedside, Menachem Begin died. I received the news from another American Begin supporter, Sandy Frank. Sandy, a noted Hollywood TV producer, happened to be in Israel at the time. He phoned me and tearfully reported the sad news to me. Sandy currently serves under me as vice-president of the Menachem Begin Heritage Foundation.

I had wanted to attend the funeral, but there was simply no time. Sandy informed me that, in keeping with Jewish tradition, Begin would be laid to rest on the Mount of Olives, next to Aliza, in about 12 hours. I learned that Begin had rejected a state funeral, to which he was entitled as a former prime minister, opting instead for a simple family ceremony. US Vice-President Dan Quayle, as well as former President Jimmy Carter and Cyrus Vance were all poised to fly in for the funeral, but their trips were canceled.

Benny Begin had insisted on a "Jewish funeral," not an international event. The graveside ceremony was a simple affair, with no eulogies. It was attended by Benny and Begin's daughters, Leah Begin and Hassia Milo, along with their families. Also in attendance were Israeli President Chaim Herzog, Prime Minister Yitzchak Shamir, and Labor Party leader, Yitzchak Rabin. Egyptian ambassador Mohammed Bassiouni was on hand, representing President Hosni Mubarak. They watched as seven former comrades-in-arms from the *Irgun Zvai Leumi*, serving as pallbearers, laid the coffin to rest and then listened as first Benny recited the traditional *Kaddish* prayer and Yechiel Kadishai chanted *Kel Male Rachamim*.

After the family and VIPs departed, thousands of onlookers broke through the human chain of police to pay their last respects. Some kissed the freshly dug grave while others laid stones on the mound. Tens of thousands of mourners, many in tears, flocked to the Mount of Olives to say good-bye. Most had walked the two and a half miles from the funeral home, through East Jerusalem to the Mount of Olives. The outpouring was extraordinary, given the fact that Begin had been out of office for nine years.

Begin was memorialized by US President George Bush at the time for his "very courageous, farsighted role in trying to bring peace to the Middle East." Israeli Prime Minister Shamir offered a eulogy for Begin, in which he called his predecessor "one of the great men of Jewish history."

Having known the man, and counted him as a mentor and a friend, I could not agree more.

With Secretary of State George Schultz and Conference of
Major American Jewish Organizations president, Morris Abram

With the 41st US president,
George Bush

With Israel Bond leader, Miles Lerman and former
Secretary of State, Henry Kissinger

With Simona and UN Ambassador,
Benjamin Netanyahu

With UN Ambassador Benjamin Netanyahu

With Israel's ambassador to the US, Moshe Arens

With Israeli president, Chaim Herzog

With Benny Begin

With General Ariel Sharon and publisher
of the Las Vegas Sun, Hank Greenspun

With Israel Bond chairman, David Hermelin
and Minister Ariel Sharon

With Minister Ariel Sharon
and his wife, Lilly

With Minister
Ariel Sharon

With Prime Minister
Sharon at the Park Lane
Hotel in New York

With Reverend and Mrs. Jerry
Falwell at the Jabotinsky Medal
ceremonies in New York

With Yigael Yadin and Indiana
Governor Robert Orr

With Deputy Prime Minister
Yigael Yadin

With Mr. and Mrs. Simon
Wiesenthal and Simona

With Simona and Indiana Senator
Richard G. Lugar

With Rabbi Alexander S. Linchner, founder of Boy's
Town Jerusalem and Minister Moshe Arens

With Sigmund Strochlitz and Elie Wiesel at an
Israel Bond dinner

With Israeli president, Ezer Weitzman

With Simona and Jerusalem mayor, Ehud Olmert

With New York City mayor, Rudolph Giuliani

With Yechiel Kadishai and Tel Aviv mayor, Roni Milo

Being hooded by my sons, Bernard and Josh, while receiving
my honorary doctorate from Touro College

With the founders of the Israel Tennis Centers
(left to right standing) Joe Shane, Harold Landesberg,
Ruby Josephs, (kneeling) Ian Froman

With actress Lynda Carter and tennis champion,
Chrissy Evert

With the two Bronze medals
I earned in Tennis at the
Israeli Maccabee Games

The Hasten Hebrew Academy of Indianapolis

Chapter Fourteen

Rubbing Shoulders

MY FRIENDSHIP with Menachem Begin provided me with many opportunities to gain an up-close look at an assortment of Israeli and American political leaders. Looking back, I would have to say that I was impressed about as often as I was disappointed.

There was certainly no disappointment when I first met President Ronald Reagan during a reception held in Prime Minister Begin's honor in the summer of 1982. We shook hands, and I could not help but be charmed by Reagan's warm, easy manner as he greeted each guest. He and Nancy circulated through the room making everyone feel welcome and comfortable. We chatted about great Jewish achievements in the arts, and I was amazed by the depth of his knowledge on the subject.

My next encounter with President Reagan was not quite so cordial. I received a call in 1986, inviting me to a meeting with the president and key American Jewish leaders. Of course, I accepted the invitation. Once I arrived at the meeting, held in the Roosevelt Room of the White House, I observed that the dozen or so top leaders present included Malcolm Hoenlein, executive vice-chairman of the Conference of Presidents of Major Jewish Organizations; Mandell Ganchrow, president of the Orthodox Union; and Marty Hecht, brother of Senator Chick Hecht. The group also included Ivan Boesky, who was about to receive great notoriety during the upcoming Wall Street scandals.

My inclusion in this group was something of a mystery to me. I was at that time serving as the national president of the Herut Zionists of America, but I suspected that my recent stint as state finance chairman for the Reagan/Bush campaign during the 1984 election might have had more to do with my garnering this invitation. As state finance chairman, I succeeded in raising millions of dollars through a series of parlor meetings held in the private homes of Reagan supporters. We focused on smaller towns where our company had bank holdings, such as Sullivan, Brazil and Tipton, Indiana. Normally each bank had a Board of Directors composed of the most prominent members of the community, and they were mostly dyed-in-the-wool Republicans and solid Reagan supporters. This made it relatively easy to organize fund-raisers.

While I have traditionally supported the Republican Party and its candidates for office over the years, my brother, Mark, has been equally active in Democratic Party affairs. This arrangement was not done by design. We both genuinely feel strong affinities towards our respective parties. Nevertheless, by covering all our bases in this way, we have been able to direct our energies to those candidates, from either party, who seem to be the most supportive of Israel. While this is not the only criterion by which we determine our support of a particular candidate, it is certainly a major one.

I have organized a number of successful political fund-raisers in my home for such politicians as Senators Richard Lugar and Dan Coats. I learned much later that, in fact, it was Senator Lugar who had recommended to the White House that I be included in this group. I'm not sure if my subsequent behavior caused him to regret this move or not, but I believe he knew me well enough to know that I'm never afraid to speak what's on my mind.

The topic of this White House meeting had to do with the US proposed arms sale to Saudi Arabia. Reagan was rounding up support and recognized the need to assuage the concerns of the American Jewish community about the sale. He was looking for our imprimatur on the deal, so he could state that he had received a green light from top Jewish leadership, and thereby diminish any concerns from within the American Jewish community about Israeli security.

I was shocked to learn that two members of our group, Marty Hecht and Ivan Boesky, were willing to go along with the arms sale plan. I recall how Boesky read from a long yellow legal pad upon which he had scribbled a lengthy two-page prepared statement. In it, he proclaimed that he agreed with the need for the arms sale and urged the group not to voice any objections for fear of being labeled "one-issue" Jews. Although the rest of us had no idea, at this point Boesky already was aware of the trouble he was facing with the federal government. His blatant kowtowing may have been influenced by a desire to gain friends in high places in preparation for the coming court battles. If so, it proved unsuccessful, since Boesky wound up serving four years in a federal penitentiary.

Before Reagan arrived, we were briefed for over one and a half hours by the National Security Advisor, Admiral John Poindexter, followed by Secretary of State George Shultz. We raised all of the security issues with Shultz, who turned out to be a delightful fellow, although he would not budge about the enormous need for this sale, in the interest of our country's foreign policy objectives.

At this point the President entered the room and took his seat at the oval conference table directly across from me. As was his custom, Reagan withdrew a little pile of 3×5 index cards from his pocket. He referred to his script as he reiterated the pitch that Poindexter and Shultz had already laid on the table. He concluded by asking for the support of Jewish leadership for the proposed Saudi arms package. He then wanted to gauge our reactions and asked that we go around the table with each of us sharing his thinking on the matter.

Several members of the group cautioned the President about selling weapons to a country that may someday use them against Israel. Reagan reassured us that these weapons were strictly to be used for defensive purposes only and, if deployed, would most likely be used against Iran. After three or four of the attendees had expressed their opinions, my turn arrived. I looked at Reagan squarely across the table and said:

"Mr. President, you may be aware that I worked very hard for your re-election," I began as Reagan smiled and nodded his head in a show of thanks. "I have always been an admirer of yours, and that's why we put out so much effort during the last campaign. I have been privileged, over the past several years, to know and to work closely with many Israeli leaders, including Menachem Begin and Yitzchak Shamir. To a man, they all believe that you are the best friend Israel has ever had in the White House. You are beloved by most Israelis and rightly so. But despite all this, my conscience will not permit me to go along with your plan to provide these arms to one of Israel's sworn enemies. And let me tell you the reason why.

"As it happens, just last night, my 21-year old daughter, Renée, a college student, returned home from a trip to Vancouver, where she was working at an international student exhibition. She explained to us that booths and pavilions were erected by many countries from around the world, including Saudi Arabia. She told me that as she stepped into the Saudi pavilion, the first thing she saw was a huge wall map of the Middle East. Of course, the map depicted the countries of the region, such as Syria, Lebanon, Jordan and Egypt. Then my daughter said to me: 'Daddy, you won't believe this. Israel was not on the map!' That is the way the Saudis regard Israel. A non-entity with no sovereign rights.

"Mr. President, I think you know that I love America just like I love Israel, but you want me to lobby in favor of selling weapons to a country that will not even put Israel on a map!? I just can't do that, Mr. President."

At hearing this, Reagan's face dropped and he became visibly flushed and flustered.

"Oh, n-n-now just hang on a minute, please," stammered Reagan, becoming quite animated, "I want you to tell your daughter that we will see to it that militarily Israel will always remain qualitatively better than all those Arab countries combined. I want you to tell your daughter that Saudi Arabia needs to protect itself against Iran. You tell her that we intend to make sure that Israel will never be threatened by these arms." How he proposed to guarantee exactly how these arms would or would not be used once they had been delivered to Saudi Arabia, he did not explain, and I was not convinced.

After the meeting all of us, with the exceptions of Boesky and Hecht, huddled up to discuss what we would say to the press corps waiting outside the door. We knew that they would ask about what was discussed during our meeting. Rather than have all of us speak to the media, we elected Malcolm Hoenlein to serve as our spokesman and agreed to direct all questions to him.

Boesky met the press first and read another prepared statement from his legal pad. Hoenlein then stepped to the microphones and stated that we, on behalf of American Jewish leadership, had been called in by the President, who had urged us to advocate support for his proposed Saudi arms sale. He went on to explain that we had a consensus of opinion that the sale posed too great a danger for Israel's security interests and had declined the President's request for support.

Mendy Ganchrow approached me afterwards to offer a compliment: "You made the best presentation," he said. "It was very impressive, what you said. It was spontaneous and very personal." That may all have been true, but it still was not effectual. The arms sale went through over the objections of the American Jewish leadership.

While President Reagan was rightfully regarded as a strong supporter of Israel, and while I felt that his heart was certainly in the right place, the Saudi arms sale was not the only time that President Reagan made a decision that went contrary to the interests of the American Jewish community. I'm referring to his highly publicized decision to visit the German military cemetery at Bitburg. Reagan opted to "stay the course" and go through with his visit during a D-Day 40th anniversary trip to Germany in 1985 – this despite the fact that it was learned, after the visit had been scheduled, that Bitburg served as the final resting place for a number of ss officers, who were known as the most fanatical of Hitler's Nazi elite. The visit was carried out over a chorus of protestations from American Jewish leaders. The most eloquent voice among them was that of noted author and Holocaust survivor Elie Wiesel, who advised Reagan during a televised face-to-face encounter that the cemetery at Bitburg was "not your place, Mr. President."

I first became acquainted with Elie Wiesel through his writing. I recall reading his landmark Holocaust memoir, *Night*, published in 1958, and feeling a strong kinship with him based on our common experiences. His powerful words have stayed with me ever since:

> Never shall I forget that night, the first night in camp, which has turned my life into one long night, seven times cursed and seven times sealed. Never shall I forget that smoke. Never shall I forget the little faces of the children, whose bodies I saw turned into wreaths of smoke beneath a silent blue sky. Never shall I forget those flames that consumed my faith forever.

My first face-to-face meeting with Wiesel came about through my affiliation with Israel Bonds on the national level. A member of Israel Bond's national executive committee, Miles Lerman, suggested during the early 1980s that the organization sponsor an annual event directed at Holocaust survivors. The thinking was that survivors who had attained success in America would, in all likelihood, be strong Zionists and hence, Israel Bonds supporters.

The national Israel Bonds president, Ijo Rager, lived in New York at the time. He had developed a friendship with Wiesel years earlier, when they had both worked together in defense of Soviet Jewry. Rager approached Wiesel to become involved in Lerman's survivor initiative. He had persuaded Wiesel to host a reception at his Manhattan home to which I was invited. As I entered, I first met Wiesel's lovely wife, Marion, and was then introduced to a gentleman with whom I soon developed a long-standing friendship, Sigmund Strochlitz. Strochlitz was a Connecticut businessman and major Bond supporter who was perhaps Wiesel's closest friend. Today, Sig is deeply involved in providing support for Bar-Ilan University in Israel.

I was to again meet Wiesel through another mutual friend, Yechiel Kadishai. Kadishai and Wiesel became close during Wiesel's days as a reporter for the French newspaper, *L'arche* and the Israeli *Yediot Aharonot*. After getting to know Wiesel, I invited him to serve as a fellow at the Simona and Hart Hasten speaker's series we had established through the Jewish Studies program at Indiana University, and he graciously accepted.

During the amazing lecture series that ensued, Wiesel brilliantly explored many areas of his intellectual interest. One lecture, during which he discussed the purges and show trials carried out under Stalin's regime in the USSR, particularly caught my interest. I had been a lifelong fan of the writings of Hungarian-born Arthur Koestler, a Jabotinskyite and author of the powerful, and now classic, *Darkness at Noon*. The book, published in 1946, as well as the 1951 Broadway stage play which it inspired, both are the result of Koestler's disillusionment with and refutation of totalitarian Communist ideology. *Darkness at Noon* deals with an old idealistic Bolshevik, Rubashov, a victim of Stalin's rule of terror, who is imprisoned in 1938 and persuaded to confess to crimes against the state, of which he is totally innocent. The book is based upon eyewitness accounts of Stalin's notorious show trials.

Wiesel discussed Koestler's work and went on to pose a question. Why would highly intelligent former Stalin supporters, such as the real figures upon which Koestler's Rubashov character was based, continue to confess to the most outlandish of crimes once they found themselves on public trial? To point out that such confessions were extracted under duress is not a sufficient answer, Wiesel claimed. If asked by the Stalinist court if they were guilty of a specific, trumped up traitorous crime, the victims would often not only admit their guilt to the charge, but also go on to lay claim to having committed even more such crimes. When it came to their defense, rather than seeking to mitigate or justify their actions, those standing accused would, with unbelievable fervor, heap more mountains of "crimes against the state" upon their own heads. This behavior, repeated over and over, did not appear on the surface to make any sense. Simply admitting to the charge was sufficient to result in the ultimate punishment being meted out. What was to be gained by adding further fictitious crimes to one's name? After all, a prisoner could only be executed once.

Wiesel's theory, upon which he expounded during the lecture series, sought to explain this seemingly irrational behavior. Wiesel believed that, by adding more and more ludicrous charges to those being brought against them, the prisoners were, in effect, communicating their innocence to the world via the only channel open to them. Had they simply confessed to the original charges and meekly gone to their deaths, those observing the proceedings might have concluded that they were, to some degree, guilty of the crimes. By insisting that they were guilty of even more crimes, the victims were actually saying to the free world: "I am innocent. Just as I could not possibly be guilty of all of the crimes I have admitted to, so am I not guilty of any of them."

While Wiesel's "doth protest too much, methinks" theory seems to make sense to me, when I shared his thinking with Menachem Begin, the prime minister did not go along with it. Begin, having been a Soviet prisoner for several years, knew of such things via first-hand experience. He believed that the victims Wiesel discusses simply parroted the words fed to them by their captors because the prisoners' families were threatened with harm if they failed to cooperate fully.

Wiesel visited the Hebrew Academy in Indianapolis on numerous occasions, and his comments were consistently the same: He was very impressed with the high quality of the elementary school, but where, he would ask, is the high school? Despite several attempts, a high school program remains an unattained dream at this point, although I do place high hopes in the initiative that is currently underway. When the high school finally does open its doors, I intend to invite Wiesel to the opening ceremony and ask that he place the school's *mezuzah* on the doorpost.

Wiesel, of course, would stay as a guest in our home whenever he visited Indianapolis, and we developed a warm friendship. We share a love of Yiddish music. Sometimes this affection was manifested in impromptu song sessions held in our living room, with Elie's robust baritone accompanied by the strains of my mandolin.

After Menachem Begin received the Nobel Peace Prize in 1979, I mentioned to him that I felt Elie Wiesel would be another deserving recipient of this award. Begin said that he agreed and would recommend his name to the prize committee. I'm not certain that there was any connection, but Wiesel was, in fact, awarded the Peace Prize in 1986. In 1990, Wiesel again visited the Academy to receive its annual HAI-Life Community Service Award, presented each year to an individual or couple who has demonstrated exceptional support for education and Jewish values. In presenting the award to Wiesel, I recall commenting:

"Professor Wiesel everyone knows that you have received numerous awards, including the 1986 Nobel Peace Prize. Well, that's all very nice, but tonight I am pleased to present you with an award you can really be proud of, because it comes from the hearts of the hundreds of Jewish children that attend our day school."

Wiesel was also on hand in 1996 when Mark and I received the school's silver anniversary medal. Elie spoke beautifully that night and was obviously moved by the honor of publicly inscribing the final letters into the new 25th anniversary Torah scroll that the school had commissioned.

These days, we see Elie frequently whenever we visit New York. In fact, if I find myself in Manhattan on *Shabbos*, I will often see Elie in *shul* at the Fifth Avenue Synagogue. I was recently prompted to contact Elie after reading the second volume of his splendid autobiography, *All Rivers Run To The Sea*. In it, he writes extensively about the role of Moshe Dayan, who was serving as Begin's foreign minister, in bringing about the Camp David Peace Accords between Israel and Egypt. Wiesel attributes much credit to Dayan for the initiation of the peace process and tends to overlook the seminal role performed by Begin himself. I wrote to Elie in order to correct this oversight. In my letter I recounted how I had personally been on hand when Begin had met with the Romanian ambassador while dealings with Egypt were in their most embryonic stages (see Chapter 13). I was pleased and gratified when Elie wrote back that he agreed with me about Begin and Dayan's relative roles, and that he would make sure the section was properly re-written with the book's next printing.

There is perhaps no greater icon of Israeli political and military leadership than General Moshe Dayan. When Begin took office as prime minister in 1977, his first task was to assemble a government and appoint his cabinet. Living in the shadow of the Labor Party for nearly 30 years, the Likud Party, at this point, had very few well-known members outside of Begin. Begin wanted someone with name recognition to add legitimacy to his new regime. So, despite the fact that Dayan was universally blamed for Israel's ill preparedness during the Yom Kippur War in 1973, Begin invited him to serve as his foreign minister.

Begin, with his enlisted man's background, was somewhat in awe of generals. At one point he boasted to me: "Do you know how many generals I have on my cabinet? Eight! No one has had more!"

It was during one of my visits to the prime minister's office that Begin introduced me to his celebrity cabinet minister. At the time I was deeply involved in the Israel Bonds movement back home, and my first comment, upon being introduced to Dayan, was: "I could use General Dayan back home to help us sell Israel Bonds." Begin's response was positive.

"Of course. By all means. He should go," offered Begin, and then, turning to Dayan: "The next time you're in the US you should stop by and help out Hart."

Although I knew that Dayan was not fond of fund-raising, he nevertheless showed his deference by saying: "I'll go wherever you want me to go, Mr. Prime Minister."

And so it was that Moshe Dayan was booked as the featured speaker at the annual Indianapolis/Israel Dinner of State in October, 1977. I had arranged to transport him in and out of our community using a private plane borrowed from Indianapolis resident, Melvin Simon, founder of Simon Malls. Dayan arrived early in the day, along with national Israel Bonds president, Michael Arnon. I escorted Dayan to the guest room of our home and suggested he get some rest before the reception. As an incentive to generate greater Bond sales, I had scheduled a private reception at our home immediately prior to the dinner. Those committing to purchase $10,000 or more in Israel Bonds were invited to our home for the reception and a "photo opportunity" with the famous general.

Although Dayan had been briefed about the reception, when the time came for him to make an appearance, he refused to come downstairs, claiming to be tired. I presumed he did not understand the nature of the program, so I tried to explain:

"Mr. Dayan, we have a few dozen people downstairs who are very anxious to meet you. These are the most prominent members of our Jewish community and they have all agreed to make additional large Bond purchases in your honor."

"I'm not coming down there. I'm tired and I want to rest," he stated, sounding every bit the prima donna.

"But, Mr. Dayan," I implored, "I invited these people here to meet you. If you don't come down and shake a few hands, they'll be very upset."

"No, no way. I'm not in the mood right now," he said brusquely. I was starting to get really peeved.

"You know, Mr. Dayan, you're not doing this for me, just like I'm not doing this for myself. We're both doing it for Bonds and for Israel."

"You don't talk to me like that," he said in a patronizing tone. "I'm the general and if I say no, it's no." There was not much I could say at this point, so I turned and began to walk out of the room. Fortunately, Michael Arnon had been standing in the hallway listening to this exchange and he motioned for me to wait another moment. Arnon understood that Dayan had insulted me and was about to cause a disaster. He went in to the room and took Dayan aside, looked him in the eye, and began speaking to him softly in Hebrew:

"Listen, it's important that you go down, otherwise it will create a real stink." I saw Dayan nod his head in agreement. He then approached me, a bit more warmly, and tried to account for his deplorable behavior:

"You know, it's because of the photographers that I didn't want to come down," he said apologetically. "Because I only have one eye, the flash from the cameras really causes me problems."

"We know that, General Dayan," I said. "We've told everyone that no photos are permitted, and the professional photographer is using lights, but no flash."

In the end, Dayan attended the reception and then spoke at the sold-out dinner, where record amounts of Israel Bonds were purchased. Despite the success of the event, I was upset all evening by Dayan's arrogant and pretentious behavior. I was so steamed that I completely forgot about the 100 copies of Dayan's recent autobiography that I had purchased to give out as gifts during the reception. As Dayan was leaving, I mentioned this oversight to him and he was livid.

"You had copies of my book?! And you didn't give them out?!" he exclaimed. "Why didn't you tell me? I would have loved to autograph them for everybody."

"Whoa, don't you remember?" I said. "You didn't even want to come downstairs. You told me you were a big general. I didn't want to upset you again by asking you to sign those books."

"You're right. I should not have acted in such a way. Please accept my apologies, Hart," he said sincerely. We shook hands and I said good-bye to the general.

Interestingly, my first meeting with Israel's current prime minister, Ariel Sharon, took place in a very similar manner to that with Dayan. I first met Sharon, known to be both charismatic and, at times, perplexing, when he was serving under Begin as Agriculture Minister. I was sitting in Yechiel Kadishai's office, adjacent to Begin's, during the early days of the first term, and I spotted Sharon seated in the reception area waiting to see Begin. The Prime Minister came out of his office and motioned for me to come into the waiting room so he could introduce me.

"This is my friend from America, Hart Hasten," said Begin in his mannered style. As I shook hands with Sharon, I looked at the prime minister and said: "I could use General Sharon back in the United States." Begin understood what I meant. I was at this time very involved in raising money for the Tel Chai Fund, and a celebrity like Sharon could help me open a lot of doors – and maybe even kick down a few of them.

"By all means," said Begin. "If he's able to go and help, he should do so."

"I'll do whatever you ask me to do, Mr. Prime Minister," said Sharon in a deferential tone. "If you tell me to go to America, I will do so."

Within a few months, Sharon and I traveled across the country together, meeting with major donors one-on-one. We succeeded in raising substantial sums for Tel Chai as we toured the US, meeting with every major Jewish phi-lanthropist we could. We stopped off to have another go at Abe Spiegel in Los Angeles, who happened to be crazy about Sharon. He grabbed Sharon as soon as we arrived and began kissing him wildly. We wound up receiving a $5,000 gift from him this time around.

It was no trouble lining up potential donors. As soon as I mentioned that "General Sharon wants to speak with you about something very impor-tant," the doors were thrown wide open for us. At one point during our tour, Sharon asked if I knew Hank Greenspun, the publisher of the *Las Vegas Sun*. I told him that Hank and I were good friends.

"So, let's go to Las Vegas to meet him," suggested Sharon.

Hank was thrilled to have the great General Sharon visit him. He set up a breakfast meeting with thirteen Jewish community leaders, at which we succeeded in raising a record amount of money, well into six figures. After Sharon addressed the group, Hank gave a stem-winder of a pitch. He was a first-class solicitor, not permitting anyone to leave the room until every donor had given him a check. Sharon and I stayed in Las Vegas for a few more hours and tried to take in some of the sights. While Sharon was not much of a gambler, his appetite was legendary. I recall dining with him at the Jerusalem Hilton some years later and watching in amazement as he ordered, and then swiftly devoured, two filet mignons one after the other.

It was during one of Sharon's fund-raising junkets to New York that the subject of his appetite came up again. I had been approached by noted television producer and good friend, Sandy Frank, to arrange for a meeting with Sharon. I had met Sandy through Menachem Begin, who was Sandy's hero and whom he had supported for many years. Sandy was, and continues to be, a very colorful and somewhat outspoken figure. He absolutely adored General Sharon, but he knew him via his reputation only and desperately wanted to meet him in person. I instructed Sandy to come up to the Gen-eral's hotel room for a brief get-together to discuss the Tel Chai Fund. Sandy showed up at the appointed time, marched into the room, shook hands with Sharon and immediately burst out with the following:

"General Sharon, I'm a big admirer of yours, but you simply have got to lose some weight. And you've got to do it right away." He wouldn't stop. "Otherwise you're going to die of a heart attack. I feel so strongly about this that I'm prepared to make you a deal. For every pound you lose, I'll donate $1,000 to your fund. Lose twenty pounds and I'll give you $20,000." Sandy presented this offer with all the enthusiasm of a Hollywood game show host.

I think he expected Sharon to immediately begin doing push-ups as Frank peeled off a $20 bill for each one.

Sharon gazed at me wide-eyed and incredulous, as if to say: "Where did you find this guy?" I just shrugged. But Sharon, as is his manner when in the presence of potential donors, remained very polite and collected.

"Yes, I guess I should lose some weight," he said feigning sincerity. "I'll start working on it right away. Thanks for your concern." Sharon was hoping to bring the conversation to a close, but Sandy was just getting warmed up.

"You know my brother, a very well-known doctor, wrote a book about obesity and heart disease. You absolutely must read his book. It will change your life, I promise you." Sharon was dumbfounded and speechless. Taking this as a sign of encouragement, Sandy grabbed the hotel telephone and dialed his New York office.

"Hi, Marlene," he barked to his secretary, "I'm over here at the Hilton with General Sharon. I want you to bring over a copy of my brother's book right away. That's right, the one about the heart attacks and fat people. Yeah, get it over here to Room 1722 right away. Thanks."

As we waited for the book to be delivered, Sharon valiantly tried to make small talk.

"So this book is by your brother? A doctor?" asked Sharon.

"That's right," answered Sandy.

"What sort of doctor is he, may I ask?" Sharon asked.

"Well, actually my brother died a few years ago," said Sandy, "but when he was alive, he was a real advocate of physical fitness and a healthy diet." Sharon nearly fell out of his chair and, to this day, still reminds me about this encounter whenever I suggest that he should meet with another American supporter. "He's not going to give me a hard time about my weight, is he?" Sharon would ask with a wink.

Over the years, General Sharon and I have kept in touch, and I have followed his political career with interest. I was very pleased when, by late 2000, it appeared that he would head the Likud ticket and run against the incumbent Labor prime minister, Ehud Barak in the February 6 election. Like many observers, I believed that Barak had been totally misguided in agreeing to partition Jerusalem during his recent talks at Camp David with Clinton and Arafat. I believed that Sharon was the right man to replace him and was prepared to do whatever I could to help his election chances. So, of course, I was pleased when I received a call in early January 2001, that General Sharon wished to meet with me. I said that I was available immediately, and so a meeting with the candidate was arranged for that afternoon.

I met with Sharon at Likud headquarters in Tel Aviv (*Metzudat Ze'ev*) and we had a long private discussion. Of course we began by reminiscing about our fund-raising days in Las Vegas and elsewhere. As we were talking, someone brought in a new portrait of Sharon's wife who had passed away less than one year before. Sharon examined the painting and was visibly moved. With real tears in his eyes, he shook his head and said softly: "I loved her so much, Hart."

"I know, Arik," I consoled him. "I could tell from that beautiful eulogy you delivered at her funeral." Sharon turned and stared at me in surprise.

"You were there!?" he marveled.

"Yes, but I didn't speak with you at the time." I explained. "There were so many thousands of people, I didn't want to fight my way up to you." I could see a new mellowness, and perhaps even a tenderness, in Sharon since becoming a widower. He seemed less overbearing and bellicose, although it was clear that his political sentiments were etched in stone.

He explained that he had asked to see me because he, and the party, needed help. He reminded me about my days as president of Herut Zionists of America and spoke to me as a fellow Likudnik. I was eager to help and told him so.

"I'll do whatever I can, Arik," I pledged. "But first, do you mind if I give you some advice?"

"Please go ahead," he said.

"You know, I'm going to be straight with you, Arik," I stated. "I'm not like a lot of these folks who advise you. I'm not looking for a minister's position or any type of job, so I'm going to be blunt." He frowned but said nothing.

"I saw you on TV last night and you know what? You looked terrible. First of all, what were you doing on TV in the first place? The polls show you're leading by about 17 points. Why risk saying something stupid on TV that could only hurt you? Here's my advice. Stay off TV and away from the reporters. Let the media grill Barak. Let him put his foot in his mouth."

"Do you know that Barak wants to debate with me on TV?" he asked. "Like in America!"

"Yes, I know. Don't you dare debate him," I proclaimed growing more impassioned.

"But I'll have to give him a few damn debates," Sharon muttered. "He's asking for ten of them, which is ridiculous. But I have to do two or three."

"Are you asking me?" I questioned. "If you're asking me, I'm telling you: No debates!"

"Okay, okay," he said, "but I can't avoid TV reporters altogether. I need to say something."

"Say something personal," I advised him. "Don't talk about how you're going to fix the economy or the highways. None of that stuff. Talk about your personal history. The other side has the public convinced that you're a warmonger. If you get elected, they say, the first thing you'll do is start a war. Go on TV and talk about how nobody knows more about the horror of war than you. Tell them the same stories you've told me. How you saw your comrades on both sides of you killed and that you survived somehow. And mention that you were injured – how many times?"

"Too many," he said.

"You carry wounds from every one of Israel's wars. Mention that fact."

"Should I tell them that I'm...." he struggled for the word in English, finally calling in his aide, Ra'anan Gissin, who held a PhD from an American university. "How do you say in English..." he said mentioning the word in Hebrew.

"Handicapped," replied Gissin.

"No, no, no," I protested. "Don't say that you're handicapped. Disabled is a better word."

"That's right," said Sharon. "I've been declared 60 percent disabled by the doctors."

"That makes you sound like a health risk," I advised. "Just say that, as a general, you know the horrors of war better than anyone and that, because of your background, you will do all you can to avoid war."

I wasn't sure at the time if any of my advice would be heeded, but I soon learned that Sharon had decided not to participate in any televised debates, not even one. I also read a Deborah Sontag column published in the *New York Times* a few weeks later, in which she quotes Sharon as saying: "I know what war is, and the last thing I would want is to start a war."

It was my intention to remain in Israel through the election on February 6, but as the result of a freak accident, I severely injured my arm, trying to break a fall as I walked along the beach in Tel Aviv. I required surgery and flew back to the United States for the operation. Fortunately, I was released by my doctor a few weeks later and was able to return to Israel in time for the election. Simona questioned my judgment on this, but I told her: "I want to be there to celebrate Sharon's victory."

I don't know how much of a role my advice played in the outcome, but the fact remains that Sharon was elected by the largest popular landslide in

Israel's history, garnering over 63% of the vote. It was clear that the Israeli public disapproved of Barak's handling of relations with the Palestinians and had decided to "throw the rascal out."

Prime Minister-elect Sharon graciously invited us to the victory celebration held a few days after the election. Simona and I had a chance to get away from the chaos and to chat privately with him for about half an hour. Sharon thanked me repeatedly for my counsel during the campaign. He went on to mention that President Bush had invited him to the White House and that he was planning to be in the US soon. Upon hearing this, I could not restrain myself from offering more advice.

"Arik, I heard you say something during the campaign that I felt was a mistake," I said. Simona immediately corrected me.

"Don't call him Arik," she scolded. "He's the prime minister now."

"No, no," said Sharon, "you two should always call me Arik."

"Simona is correct," I continued, "Mr. Prime Minister-elect, I heard you state on TV that you were not a religious man. This is a mistake. Especially when you meet with Bush, who is a deeply religious man."

"You're right," he said, "but I was answering a question about the difference between me and some of the religious party candidates."

"But you didn't mean that you're not religious," I pointed out. "You meant that you're not observant. You are religious. I saw your picture in the newspaper yesterday. I saw how you went to the *Kotel* to pray after winning the election. I saw you at your wife's funeral wearing a *kippa*. That means you are definitely a religious man. You're just not an observant Jew."

"That's exactly what I was trying to say," he exclaimed.

"But you're not coming across correctly," I told him. "In America, if you say you're not religious, that means you're an atheist. And that would not sit too well with Bush who, you know, is a born-again Christian just like Jimmy Carter." I alluded to Carter, since Sharon knew that one reason Carter had so much respect for Begin in the 1970s was because he perceived Begin to be a deeply religious man.

"Wait, wait, don't say another word," Sharon admonished. "Let me write this down." Sharon had developed the habit of jotting down notes in a little notebook he always carried. He would pull it out whenever he heard something he felt was worth remembering. I watched as he wrote down the word "observant" in his little notebook and committed it to memory.

I'm pleased to report that, these days, Sharon has stopped referring to himself as "not religious," preferring the term "not observant."

Sharon did travel to the US the following June and we flew to New York to meet with him at his hotel. Sharon was scheduled to meet President Bush for the first time the following day in Washington. The meeting was taking place shortly after a horrific act of terror in which a suicide bomber had murdered 21 teenagers at a Tel Aviv nightspot.

I suggested to Sharon during our meeting that he stress the fact with Bush that the victims were teenagers. "Bush will be able to relate to that, since he is the father of two teenage girls." Sharon went for his notebook to jot this down, but found it was missing. "Who has my notebook?" he bellowed and four or five aides scurried around the suite searching for it. Luckily, it was soon retrieved and Sharon marked down: "Bush / teenage daughters." We wished him luck at the White House and said our farewells. According to news reports, the meetings with Bush went very well.

In July, we once again traveled to Israel for my participation in the Maccabiah Games. I was a member of the American team, competing in Men's Tennis, in this quadrennial athletic event that has been dubbed "the Jewish Olympics." The prime minister was always aware of my presence in Israel, so I was not too surprised when, after the games ended, I received a message from one of his aides, Meirav, requesting that Simona and I meet with him at his home. The meeting venue was changed, first to his office, and, finally, I was instructed to come to the Knesset at 12:30. Meirav met us at the gate and ushered us through security. She began directing us towards the Prime Minister's Office.

"Thank you for guiding us, but we know the way," I told her.

"You do?" she responded.

"We visited Prime Minister Begin here many times," Simona explained. "Netanyahu, too."

We were shown to a private dining room off the large main dining hall, where some refreshments had been laid out for us. Sharon arrived a few minutes late and apologized for being tardy. He explained that a security matter had detained him.

"One of our rockets hit a Hamas terrorist in Nablus just now," he explained. "I'm not sure if we killed him or not, but his car was completely destroyed." A few moments later he received a phone call confirming the kill.

"You know, Mr. Prime Minister," I said after the phone call, "you are being accused in the media of assassinating Palestinians." He shrugged, palms up, as if to say "What can I do?"

"If I were you, I would say 'We're not assassinating anyone. What we are doing is killing the assassins.'" Sharon appeared to like this phrase and immediately pulled out his notebook and jotted it down. He next phoned his press secretary and instructed him, in Hebrew, to use this wording when discussing today's action.

"I wish I had someone on my staff who understood these public relations matters as well as you do, Hart," he complimented me. Feeling encouraged, I decided to offer further advice.

"Another point, Mr. Prime Minister," I went on. "Whenever an incident is reported in the American media, they always use a phrase like 'the cycle of violence continues.' Sometimes it's the 'circle of violence' or 'the spiral of violence.' But it's always depicted like two feuding gangster families carrying out vendettas against each other. If we accept this, we are agreeing that our actions have a moral equivalency to theirs. And this is not the case. You must do all you can to dispel this image. There is no 'cycle of violence,' there is only 'crime and punishment.'"

From his hurried scribbling, I could tell he liked this phrase as well. Once again, he picked up the phone to his press secretary and directed: "You tell them, when you talk to the media today, it's not a 'cycle of violence.' It's really 'crime and punishment.'"

I was pleased to see that, from this point on, Sharon, as well as other Israeli and American leaders, have refrained from using the "cycle of violence" euphemism. For example, I read that during a meeting with Egyptian Foreign Minister Ahmed Maher on December 6, 2001, Sharon told him that there is "no cycle of violence; there is Palestinian terror and Israeli efforts to end it." Sharon's statement was in response to a call made by Maher for the two sides to end the cycle of violence that has plagued the region for the past 14 months.

Sharon thanked me for the suggestions, but I still had a more serious bone to pick with the prime minister before I left.

"Mr. Prime Minister," I began and then presented him with a reporter-style question: "When we spoke in New York last month, you assured me that you would not permit your foreign minister, Shimon Peres, to meet with Yasser Arafat. Yet, I read that the two did meet last week in Portugal. Why did you change your mind?"

"Oh, Hart, it's just politics," he said with an exasperated motion. "Keeping this unity government together is very important to me. I remember that you were afraid that, if Peres spoke with him, then the next thing would be Arafat getting an invitation to the White House. Well, Bush told me that there is no way that Arafat would ever be invited, so I felt it would not be a problem for Peres to speak with him." I didn't fully accept this explanation, since it gave the appearance that Peres was conducting his own unilateral foreign policy, but I decided to back off. My next question was a cream puff:

"By the way, Mr. Prime Minister, could you tell me what they talk about when they meet? Does Peres report back to you after such a meeting?" Sharon gave a half-smile and looked over both shoulders before responding.

"Whatever they talk about – it's irrelevant," he said, waving his hand dismissively. "Besides, if I really want to send a message to Arafat, I have my son, Omri, who I use to communicate with him. I don't rely upon Peres for this."

I could not help but recall this conversation with Sharon when, in December 2001, after a series of devastating terrorist attacks, he wisely terminated relations with Arafat and publicly labeled him as "irrelevant."

There was more I wanted to say to Sharon about Peres, and this seemed to be the right time. "Can't you control his statements?" I asked. "For example, not long ago he came out with this: 'Everyone knows that there is no military solution to the Arab/Israeli conflict.' Somehow this nonsense got picked up by the media and now our own Secretary of State, Colin Powell, is going around saying the same stupid thing. You should clarify this point, Mr. Prime Minister. Tell them that there is always a military solution, but we prefer to avoid it if possible." Sharon nodded in agreement as he scribbled this down in his notes.

Finally, after so much berating, I felt I should say something positive. "Mr. Prime Minister, I was at the recent Maccabiah Games, and I was impressed with your remarks at both the opening and closing ceremonies." Normally the prime minister only appears to open the games. Merely holding the games this year was an act of great courage on his part, as I pointed out, since there was much pressure to have them cancelled for security reasons. Sharon, I was sure, presumed that I had attended the games strictly as a spectator.

"You may not be aware of this, Mr. Prime Minister, but I participated in the competition. I played tennis."

"You?! You are an athlete?" he said in a shocked tone. I pulled out the silver medal I had won and showed it to him. He could not get over it. He examined the medal closely and called over several of his aides. "Come here. Look at this. I want to show you what my friend has won. Hart won a silver medal in the Maccabiah. Look. I want you to see this." He seemed more excited about this medal than even I was.

Over the past year I have observed Sharon's stature as premier grow, as he valiantly executes a delicate political high-wire act, maintaining a unity government while remaining true to his guiding principles. As of this writing, Israel is still being plagued by suicide bombings and other terrorist attacks against innocent civilians. Sharon is courageously leading the Israeli nation in a war of national defense and has gained US support in the campaign to root out world-wide terrorism. I believe that under his leadership, Israel, with the cooperation of the US, will prevail and eventually succeed in eliminating this scourge.

Sharon's predecessor as Likud prime minister was Benjamin Netanyahu who, despite having committed major blunders while in office, still enjoys popular support and may soon seek a political comeback. I was first introduced to Netanyahu by the former Israeli ambassador to the US, Moshe (Misha) Arens in 1988. Netanyahu was serving as Minister in Washington under Arens' successor, Meir Rosenne, and was something of an Arens' protégé. I was immediately impressed with this young, handsome man and his total command of American English. I, of course, was aware of his family background. His father, Ben-Tzion, was a noted professor and Jabotinsky supporter, and his late brother, Yonatan, was the hero, and sole Israeli casualty, of the incredible "Raid on Entebbe" rescue mission in Uganda back in 1976. Over the course of several meetings, I became even more impressed with Netanyahu and his deep commitment to the principles I held dear, as well as with his understanding of international terrorism and how to go about combating it. He knew of my relationship with Menachem Begin, and since he was also an admirer of the man, he wanted to learn all he could from me about the reclusive former PM.

Shortly thereafter, Netanyahu was appointed by Prime Minister Shamir to serve as Israel's ambassador to the United Nations, and Simona and I were able to visit with him whenever we found ourselves in New York. My daughter Renée was a student at Indiana University at the time and was deeply involved in pro-Israel activities on campus. This was a time when anti-Zionists and Holocaust revisionists were waging a campaign on American campuses to win over the hearts and minds of America's young people. Renée worked very hard at supporting Israel and combating this wave of anti-Jewish propaganda. She had asked me to contact UN Ambassador Netanyahu and request that he appear at a pro-Israel student rally she was organizing. I did call him with the request and he gladly complied, delivering a memorable and inspiring speech to the large student gathering. Naturally there were some pro-Arab hecklers planted in the crowd. But Netanyahu made quick work of them, disarming their attacks with humor and a razor-sharp wit.

I saw in Netanyahu the ambition, the leadership qualities, and the intellectual capacity of a future Israeli prime minister. I would always encourage his political aspirations and was pleased whenever I would spot one of his many appearances on American television. The us media had made him their favorite Israeli spokesperson because of his excellent command of English and his charming onscreen presence. This fact made him a more popular politician in America than in Israel.

I was approached by Harry Nadler, Frank Newman's successor as executive director of the local Jewish Federation, to learn if I could invite Ambassador Netanyahu to Indianapolis for the Federation's annual fund-raising dinner. I said that I would do so, although I recalled that Netanyahu had a reputation for canceling out on speaking engagements at the last minute. I remembered friends advising me: "Don't bring in Bibi (his nickname), because he'll tell you that he'll be there and then cancel for no reason at the last minute." I mentioned this concern to Harry and then assured him not to worry because "...he might pull that stuff with someone else, but he's not going to do that with me." So the appearance was booked and the publicity went out.

Sure enough, on the morning of the event, I received a phone call from Netanyahu:

"Hello, Hart. This is Bibi," he said. "Listen, I'm awfully sorry but I won't be able to make it tonight. I just learned that I have to be at the un tomorrow morning at 8 am for a vote."

I would have none of it. I said: "Bibi, you're going to be in Indianapolis tonight because you promised you would be. I told my friends you're not going to do this to me. If you don't show, it will be humiliating for me."

"But Hart, I have to be here for the vote in the morning," he pleaded.

"I'll see that you get back alright," I assured him.

"How will you do that?" he asked.

"How about a private plane to pick you up and deliver you back?" He agreed that this would work, and so I chartered a Cessna and a pilot from New York who flew Bibi back and forth on the 800-mile trip.

Since I had made a sizable investment in getting Netanyahu to the dinner, I wanted to enjoy some sort of mileage from his visit. It was during this period that attitudes were beginning to change at the Federation and there was some movement, thanks in large part to Harry Nadler's efforts, towards extending financial support to the Hebrew Academy for the first time. I felt that a solid endorsement of our school, or at least of Jewish day school education in general, by someone of the ambassador's stature would go a long way towards changing attitudes at the Federation.

I asked Bibi to insert a plug for the Academy into his remarks, and he agreed to do so. Sadly, and to my disappointment, he either forgot or some-one from the Federation got to him, because he made no mention whatso-ever of either the school or of Jewish education.

I was also able to enlist Bibi's assistance during this period on behalf of another project with which I was deeply involved. We were attempting to excavate Fortress Betar. The word "Betar" had been selected by Jabotinsky as the name of the Revisionist youth movement in the 1930s. The name is an acronym for Brith Trumpeldor, and it also is the name of an historic loca-tion mentioned in the Talmud's account of the legendary anti-Roman zealot and last president of ancient Israel, Simon Bar Kokhba.

The citadel at Betar was the site of Bar Kokhba's heroic last stand against the Roman siege during the Second Revolt in 135 CE. Fortress Betar is con-sidered to be a somewhat smaller version of the well-known Masada fortress conquered by the Romans during the First Revolt. Vestiges of the Roman encampment are visible surrounding Betar, just as at Masada, and evidence remains that shows how the Romans used the same sort of ramp to assault the rebels at Betar. Whereas, at Masada, the trapped zealots opted to com-mit mass suicide rather than to fall under Roman conquest, at Fortress Betar, the Jews fought on until the bitter end and were finally vanquished by thirst and starvation.

In 1960, the famed Dead Sea Scrolls had provided evidence that, for the first time, established Bar Kokhba as having been a real historical figure and not merely the subject of Jewish legend. This spurred the work of famed Israeli military leader and archeologist, Yigael Yadin, who was responsible for the excavations at Masada.

The Betar project was brought to my attention by Yadin in the mid 1980s. I agreed to support it and began to educate myself about its history. Begin, as well, was extremely interested in the project and would question me about it extensively during those years.

When Yadin died in 1984, the project was taken over by his assistant, David Ussishkin. After many months of preparation, the actual excavations were just getting underway when the Palestinian uprising known as the *Inti-fada* commenced, and the project had to be abandoned for security reasons. The site is now in Palestinian hands and is no longer being excavated.

Among the VIPs I escorted around the excavation site while it was active, were Netanyahu and his second wife, Fleur. I recall how she came across an ancient stone used by the Roman catapults to assail the fortress. Although no artifacts were to be removed from the site, she managed to smuggle it out. As a result of their visit, Bibi and Fleur agreed to hold a fund-raiser at their home in New York on behalf of the Betar project. Fleur passed around the stone missile and told its history to the group.

Thanks to this fund-raiser, we succeeded in raising enough money to pay for the excavations. Unfortunately this investment has been lost. I maintain hope that someday Fortress Betar will once again be under Israeli control and that we may continue to search for evidence of our people's heroic past.

In 1996, Netanyahu was running for prime minister against incumbent Shimon Peres, who had taken the reins of government after the assassination of Yitzchak Rabin. It was a very close race, and Bibi felt that he needed my assistance in garnering support from Menachem Begin's son, Benny, who was a member of the Knesset and a strong force within the Likud Party. I was vacationing at our condominium in Herzliya Pituach. You might even say I was hiding out, because very few people knew how to reach me. I have learned, however, that if an Israeli politico wants to find you in Israel, he will find you by hook or by crook. When it comes to politicians, you can always count on them to be there when they need you! Bibi found me and asked to meet with me at the King David Hotel in Jerusalem.

Netanyahu was seated in the lobby, smoking an enormous cigar, as I walked in. I sat down and he got right to the point.

"Benny is not supporting me in this thing and unfortunately we need him." Benny and Bibi were referred to, among party insiders, as "The Princes," and there was little love lost between the two rivals. Both men were from prominent Israeli families, and both had designs on the party leadership. They were at odds over the Likud Party's position on the Oslo Accords. Both men served on the party's executive committee, where they often wrangled over planks in the party platform. According to Bibi, the dispute had gotten so heated that Benny was on the verge of going public with his opinion that Netanyahu was "the wrong man for the job and I don't intend to vote for him." I agreed with Bibi that this sort of internecine squabbling could doom Likud's chances in the coming election. I offered to do what I could to resolve this matter.

"I know, Hart," said Bibi in desperation. "If your friend Benny goes public against me, I'm sunk." Bibi always enjoyed spicing up his speech with American idioms.

"Well you know that Benny's not very pragmatic. He's a very principled guy," I stated. "If his actions result in handing the election to Peres, he doesn't care. He'd rather be right than prime minister."

"Will you help me, Hart?" he pleaded. "Will you talk to him?" I certainly did not wish to see Peres get elected, so I responded instantly:

"I'll do all I can and I'll start right away," I pledged. Thus began several days of shuttle diplomacy. I ping-ponged back and forth between the two men's homes and offices trying to work out an agreement that would stave off political suicide. Benny Begin was intense in his dislike of Netanyahu.

"You don't know him like I do, Hart," Benny told me. "He is not very principled, and who knows what he might do as prime minister?"

After several days of haggling, there remained only a single issue dividing the two camps. It had to do with a plank, proposed by Netanyahu for inclusion in the party platform that was under consideration by the executive committee. Once I realized this, I devised a compromise that I hoped would provide us with a way out. I approached Benny:

"Benny, I know that in spite of how you feel about Bibi, you would not go against the party. Am I right?" I asked.

"Well, not publicly, at least," he replied.

"What if the executive committee should vote to accept Bibi's plank? Could I count on you then not to oppose him publicly?" Benny pondered this for a few moments.

"Well, I suppose if a majority of the committee supports Bibi, I'll have to keep silent," he agreed. When the meeting was convened and the vote taken, Bibi's plank did, in fact, receive approval. Benny, true to his word, did not voice his opposition to Netanyahu publicly during the campaign and Netanyahu was elected by a narrow margin. In the spirit of mending political fences, Prime Minister Netanyahu named Benny Begin to his cabinet to serve as minister of science.

I don't believe my actions resulted in Netanyahu's victory, but I do believe that if I had not acted, Benny's public condemnation of Bibi would have caused such a rift in the party that Peres would likely have wound up as the winner.

Once Netanyahu was elected as Israel's ninth prime minister in 1996, and with the new Likud regime in place, I was once again welcomed to the Knesset and the Prime Minister's Office in Jerusalem. My first impression when entering the Prime Minister's Office was that he had enlarged the clerical staff to include some very attractive young women. I'm sure they were all highly competent, as well as beautiful.

To a large degree, Benny Begin's warnings about Netanyahu proved to be warranted. Benny felt compelled to resign from the cabinet after witnessing Bibi give away Hebron in 1996 in an effort to keep the so-called "peace process" afloat. Bibi's willingness to alienate his party's right wing in his quest for international acclaim also cost him the support of a man who was soon to become his political rival, Ariel Sharon. While I was by no means happy with Bibi's performance as prime minister, I still believe that, had Peres been elected, things would have been much worse.

My most recent contact with Bibi took place during Passover 2001. We were observing the holiday at the Fontainebleau Hotel in Miami Beach, Florida. The hotel offered its annual kosher Passover package, in which our family had participated for many years. We were in the pleasant company of my daughter-in-law's family from New Jersey, the Laulichts and the Kushners. Laurie's uncle, Charlie Kushner, one of the nation's major apartment developers, had received a call from his friend, Bibi, who wanted to meet with him over breakfast. Charlie, knowing of my friendship with Bibi, asked me to join them.

The following morning Simona and I met up with Charlie and his wife, Seryl, at their table and a, few moments later, Bibi and his third wife, Sara, arrived. My son and daughter-in-law, Bernard and Laurie, stopped by for a while as well. After we had exchanged the requisite pleasantries, Bibi soon got to work expounding on his political vision and his need for support from American Jews, such as Charlie and me, who presumably shared that vision. I decided to speak up.

"You know, Bibi, if you really wanted to become prime minister again, then you made a terrible mistake," I announced. "You missed the opportunity to become the party leader because of your stance on general elections."

He immediately understood my reference and responded with a barely audible denial: "I did not make any mistake," he whispered. Then, speaking up: "You're a Sharon supporter. I know that." I agreed that I was a supporter of all the Likud prime ministers.

The mistake to which I was referring took place during the most recent Likud conference, held to name a party leader who would then become their nominee for the prime ministership. Netanyahu enjoyed a good deal of support among the party faithful who, because of his high standing in the polls, regarded him as electable despite his defeat back in 1999. But Bibi succeeded in alienating the Likud leadership through his stubborn insistence on calling for general elections and for his support of the popular election of Knesset representatives. At that time, only the prime minister was elected via a nationwide popular vote. He wanted to extend this practice to the entire Knesset, moving Israel further from the British parliamentary model and closer to the American electoral system. He argued that such a move would provide him with a clear majority in the Knesset and a strong mandate to govern. He would not be forced, he argued, to join into flimsy coalitions with his political enemies in order to form a government.

Bibi had seriously miscalculated, because the Likud Knesset members had no desire to see a general election called which would place their own seats in jeopardy. The idea of popular elections also did not sit well with them. Because of the party's unwillingness to call for general elections, Bibi withdrew his candidacy for the premiership, and the party stalwarts lined up behind his chief opponent, Ariel Sharon. Sharon had expressed his willingness to form a Unity Government and had assured everyone that he would not call for new elections. Sharon was named party leader and went on to a landslide victory in February, 2001.

Another reason for the collapse of support for Netanyahu within the party was the dismal job he had done as party leader during his years in office. When Netanyahu was defeated in his quest to be prime minister, he pulled the plug on his entire political career. He resigned from the Knesset and turned over party leadership to Sharon. According to all accounts, he had left the party organization in shambles and its coffers next to empty. Likud loyalists respected Sharon for the job he had done in cleaning up Bibi's mess. He had restored the party to a stable financial footing and had worked hard to rebuild the party structure.

After listening to my comments, Bibi remained in a state of denial and declined to acknowledge my interpretation of recent events. It's a fact that Netanyahu is young and still quite popular among the Israeli electorate. In Israeli politics, as in America, a politician's ability to garner votes is his most important single quality. Despite the antipathy of his party, I would certainly not discount the possibility of Netanyahu's making some sort of political comeback in the next few years.

It was during our stay in Miami that I was asked to deliver a speech on the Middle East situation to the Fontainebleau Passover attendees. These Passover packages typically attracted between 800 and 1,000 guests and, in addition to the Passover religious observance, the program always included addresses by prominent speakers on topics of interest to the Jewish community. I had decided to talk about Arafat. When I announced my choice of topic to my *mechooten*, Murray Laulicht, he expressed some dismay. Murray, whose political leanings are far to the left of my own, did not share my opinion that Arafat was a "master terrorist." In fact, when I so characterized Arafat, Murray responded with: "Well, wasn't Begin also considered a terrorist?" I was speechless.

"Murray," I finally said, "that's not the smartest thing I've ever heard you say!" While it's considered glib to suggest that one man's terrorist is another man's freedom fighter, the ability to distinguish between the two is of paramount importance. To label Begin as a terrorist is every bit as absurd as equating Samuel Adams with Osama bin Laden.

Despite Murray's apprehensions, I proceeded to deliver a thirty-minute address about why Arafat was not a suitable peace partner for Israel. I concluded with the following comments:

"People often ask me, 'Well, if the Oslo Accords do not represent the correct path towards peace, what would you propose in their place?' or, more simply: 'How would you deal with Arafat?' I answer by telling them a little story. How many of you here remember the movie or the play called 'Stalag 17' about life in a World War II prison camp? Raise your hands if you do." About half the people in the room raised their hands.

"I see that quite a few of you do remember it. Good. Let me remind you about one particular scene that I thought was quite memorable. It has to do with one of the prisoners, Animal, and his good friend, Shapiro. Animal, who is desperately in love with movie actress Betty Grable, is being driven crazy by his desire to visit the adjoining camp filled with beautiful Russian women prisoners. It is the task of his buddy, Shapiro, to restrain him and keep him from this deadly desire. 'You can't go over there, Animal,' he would plead. 'Do you see that line? If you cross that line, those guards will kill you?' But Animal doesn't care about the danger. He hurls himself through the mud, in a desperate drive to reach the women's camp. Shapiro, using all his available strength, attempts to drag him back. 'Animal. You can't do this. Do you see the Nazis in those guard towers? They're getting ready to shoot. Come back, do you hear me?'

'I don't care what happens. I gotta go,' shouts Animal. Finally Shapiro hits on an idea.

'Listen to me, Animal. If you come back with me, I promise you a date with Betty Grable as soon as we get back to the States.' Animal is skeptical, but at least he's momentarily distracted from his foolhardy quest.

'How are you gonna get me a date with Betty Grable?' he asks sullenly.

'Well, it's like this,' shoots back Shapiro. 'I have a cousin who lives in Los Angeles and he works for the gas company. My cousin knows Betty Grable's address. I'm going to find out her address, and then you and me – we're going to go to her house and knock on her door. And then Betty Grable will come to the door, see? And when she does, I will say to her: "Betty, you have won the 'Girl I'd Most Like To Be Behind Barbed Wire With' and here is your prize, a date with Animal" And then I point to you.'

Animal considers this for a moment and then asks, laconically: 'And what if she don't want me?'

'Well, if she don't want you then she don't get nuttin!' snapped Shapiro in his best Brooklynese.

Well, ladies and gentlemen, this is how I would deal with Mr. Arafat, who has not seen fit to accept Israel's most generous offers. If he don't want 'em, then he don't get nuttin! How would I deal with Arafat? I would put my best offer on the table and say take it or leave it."

This was not the first time that the subject of Arafat had come up during one of these Miami Passover programs. Six years before, in 1995, I was a participant in a Middle East panel discussion featuring Senator Joseph Lieberman and Rabbi Yitzchak Greenberg, the head of the CLAL movement, a trans-denominational Jewish unity organization. Greenberg was later named by President Clinton to serve as the director of the United States Holocaust Memorial Council in Washington, DC. He was highly instrumental in convincing Clinton to issue an eleventh hour pardon for Jewish fugitive financier, Marc Rich.

The panel discussion took place shortly before the famed handshake on the White House lawn between Yitzchak Rabin and Yasser Arafat. Greenberg had just delivered a strong endorsement of the Oslo peace process and expressed his confidence in Arafat as a true partner for peace. I could tell from the crowd reaction that he had the support of about half of the audience. Not surprisingly, I was not among them.

What bothered me the most was that Yitz Greenberg enjoyed a well-deserved reputation as a leading Jewish intellectual and philosopher. Because of his standing, his misguided view of the situation was capable of influencing a great many people. This fact was getting under my skin and I decided to speak up.

"You know, Rabbi Greenberg," I said as I stood up, "with all due respect, you remind me so much of those left-wing pre-World War II Jewish intellectuals. I'm talking about the socialists, the communists and the Bundists who embraced Stalinism in the face of the Nazi onslaught. They also knowingly misled our people into thinking that they could find refuge from Fascism under the banner of Communism. My father, of blessed memory, was no intellectual. He was a simple man, with a lot of common sense, who believed in seeing things the way they really were. He taught us that Communism was wrong and that it represented a worthless ideology. Those Jewish leftists flying the red banner were also intelligent enough to understand this, but yet they chose to be intellectually dishonest." Turning my remarks to the audience, I went on.

"And it is that same sort of intellectual dishonesty that I am reminded of when I listen to Yitz Greenberg's statements. He knows the truth; yet, for whatever reason, he chooses to mislead others into believing that appeasement will bring us closer to peace. It is the responsibility of the intellectual leadership among us to honestly apply their intellect to the problems we face and not be swayed by what is considered politically correct or expedient at the moment."

I could see that my words were getting through to the audience. Emboldened, I pointed my finger at Greenberg and announced passionately "Yitz, stop misleading our people! Stop telling us stories about all the great things that Arafat is going to do and all the good things that are going to happen. You know better. You know that Arafat is a master terrorist and that nothing of the rosy picture you are painting will ever materialize. You are intentionally misleading our people and I insist that you stop doing it."

I sat down to the sound of enthusiastic applause and waited for a response to my indictment. But there was none forthcoming from Greenberg. He had evidently chosen to ignore my accusations, although a number of others rose to his defense. Among them, surprisingly, was Sam Halpern, a prominent Jewish philanthropist and a lay leader of the Religious Zionist movement. Despite my call for intellectual honesty, Greenberg and others continued their public pronouncements and misrepresentations until, finally, the events of 2000 and 2001 convinced them that Oslo was a failed formula for peace and that they were wrong to place their faith in the likes of a self-serving, unrepentant terrorist like Arafat.

It was during Rabin's second term as Prime Minister that Ehud Olmert was elected mayor of Jerusalem. Ehud is another of the young princes of the Likud Party. We first met during one of his tours of the US on behalf of Israel Bonds. He was being billed as the "youngest person ever elected to the Israeli Knesset." A cigar aficionado and a brilliant attorney, Ehud attempted to interest me in a number of Israeli business ventures over the years, including the purchase of the Jerusalem Hilton. When he decided to run for mayor of Jerusalem, I gave him my full support. These days we enjoy a standing invitation to stop by City Hall, whenever we are in Jerusalem, for a good *schmooze* with the city's charismatic and highly capable mayor.

I first met Begin's successor, Yitzchak Shamir, when he was serving as the Speaker of the Knesset. He was known as a dedicated and highly capable leader and had served as one of Begin's comrade-in-arms during the struggle for Israeli independence. Shamir had been the chief of the Lehi underground detachment, also known as the Stern Group, during the British mandate. Begin had great respect for Shamir and had always envisioned him as his successor. Shamir recognized that Begin's prime ministership was going to be a hard act to follow and decided to adhere closely to Begin's policies. In so doing, he won the admiration of many both within and outside the party.

As explained earlier, by 1985 Shamir and Peres were serving in a National Unity government that provided for a two-year rotation of the premiership between the Likud and Labor parties. A decision was made while Peres held the office that allowed for over 1,000 convicted Palestinian terrorists, released via a prisoner exchange, to return to their homes in the territories. This decision led directly to the Intifada uprising later that year. The Intifada erupted during Shamir's turn in office and placed enormous stress on his leadership. Yitzchak Rabin was serving as minister of defense at the time and was widely quoted when he boasted: "We will break their bones!"

The Intifada was marked by intense street fighting, pitting young Palestinians, armed with stones, against well-equipped Israeli troops assigned to quell the disturbances. But all was not as it seemed. It became clear that the Intifada was not so much a popular uprising of liberation as a finely orchestrated exercise in media manipulation. Under the direction of Yasser Arafat, the street fighters would put on daily performances just as soon as the television cameras were set up. Arafat himself was quoted at the time cynically remarking: "We are only a stone's throw away from achieving our goal." Arafat, a student of the American civil rights movement, was early to understand the vast power of the new media phenomenon CNN. He wisely recognized that the staging of such scenes day after day would be transmitted around the globe and would serve to build up enormous world sympathy for his cause. Every half hour, on the half hour, CNN would show how poor Palestinian kids were being beaten up by vicious Israeli soldiers. As the media campaign forged ahead, Israel, under Shamir's leadership, was coming under more and more stringent criticism from the international community.

Unfortunately, Israeli leadership was not as quick to understand the political power of global public relations. As the situation continued to worsen, I became increasingly concerned and decided to see if I could be of some help. During my next visit to Israel, I requested and arranged for a meeting with the prime minister to specifically discuss this matter. I enjoyed similar access to Shamir as I had had to Begin, so a meeting was quickly scheduled through Mati Shmulevitch, one of Shamir's closest Lehi comrades, who had been appointed to serve as his Director of the Office of the Prime Minister.

After welcoming me into his spartan office and exchanging greetings, Shamir bade me sit down. I got right to the point.

"Mr. Prime Minister, I'd like to talk to you about the *Intifada*," I began. "You've got to do something about this." Shamir is a pugnacious and compact man, whose face bears a permanent frown due to his bushy brow. His eyes bore through me as I continued. "This is an either/or situation. Either you conduct this like a wartime action, or you walk away."

"What do you mean?" he asked.

"Number one, you do not permit the media to have such free access," I said. "You are getting pummeled in the press all around the world." Shamir retorted with the standard Israeli line.

"Hart, if we let world opinion determine our course, we would no longer have a state." I could see that I needed to explain some of the new realities to the man.

"Mr. Prime Minister, we're living in a new age. CNN and other cable news networks are feeding non-stop news coverage to the entire world 24 hours a day. They constantly need colorful news stories to grab the attention of their viewers. And the bloodier the better. Images of big Israeli soldiers clubbing poor little Palestinian children are exactly the type of thing they're looking for. They show these images over and over every half hour in every country in the world. Do you realize what's going on here?" Shamir looked a bit taken aback as he pondered my question for a moment.

"Yes," he said weakly. "Yes, we do know about this." But I did not believe him. I did not believe he had an inkling of how Israel was being depicted around the world. Israel, due to its many cumbersome and bureaucratic government regulations, had been slow to embrace cable TV. While I would soon begin a project to help remedy this situation, at this point most Israelis, including Shamir, were unfamiliar with CNN.

"If you understand the seriousness of the situation, Mr. Prime Minister, then I urge you to do something about it one way or another," I stated. He indicated that I should continue.

"Either you get tough or you walk away. For example, one thing you can do to squelch this thing, once the cameras are no longer filming, is mass arrest. You instruct the troops to surround a group of rioting kids and then haul them off in trucks to a detention center. You require that their parents come to bail them out after hitting them with a large fine. In our country, a parent is legally responsible for the criminal actions of his minor child. If you do this here, these disturbances will come to a stop." Shamir said he liked this suggestion and agreed to discuss it with his military leadership.

"But whatever you decide to do," I urged him, "keep the media out of it. Keep them out of these areas entirely. You may suffer negative press reaction for a little while. They'll criticize you strongly for this, but after a week they'll forget about it. They'll understand that there's no more bloody scenes to be filmed here and they'll move on to some other, more accessible trouble spot."

I left the meeting believing that I had gotten through to Shamir on the importance of maintaining Israel's public image in the world. His subsequent actions, however, demonstrated that he chose only to heed my advice about getting tougher with the rioters. He continued to permit full media access as the violence escalated. Israel continued to be depicted as a cruel oppressor and the rock-throwing Palestinian children continued to be labeled as freedom fighters for years to come.

The following year I returned to Israel for a meeting of the Conference of Presidents. Shamir was to address our group, and I was given the honor of introducing him. We chatted briefly beforehand, and he recalled our meeting about the Intifada, which was still going on at the time. He explained how weary he was of dealing with the situation in the territories and explained how such problems were never envisioned when these lands were conquered in 1967.

"Well, you know, Mr. Prime Minister," I said, "America deals quite differently with the territory it conquers in war. After defeating Germany we created the Marshall Plan to help the people get back on their feet. We did the same thing in Japan."

"That's true," he said with a smile, "but before you could help them you had to defeat them. Didn't Churchill say, 'First we must be victorious, then we can be magnanimous?'" I returned the smile and nodded my agreement as I rose to make the introduction. Shamir spoke plainly, delivering an overview of Israel's security situation and stressing the need for American moral and financial support. He was never able to effectively deal with the Intifada, and I believe the Israeli public recognized this when they voted a Labor government into power after Shamir's term had ended.

When I share accounts of my dealings with Israeli political leaders, friends are often surprised by my level of access and my ability to be completely candid with them. They say: "These fellows have advisors at their beck and call. Why do they choose to consult with you?"

The fact is that, for the most part, Israeli leaders, and particularly prime ministers, lead rather lonely lives. When they are not out in front of a crowd delivering a stirring speech, they often find themselves quite alone and cut off. They are surrounded by aides and advisors, all of whom have some sort of ax to grind. Other than their spouses, there's really no one who will extend an unvarnished opinion. I found, for the most part, that they welcome the opportunity of discussing the affairs of state with someone like me, who has no agenda, and who wants absolutely nothing from them in return. Begin, Shamir, Netanyahu and Sharon all permitted me – no, they encouraged me – to speak my mind freely, and that's exactly what I did. That is why I had no reservations about looking Prime Minister Sharon in the eye and telling him, "You look terrible on TV." If I sugar-coated my opinions out of some sense of deference, I would turn into just another yes-man sycophant and soon find myself rendered irrelevant.

While my connections to Israeli politics were mostly through the Likud Party, I had occasion to meet many of the top Labor Party leaders as well. Perhaps the most venerated of these, particularly since his tragic assassination in 1995, was Yitzchak Rabin.

In 1994 I made a special trip to Israel as part of a world Rabbinical conference. I joined the group because I learned that they would be meeting with Prime Minister Rabin. By this time Rabin had already signed the agreement and gone through the famous handshake on the White House lawn with Arafat. I wanted an opportunity to ask him about how certain he was that he was moving down the correct path.

On the afternoon of our arrival, we were convened in a small meeting room at our Tel Aviv hotel. The room was filled with Orthodox Rabbis from around the world awaiting the prime minister who, we were told, was running late. Finally Rabin entered the room, and I could tell from his ruddiness and slurred speech that he had been drinking. Rabin rambled on for over an hour, reciting the standard speech he routinely delivered to visiting foreigners, and then promptly left the room without taking any questions.

I was outraged! I had traveled all the way from Indiana for this opportunity to ask Rabin face-to-face, "Are you sure you know what you're doing with this agreement?" Sadly, I never got the chance to ask him the question.

Simona and I were at our home in Herzliya when Rabin was shot and killed by an Israeli right-wing fanatic. In shock, we watched on live TV as his killer was captured and we witnessed the enormous outpouring of emotion that flowed from the Israeli people. Of course the media had immediately gone into one of their typical frenzies, inflating Rabin to a larger-than-life figure. The news accounts had dubbed him a "soldier for peace" and a martyr. He was being depicted as the greatest prime minister and military hero in Israel's history. In addition, he was touted as a skilled tennis player, the greatest this and the greatest that, *ad nauseam.*

I was contacted at the time by several US reporters who knew of my close ties to the Israeli government. They wanted my reaction to Rabin's assassination.

"It's been reported that Yitzchak Rabin was a great statesman and peace-maker and I can go along with that." I told them. "It's being said that he was the greatest military leader in Jewish history, and I will not dispute that. But when they start to say that he was a great tennis player – that's where I draw the line." I had observed Rabin play tennis, and he was truly an atrocious player. A mutual friend, Sidney Cooperman, the chairman of the Be'ersheva Foundation, had arranged a tennis match with me and the prime minister during Rabin's first term in office. We were supposed to play doubles together, but then Rabin asked someone about me. He was advised about my Herut Zionist background and promptly backed out of the match. Sidney apologized profusely, and I made a joke that Rabin sounds to me like an unstrung tennis racket – no guts!

The anti-right wing and anti-religious atmosphere that permeated Israel in the wake of Rabin's assassination was utterly pervasive. Since Rabin had been killed by a religious right-wing fanatic, all who stood to the right of center had become suspect and targets of self-righteous rage. I recall walking to synagogue from our home in Herzliya on the Sabbath after the killing. A teenage girl spotted my kippa and loudly began to publicly berate me as one of Rabin's killers. I never would have believed that simply wearing a kippa on the streets of Israel would label me as a murderer.

I could never understand why Rabin saw fit to trust a man like Arafat who had the blood of so many terrorist victims on his hands. How could he agree to give away parts of Eretz Yisrael, relying upon his faith in a master terrorist like Arafat? Did the Holocaust mean nothing? What did the term "Never Again" mean to a man like Rabin? I firmly believe that his decision to pursue the false promise of the Oslo Accords will go down in history as the most monumental mistake made by any Israeli government.

I saw so many parallels between the self-delusional sleepwalking engaged in by many Jews during this period and the pre-Holocaust mindset I had observed in Europe. "Oh, maybe that Hitler fellow is not as bad as they say." I remember those words whenever I hear a Jew saying: "We need to work with Arafat to achieve peace." Perhaps the greatest lesson I learned from my father was the importance of seeing things the way they actually are, not the way you'd like them to be. We Jews must face the reality of the situation and never allow ourselves the luxury of indulging in pie-in-the-sky dreams. The reality is that Arafat wants to destroy the Jewish state, and he enjoys widespread support among his people in this quest. He has never said otherwise, and I cannot understand why Israeli leaders such as Peres and Barak are unwilling to take him at his word.

I first met Barak when he was seeking his party's nomination for prime minister in 1997. The annual UJA General Assembly (GA) was being held in Indianapolis. Thousands of delegates flocked to our city in this once-a-year conclave of top Jewish leadership. Prime Minister Netanyahu delivered the keynote address, and Barak was introduced to the convention as the spokesman for the opposition party.

One of Barak's major supporters in the US was Murray Laulicht, my son Bernard's father-in-law. Murray was also speaking at the GA in his capacity as president of the United Jewish Federation (UJF) of MetroWest and had put together a private reception for Barak prior to his address. Murray introduced me to the future prime minister as a Likudnik, and we naturally spoke about my long-standing friendship with the late Menachem Begin. I was not particularly impressed with Barak and had difficulty picturing him as prime minister. Despite my disaffection with Netanyahu, I was not at all pleased when Barak was elected in 1999.

My initial impressions were borne out in the summer of 2000 when Barak met with Clinton and Arafat in an attempted replay of the 1979 Camp David summit. How I longed for Begin's leadership as I observed Barak's willingness to negotiate away Israel's sovereignty over Jerusalem. Like many Jews around the world, I was incensed by Barak's actions. How dare he presume to give away even a portion of Israel's – of MY – eternal homeland!? I believe that this was a mistake of gross proportions and one that will plague Israel for years to come.

I had the opportunity to meet Israel's first prime minister, David Ben-Gurion, in 1972 during a large UJA mission. At this point Ben-Gurion was 86 years old and living in retirement at Sde Boker. He had left the Knesset in 1970, where he had served as the head of the Rafi Party, a political faction he had established and which would eventually form the nucleus of today's Labor Party. He was universally regarded as a venerated elder statesman and one of Israel's beloved founding fathers.

I listened as, despite his years, Ben-Gurion delivered a highly impassioned speech covering the history of Zionism, although it was clear that his memory was giving him some trouble. For example, as he recounted the founding of the Israeli state:

"The first three settlements in Israel were at Petach Tikvah, Zichron Ya'acov and…" He struggled to recall the third settlement until, finally, an aide approached him and whispered in his ear. "…and Rishon LeTzion, of course. That's the third one." As he concluded his speech, he got stuck once again:

"And I want you to go home, all of you, and remember these three things that you should teach to your children. The Hebrew language, Hebrew literature and, and…" His features frowned as he strained for the third point until, once again, an aide whispered to him and he nodded. "The Bible. Teach your children the Bible." Ben-Gurion died the following year at age 87.

My first encounter with Prime Minister Golda Meir came about during an Israel Bonds mission several years later. She met privately with our leadership before delivering a speech to our group. I was introduced to her as "Mr. Hasten from Indianapolis." She immediately reacted.

"I must tell you something that happened to me in Indianapolis," she said with a slight smile, as she stubbed out her cigarette. "This was in the early 1950s and I was traveling in America trying to get things going with Israel Bonds. I arrived in Indianapolis and one of your Jewish leaders told me 'We aren't interested in selling Bonds here. This town is very UJA oriented and we don't like the competition from Bonds. You'd better go elsewhere to sell Bonds.' So these guys tried to run me out of town. 'You can't come in here to raise money from the Jews of Indianapolis,' they told me. 'Is that so?' I told them right back. 'It so happens that I have a visa for the US, and you know who gave it to me? Secretary of State Dean Acheson, that's who! And it says I can go anywhere in America I want to.'"

I laughed at the story, despite the fact that I had heard it countless times before. "Well, things have sure changed, Madame Prime Minister," I told her. "We're selling a lot of Bonds in Indianapolis these days."

"That's wonderful," she said with a wrinkled smile and shook my hand warmly.

My most salient memory of Labor Party leader Shimon Peres came about due to my service as president of the Herut Zionists of America, a post I had accepted at the behest of Menachem Begin. HZA is a US lobbying and fund-raising organization that offers support for Israel's conservative agenda. I represented the Herut Zionists at meetings of the *Sochnut* (Jewish Agency) which provides global oversight for Jewish fund-raising and social service activities.

As president I strove to enhance the legitimacy of the Herut Zionists and, in this regard, was successful in creating a new seat for our Herut Zionists group within another umbrella organization, the Conference of Presidents of Major Jewish Organizations. During my service with this organization, I was instrumental in recruiting its current executive vice-chairman, Malcolm Hoenlein. I encouraged him to accept the position. He did and still holds it to this day. After my term as president of Herut Zionists ended, my brother, Mark, took my place and succeeded in making great strides towards building support for the conservative Israeli agenda in the US. Since my departure, the organization has changed its name to Likud Zionists and remains active as an advocate of the Likud Party platform and principles.

It was my involvement in the Conference of Presidents that led me, in 1987, to New York to attend a special meeting. I was anxious to listen to the scheduled speaker, Shimon Peres, who at that time was serving as foreign minister under the Unity Government arrangement. Under this scheme, Likud leader Yitzchak Shamir and Peres would take turns serving as the Israeli prime minister. When either man was not serving as prime minister, he would then become the other's foreign minister and hold the title of vice-premier.

Peres had indicated that he had some extraordinary plans for bringing about a new peace agreement between Israel and its Arab neighbors. When he addressed our group, he hinted that he had been negotiating secretly with an unnamed Arab leader, who we later learned was King Hussein of Jordan. Peres announced his support for a proposed international conference that would ostensibly be convened to seek out solutions to the Palestinian/Israeli conflict. Prime Minister Shamir had stated his opposition to the conference fearing that it would degenerate into an Israel-bashing propaganda forum. Peres concluded by ticking off his breakthrough foreign policy accomplishments and then opened the floor for questions. After a time, I approached the microphone and posed my first question:

"Mr. Foreign Minister. Does your support of an international conference enjoy the blessing of the prime minister?" Peres glowered at me, and it was clear that he understood the intent of my question.

"No," he answered, "I do not believe that it does."

"Did the cabinet approve this position?" I pressed.

"No," he replied, somewhat warily.

"Did the Knesset vote in favor of the conference?" He shook his head. "Did the prime minister approve of your participation in the secret talks you mentioned?" I pressed further.

"I don't need anybody to approve anything," he said in patronizing tone. "I am the foreign minister."

"When you speak to these Arab leaders, are you speaking for the Israeli government or for yourself?" My tone was becoming more strident by this point.

"I don't need anybody to tell me what I can or cannot do," he began shouting, red-faced. "Fifty percent of the Israeli population voted for me for prime minister. I have a mandate and I speak for the people of Israel." By now others in our group were trying to shout me down. They were insisting that I sit down and shut up. But I had no intention of letting Peres' arrogance go unchallenged.

"You say you do not need permission from Shamir," I said. "But did Shamir act this way when you were the prime minister and he was the foreign minister?" Everyone knew the answer to my rhetorical question since, of course, Shamir had always acted deferentially to the prime minister, out of respect for the office. I finally took my seat without waiting for an answer and watched as Peres made his hurried exit from the room.

I reinforced my reputation as being an outspoken American when, in the mid-nineties, I participated in an AIPAC President's mission to Israel and Jordan. In Amman, we had met with King Hussein and had just returned to Jerusalem where we had a meeting scheduled with the president of Israel, Ezer Weizman. Weizman greeted us and explained that he had just returned from Egypt where he had conferred with Egyptian president, Hosni Mubarak. I was the first to rise when Weizman opened the floor to questions.

"Mr. President," I stated, "you said you recently visited President Mubarak in Cairo. Are you aware that, aside from attending Rabin's funeral, Mubarak has never once visited Israel?" Weizman nodded to indicate that he was aware of this fact.

"Well," I challenged, "did you invite him to come to Israel?"

"No, I did not," he replied.

"And why not, might I ask?" I said.

"Because I know he would not accept," answered Weizman lamely. Everyone understood that for Mubarak to pay a visit to Israel, it would require an act of denigration on his part. But that was his problem. It would nevertheless behoove Weizman, out of a sense of *hadar* or Jewish pride, to extend the invitation anyway. I decided to tell him so.

"You know, President Weizman," I said firmly, "you should have invited him anyway." At this point Weizman looked directly at me.

"Oh, yeah. I know you. You're the Begin guy," he said dismissively. "What we're concerned about here is peace. We don't get hung up about who visits where. That's not the important thing."

I disagreed. Where was Jewish honor, Jewish pride, I wanted to know. What these Israeli liberals were lacking was not only a sense of *hadar*, but also a sense of history. Why did they fail to understand that this is the land where the Jewish odyssey began? If it were not for this land, there would be no Jewish people today. Why didn't they get it?

Another Israeli leader that "just didn't get it" was, perhaps the most outwardly impressive politician I had ever met. Abba Eban had served as Israel's first UN ambassador. I joined him at a breakfast meeting years after he had left that office, at the same Conference of Presidents gathering mentioned earlier.

Eban addressed our group and explained that he had just returned from conferring with US administration officials and State Department Middle East advisors. Eban had been urging the American foreign policy establishment to pressure the Israeli Likud government into yielding on the issue of returning the Golan Heights to Syria. Unlike Begin, who as opposition leader would never publicly criticize the Israeli government when he traveled abroad, Eban had no compunction about doing so. His polished and refined manner was amply evident as we took our seats. Eban's eloquence and splendid command of the King's English were astonishing. Yet, when it came to his thinking, he was dead wrong. And I told him so.

"You have an amazing ability to express the ugliest ideas in the most beautiful manner." I managed to get a chuckle out of him with that comment.

Perhaps the most misguided, and reckless, of Israel's political leaders is Yossi Beilin, considered to be the chief architect of the ill-fated Oslo Peace Accords. Beilin served as minister of justice in the Barak government and, to my mind, is the embodiment of the self-hating, masochistic and dishonest Israeli intellectual. I had the opportunity of meeting and confronting Beilin during an Israel Bonds mission in the mid-seventies. Beilin was on the program, billed as a foreign policy expert, and was continuing to use the term "West Bank" to refer to the territories of Judea and Samaria. I decided to challenge this.

"Dr. Beilin," I said politely, "why do you use the term West Bank to refer to the territories of Judea and Samaria?" He gave me an annoyed look.

"I don't care what you call it," he said, waving his hand dismissively. "You can call it the West Bank or Judea or whatever. You can even call it Moishe. What's the difference? The main thing is we should have peace."

"Dr. Beilin," I replied, "since it doesn't matter to you what we call it, why don't we refer to these areas as Judea and Samaria from now on?" Beilin gave me a smirk and continued answering questions, pointedly using the "West Bank" appellation, never once mentioning Samaria and Judea.

Similarly, when Shimon Peres was asked to refrain from employing the term "West Bank" during a speech in the Knesset, he responded in the same way. "I will always use the name 'West Bank'," he announced defiantly.

It is attitudes such as these that so characterize the Israeli left. Intellectually bankrupt, with no moorings in our rich Jewish history, such leadership has served to hamper and hold back the development of Israel as the embodiment of the Zionist dream. Fortunately, the tide is turning, as I discuss in Chapter Eighteen, and it appears that Israel may finally be dispensing with such leftist leadership that has served her so poorly in the recent past.

Chapter Fifteen

Serving on the Court

I USED TO SAY that middle age would always be "fifteen years older than I am right now." But by the time I was approaching forty, I started to see time taking its toll. As is the case with many men who are devoted to their careers and their volunteer work, there was little time in my life for athletics. I had entirely abandoned soccer, although I was an outstanding player in my youth and had played sporadically in Minneapolis. And though I remained active on the job, I was involved in no sports or fitness program of any kind. All this was to change dramatically in 1974.

Seated at my desk, puffing on my sixty-fifth cigarette of the day, I never could have imagined that twenty years later I would enjoy a reputation as a world-class tennis player. Interestingly, my introduction to tennis came about due to an accidental event which took place in the late sixties.

After five years of enduring the stresses of the nursing home business, I had watched as my cigarette addiction rose to four packs per day. I was chain-smoking without interruption all day long and would even smoke during the night, as my nicotine cravings would disturb my sleep. I started the smoking habit shortly before I got married. In fact, my mother, who disapproved of my smoking, would accuse Simona of having caused me to start. "He was smoking when I met him, Mama," Simona would tell her, and she was quite correct.

By the late 1960s, many of the hazards of cigarette smoking were becoming widely known. I was defiant in the face of the mounting evidence linking smoking with cancer and other diseases. I liked to smoke and, by G-d, I was going to do it.

On August 13, 1969, I came home after a long day at work. After dinner, with a freshly lit cigarette dangling from my lips, I picked up our 3-year old, Bernard, and placed him on my lap for some playtime. Bernard, at this point, always carried his security blanket with him, which he now began waving about wildly as I tickled and bounced him around. Suddenly, Bernard began screaming in pain. At first I didn't know what had happened, but I did notice that my cigarette was no longer lit. Evidently the blanket had caught on the lit tip of my cigarette and pulled it off. The burning tobacco adhered to the blanket for a moment and then fell loose, landing on the front of Bernard's neck, burning him severely. He reached for his throat, pressing the ash against his flesh and screaming horribly. Pulling away his little hands, I was shocked to see what looked like a black hole in his flesh. I realized later that I was looking at the black sooty tobacco from my cigarette, but to my hysterical mind at the moment, I believed that I had burned a hole right through my little boy's throat!

So many crazy thoughts run through a parent's mind at a moment like this. For a split second I panicked and feared that my carelessness would actually cost Bernard his life. I imagined him unable to breathe due to the cigarette hole. I removed the burning ash from his neck and ran to put ice on the area before treating the burn. Bernard soon recovered, but he carries a large burn scar on his throat to this day as a reminder of this episode.

After I was assured of Bernard's safety, I made a solemn *neder,* or oath, to myself: "I shall never smoke again." I am proud to say that I have kept that pledge for over 32 years. I quit smoking on the spot, going from eighty cigarettes per day to zero cold turkey. Amazingly, I suffered absolutely no withdrawal symptoms. Like all smokers, I had attempted to quit several times before, but the strong cravings would always overcome my willpower and cause me to light up again. This time, however, due to my extreme motivation, things were different. Whenever I would even think about a cigarette, I merely had to conjure up my little son's face, twisted in pain and anguish, and remember that my smoking had been the cause of it.

For several years after I had quit, I would continue to suffer nightmares in which I would observe myself smoking. I would wake in a cold sweat and turn to Simona with "What am I doing smoking? I'm not supposed to be smoking."

"It's just a dream, honey," she would assure me. "Go back to sleep."

Like many people who quit smoking, I began putting on weight, ballooning up to 230 lbs. by 1973. I had always been athletic, and the extra weight made me feel awkward and uncomfortable. By 1974, I finally decided I had to do something about it.

At this time we were living in a north side housing development in suburban Indianapolis, North Willow Farms. We enjoyed access to a community clubhouse and the attached outdoor tennis courts. Driving through the development in the summer months, I would invariably observe our neighbors out on the courts. They all looked healthy and seemed to be having a good time. One sunny day, in the late afternoon, I walked over to the courts wearing shorts and tennis shoes. I spotted one of my neighbors on the court, and he asked if I wished to join him for a set. I told him I didn't know how to play. In fact, I didn't even know what a set was. I started asking questions, and he kindly let me use his racket and try my hand at knocking a few balls over the net.

I guess you could say it was "love" at first grip. I was soon the owner of my own racket and began making daily trips to the community courts. Initially, I wasn't good enough to play with anyone else and besides, I didn't even know the rules of the game. But I soon caught on and began playing regularly with my friend, Rabbi Ronald Gray. It was Rabbi Gray who taught me the rules and about scoring. He advised me that the best thing I could do to improve my game was to regularly attend Sabbath services at his synagogue each week.

"If you want to improve your golf game, you need to go to the Reform synagogue, but mine is the tennis shul," he explained with a twinkle.

By this time Simona and I were making plans to construct our new home. We had purchased a scenic wooded parcel a mile south of our current home and were working with an architect who had designed a magnificent Spanish style villa. We were meeting with the architect and going over the floor plans when something occurred to me.

"How am I going to play tennis after we move in?" I asked. "I can't keep coming back to North Willow."

"You've got plenty of room to build a court on this lot," suggested the architect. "Do you want me to put together some designs and cost figures?"

"Definitely," I responded enthusiastically. With my own tennis court I could really become serious about the game. I approved the court designs and had them installed right away, enabling me to begin using them while the house was still under construction.

In addition to the Rabbi, my regular partner was my new next-door neighbor, Walter Wolf.[1] A prominent attorney and a member of the Jewish Federation leadership who opposed funding for the Hebrew Academy, Walter was an avid tennis player. He took me under his wing and began teaching

---

1 Not to be confused with the bank president, Walter Wolff, mentioned in Chapter 12.

me the finer points of the game. He would instruct me on how to improve my backhand while I would instruct him about the many advantages of day school education. I know we both learned a great deal from each other.

Before long, my game began to improve. The exercise was having the desired effect on my body and tennis was soon becoming a central feature of my life. Until I got back into shape, I did not realize how badly my years of smoking and physical inactivity had affected me. I promised myself that I would never return to that unhealthy lifestyle, and I'm proud to say I have kept that promise.

As my skills improved, I felt the need to move to the next level and decided to begin working with a pro. I was referred to Prem Gupta, an Indian-born tennis instructor who began working with me once a week. Prem was a great teacher who offered me strong encouragement. He instilled a love of the game in me that was based on my desire for competition and my appreciation of physical skill. To the untrained eye, tennis looks like a rather rudimentary endeavor. You simply have to hit the ball over the net. Prem showed me how to achieve precision placement, enabling me to control where the ball traveled and how it would bounce. Most players, he explained, have a difficult time with their backhand and favor using their forehand swing. While my forehand is stronger, my backhand is steadier and is able to execute better control of the ball.

"You know, Hart, if you put your mind to it, you could become an excellent tennis player," he advised. "Physically, you're an athlete, and if you start playing against some decent competition, you have the potential to become a champion."

I didn't know if Prem was simply flattering me or not, but I decided to find out by heeding his advice. I joined the Broadmoor Country Club and the Indianapolis Racquet Club where, Prem informed me, many of his clients competed. He set up matches for me against other players and tried to find opponents who were always a bit better than I, in order to stretch my limits and thereby improve my game. It worked. Over time, my game steadily got stronger as my competitive instincts drove me on.

It was not long after I became seriously involved with tennis that I discovered a way of combining two of my passions. I was contacted by a group wishing to establish something called the Israel Tennis Center. They wished to construct a series of facilities throughout Israel in order to promote the game and to develop Israeli tennis athletes. I soon became an avid supporter and helped to launch the first Tennis Center in Israel. In this context I got to know and play against many Israeli tennis enthusiasts. Tennis soon became part of my routine, both in the US and in Israel.

Little by little, I watched my skills improve over the next ten years. As I moved up, I was able to defeat opponents who had initially beaten me. I began to enter amateur tennis competitions at the racquet clubs and started earning a modest reputation as a serious player. In 1983, at age 52, I took the number one spot at the Broadmoor's annual men's tennis tournament, beating out players in all age categories. The following year I did the same thing at the Indianapolis Racquet Club.

Amateur and professional tennis players are seeded in tournaments, based on a seven-point scale, with 7.0 as the top seed rating. By the late 1980s I was being seeded at the 4.0 level, which is where I have remained to this day. As my skill level advanced year by year, I eventually discovered that I had outgrown the local competition of weekend tennis players. If I was going to continue to improve my game, I needed stiffer competition. That's when I began to think about the Maccabiah Games. This worldwide competition was sometimes known as the "Jewish Olympics." The Maccabiah Games are held every four years in Israel. There is also a Jewish equivalent of the Pan American Games, held in the Western hemisphere two years after every Israeli Maccabiah.

In 1993, at the suggestion of my Israeli tennis partners, I completed the application forms for entry into the upcoming Maccabiah Games. I traveled to Miami to try out for the US tennis team and, while I did not make the team, I succeeded in being named an alternate. I traveled with the team to Tel Aviv and got to know many of the top-seeded Israeli competitors.

Two years later, in January of 1995, I did make the team and competed at the Pan Am Maccabiah in Buenos Aires, Argentina. I captured my first two medals, both bronze, in men's singles and men's doubles. While in Buenos Aires, I had the chance to meet two of my cousins for the first time, Teodoro and Guillermo Halpern. They were the sons of my mother's brother, David, who had immigrated to Argentina along with another brother, Joseph, after World War 1. I was struck by the strong family resemblances, particularly in Guillermo's facial features, nose, receding hairline, as well as his voice and certain distinctive mannerisms.

I again qualified for the US team in 1997 and traveled to Israel for the competition. I was lined up with all the other athletes outside of the stadium as the opening ceremonies were getting underway. Teams from each nation were to enter the stadium for the traditional grand promenade. Just as the Australian team was crossing a short footbridge temporarily constructed to provide access to the stadium over a small ravine, the bridge started to sway and then gave way, dumping the terrified athletes into the highly polluted stream. There were four fatalities, all Australian athletes, and numerous injuries. Directly following the Australian team were the Austrian athletes, followed by our American team. After a delay, the opening ceremonies continued with no public mention of the incident. Spectators in the stands, unaware of the tragedy taking place just outside of the stadium, were placing cell phone calls to their families at home watching the live TV coverage. Eventually the ceremonies were curtailed and, after an announcement was made, they were aborted.

As is the case with all large gatherings in Israel, there was abundant security on hand to offer protection against Arab terrorists. But, sadly, there was no protection against the threat posed by shoddy, hurried workmanship. A year-long government investigation ensued and resulted in a lot of finger-pointing by the building trades and the labor unions. A few short jail sentences were handed down, but in the end, no real culpability for the disaster was determined.

The games went on as scheduled, despite the bridge disaster, and I succeeded in once again bringing home a bronze medal for my performance in the men's singles competition.

Two years later, at the Pan Am Maccabiah in Mexico City, I succeeded in garnering my first Silver Medal in men's singles. Back in Tel Aviv for the Israeli games in 2001, I again managed to earn another Silver Medal in men's doubles. As of this writing, I intend to compete in the upcoming Pan Am Maccabiah to be held in Caracas, Venezuela in 2003. I will be competing in the over 70 age category for the first time and will be working very hard to win my first Gold Medal.

Tennis has opened many doors for me over the years and permitted me to meet and enjoy playing with many well-known professionals such as Bobby Riggs, Christine Evert, Stan Smith, Pancho Segura and Fred Stolle. One of my other memorable tennis partners was TV game show host Monty Hall, a guest at my home and a fairly good player. The former junior senator from Indiana, Dan Coats, is a first-class tennis player. When Senator Coats was in office, I would occasionally be his guest at the indoor tennis courts at the Senate Office Building where I witnessed the true meaning of the term "public service."

Through my involvement with the Israel Tennis Centers I have become friendly with the top Israeli tennis champions such as Shlomo Glickstein and Amos Mansdorf. People are astounded when I tell them that I beat Mansdorf in a tennis match. But it's the truth. Of course, sometimes I fail to mention that Mansdorf was only ten years old at the time! Both players, along with many others, rose to prominence on the world tennis circuit, thanks to the work of the Israel Tennis Center.

The first Tennis Center was constructed in 1975 in Ramat HaSharon, and it soon became obvious that there was a serious traffic access problem. In order to drive to the center, one had to pull off of the main highway and take a dirt access road through a neighboring *pardes* (orchard), in order to reach the front door. When Menachem Begin became prime minister in 1977, I was asked to exploit my political connections to see about improving the highway connections to the site. The group was requesting that an access road be constructed leading to the Tennis Center from the main highway. I mustered every bit of my *protekzia* (influence) and finally managed to convince the prime minister to order the building of the needed road. Ironically, once Begin left office, the road was promptly closed.

It was actually through my work with the Tennis Center that I became an Israeli homeowner in 1985. The original founders of the Tennis Center, successful American businessmen, all shared a twin passion for Zionism and the game of tennis. The group decided to form a syndicate, in order to create a six-story high-rise condominium development along the Mediterranean seaboard at a prestigious Israeli resort area known as Herzliya Pituach. This scenic beachfront area is often referred to as the Israeli Riviera. A founding member of the Tennis Center group was Ruby Josephs, a real estate developer from Monsey, New York, whom I had met through my involvement with Israel Bonds. Ruby had located an available parcel in the Herzliya Pituach area and brought it to the rest of us for consideration. Simona and I joined Ruby at the site and listened as he explained:

"Hart, we need one million dollars to put this deal together," he began. "I'm thinking each of the ten Tennis Center guys should put in a hundred thousand. That gets you a ten percent interest and your first choice of a condo for yourself. What do you think?" Without waiting for me to say a word, Simona chirped up enthusiastically.

"Let's do it, Dad," she told me. "Remember what Menachem Begin was always telling American Jews? You should have a foot in the door. Have a home in Eretz Yisrael."

I agreed with Simona, and so we went ahead and joined in and watched as the building, housing fifty luxury condo units, was erected in short order along the Mediterranean shore. After assigning a unit to each of the partners, we quickly filled the place up and were happy to observe property values continue to increase. As investors, we were delighted to watch our equity appreciate and, on top of that, Simona and I loved living so close to all of my tennis buddies.

Curiously, because of limited space, our tennis development group was unable to build a single tennis court on our own property. We frequented the courts a few blocks away at the Accadia Hotel (Yitzchak Rabin's favorite tennis spot).

Like many resort communities, Herzliya Pituach eventually became overdeveloped. Continuous traffic jams and huge crowds on the beach began to impact on the quality of life. A public park was erected next door to the building, and on Friday nights we were now treated to the sound of Russian immigrant picnickers' desecrating the Sabbath with their drunken singing and reveling all night long. To top things off, the city had erected a new marina a few miles south of our property. The result was the ruination of our beach as the shoreline now encroached on the sand, making any sort of walking or jogging impossible. In 1998, we placed our condo on the market and were able to sell it at a handsome profit not long thereafter.

Coordinating the work of the Tennis Centers in Israel was the responsibility of Dr. Ian Froman. Ian, a respected dentist, was a world-class tennis player who had made Aliyah to Israel from South Africa. His passion for tennis, and his desire to see the game flourish in Israel, drove him to contact other tennis-loving Zionists from around the world and enlist their support for the Tennis Center cause. One such devotee was Dr. Bill Lippy from Youngstown, Ohio. Dr. Lippy, a noted ear specialist, was fulfilling his commitment to the Jewish state by working pro bono in Israeli teaching hospitals and medical schools. Another of Dr. Froman's tennis disciples was Harold Landesberg, a Pennsylvania businessman.

Perhaps the most illustrious member of this Israeli tennis clique was Joe Shane, who was considered by many as the father of Israeli tennis. Joe, a successful American businessman and very active in the UJA, had observed years ago that Israel was plagued by an overabundance of wars. He wished to introduce some normalcy into the lives of Israeli children and felt that tennis was the best way to go about it. Shane decided to go to the prime minister with a proposal. He met with Ben-Gurion and announced that Israeli children needed to learn how to play tennis, and that he would be willing to pay for the building of new public tennis courts.

"Just give me the land, Mr. Prime Minister," he said, "and I will put the tennis courts on it."

"That sounds like a good idea, Mr. Shane," responded Ben-Gurion, "but in order to acquire the land, you must confer with the minister of culture who handles everything related to sports." Ben-Gurion made the appropriate phone call and Shane set off to see the minister. Once again, Shane made his pitch, this time to the minister, explaining the importance of tennis in helping to shape the youth of Israel. Joe again pointed out that all he needed was a parcel of land, and that he would construct the actual tennis courts free of charge.

"I'll build as many courts as we have room for," Joe pointed out. "If you give me a parcel that will hold ten courts, I'll build ten courts. If you give me one that can hold twenty courts, I'll build twenty." Joe went on for over two hours, making his case as the minister listened and nodded approvingly. Finally, he spoke:

"Yes, that all seems good and fine, Mr. Shane," he said. "I'll be happy to work with you, and you may count on my full cooperation." Joe was overjoyed and thanked the man profusely for his help. Just as Joe reached the door of the office to leave, the minister called him back.

"Oh, there's just one more thing, Mr. Shane," he said. "Could you tell me please, *Vos is Tennis?* " (Yiddish for "What is tennis?")

Joe Shane was an amazing, and a decidedly single-minded, individual. Bill Lippy tells the story of how Joe surprised him one day by flying into Youngstown, Ohio, from his home in Los Angeles and then showing up at his office asking to speak to him.

"Of course, Joe," said Bill, greeting him in the waiting room. "Come on in and have a seat in my office. Can you join us for dinner, tonight?"

"No, I can't, Bill," replied Joe. "I just flew straight in to talk to you for a few minutes, and then I have to leave for the airport to catch the next plane back to LA."

"What did you fly all the way out here to tell me, Joe?" asked Bill, his curiosity piqued.

"I came to plead with you to quit smoking, and I wanted to ask you face to face," was Joe's only reply. Bill was so impressed by this gesture that he quit smoking that very day and has never returned to the habit. Joe's fanatical devotion to fitness prompted him to found a smoking cessation organization in Israel to help Israelis quit smoking.

I am still in contact with the surviving members of the Tennis Center group and count several of them among my closest friends. These friendships illustrate why tennis will always mean so much more to me than merely a game of smacking a little ball over a net.

Chapter Sixteen
Relations & Relationships

"…and Zayde made us laugh, and Zayde made us cry, and Zayde made a Kiddush Friday night…"

— song lyric from "My Zayde" by Moshe Yess

As this song lyric indicates, the *Zayde* (grandfather) holds a special place in the heart of the typical Jewish family. Today my greatest joy is derived from the smiles and hugs of my ten grandchildren. I have come to understand why my own beloved Zayde cared so much for me, Lonka and his other grandchildren back in Bohorodczany. It goes beyond love. Gazing into the faces of my grandchildren, I see the future, full of hope and anticipation. When my own children were small, we were struggling and scrambling too much to think about such philosophical matters. But today, it's different. I have the time and the ability to cherish not only who they are, but who they are becoming.

I'm pleased to say that all three of my children have established wonderful Jewish homes, full of warmth and the type of nurturing that children require. I am blessed not only with extraordinary children, but also with three sets of terrific *machetonem* (in-laws). All three of my children's in-laws are not only relatives, but have become close personal friends.

My daughter Renée is married to Eyal Halevy, an Israeli businessman. They have lived in Israel since their marriage. Eyal's parents, Yehuda and Leora Halevy live in both Manhattan and Tel Aviv. General Halevy was the international president of Israel Bonds for many years and today serves as vice-president of Bar-Ilan University. Renée and Eyal are the parents of four of my beloved grandchildren: Shane, Ely, Leny and Dorayah Halevy.

Bernard's wife, Laurie, is the daughter of Linda and Murray Laulicht of West Orange, New Jersey. Murray is a prominent attorney and former president of the Jewish Federation of MetroWest. He is a nationally recognized Jewish community leader, holding positions with the New Jersey Commission on Holocaust Education, United Jewish Communities, Union of Orthodox Jewish Congregations and Stern College, among others. Bernard and his family live in the Chicago area, where he serves as CEO of our family banking and real estate operations along with tending to a number of other business interests. Bernard and Laurie are also the parents of four of my beloved grandchildren: Erica, Joseph, Samantha and Hannah Hasten.

Our youngest, Josh, is married to the former Shuli Goldberg whose parents, Ysachar and P'nina I respect and admire greatly. Ysachar was born in Kazakhstan and shares a background similar to my own. He is retired from the printing business and used to live in Staten Island, New York. P'nina is a retired Hebrew teacher. They have recently moved to Israel and are today living in a settlement in a community in Samaria. Josh and Shuli are the parents of two of my beloved grandchildren: Adin and Benny. Through 2001, Josh was heading up our family's property management company in Indianapolis. He made *aliyah* with his family in early 2002 and they are now living in Jerusalem.

I'm equally proud of my brother Mark's children: Eddie Hasten, Rabbi Michael Hasten, Monica Rosenfeld and Judy Kaye. Rabbi Michael is a recognized scholar and a true *Talmid Chacham* (learned person).

I have attempted to transmit to my children and grandchildren the value of community service. As has been mentioned, I have devoted a good portion of my energy and resources towards the advancement of the causes in which I believe. I have done this not so much out of obligation, or because of any glory that might come my way. I believe that a person must make clear where he stands and what he stands for. These values can most easily be determined by how he or she volunteers his time and contributes his or her money.

As mentioned earlier, one of the first organizations with which I became involved was State of Israel Bonds. My association with the Bonds movement exposed me to many of the top lay leaders of the American Jewish community, as well as to many of Israel's political officials. As I accepted these principal positions on the national level with Israel Bonds, I continued to remain in touch with local activities in our community. It was for this reason, in the fall of 1986, that the director of our local Israel Bonds office, Mike Blain, turned to me for help when he found himself facing a real crisis.

As it did every year, the Bond organization was putting on its annual "Man of the Year" fund-raising dinner at which a majority of the year's Bond sales took place. They had very high hopes for this year's event, since they were honoring a prominent local businessman, Bart Kaufman, who enjoyed a national reputation and maintained numerous political connections. Kaufman was a good friend of the current Israel Bonds lay chairman, Ezra (Zeke) Fried-lander, who had convinced Bart to serve as the honoree. Bart had made it clear that he wanted the dinner to be a truly stellar event. When consulted about his choice for a guest speaker, Bart indicated that former Secretary of State, Henry Kissinger was his first choice. Mike explained to Bart that the Bond organization did not have the funds to pay Kissinger's $25,000 speaker's fee, whereupon Bart volunteered to raise the money by tapping his buddies to kick in the cost. It was several weeks before the dinner that Mike Blain phoned me in a panic.

"Hart, I got big trouble," said Mike. I could tell he was highly agi-tated.

"What's wrong, Mike?" I asked.

"It's Bart Kaufman. He doesn't like kosher," Mike said with a nervous laugh. "Can you believe it? He says he doesn't want the dinner to be kosher."

"What's he got against kosher?" I said.

"He says that kosher food tastes lousy, and he doesn't want to force his friends to come to the dinner and eat lousy food," Mike explained incredu-lously.

"Is this guy kidding?"

"No, he's serious. He says if we don't agree to make it a non-kosher event, he's pulling out. And he's taking Kissinger with him. I don't know what to do, Hart. The invitations have been designed and we're ready to send them out. He's got us by the *kishkes*."

"Oh no, he doesn't," I assured him. "Give him another call and try to talk some sense into him." Mike's appeal to reason fell on deaf ears. Despite all his patient explanations that the welfare of Israel is far more important than the menu at some Bonds dinner, Kaufman remained adamant. If we weren't going to play by his rules, he was taking his ball and going home. He had also convinced his friend, Zeke, to resign as chairman, unless his demands were met. I decided to personally call Zeke, who picked up the phone and said right away: "Now before you say anything, Hart, please don't yell at me."

"I'm not going to yell at you, Zeke," I assured him calmly, "but I want you to know that this dinner is definitely going to be a kosher event. This is not subject to negotiation."

"Well, in that case you'd better count me out," he said. Zeke turned in his resignation letter the same day. I called Mike back and gave him the bad news that I got nowhere with Zeke.

"What are we going to do now, Hart?" asked Mike with a desperate tremor in his voice. "I think we've got to cancel the dinner."

"I'll tell you what we're *not* going to do. We're not going to give in to extortion and we're not going to cancel the dinner. Kaufman thinks that we don't have the guts to put on the dinner without him. He thinks that he can tell us what to do, even when it comes to violating Jewish law. We've got to show him and the whole community that we can't be pushed around so easily. I want you to call up Kaufman and explain that it is National Israel Bonds policy for all dinners to be kosher. And tell him that rather than compromise that policy, we'd find another honoree."

With only a few weeks to go, Mike and I scrambled to find another deserving community leader to honor. I immediately thought of long-time Bonds supporter Morrie Katz.

"Morrie, this is Hart," I said after phoning him up. "I want you to be the honoree at the Bonds dinner next month."

"What do you mean, Hart?" he said puzzled. "Bart Kaufman is the honoree, isn't he?"

"Morrie, don't ask me any questions. You are the honoree, and that's that."

"Okay, if you say so," he said agreeably.

We next had to secure a speaker, since Kissinger was obviously out. I called up my former "boss" at the Conference of Presidents, Morris Abram, and explained the situation to him. Morris was a highly respected national Jewish spokesperson and a good friend.

"Morris," I said, "you've always been an advocate of free speech, haven't you?"

"Of course," he agreed.

"Good, because you're giving one in Indianapolis next month at our Bonds dinner." Abram said he'd heard that one before and asked me to hang on. He checked his calendar and then readily agreed to pinch hit for Henry Kissinger. Abram turned out to be a great speaker, as I knew he would be, and the dinner was well-attended and a tremendous success in every way, including Bond sales generated.

This episode once again illustrated the attitudes of the highly assimilated Jewish population amongst whom we lived. Kaufman and Friedlander were products of this community whose values embraced, and even flaunted, a strong disdain for Jewish tradition. The incident also helped to reinforce my commitment to Jewish education as a means of building a generation who will regard Jewish traditions as a source of pride rather than shame.

Through my membership in the Conference of Presidents, as a representative of the Herut Zionists of America, I got to know many of the country's top Jewish leaders during the 1980s. One of the most intriguing of these was Rabbi Alexander Schindler, the head of the Reform Judaism movement in America. Schindler was also good friends with Menachem Begin, as well as an avid tennis player. Despite the fact that Schindler and I had many points in common, we did not see eye-to-eye on certain fundamental issues.

Schindler, facing the declining numbers among the ranks of Reform Jews, devised a strategy to halt or even reverse the trend. In complete contradiction of Jewish tradition, Schindler had begun advocating the doctrine of patrilineal descent. Historically Jews have looked to the mother to determine if an individual is to be considered a Jew or not. The religion of the father is not taken into account. Schindler advocated that a child of a Jewish father and a non-Jewish mother should be considered as legitimately Jewish. By accepting such a standard, Reform synagogues are able to draw from the ever larger pool of intermarried couples as they seek to recruit new members.

I attempted to convince Schindler that by adopting such a position, not only was he flying in the face of two thousand years of Jewish tradition, he was also encouraging interfaith marriage. By accepting the children of a Jewish father and a non-Jewish mother as Jews, without first requiring a conversion, Schindler was removing one of the negative consequences associated with intermarriage. Under the doctrine of matrilineal descent a Jewish man who wishes his children to be regarded as Jews is required to marry a Jewish woman. Patrilineal descent, on the other hand, permits the same man to marry whomever he chooses and still be assured of fathering Jewish children.

Schindler defended his doctrine by calling up Biblical precedents and by extolling the virtues of "inclusiveness." He also pointed out that Judaism must remain flexible and change with the times in order to survive. To date, I have not been privy to any statistics that support the claim that patrilineal descent promotes Jewish survival. In fact, it appears that just the opposite is the case. I was never able to convince Rabbi Schindler of the error of his ways, but I remain hopeful that the Reform movement will one day move away from this dangerous doctrine.

At times, my involvement with the Conference of Presidents resulted in some rather furious conflicts. I recall how, in 1987, during the first Palestinian *Intifada*, Rabbi Schindler, along with Rabbi Henry Siegman, the executive director of the American Jewish Congress at the time, were actively supporting a resolution intended to lay out the organization's position on the current situation. The resolution, placed before the Conference during its annual meeting in New York, did not overtly endorse the Oslo Accords, but rather stated that the current status quo was unacceptable and that Israeli domination of the territories must be halted. The resolution also enjoyed the support of Ruth Popkin, head of Hadassah. I rose to question the resolution and thereby triggered an impassioned debate that lasted until 4 AM the next morning.

I argued the point vigorously and stated: "Who are we to say that the status quo is unacceptable?" Simply advocating a change in the present situation overlooks the possibility that such a change may worsen Israel's security interests. Finally, a vote was called and the measure was narrowly defeated.

Another organization that I have proudly supported over the years is the Simon Wiesenthal Center in Los Angeles. The SWC is a human rights organization that preserves the legacy of the Holocaust by fighting anti-Semitism around the globe. In 1977, I was approached by the organization's founders, Rabbi Marvin Hier and famed Austrian Nazi-hunter, Simon Wiesenthal, to assist them in raising the funds needed to launch the Center. I had arranged for a number of local fund-raising meetings during a visit they had scheduled in Indianapolis.

One of the prospective supporters I had contacted to meet with Wiesenthal was Eugene Glick, a highly successful residential real estate developer and a noted philanthropist. I had gotten to know Gene through his active support of the Israel Bonds movement and was aware of his background. As a member of the US Army in Europe during the closing phase of World War II, Gene had served as a liberator of the Dachau concentration camp near Munich, Germany. The experience had deeply affected him and resulted in a lifelong commitment to preserving the security of Israel. I was also aware of the fact that Gene was a prominent supporter of various high profile cultural causes in the general community, such as the local symphony orchestra, art museum, opera and ballet. I reached Gene by telephone and discussed the importance of establishing the Wiesenthal Center.

"Gene, I'm going to have a very important visitor here next week," I told him. "Simon Wiesenthal will be in town, and we want to come and see you to discuss your becoming a founder of this new Center."

"By all means, Hart," he said brightly. "Bring him around. I definitely want to meet Simon Wiesenthal," and we proceeded to set up the appointment.

Gene welcomed us warmly into his office and then started to regale us with stories about his wartime experiences. He expressed a good deal of verbal support for the Center's mission and mentioned repeatedly how honored he was to receive Wiesenthal as a visitor. Finally it was time to come to the point; so I put it to him: "Gene, are you prepared to come aboard as a founder of the Wiesenthal Center?"

"You said that involves a gift of $25,000. Am I correct?" he said. I confirmed the amount of our request, as Gene leaned back in his chair. A faint smile passed his lips as he looked at me and said:

"I'll tell you what, Hart. Let's make it a quid pro quo. Whatever size gift you make to my favorite cause, which is the Indianapolis Symphony Orchestra, I will match and donate to the Wiesenthal Center." I could not believe my ears.

"What?" I said, quite startled by this unexpected proposal. "If you wish for me to make a gift to the Symphony, I'll be glad to discuss it with you, but linking it to your support of the Wiesenthal Center doesn't make much sense. This is not what I had expected, and I must tell you that I'm very disappointed by this."

He shrugged and said: "That's the way I do things, Hart. You help me and I'll help you. That's the way it works."

At this point Wiesenthal, visibly dismayed by Glick's proposal, chimed in with: "I will make a contribution to your orchestra, Mr. Glick." Wiesenthal was as good as his word and sent Gene a check made out to the Symphony in the amount of $25. But even this gesture failed to win him over and Gene never gave the Center any financial support. He even failed to match the $25 tendered by Wiesenthal.

Dejected over having wasted two hours listening to Glick's recollections and walking out empty-handed, Wiesenthal quipped: "His name is Glick? His name should be *Umglick*!" using the Yiddish term for misfortune.

Despite his attempt at humor, I could see that Wiesenthal was dejected over the outcome of our meeting with Glick. In an attempt to cheer him up, I suggested a visit to the Hebrew Academy and Wiesenthal agreed. I phoned Dr. Raymond Stern, the school's principal, and asked if he could quickly put together a school assembly in order to welcome an important visitor. He said that he could and, when our group arrived at the school soon thereafter, we were greeted by young students standing in the hallways clapping and singing *"Heiveinu Shalom Aleichem."* Wiesenthal was visibly moved by the visit, the details of which are recounted in Chapter Eleven.

Despite Glick's lack of support, other donors came through and the

Center was successfully launched. It has grown to encompass a Museum of Tolerance and a documentary film studio. It continues to serve as a vocal defense organization against the forces of anti-Semitism around the globe.

Over the years I have been most fortunate to receive a number of awards and honors in recognition of my volunteer activities. I'm not certain if I was always deserving, but I do know that I'm appreciative of each such distinction. One such award that I am most proud of, was the Jabotinsky Medal, presented in 1980 to one hundred distinguished Americans by an ad hoc committee, initiated through the Herut Zionists of America, in order to mark the centennial of Ze'ev Jabotinsky's birth.

I recall attending the awards ceremony in New York along with the other 99 recipients. Since we were seated in alphabetical order, I found myself sitting next to the well-known televangelist, Jerry Falwell, who had also been named as a recipient. Israeli Prime Minister Menachem Begin flew in to New York to present the medals. I recall how proud I felt when, after shaking hands with all of the prior recipients, including Falwell, it came to my turn, and Begin placed the medal around my neck and embraced me in a warm public hug.

When my pending award of the Jabotinsky Medal was announced, I began receiving a tide of congratulatory messages. One response to the news, however, was anything but laudatory. I was advised by my secretary that Gabriel Cohen was holding on line one. Gabe was, and still remains at age 92, the irascible editor of the *Indiana Jewish Post and Opinion*, a Jewish weekly tabloid published in Indianapolis. I knew I could count on Gabe for something lively.

"Hart, I understand from reading my newspaper that you're about to receive the Jabotinsky Medal," he said without preamble.

"That's right, Gabe." I replied. "Nice of you to call. You know they're actually giving it to one hundred Americans."

"Yes, I know. That's why I'm calling," he said testily. "How come I didn't get one? Did you know that I was on the Zionist welcoming committee when Jabotinsky came to America in the 1930s? I was very involved with Jabotinsky. I even wrote editorials about him in the paper."

"Oh, I see," I responded. "I wasn't aware of all that. Let me look into it and see what I can do." This intrigued me since I knew that Gabe, like many American Jewish liberals, arrived rather late to the table when it came to supporting a Zionist state. Before I would go and recommend him for any sort of medal, I felt I should, like any good reporter, check out his story. I visited the small archive of bound volumes containing all the back issues of the *Jewish Post*. I sought out, and soon located, the Jabotinsky editorials that Gabe claimed to have written in the 1930s. Yes, it was true. He had written several pieces that mentioned Jabotinsky, but none of them was flattering, to say the least. I did not mention my research expedition to Gabe when I phoned him back in order to beg off, explaining that I really did not have any input into the selection process.

During the very moving awards ceremony, the story was once again told of Jabotinsky's legacy. He had died suddenly in 1940 while visiting New York and was buried there. His widow announced at the time that Jabotinsky had left instructions that it was his desire for the head of state of the new Zionist nation to order his remains moved there once such a state had been established. It was eight years before the State of Israel was born under the leadership of David Ben Gurion. But, so strong was Ben Gurion's revulsion towards the Revisionist movement, that he could not bring himself to issue the order, leaving it, instead, to his successor, Levi Eshkol, to bring Jabotinsky's remains to Israel for burial at Mount Hertzl. I recall how Menachem Begin served as one of Jabotinsky's pall-bearers at the time.

A number of groups have sprung up since Begin's death to preserve his legacy and secure his place in history. The most prominent of these is the Menachem Begin Heritage Foundation, a group that I, along with its director Harry Hurwitz, helped to found. The Foundation is headquartered in Israel and is currently involved in building the Menachem Begin Library, which will house all of Begin's papers and serve as a learning center for students and historians. I am proud to serve as the president of the US branch of the organization, Friends of the Menachem Begin Heritage Foundation, which is currently being managed from my office in Indianapolis. Over the coming years, the Begin Library will help to preserve the memory of Begin's leadership and to promote his values of free enterprise and Jewish national pride.

Not many people outside of the Jewish community are aware of the existence of Boy's Town Jerusalem. This worthwhile organization works diligently in Israel to provide economically disadvantaged boys of limiting backgrounds with unlimited futures. The organization was founded in 1949 by Rabbi Alexander S. Linchner, a Brooklyn-born clergyman inspired, after the Holocaust, to devote his life to building a school that would provide a home and outstanding education to the children who poured into Israel from countries around the world. It would also prepare them to build the State of Israel with both technical skill and traditional Jewish idealism. Boy's Town Jerusalem operates a fund-raising office in New York under the direction of Rabbi Ronald Gray, who, during his years as rabbi of Congregation

B'nai Torah in Indianapolis had founded the Hebrew Academy day school (see Chapter 11).

My involvement with Boy's Town goes back to its earliest days. Given my own background in the postwar DP camps, it is not surprising that I support the opportunities they are extending to Israel's youth. I currently sit on their Board of Directors and have been called upon to invite, and then introduce, Benny Begin as a speaker for a New York fund-raising event. I would encourage anyone traveling to Israel to pay a visit to the amazing Boy's Town 18-acre campus located in the Bayit Vegan area of Jerusalem.

One of my most important affiliations is with the American Israeli Public Affairs Committee or AIPAC. AIPAC is a grass roots lobbying organization that works to promote Israeli interests in Washington. I believe that, along with the Conference of Presidents, AIPAC is perhaps the most important Jewish organization in the United States. My relationship with AIPAC has been a mercurial one, primarily because of their tendency to support, without question, the policies of whatever government happens to be currently in power in Israel. This policy places the group in a position of support for the various unworkable and ill-conceived peace process schemes devised by the Labor governments. I have urged AIPAC leaders, such as Tom Dine and his successor Howard Kohr, to develop positions that are based on what is best for Israel, regardless of which party happens to be in power at the moment. Unlike foreign lobbying groups who must register with the State Department, AIPAC is made up entirely of Americans and should therefore, I feel, articulate the opinions of American Jews, even when they may conflict with the policies of the current Israeli government.

Despite my differences from time to time with AIPAC, I find them a more effective group than the other major Jewish defense organization, the Anti-Defamation League (ADL). Interestingly, the ADL's national chairman, Abe Foxman, and I knew each other in the DP camps of Austria after the war. I served as Abe's Betar commander in those days and have maintained my friendship with him over the years.

As mentioned earlier, I succeeded during my presidency of the Herut Zionists of America to gain the organization a seat on the Conference of Presidents of Major Jewish Organizations. More than any other group, I feel that the Conference of Presidents, a congress of leaders from fifty major Jewish organizations, can best lay claim to the title of the "Voice of the American Jewish community." They are frequently called upon by the President and by Congress to express the attitudes and opinions of US Jews. The Conference of Presidents often plays host to visiting foreign leaders, such as Egyptian president, Hosni Mubarak, among others. It is one of the few organizations to actively come out in support of leniency for Jonathan Pollard, the convicted American serving a life sentence for spying on behalf of Israel. Before taking such a position, the Conference must first arrive at a consensus from among its members. The Conference is ably served by its executive vice-chairman, Malcolm Hoenlein, perhaps the most capable Jewish professional on the scene today.

I am also a proud supporter of the Be'ersheva Foundation, established in 1989 by the mayor of Be'ersheva, Ijo Rager. The group raises funds around the world to assist in the development of this beautiful ancient city, considered to be the Biblical home of the Patriarch Abraham and known as the "Capital of the Negev." I have visited Be'ersheva frequently and have seen how this group has succeeded in improving the quality of life for the new immigrants, Jews, Christians and Bedouins who populate this central Israeli community.

In terms of non-sectarian organizations, I proudly count myself as a Senior Rotarian. While no longer actively involved in Rotary projects, I still follow their activities and offer my ongoing support. I first became involved with Rotary after moving to Indianapolis, and while still working for Bemis. I recall being placed on the Board of the Mary Riggs Neighborhood Center, an inner city community agency located on the city's south side. This tour of service was extremely rewarding and provided me with an excellent foundation for my later involvement with Jewish community work.

My brother Mark and I have been supporters of the good work carried out by the City of Hope comprehensive cancer center located northeast of Los Angeles in Duarte, California. The center is supported almost entirely through philanthropy and provides assistance to millions of people fighting cancer and other life threatening diseases, such as diabetes and AIDS. Over 300 scientists and physicians, along with 2,500 employees, are actively seeking the causes and cures of these and other diseases. Mark and I have been honored by the City of Hope for our efforts on behalf of their important mission.

I am also very pleased to be associated with one of the oldest Jewish organizations in America, the Orthodox Union. The OU is the largest and most dynamic Jewish movement of its kind in the world. It serves as the national voice for over 1,000 Orthodox synagogues. It is also a non-profit educational, outreach and social service organization, conducting far-reaching activities as a coordinating agency for American and Canadian Orthodox congregations. Among their major programs are the National Council for Synagogue Youth

(NCSY) and the Joint Kashruth Certification Service, whose OU is the world's preeminent *kashruth* symbol. The OU is very politically involved. Their faxed update on Jewish and Israeli news topics is a daily must-read.

I have also become involved with a number of Israeli charitable organizations, such as the College of Judea and Samaria. And through the efforts of Aliza Begin, I was asked to join the Board of Asaf HaRofeh, a hospital located outside of Tel Aviv. Aliza had also asked me to carry out a special charitable function after Menachem Begin had won the Nobel Peace Prize jointly with Anwar Sadat in 1979. Begin elected not to keep the several hundred thousand dollars that represented his portion of the prize money. Instead he wished to donate the funds to a worthy cause. Aliza asked me to serve on the Board of a trust fund that was established to distribute the money to needy Israeli college students. We set up a committee to review the applications and put the money to good use by providing college educations to bright and deserving young men and women.

Not all of the groups with which I became involved resulted in positive experiences. As was recounted in Chapter Six, I traveled to New York several years after arriving in America to reunite with a number of my Ebelsberg DP camp buddies who had re-settled in Brooklyn. I maintained sporadic contact with this group over the years and, beginning in the early 1990s, I was asked to join them at an Ebelsberg Camp reunion held every year in Fort Lauderdale, Florida. Finally, in February of 1996, I decided to attend for the first time.

About fifty survivors and their spouses gathered at a private banquet hall for a sit down luncheon. Simona and I were a bit surprised to see that a non-kosher meal was being served. Most of the attendees lived in New York, but a number had already retired to Florida. There were even a few participants who had traveled from Israel. I moved around the hall in an almost dreamlike state. Here were faces I had not even thought about for fifty years. Some were unchanged but for the white hair and deeper facial furrows. Others clearly showed the toll of their years. "Did I look to them as they looked to me?" I wondered.

Simona and I were disappointed by the fact that we were served a non-kosher meal, but even more disappointing was the fact that most of the attendees were more interested in the menu than in catching up on the lives of their old campmates. I expressed my feelings and told them all plainly: "Simona and I did not come here for the food. We came here to learn about all of you. I want to know who was the ultimate winner in the struggle that placed us into Ebelsberg. Did we prevail or did our enemies? Do we have

Jewish grandchildren or not? Have we been keeping *Yiddishkeit* alive in our respective communities? These are the things I am most interested in." My remarks succeeded in prompting a few of the attendees to open up, but most of them, I'm afraid, continued to restrict their conversation to small talk and trivialities.

The highlight of the experience was reuniting with Mr. Lifschitz, who had served as the director of the ORT school at Ebelsberg. At age 90, Mr. Lifschitz was the oldest attendee and still quite mentally sharp. He had traveled to the event from California and he fully agreed with my comments.

"Oh, I've heard so much about you, Hart," he said warmly, extending his hand to me after having sought me out. "I've heard about your many accomplishments and am delighted to finally meet up with you again." The bulk of my time at the reunion was spent in Mr. Lifschitz's pleasant company, retrieving and reliving those cherished memories of "the good old days."

Of course, my curiosity prompted me to locate some of the women with whom I'd been romantically involved way back when. Was any trace of the old infatuation still alive? Had their beauty succumbed to the winds of time? And how did I appear to them? What if I had married that young girl fifty years ago and today this woman I'm now looking at would be on my arm instead of Simona? Despite all of these "what if" questions, I came away with a sense of gratitude that the Almighty has consistently guided me towards making good decisions.

After returning home and reflecting about the experience, I came to understand the underlying causes of my disappointment with the reunion. I had observed that only a few of the attendees were at all involved in Jewish community affairs. Why was I so different? The same forces that had shaped me as a Betar zealot in the crucible of my youth had also been at work in the case of many others in my situation. Why had I gone on to continue my activism while most of these folks obviously had not?

The answer, I determined, lay in the fact that almost all of the passionate Zionists with whom I had associated in Ebelsberg made *aliyah* to Israel after leaving the camp. Those who were more interested in economic opportunity opted for immigration to America instead. Somehow, I became the hybrid. I embraced the American Dream with all of my being, while at the same time never abandoning my strong Zionist ideals. In fact, these twin passions have never competed for primacy in my life. Instead there has always been an ongoing synergy. The more successful I found myself as an American businessman, the more devoted I have become to the ongoing strength and survival of the Jewish people. And the reverse, I feel, is equally as true.

One of my proudest affiliations is with Dr. Bernard Lander and Touro College. In 1997, in recognition of our support for their work, Touro invested Mark and me with Doctor of Letters degrees. While I always felt that there would someday be a few Dr. Hastens in our family, I never suspected that the first would be Mark and I.

While my personal religious beliefs could be characterized as traditional, I have never been a part of any Chassidic movement. At the same time, I am an admirer of the Chabad organization, also known as Lubavitch. This group has accomplished a great deal in terms of bringing assimilated American Jews back to Judaism. They approach social service endeavors with an almost missionary zeal, although their outreach is directed only at Jews, never at gentiles. The movement's spiritual leader, the late Rav Menachem Schneerson, of blessed memory, was an extraordinary and highly charismatic figure. I recall meeting with him on the wedding day of my older son, Bernard. We had traveled to Schneerson's Brooklyn home in order to receive his blessing for the match. It must have been effective, since the marriage has already lasted close to fifteen years and has produced four adorable grandchildren.

This last fact points to a relationship between the relationships in my life. Viewing the community as an extension of the family is not a uniquely Jewish concept, but it is certainly a widely held point of view among many Jews. In light of this, it is not surprising that my experiences in the world of community service have mirrored my own family dynamics. The fraternal fellowship of the Rotary, the sibling rivalries between the ADL and the JCRC, and the fatherly respect afforded to the Orthodox Union and Chabad. I believe that strong family values tend to generate strong community values and vice versa. The Torah talks of G-d's promise to Abraham in both domestic and global proportions in Genesis, Chapter 35, Verse 11:

> And G-d said to him, "I am G-d Almighty; be fruitful and
> increase in number. A nation and a community of nations
> will come from you... "

Here, as well as in other instances, the community is seen as the extension of the family, just as the nation is the outgrowth of the community. They are all constructs along a continuum of societal structures that, as a people moves further up the ladder, results in ever increasing strength and stability.

The basic societal unit, of course, is the individual. But the lesson I take from our heritage is that the individual is merely the starting point. As civilizations have developed over time, the needs of the family took precedence over the needs of the individual, and so on. Just as I believe that engendering more intensive family ties results in stronger families, I feel that greater community service results in a stronger and more secure Jewish people. It is this outlook and these sentiments that I hope to have embedded in my children and my grandchildren.

Chapter Seventeen
Full Circle

ONE OF THE MOST memorable experiences of my life was a special vacation that I planned in honor of Simona's fiftieth birthday in 1990. It was an adventure of a lifetime, as we traveled from the US to the Far East, India and Europe, visiting a dozen cities all around the world.

Three years after our return, we decided to plan a trip in the other direction. The dimension we traveled through this time was not space, but time, as we embarked on an extraordinary odyssey. Instead of traveling to the lavish fun spots of the globe, we headed for one of the most dismal and unglamorous venues imaginable. Instead of jetting around the globe in bright futuristic style, on this trip we would ride the rails back into our dark and disparate past. Instead of filling my senses with new and exciting tastes, sights and sounds, this was to be a journey to satisfy a hunger of the heart. A journey back to where all things began for me. A journey that would bring me full circle, some 52 years after first setting out from my *shtetl* on that lonely night back in June of 1941. Not a visit to faraway lands, but rather a journey to the familiar and pungent soil in which my earliest memories are firmly planted. We were going back. Back in time; back to the beginning. We were going back to Brotchin.

Not surprisingly, I never had the urge to return to my homeland after arriving in America. Unlike some immigrants who feel a desire to re-visit their county of origin in order to flaunt the success they had achieved in America, I did not harbor any such emotions. I had made a clean break with Europe, and I really was not interested at any time during all those years, in returning to my native soil. I wanted nothing whatsoever to do with the old world I had left behind. Then, in 1993, something happened that changed all of this.

During a conversation with Simon Wiesenthal, he confirmed the circumstances surrounding the killing of my grandfather and my cousin, Lonka, as recounted in the introduction to this book. Additionally, Wiesenthal showed me an entry in a remembrance date-book entitled *Every Day Remembrance Day*. The book details hundreds of atrocities committed against the Jews over the centuries, with the entries arranged date-book-style according to the month and day upon which they occurred. Among the entries for June 16 is the following one:

June 16, 1942: From Bohorodczany, Poland, 1,200 Jews are brought to Stanislav (*sic*) and murdered by Ukainian police in the *Rudolfsmühle* (Rudolf's Mill).

This entry represents the first documentation I had seen that mentions the exact date of the probable extermination of my family. For nearly fifty years, I had been unable to light a *yahrtzeit* candle for my family members, because I was not certain of the date of their deaths. Although I am still unsure about the exact date of my Zayde and Lonka's vicious murder, I now had evidence that most of my family were, in all likelihood, killed on June 16, 1942 (*1 Tamuz 5702*) in a place called Rudolf's Mill, in a town that was now called Ivano Frankovsk, in the Ukraine. I was now able to light a memorial candle in their memory on the first day of the Hebrew month of *Tamuz*. Although my family may have been among the roughly 1,300 Jews who died in Bohorodczany due to extreme deprivations before the deportations to Stanislawow took place, I believe that the first of *Tamuz* is the appropriate date for me to honor their blessed memories.

It was as if a burden had been lifted from my shoulders, perhaps by a divine hand. I suddenly felt an overwhelming desire to visit the spot and to recite a *Kaddish* prayer for my family and for my murdered landsmen.

So it was that in the summer of 1993, Simona and I, along with our 17-year-old son, Josh, packed up for an overland odyssey across Eastern Europe to reclaim the memory of our family.

The journey was not an easy one. The largest city in the region we wished to visit was Lvov, but scheduled flights into Lvov were an iffy business. We were advised to fly in to Budapest and then take a train to Lvov, where we would arrange for a minivan to drive us into Ivano Frankovsk. From there we could drive to Bohorodczany, if we so chose.

The flight into Budapest was a breeze, and we were met by a guide who escorted us to the train station for our trip to Lvov. According to the map, we expected the train ride to last no more than five or six hours. In actuality, it took nearly 14 hours to get there. One reason for the slow progress was the fact that the train was a local, stopping at every point along the way. The major reason for the delay, however, became plain to us around 3 AM. The train came to a complete stop as we approached the Ukrainian border. Once we were stopped, we were greeted by an incessant, loud, metallic pounding. Sleep was impossible, so we stepped out, weary-eyed, onto the platform to investigate the matter. We observed hundreds of train crew workers placing each rail car on a special hydraulic lift that raised the car several feet into the air. After making some inquiries in an effort to understand this mysterious behavior, we were finally informed about what was going on. It appeared that the train tracks on the other side of the border are of a different gauge than the type found throughout Europe. Because of this difference in rail width, trains from Europe cannot travel on Russian-built rail lines without undergoing serious modification. It was this modification, we learned, that must take place on every train entering or exiting a former Soviet republic and bound into or out of western Europe. The crews were elevating every train car and replacing the wheel assemblies on each one. The process was long, arduous, labor intensive and extremely noisy.

After about four hours of this, the work was completed. Of course it would all have to be undone a few hours later when the same train came back across the border going the other way. I calculated that if the hundreds of hours of manpower being expended daily in this absurd activity were to be deployed towards laying new rail track, this problem could be permanently eliminated in a little over one year. I happened to think back to a pundit's comment about how best to understand the Soviet system. "The best way to comprehend it," he opined, "is that in the USSR, time is not money." I figured that this observation still held true today in many parts of the former USSR.

Once we observed that the work was finished, we made our way back to our private compartment. We had been given a "first class" seat that simply meant that we did not have to share our compartment with other passengers. Otherwise, our space was just as stinky and run-down as the rest of the train. Every car on the train was supposed to be managed under the watchful eye of a female monitor whose single responsibility seemed to be dispensing the key to the only available toilet. Unfortunately, after the wheel exchange, our monitor lady had disappeared, along with her bathroom key. This situation made the balance of the journey particularly uncomfortable for us. The sole refreshment facility was a pot of boiling water at the front of our car. Fortunately, because of our need to observe kosher dietary laws, we had brought along our own food supply. This was a blessing, since there was literally not a crumb of food commercially available to passengers anywhere on this train.

I soon realized that I was guilty of a serious oversight. I had failed to bring cigarettes along with me. As we entered the Ukraine, the border guards, seeing our American passports, asked us for Western cigarettes. I explained that I didn't smoke, but this fact seemed to be completely irrelevant and only served to make the guards even more upset. They soon made off with our passports and, after what seemed like several hours, had still not returned them to us. I was afraid that they were holding our passports hostage until we could "cough up" some American smokes. Fortunately, the passports were returned to us without incident before we arrived in Lvov.

Finally we pulled into Lvov, a city of three million, with all the charm and excitement of a municipal drunk tank. The once proud boulevards were littered with human wreckage. Young, derelict men, shouting in vodka-induced rage, were visible even during the morning hours. We viewed others shamelessly urinating in public as if to say: "Piss on this town!" This was Josh's first exposure to this sort of crude, brutish life-style, and his reaction was, at first, one of shock that people actually lived like this. Rather quickly, however, Josh's sense of humor got warmed up and he used it to combat his obvious culture shock. He soon had us laughing over the primitive toilets, the bizarre restaurant fare, the unbelievably bad four-star hotel and the many other outrageous aspects of trying to be a tourist in post-Soviet Ukraine.

We were shown around the city by a former government issue tourist guide. Lydia was a stocky lady who sported 1970s vintage eyeglasses and a large facial wart. Her classroom English was passable, and she was glad to have the opportunity to practice it on real, live Americans. We traveled via a brand new Mitsubishi minivan, complete with driver, that succeeded in creating quite a stir along the streets of Lvov. Ours was the only vehicle on the road since traffic did not exist in Lvov until around 9 AM. When we inquired, we were advised that only big shot government officials traveled to work in private cars, and they're all late sleepers. The sight of a brand new Japanese minivan on the streets of Lvov at 7 AM was unusual enough to draw the stares of all who laid eyes upon it.

There was already a crowd gathered around the vehicle as we boarded. As we got in, a small ten-year-old Ukrainian boy decided to wipe off our exterior mirrors and windshield. I felt obliged to offer him a tip and asked our guide what would be an appropriate amount.

"Do you have one dollar?" she asked, and I said that I did. I took the one-dollar bill and handed it to the boy, who nearly fell over with excitement. He took off at top speed to show the precious bill to his mother. Lydia explained that one US dollar was the equivalent of 3,900 Ukrainian *Koupons* (local currency). I didn't know what that would buy, but it sounded like a great deal.

I did not reveal to Lydia the true reason for our visit, since she was not Jewish and probably would not understand my motives. But after a few hours of riding with us, she was beginning to get the picture. After directing us to the standard government approved tourist sites, I asked her to show us the sole active synagogue, which she eventually did. While there, I learned that Lvov has a Jewish population of roughly 5,000, many of whom help to maintain a Jewish day school, which we also visited. I was impressed with how Jewish life refused to die out here, despite Hitler's best efforts and fifty years of Soviet domination.

I had heard that Lvov had erected a rather impressive monument to the city's Holocaust victims. I asked Lydia to please direct us there because we wished to see it. She appeared puzzled, at first. "Why would you want to go there?" seemed to be her attitude. "I'm not exactly sure where it is." she offered weakly and tried to interest us in some sites that depicted the history of Lvov.

"Well, then, look it up and get us there. And please don't forget that your job is to take us wherever we wish to go. I'm sorry, but I'm really not very interested in the history of Lvov. But I am interested in learning about what happened to my people. Understand?" She got us there, and it was, indeed, a very impressive monument. When we were done, she again tried to steer us back to the official party-line visitor's tour.

I insisted we deviate from the textbook tour and visit areas where people actually lived and worked. The economic deprivation under which the population was forced to live was shocking to witness. Store shelves were empty but for the most paltry of goods. Sights of shoppers standing in long lines for bread and other staple items were common. Perhaps it was out of nostalgia for my youthful days spent standing in such lines back in Alga, but I wanted to experience this for myself. I got out of the minivan and stood at the end of a moderately long breadline. The memories came flooding back as I finally reached the head of the line and was permitted to purchase a single loaf of bread. Just one whiff of the loaf succeeded in erasing a half-century of my life, and I was once again a scruffy little kid back in pre-war Poland. Not only that, but I felt that the bread tasted delicious, although my family did not fully agree with this assessment. The locals standing in line with me didn't quite know what to make of me, either. I could sense them thinking: "Who is this guy with his new Mitsubishi and his American jeans who can speak our language and for some reason has taken it into his head to stand in line with us today for bread?" I'm sure they all concluded that I was some sort of nut case.

The following morning we boarded the minivan for the drive towards Bohorodczany. Our first stop was in Ivano Frankovsk (formerly Stanislawow). This, of course was the central collection point in this region for all the Jews targeted by the Nazis. Over 100,000 Jewish men, women and children were ruthlessly, and pointlessly, murdered in this quiet Carpathian town between 1941 and 1943. Although the town was declared *judenrein* (cleansed of Jews) by the Nazis, today a spark of Jewish life still exists amidst an overall population of over one million.

We sought out and met with the community's sole Rabbi, a Lubavitcher named Victor Kolesnik. Oddly, Rabbi Kolesnik spoke no Yiddish. He was born after the war to a Jewish Communist father, whose ideology Victor eventually came to reject. He had traveled to Moscow and connected with a Lubavitch seminary where he rekindled his Jewish identity and became ordained. He was now working to keep Judaism alive in remote areas such as Ivano Frankovsk. Fortunately, our Hebrew was adequate to communicate with him effectively.

When we informed Rabbi Kolesnik that I was born in Bohorodczany and then told him my story, he insisted that we meet with Shimshon Tabak without delay. Shimshon was another Jewish Holocaust survivor from Bohorodczany, now living in Ivano Frankovsk. Shimshon's tale of survival was very similar to my own. He had also managed to flee to the Soviet Union as the Germans were advancing across Poland in 1941. He remembered my father quite well, and he even remembered my brother and me and called me by my Yiddish name, Hetche. Of course, I was too young to remember Shimshon, but when I returned home I showed a video interview that I had conducted with him to both my mother and to Sam Hipschman. They both remembered Shimshon clearly and were delighted to learn that he had survived.

Shimshon had been swallowed up into Russian society after the war, marrying a non-Jewish Russian woman and working at menial government jobs. At this point, as a widower in his eighties, Shimshon was living simply off his pension close to the town where he had been raised. Although he managed to get to Russia before the deportations from Bohorodczany, he recalled with horror the eyewitness accounts he had heard about the bloody massacres that had taken place here in the former Stanislawow. Speaking with Shimshon was like opening a history book. His memory was remarkable and all his testimony bore the unmistakable ring of truth.

At our request, Shimshon accompanied us to the place once known as

Rudolf's Mill. This was the charnel house used by the Ukrainians to slaughter thousands of Jews brought to their town from the countryside. Today, the building is an ordinary, functioning factory. As we stood across the street, staring at what once was a house of horror for so many innocent victims, I could picture the rivers of Jewish blood pouring from the building into the overflowing street gutters. No marker or sign has ever been erected to identify this infamous spot, and hence, very few of the workers who enter this building every day are even aware of its notorious history. The specter of the evil that once occupied this place was palpable to me and to my family. Yet today, it's as if nothing had ever happened in this seemingly banal and quite ordinary-looking factory building.

Likewise, the once thriving Jewish community, today reduced to no more than 150 souls, is not commemorated in any fashion. It's as if the hundreds of thousands of Jews who called this town their home for over 500 years, had never even existed.

After our touring what was once the Jewish ghetto, Shimshon finally took us to the cemetery. According to reliable accounts, the Jews of Bohorodczany were murdered at Rudolf's Mill on June 16, 1942, and their ravaged bodies dumped into a mass grave located about one kilometer away, near the Jewish cemetery.

Arriving at the scene, Rabbi Kolesnik pointed towards the spot. We gazed out across a wide, grass-covered meadow, and I could see the dip, or depression, in the landscape that indicated where the mass grave had been dug. Shimshon pointed out other, similar nearby depressions, where the Jews from other rural communities had been deposited. A warm breeze swabbed our faces as birds flittered across a blue, cloudless sky. It was probably a lovely day like this one, back in June of 1942, at this very spot, that the lifeless, tortured bodies of my family members were flung into a human landfill. How could people on G-d's green earth go out on such a beautiful day and smash the skulls of innocent babies until the killers were knee-deep in Jewish blood? What level of hatred can drive people to commit such atrocities?

I stood in stoic silence, without tears, attempting somehow to grasp what had happened here to all those Brotchin *Yidn* (Jews) who were fondly retained in the memories of my youth. I wondered quietly, "What were their last thoughts?" When they could see what was being done to the others ahead of them and they understood that their turn was coming soon – what were they thinking as they prepared to meet their fate? Were they praising the glory of G-d? Were they plotting some sort of desperate resistance? Were they too tired, hungry or weak to think of anything at all? Actually, I was pondering what would have been going through *my* mind had a miracle, and my father's courage, not intervened, and had I not been spared the fate of my fellow Jews.

I concluded that, had I been there and had I been faced with no way out, my final thoughts would have been a prayer to G-d asking that we not be forgotten. That our lives be remembered and that the manner of our deaths be revealed to the entire world. This is the sentiment I felt from the spirits of the victims whose remains lay beneath my feet. "Don't forget about us. We were people just like you. Don't forget about us. Avenge our deaths by finding justice. And, most of all, never again. Never permit this to happen again." This is the message I received that day from the *neshamot* (souls) of the Brotchin Jews. This is the message I came full circle to hear. And this is the message that I shall carry with me for the rest of my days.

For some divine reason, my pleadings of "I Shall Not Die!" were heeded and I was permitted to live while nearly everyone around me, including my Zayde and my little cousin, Lonka, were destined for death. Standing in the sacred presence of my martyred, murdered family that day, I fully understood, for the first time, why I had been permitted to live. It was to fulfill the wishes of the Brotchin Jews by not forgetting them and by working to insure that such things would "Never Again" take place. "Never Again" let yourself become so weak that your enemies are tempted to try and destroy you. Learn how to shoot back. Don't sit back idly when you are attacked in words or in deeds waiting for things to get better or for a Messiah to come and rescue you. Until the *Maschiach* arrives, rely upon yourself and do what must be done in order to survive. In a certain sense, we must become our own redeemers, rescuing ourselves and our people from the abyss of historic extinction. This attitude applies to the nation of Israel as well as to each individual Jew.

An uneasy ambivalence overtook me at this point, as these thoughts came gushing forth rapidly. On the one hand, I felt burdened by such an awesome responsibility, while at the same time I felt incredible relief in finally making sense of the dramatic events of my life. By serving as a lifelong advocate of Jewish strength and an enemy of appeasement, I have been working to make sure these horrors will never recur. And by visiting their final resting place, I was doing something to guarantee that these unfortunate victims would not be forgotten. I felt, however, that there was something more that I could do towards this end.

I observed that no marker had been erected to honor the memory of those who had perished here. Had the Rabbi not been there to point out the exact spot, I would not have been able to identify it on my own. I decided that I could do something about this situation. I informed the Rabbi that I wanted a *Matzayvah* (stone memorial) erected at this spot, relating what happened here to the Jews of my home town. I explained that I would underwrite the costs, but I wanted him to make all the arrangements. He agreed to do so. Rabbi Kolesnik has been working on this project ever since and it is finally near to completion. It is our hope that the *Matzayvah* will be unveiled on June 16, 2002, the sixtieth anniversary of the slaughter.

At the site of the mass grave, I bowed down and recited *Kaddish* for our departed ones. My heart went out to my son Josh, who was deeply touched by the experience and fought to hold back his anger and his tears.

Our guide, Lydia, had been taking all of this in without saying a word. Walking back from the site together, she asked me why I had paid so much attention to what this bearded man was telling me? I was surprised by the question and responded by saying: "He's a Rabbi and he knows a lot." What she said next surprised me even more.

"You know he's not a Jew," she pronounced under her breath.

"Of course, he's a Jew," I protested. "In fact, he's a Chassid. A very serious Jew." She gave me a confused look.

"But he is Ukrainian," she said. "The way he speaks. His Ukrainian is perfect. Only a true Ukrainian can speak this way. Also, Victor Kolesnik is a Ukrainian name, not a Jewish name."

Despite my efforts, I could not get her to understand that a person could be both a Ukrainian and a Jew at the same time. To Lydia, these were matters of blood. Years after the demise of the Soviet system and long after the fall of Nazism, in Lydia's world, a Jew was one thing and a Ukrainian was something else.

After several hours at the burial ground, we re-boarded the minivan and headed south to Bohorodczany. We passed the little village of Lisec that I recalled lay on the road between our town and what was then called Stanislawow. I was uneasy and somewhat anxious as we approached the road sign, now bearing the Ukrainian instead of the Polish spelling, directing us to the town of my birth and early childhood. The last time I traversed this road, it was as a ten-year-old boy on the back of a horse-drawn wagon, fleeing from the Nazi onslaught. Strange and powerful feelings began to surface as buildings popped into view.

Fifty-two years is a long time, and I found almost nothing as I remembered it. Nothing was the same. None of the buildings that lined the avenues of my memory were in sight. Finally we arrived at the center of town at what used to be the town square. Right at the edge of the old square used to sit our big house, occupying a full city block, and serving as home and place of business for our entire extended family. It was in this square that my Zayde and little cousin Lonka were publicly executed. But the square was no more. And from the looks of things, it was clear that the Jews of Bohorodczany were also no more. Our *shtetl*, "cleansed" of its 2,500 Jews by the Nazis in 1942 had remained "*judenrein*" ever since.

What used to be the town square was now built up with ugly, Soviet-style office buildings and non-descript shops. One corner contained a memorial statue honoring the Ukrainians who lost their lives in World War II. No mention of Jews anywhere. It's as if we had never existed. We searched in vain for any trace of the several synagogues and of the *cheder* I attended as a child. All were gone.

I could see that killing Jews was such a natural instinct for these Ukrainians that they continued doing so indefinitely, by altering history and denying that Jews ever lived amongst them at all. Merely destroying a Jew's life was not sufficient for them. They wanted to go even further and destroy the very memory of the Jew's existence. According to these Ukrainians, my Zayde didn't live and then die at the hands of the Nazis. He never even existed at all. This, I imagine, is what is meant by the term "a fate worse than death."

Suddenly my eyes finally fell on something that looked familiar. Ironically, it was the church cathedral that I remember dominating the city square. How much smaller it now appeared than when it was viewed through the eyes of a ten-year-old boy. Walking closer, I could tell how run-down the church had become. I also saw that the streets had become all shifted around and dreary avenues now ran where houses once stood. Feeling a bit like old Rip Van Winkle, I used the church steeple to gain my bearings. I remembered how tall the steeple appeared from the backyard of our home and, using navigational triangulation, I was able to pinpoint the exact location of our old house. The building was gone and in its place there now stood a modest Post Office.

Memories began flowing once I had my bearings. For instance, I remembered that we drew water from a well in the backyard. I located the general area and began to poke around behind the Post Office. I spotted what appeared to be a little circular doghouse designed to keep something on the ground protected from the weather. I told Simona: "That's where our well was located."

Simona was impressed with my navigational skills, but we both had something more pressing on our minds. "I need to use the bathroom and I'll bet you do, too," she said. She was right.

"Let's go inside the Post Office and ask to use theirs," I suggested. When I inquired, I was directed back outside to an outhouse of the most dirty and disgusting variety. Despite fifty-two Jew-less years of progress, indoor plumbing had not yet arrived in Bohorodczany.

There were other signs of "de-evolution" in evidence as well. I have a clear recollection of the public bus that, back in my day, made a daily run between Bohorodczany and Stanislawow. I rode this bus frequently as a child and, to this day, the smell of its diesel exhaust will transport me back to those carefree pre-war days. When I inquired, I was told that, yes, a bus still runs between the two towns, but nowadays, because of the fuel shortage, it just runs once a week. The clock of history was definitely turning backwards.

Would Bohorodczany be any better off today had all the Jews not been killed off or driven out? Who knows? But I am just enough of a Jewish chauvinist to believe that the answer might be "yes!"

My final desire before leaving Bohorodczany was to visit the Jewish cemetery and the grave of my grandmother, Yonah. Bubbe Yonah died when I was just five years old, but I still remember the unveiling of her tombstone the following year. The name Yonah means "dove," and the handsome stone was decorated with two sculpted doves. To the eyes of a six-year-old boy, it was extremely beautiful.

I also wished to visit the cemetery because, since there were no living Jews in the town, perhaps I could visit with the dead ones. Unfortunately, this was not to be. The Jewish cemetery was long since gone, replaced by a heap of stones. Learning of this only served to compound my depression and my desire to get out of this place and never to return.

We boarded the minivan and headed back through town towards Ivano Frankovsk, stopping from time to time in order to permit a herd of sheep, or a farmer with his oxen, to pass. Some might have found this bucolic way of life idyllic and rather charming, but not I. Every time I spotted a Ukrainian farmer, I could not help but think to myself: "Is this the one, or is this the son of the one, who murdered my family?"

I came away demoralized and concluded that the Nazis, along with their zealous Ukrainian partners, had done an amazingly effective job of erasing Jews forever from their midst. Not only had they murdered or run out all the Jews and destroyed any trace of their ever having lived there, they also vanquished any desire of returning to Bohorodczany that might have existed in my heart.

I still had not directly explained to Lydia, our guide, why I wanted to visit Bohorodczany, although I presumed she might have guessed by now. On the return trip, I decided to lay my cards on the table. As we drove through the town for the last time, I pointed out the window and told her:

"I was born here. This town is my birthplace." She said nothing and sat stone-faced and impassive. But I could tell what she was thinking: "Damn it. I thought we got you all. How did you slip through?" Maybe I was suffering from some lingering paranoia, but that was what the body language was telling me.

We returned to Lvov that evening and retired to our rooms at the Intercontinental Hotel. This was supposed to be the finest luxury hotel in the city, but we encountered a rather bizarre problem. Josh was unable to sleep in his room because it was permeated with an overwhelming odor of kerosene. This seemed odd since the weather was warm and no heating fuel was being used. But then it came to me. In this part of the world, they clean everything with kerosene in order to kill the bedbugs. With this pleasant thought in mind, I attempted to take a shower, until I noticed that the bath towel was the size of a dishtowel and half as absorbent.

We were so delighted to get out of that place that we didn't even complain when the Lvov to Budapest train was again stopped at the border for four hours in the middle of the night in order to change all of the wheels back to their original size.

Once in Budapest, I wanted to get to Israel, and back to civilization, as soon as possible. We caught the next El Al flight and never felt more grateful to be in *Eretz Yisrael* than after this nightmare visit to Ukraine. We literally felt like kissing the ground when we arrived at Ben Gurion airport.

Looking back, this "return to my roots" trip turned out to be a mixed bag. In many ways I was thankful for the opportunity, after so many years, to be able to properly pay my respects to the dead. On the other hand, walking the streets of Bohorodczany was a traumatic and painful experience that I probably could have done without. There was, undoubtedly, a feeling of closure, of having come full circle — not physically as we had done during our circumnavigational trip a few years before. But spiritually, I felt as though I had, at last, come to terms with my past, and this fact has helped me to live a calmer and more grounded life ever since.

Perhaps the most wonderful aspect of the journey was an unbelievable surprise reunion that I never would have expected.

As mentioned earlier, I conducted a videotaped interview, in Yiddish, with Shimshon Tabak, during which he recounted, in horrid detail, what had become of the Jews of our shtetl after they were deported to Stanislawow. During this interview, he also disclosed a somewhat earth-shaking revelation. He knew the whereabouts of the two surviving Friedman brothers with whom our family had shared our horse-drawn wagon back in 1941. In the 1960s the two younger surviving brothers and their families had emigrated from Kazakhstan and settled in Stanislawow where they had met up with Shimshon. After several years there, the brothers moved on to Israel and were now living in Be'ersheva, I learned, along with their extended families. This was incredible news. Shimshon had given us the Friedmans' addresses and phone numbers, and this was another reason we decided to travel to Israel as soon as we got back to Budapest.

I had learned that the older Friedman brother, Sioma (Shlomo) had adopted his mother's maiden name, Druker. Once we arrived in Tel Aviv, I phoned Sioma Druker and listened to his shocked reaction when I identified myself.

"Hetche? Hetchele?" he gasped, almost in hysterics. "You found us! After so many long years! *Baruch HaShem.*"

"How is Laib?" I inquired, asking about his younger brother.

"You know, we're both getting old, but I know he'll be so happy when I tell him I spoke with you. When can I see you and your family?"

"I'm here with my youngest and my wife, and we're coming to see you in Be'ersheva tomorrow." And the following morning we got into our Volvo and drove south for our date with destiny in the desert.

It was a tearful and emotionally charged reunion. I had no difficulty in recognizing Sioma, despite the passage of nearly fifty years. He also claimed he would have recognized me anywhere, although I can't be sure he was being truthful.

We found Sioma and his wife living in a beautiful apartment. They had two grown children who lived nearby – a daughter who was a physician and a son who was a trained engineer. Both children and their spouses were out of work.

We spent the entire day reminiscing and passing on family stories to the children and grandchildren. Sioma told the story of how my mother always divided the bread evenly during our escape journey…never giving more to her own two boys than to the Friedmans. He was delighted to learn that she was alive at age 99 and took this as evidence that G-d agreed with his assessment of her as a true *Tzadekes.*

I recounted our recent experiences in Ivano Frankovsk and Bohorodczany and brought regards from Shimshon Tabak. The wives prepared a wonderful feast, and we celebrated with laughter and with tears for hours on end. At times we simply said nothing as words failed to express the joy in our hearts.

Sioma, of course, inquired about how we were faring in America. I was honest and told him that America had been very good to our family and had given us freedom and enormous economic opportunity. I must have sounded pretty patriotic as I credited all of our success to Uncle Sam. But that's really the way I do feel about it. Sioma could see that we were doing well, and he showed no hesitation when he turned serious and extended the following plea:

"Years ago, your dear father, may his name forever be blessed, saved us from certain death. Now I want you to do the same thing for my children. I want you to save them. My children cannot find work, even though they are highly trained professionals. When you told me you were friends of the mayor, Ijo Rager, I understood why G-d sent you to us at this time. They need your help. Will you help them, Hetche?"

I let my actions do my talking. I got into the car and drove immediately to the mayor's office. I explained the whole situation, including the history involving our wartime rescue.

"Mr. Mayor," I told him frankly, "you must help them find work here in Be'ersheva. Can you speak with your wife, Bracha, and find out if there are any openings at Soroka Hospital?" Bracha was a doctor and a professor and served as director of the hospital.

"What a wonderful story, Hart," said the mayor. "Of course we'll help them. I'll get on this right away." He was as good as his word, and within a few weeks both of Sioma's kids had found work with the local government.

Of course, in Israel, as elsewhere, no good deed goes unpunished. A few weeks later, Ijo Rager came to visit me at my home in Herzliya. He presented me with an accounting statement.

"This is what I need from you, Hart," he explained. When I asked what this was for, he laid out the cold facts.

"The woman went to medical school in Russia, where anyone who was a party member could get such a degree for the asking. Her credentials are not recognized here. If she works as a doctor for three years, however, she'll be able to get an Israeli license – as long as she doesn't kill someone in the meanwhile. This money is needed to underwrite her salary, until she is able to start earning on her own."

I was beginning to get the picture. "What about the rest?"

"Hart, every *oleh* (immigrant) who arrives here from Russia and isn't carrying a violin case is an engineer. The fellow who painted Lenin's lipstick on his face every day was called a cosmetic engineer. In other words, being a Russian engineer is the same as having a blank résumé. We found him a public works job, and his salary also needs to be underwritten until he can be trained."

"Let me ask you a question, Ija," I said. "Why don't I just give this money directly to them?"

"What?! That way there would be no public service. This isn't just *tzedakah* (charity)," he said. "You're also helping to build a solid infrastructure in Be'ersheva."

"Spoken like a true public servant," I told him.

I noticed that Sioma was not too anxious for me to meet his younger brother, Laib. In fact, I did not get to meet him until several days later, and when I did, I understood Sioma's reluctance. Laib had married a non-Jewish Russian woman, and Sioma felt that I might disapprove. When I finally did get to meet face-to-face with Laib, I got the feeling that he didn't really remember me all that well. Thinking back, I recalled that I was much closer to Sioma than to Laib during our months on the open road together. It's amazing that such original ties of friendship can still have a lasting effect on a relationship more than fifty years later.

Sioma died in 1996. His brother Laib died two years later. Both were 75 years old at the time of their deaths. Simona and I still keep in touch with their children and visit with them whenever we travel to Be'ersheva.

We had witnessed how little progress had been made over the previous half-century back in our European homeland; in fact, in many cases, regression was the rule. How wonderful it felt to see a new generation transplanted from that dead-end environment into a land that could offer them a brighter future, as well as a sense of Jewish pride.

The situation was undeniably ironic. I had embarked on this journey to pay tribute and finally to bury my past. Instead, at the end of the road, I had come away with a new confidence and optimism about the future. A decidedly sweet, and surprising, outcome.

Chapter Eighteen

Summing Up

I'D LIKE to close this volume by devoting a few words to what might be called my personal philosophy and how it relates to my political point-of-view. Also, after so many words of retrospection, I would like to present the results of some personal introspection. And, finally, I'd like to share some aspects of my vision for the road that now lies ahead.

Unquestionably my earliest, and perhaps most profound, influence was Ze'ev Jabotinsky. His lessons of Jewish pride resonated strongly among the displaced youth of post-war Europe. He coined the word *hadar*, which literally means splendor, magnificence or chivalrous honor, to describe this sense of proud Jewish identity. Jabotinsky's strong nationalistic message, even when there was as yet no nation in existence, took great courage and still serves to inspire me to this day. Jabotinsky would exhort young Jewish people with the oft-repeated message: "The blood of King David, King Solomon and the Maccabees runs in your veins!" This was a message that embodied the essence of *hadar*. Menachem Begin had a keen sense of *hadar* and Benny Begin carries on that tradition today.

As we now stand in the ashes of what was known as the "peace process," Benny's sense of *hadar* has clearly been vindicated. He is recognized as one of the few Israeli politicians who accurately predicted the failure of the Oslo Accords.

Hadar, among those who possess it, is visible in every aspect of the way they conduct their lives. It was clearly *hadar* that drove Menachem Begin, unlike his predecessors, to wear a necktie everyday while serving as prime minister. This was done out of pride and respect for the office. Left-wing Israeli politicians do not share this outlook, not only when it comes to neckties, but also in more significant areas; they seem to lack this sense of *hadar*.

The concept of *hadar* should not be confused with religious fundamentalism. While detractors may compare Jewish pride with extremist movements within Christianity and, in particular, Islam, this comparison is misguided and without merit. Yes, I believe that the territories of Judea and Samaria should be called by their ancient Biblical names. Yes, I believe in Jabotinsky's heroic call to action when he invoked our royal lineage, Yes, I believe that Israel should be guided by Jewish law and principles laid down in the Torah and other sacred texts. Do these attitudes make me a fundamentalist? A fascist? A chauvinist? To mistake my zeal for jingoistic fervor is to miss the point. Important distinctions exist and need to be kept in mind.

Unlike Muslims, the Jews are a people small in number and smaller still when it comes to territory. Unlike Christians, we Jews are not trying to convert anyone to our beliefs. In fact, Jewish thinking does not encourage proselytizing. Jews have always clung to a "live and let live" philosophy. Historically, Jews have never embarked on holy crusades to vanquish the infidel. We have never initiated "inquisitions" or "final solutions" to eliminate those who hold differing beliefs. We wish to be left to live in peace on the land granted to us by the Almighty and we recognize we must be strong in order to defend ourselves against our enemies who wish to prevent us from doing so.

To most Palestinians, the very existence of a Jewish state in their midst is unacceptable and must be combated by any means available – including the killing of innocent children by fanatical suicide bombers. Do right-wing Israeli leaders call for the destruction of Arab states? Never.

Hatred of Israel is a main component in the curriculum of most elementary level schools in Palestinian communities, while Israeli teachers, in contrast, attempt to spread understanding and tolerance of Israel's neighbors. These are not trivial differences. They represent a "fundamental" divergence in world-view. To paint those of us who believe in a strong and proud Jewish people with the brush of "fanatic" is to overlook these crucial distinguishing characteristics.

Many are puzzled by the inability of Israel to reach an agreement with Palestinian leadership over the creation of a Palestinian state. What they fail to understand is that the central core of Arafat's agenda is the elimination of the State of Israel. In other words, Arafat's primary interest is not in the creation of a new nation, but rather in the destruction of an existing one. Arafat does not visualize himself ever serving as the first president of the peaceful nation of Palestine, coexisting with its Israeli neighbors.

The reason Arafat has been reluctant to declare a Palestinian state is that if he did so, he would be forced to live there – and that is something he would rather not do, preferring instead to globetrot as a world-class celebrity. I am encouraged by the fact that, thanks to Prime Minister Sharon's leadership, the world is finally awakening to the fiction of Arafat as a partner for peace.

I am also cautiously optimistic that under the administration of George W. Bush, who has been exhibiting outstanding leadership skills in the wake of the September 11, 2001 attacks, United States foreign policy may be moving in the proper direction. At this juncture, the opening weeks of 2002, the US appears to be mopping up a successful military operation in Afghanistan and pondering where to next direct its forces in its ongoing War on Terrorism. If Iraq becomes the next target, as many feel it could and should be, then Israel's defense against external attack will once again become a major concern. The US has assured Israel that if it decides to move against the Saddam Hussein regime in Baghdad, it would provide Israel with adequate time to prepare for any retaliatory strikes.

The key point to remember, when struggling for solutions to Israel's security needs, is that peace may be proposed, but it can never be imposed. No lasting resolution of the conflict can ever be thrust upon the parties from without. Just as the historic peace agreement between Israel and Egypt came about because the right people were in the right places at the right time, the eventual answer to the current conflict will emerge only when the parties themselves are prepared to move forward.

For too many years Israel has been playing chess with itself; seeking a negotiated peace agreement with a non-existent partner – one committed to its eventual destruction. As the naïve notions that led Israel down blind alleys such as Oslo begin to fall away, the new realities are becoming more widely understood. It is in this real-world environment, and only in such an environment, that true peace will be achieved.

Part of the blame for Israel's willingness to proceed down this misguided road, must be attributed to Bill Clinton. Clinton was widely touted as the best friend Israel has ever had in the White House. The highly stage-managed "handshake on the White House lawn" between Rabin and Arafat helped to contribute to this popular image. I recall how my liberal friends, including members of my extended family, reported having tears in their eyes as they watched the proceedings. They felt as though we were entering a new utopian age of peace and understanding between Arab and Jew. I, too, had tears in my eyes, but they were tears of sadness at the massive naïveté that had placed Israel on the road to eventual disaster.

I find it unconscionable that in January 2002, The Hebrew University of Jerusalem opted to award Bill Clinton an honorary doctorate degree. I wish I could have been at the award ceremony and been permitted to ask him a few direct questions.

"Mr. President," I would have asked, "you urged Israel to take chances for peace by agreeing to participate in the Oslo peace process. Now, as that process lies decimated and has resulted in ongoing tragedy and bloodshed, do you experience any remorse? Do you feel you were mistaken in pursuing your quest for a Nobel Peace Prize in this way? And if so, do you feel you owe anyone an apology after 250 innocent Israeli civilians and nearly 1,000 Palestinians have lost their lives to date?"

I would like to know how Clinton could, in good conscience, advocate that Israel comply with the terms of the Oslo Accords, while not at the same time demanding that the PLO comply with one especially important requirement that was demanded of them. Mainly, the complete revocation of the PLO covenant that calls for the destruction of the so-called "Zionist entity." This provision was the linchpin of the entire agreement. It was all that was asked of Arafat. Yet, it was never carried out. The covenant stands today, and this fact speaks volumes. Arafat's failure to revoke this covenant says plainly: "We have no interest in making peace with you. It is our desire to destroy you." It speaks to the heart of the matter, and yet it continues to be minimized by self-deluding Jews who prefer to turn a blind eye to this obvious truth.

Despite the events I've lived through, I continue to be amazed at people's unwillingness to accept the truth. Hitler wrote in *Mein Kampf* in 1922[2] that he intended to target the Jews if he were ever to gain power. Why do Jews refuse to believe it when our enemies announce that they wish to kill us?

I feel that countless American Jews are misled by the standard rhetoric employed by the media to portray the situation in the Middle East. I have often attempted to understand why the majority of the American Jewish population overwhelmingly gravitates towards the liberal end of the political spectrum. I believe this phenomenon is connected to the prevalence, in America, of the self-hating, self-flagellating Jew. In discussing this subject with my friend, Professor Alvin Rosenfeld, head of the Indiana University Jewish Studies Program, I floated my theory that perhaps there is a genetic rationale. Isn't it possible that Jews harbor some sort of faulty masochistic gene that prevents them from experiencing joy without guilt? Could it be

---

2 "…if twelve or fifteen thousand of these Jews who were corrupting the nation had been forced to submit to poison gas, …then the millions of sacrifices made at the front (by Germans) would not have been in vain." Adolf Hitler, *Mein Kampf*, (Transl. Ralph Manheim; ed. John Lukacs), Houghton Mifflin Co., 1998, Vol. II, p.772

that, when our ancestors were bred to serve as slaves in Egypt, this gene was cultivated and wound up in our DNA? How else may we account for such aberrations as Jewish electoral voting patterns in the US, for example.

In the last presidential election, the overall voting population was precisely divided into Republican and Democratic voters. Yet over 80% of the Jewish vote went to Al Gore – when George W. Bush was clearly the candidate with the stronger pro-Israel stance. It is abnormal, unnatural and essentially dysfunctional for an intelligent group, such as American Jews, to vote against its own self-interests. Yet, they do it! Why do Jews seem to enjoy being victims? I, for one, somehow managed to avoid this self-destructive pathology and can state with certainty that I do not ever wish to be a victim.

Taking this point a step further, I discussed the situation with my friend, Rabbi Marvin Hier, the director of the Simon Wiesenthal Center.

"Why do you believe that so many problems exist between Jews and African-Americans these days?" I asked him. "Didn't Jews play an active role in the civil rights movement of the 1960s? Didn't we always assist them in defending their human rights in society?" Hier agreed that we had.

"Then why do so many hate us?" I demanded. Hier began to recite the common wisdom, naming various sociological factors and linking anti-Semitism with lack of educational opportunities. I stopped him right away.

"What you say is certainly true enough, but it doesn't fully answer the question. I believe that the real reason they hate us, Rabbi, is that they covet the role of victim." I explained. "Blacks want to hold the franchise on public sympathy and they do not wish to share it with Jews. 'Oh, you had a Holocaust for seven years and lost six million? That's nothing. We were slaves for three hundred years and lost sixty million. We are the true victims, not you.' And of course, Jews do not care to relinquish this crown easily and so friction is the result." Rabbi Hier's smile at this point indicated that he took my opinions to be somewhat tongue-in-cheek.

"I say to them: 'You want to be victims? Go ahead. Be my guest.' I would rather that Jews give up this role forever. To me, respect is worth much more than sympathy. If more Jews felt as I do, Jewish-Black relations would improve tremendously."

I shared these opinions with one other person whom I happen to admire greatly, Ruth Roskies Wisse, the noted author and Harvard professor of Yiddish literature. Ruth was born in Czernowitz (then Romania, now Ukraine) and raised in Montreal. She has written extensively about the "liberal betrayal of the Jews," which is the subtitle of her book *If I am Not for Myself.* Ruth had been invited to deliver a guest lecture as part of the Simona and Hart

Hasten Visiting Fellows Series at Indiana University's Jewish Studies Program. Ruth fully agreed with my analysis. In fact she went a step further.

"You're right, Hart," she confided. "The American Jews you refer to are not only self-hating masochists, they actually operate under a death wish." I don't know if I would go quite that far, but the fact remains that American Jews have a tradition of supporting so-called liberal causes. And the more successful the Jew is, the stronger is the support. Jewish families who have accumulated great wealth in America, such as the Bronfmans and the Simons, continue to channel enormous support towards the very left-wing politicians who would, if permitted, re-distribute that wealth through onerous taxation. Can't these wealthy Jews be comfortable with their success without insisting that their resultant guilt be assuaged via virtual victimization? Political pundits have observed, more than once, that Jews prefer to live like WASPs and vote like Puerto Ricans. Why are we like this?

I have never observed this mindset among the gentile community. It is a peculiarly Jewish neurosis that forces a successful Jew to ask, "Why am I so blessed when there is so much suffering in the world?" and then act to punish himself to the point that he is once again back in the classic and psychologically comfortable role of history's victim. Most non-Jews do not suffer from such hang-ups. That is not to say that only Jews are true philanthropists. I simply have not observed gentiles providing financial support for those causes that are contrary to their own self-interests. This unnatural practice, I'm sorry to report, is the peculiar province of the Jews.

Historically, Jews have raced to support political causes promising social justice but that have, in reality, delivered more suffering. Two examples come to mind and, as Natan Sharansky has recently pointed out, there is a thread linking the two. First is the specter of Soviet-style communism. Supposedly this ideology, which was embraced by many misguided Jews during my youth in Europe, died out with the end of the Cold War in the early 1990s. Yet, the body of the Bolshevik messiah himself, V. Lenin, still rests above ground today.

Similarly, the Oslo Peace Accords, a fatally flawed plan for appeasement between Israel and the Palestinians, still claims adherents today; long after it has been discredited as disastrous and delusional. Why do both of these stinking, rotting corpses still remain with us? Why haven't both cadavers been long-since buried, as common sense and history would dictate? The answer is that, despite all evidence to the contrary, both still enjoy a cadre of adherents who believe they can blow life back into these long-deceased carcasses.

It seems that our own government still hasn't fully gotten the message.

In a recent foreign policy address delivered at the University of Kentucky, Secretary of State Colin Powell continued to assert that the Israelis and the Palestinians must walk side-by-side on the road to peace. This vacuous rhetoric overlooks the fact that if the parties are to arrive at their peaceful destination, Arafat must be removed from the road. Israel will never be able to achieve peace as long as Arafat holds on to power. It is Arafat's lack of courage that renders him an ineffectual leader.

There are many who cynically caution that whoever replaces Arafat would probably be even worse. I disagree. In all probability, Arafat's successor would necessarily be a strong and courageous individual. Even if his views were more extreme than Arafat's so-called moderate position, if he were, in fact, a truly viable leader, Israel would be able to deal with him. At least with a strong effectual leader, you know where you stand. I believe, therefore, that deposing Yasser Arafat must be the first step towards achieving a Middle East peace.

The next step must be a strong and unflinching US foreign policy on the issue of terrorism. As evidenced by the willingness of Arab nations, such as Syria and even Libya, to offer cooperation to America as it combats global terrorism, an aggressive posture will earn the respect of Israel's neighbors and eventually lead to peace.

Once Arafat is gone and Israel's enemies halt the flow of support to Palestinian terrorists, the next step must be the democratization of these Arab nations. A government that is held accountable to the constituency that elects it to power, is much less likely to engage in war or acts of state-sponsored terrorism. If we hope to ever witness a true stability in this part of the world, we must work towards the day when Israel is no longer the sole democracy in the Middle East. If true democratic institutions such as a free press, free assembly, and freedom of religion were to emerge in these nations, they would serve not only to economically revitalize them, but also to establish true safeguards against conflicts that have erupted there for centuries.

While such a wave of democracy washing over the Middle East, as it did in Eastern Europe after the end of the Cold War, seems rather unlikely, given the deep cultural obstacles in the way, we must never rule out this objective. I believe that democracy and free market economies represent man's natural state. I have faith that someday all totalitarian systems, such as sheikdoms and dictatorships, will eventually crumble and give way to more democratic societies. Arabs residing in Jerusalem, for example, have become used to living under Israeli-style democracy for the past thirty-five years. Arafat holds very little attraction to these Palestinians. They understand that it is preferable to live as a minority in a democratic state that respects the rights of each citizen than to be part of the majority under an Islamic dictatorship.

Despite the all too frequent terrorist attacks splattered across the headlines these days, I do find cause for optimism. I am encouraged because I feel that the current Israeli leadership shares my views about how to go about achieving long-term peace in the area. I did not, however, anticipate how long it would take Prime Minister Sharon to get things turned around.

I have often compared Israeli participation in the Oslo Accords to a runaway automobile being driven at top speed towards the edge of a cliff. Sharon took over the controls in early 2001 and has been trying to turn the car around. Of course, stopping the car abruptly at high speed would be disastrous, so he must first slow it down before turning it in the opposite direction. At this point, in early 2002, I feel he is making the U-turn and will soon be in position to start heading in the right direction. More slowly than perhaps some would like, but piece-by-piece, Prime Minister Sharon is undoing the harm done by his predecessors. He is making the turn. We will know that Israel is headed the right way once we no longer bear witness to the spectacle of the prime minister declaring Arafat to be "irrelevant" to the peace process, while his own foreign minister continues to carry on negotiations with him.

Like most, I tend to regard myself as an optimist. Very few pessimists would ever admit to being one. But beyond that, my conviction that life is truly worth living has, in many ways, accounted for my survival despite the long odds against it at times. As mentioned before, I feel that I inherited my father's common sense, pragmatic approach to life's problems and challenges. My father, may his memory be for a blessing, fancied himself something of a *maven* (expert) when it came to the behavior of the European intelligentsia before the War. He observed with dismay how many intellectuals, with their degrees and PhD's, would enjoy widespread respect among the Jewish population, as they wrong-headedly espoused their worn-out socialist philosophies. My father considered them to be fools. His favorite expression was: "You send a fool to college and what do you get? An educated fool."

Most of the time such educated fools are harmless, but they do become dangerous if they should happen to gain political power. This phenomenon is most evident in Israel today, where the general population, unlike in America, still holds such intellectuals in high esteem. These Israeli political fools are characterized by their unmitigated chutzpah and arrogance. They look down their noses at the general population as they display a shameless disdain for democratic principles. They prefer to believe that, because of their intellect and level of education, they know what's best for the country and are under no obligation to consider the will of the majority. It is this reckless, cavalier and ultimately elitist attitude, as exhibited by its leading exponent, Yossi Beilin, that is so dangerous and has placed Israel into so much jeopardy in recent years.

Beilin served as minister of justice under the Barak administration and he is best known for the dubious distinction of being the architect of the Oslo Accords. It was under the provisions of Oslo that the Israeli Labor government approved the delivery of 40,000 rifles to the Palestinian Authority, allegedly for use by their domestic police force. Even though the serial numbers of these weapons were registered with Israeli security, it still amazes me why no one raised a question about the need for so many rifles for purported police deployment in the first place. It is these very same rifles, approved by Israel, which have been used in terrorist attacks against Israeli civilians.

The Second Intifada, which began in September of 2000, broke out shortly after these arms were delivered. It is my allegation that this outbreak of violence was instigated as the direct result of advice received by Arafat from Yossi Beilin, and not by Sharon's visit to the *Kotel* as is often misreported in the media. I suspect that Beilin, in his many private meetings with Arafat, counseled him to call for violence, referring to it as "resistance to occupation," as the most expedient means of achieving Arafat's objectives. This is not to mention the false hope that Beilin has publicly held out to Arafat regarding full Israeli withdrawal from Jerusalem. I suspect that Beilin and his crowd hold few religious convictions and are disdainful of Jewish history. Hence Jerusalem holds no special meaning to him as a Jew. From where I sit, Yossi Beilin's actions border on criminality. I sense that he is guilty of providing aid and comfort to the enemy. I only hope that someday he will be forced to face Israeli justice.

Another reason for my current optimism is that it appears that the political left-wing is finally waking up to the error of its ways. A recent editorial in *The Jerusalem Post* by Isi Leibler, senior vice president of the World Jewish Congress, an organization widely known for its liberal point of view, addresses the disillusionment of the left and clearly illustrates my point.

In a piece entitled "Disloyalty and Patriotism" (*The Jerusalem Post*, December 30, 2001), Leibler states that now, with Israel in a virtual state of war and taking civilian casualties almost daily, it is the proper time to revisit concepts such as patriotism, disloyalty and solidarity. Leibler points out that he was heretofore a supporter of the so-called "irreversible" Oslo peace process that he now regards as "such a cruel illusion." He states that Yitzchak Rabin, under the urging of the US, took a huge gamble and lost. He is entirely correct and on the mark with this assessment.

I recall how President Clinton would urge Israel to take "risks for peace." To me the concept of "risks for peace" is an utter oxymoron. Peace, by its very definition, is the elimination of risks to one's security and well-being. Some might argue that Begin took a great risk when signing the Camp David Treaty in order to achieve peace with Egypt, but, in fact, Begin had wisely made sure that all risks were eliminated before signing off. Most importantly, he made sure that his counterpart, Anwar Sadat, was operating in good faith and had the power to carry out the provisions of the treaty. This was certainly not the case with Rabin, who foolishly agreed to risks that would have been deemed wholly unacceptable by Begin. At the misguided urging of the President of the United States, Rabin and his crew were willing to risk everything. Sadly, Israel today is paying the price in blood for the risks that Rabin wrongly found acceptable.

Despite Rabin's standing in the pantheon of martyred Jewish leaders and despite his good intentions, Leibler believes that history will judge him harshly and I fully agree. Had he lived, speculates Leibler, he would have long ago admitted failure, cut his losses and worked to unite the people of Israel against the common enemy – unlike his many Labor Party colleagues have done.

Leibler goes on to point to the "irresponsible behavior of some of our rejected political leaders (who)...challenge the fundamentals of Israel's democratic ethos." He points an accusing finger at Yossi Beilin when he observes that, "In the most liberal of democracies it would be unacceptable that a former justice minister – in this case Yossi Beilin – would be given sanction to lobby foreign governments, including the United States, urging them to reject the policies of their own democratically elected government. It is simply not done." Leibler condemns as scandalous Beilin's providing tactical advice to Arafat and his cohorts, who advocate the killing of Jews, on how to respond to the Sharon government. He condemns Beilin and Meretz Party leader, Yossi Sarid, for their outspoken campaign to undermine the Sharon government's policies and for publicly urging the US to reject them and impose a settlement. "...Here we have the leader of the opposition and other diehard Osloists, such as Beilin, displaying utter contempt for the democratic process..."

Finally, Leibler suggests that such wayward politicians, along with the Israeli media which support them, should look to America's closing of political ranks and unified support of the government in a time of crisis after the

September 11th attacks. He also summons the memory of Menachem Begin "who, as a highly outspoken leader of the opposition, always stressed that divisions in Israel were not for export and had to be resolved in Israel within a democratic framework." He correctly observes that Begin consistently refused to criticize the government when abroad.

In America, we say that "party politics end at the water's edge." This principle seems to have no meaning when it comes to the Israeli left. The Labor Party has a history of undermining the policies of the government whenever the Likud Party is in power. As they did with Begin and Shamir, Peres and his supporters travel the globe today, publicly denouncing Sharon, who enjoys more popular support in Israel today than when he was elected by the largest margin in history. Imagine for a moment, if during Clinton's presidency, his own defense secretary, Republican William Cohen, would have visited our allies and publicly criticized Clinton's defense policies. Such action would have rightly been regarded as outrageous and unacceptable. Why this is not the case in Israel is beyond my understanding.

Finally, I am optimistic about the future of Israel because I believe that today the post-Zionists have been discredited and their era is drawing to a close. Post-Zionism, as outlined in Yoram Hazony's excellent book on the subject (*The Jewish State: The Struggle for Israel's Soul*)[3] is a philosophy that contends that Zionism's work is finished and must now depart the world stage, in order to make way for a new more relevant ideology. Post-Zionism's adherents are the same sort of quasi-intellectuals who so misled the Jews of Europe in the 1930s. While their voices are still being heard in Israel, fewer and fewer are bothering to listen. Zionism, the dream of a displaced people for a sovereign homeland, where they are permitted to live in peace and security, has, sadly, not yet been attained. When that day arrives, I will be the first to call myself a post-Zionist.

The question of how to find a solid road to lasting peace is crucial as I look ahead and assess the outlook for Jewish survival in Israel. But Jewish survival in the Diaspora is another concern that has involved much thought and discussion among Jewish leadership. After spending the better part of my seventy years studying and analyzing the realities of Jewish survival, I come away with a single unquestionable conclusion: Jewish survival depends upon an adherence to traditional Jewish values and practices. Without a solid grounding in authentic Judaism, American Jews are too easily swayed by the winds of assimilation. None of the non-Orthodox movements in the

---

3 Basic Books, 2000

Diaspora have succeeded in increasing our numbers. I am afraid that if it were left to the non-traditional denominations, Judaism would eventually disappear from the American scene. I believe that we are here today as Jews, and our offspring will continue to live as Jews, because of traditional Judaism and in spite of the other movements.

I don't make this statement because I am an Orthodox chauvinist, and I don't hold to this belief because I am such a pious person. Believe me, I'm not. I make this statement because of what my father always taught me. See things as they really are. Don't kid yourself. A simple review of American intermarriage statistics for the major Jewish denominations will illustrate the correctness of my position. I am sympathetic to those who wish to integrate traditional Judaism into modern American life. This, however, must not be carried out at the expense of basic Jewish beliefs and values. To forget this fact is to contribute to the decimation of our people.

A deep and dynamic interconnection exists between strong Jewish values and Jewish political strength. You cannot presume to have a viable and lasting Jewish state in the absence of traditional Jewish values and beliefs. I believe that the opposite is also true. You cannot truly be an observant Jew and not be a strong Zionist at the same time. These two ideals go hand in hand.

In this regard, I was very moved by the remarks offered by Prime Minister Ariel Sharon, at the March 2001 AIPAC conference I attended in Washington. Mr. Sharon, at the outset of his address stated: "I stand before you today first and foremost as a Jew. This strong Jewish identity is a central theme in my life, and will be, in carrying out my responsibilities as prime minister." He could have said, "First and foremost, I am an Israeli, a Likudnik, a general, a prime minister." But he did not. He defined himself, first and foremost as a Jew. This was said without arrogance or hubris. But it was said with unabashed pride in the three thousand years of history that have defined us and brought us, as a people and as a nation, to this day. It is this connection to our land and to our history that most Jewish day schools seek to instill in our young people. To answer not only the question of "Who am I?" but also "What am I?" and "In what do I believe?"

I recall once listening to a friend, a well-known Jewish community and business leader, commenting about his adult son to a noted sociologist and guest lecturer. "My son is a good person," my friend explained to the visiting sociologist. "He's compassionate. He's a humanitarian. He's literate. He cares about the less fortunate. He just doesn't happen to be a good Jew." The sociologist sighed and replied: "Once all you had to say was 'He's a good Jew' and all the other qualities would follow."

This point is not lost on the students we educate at the Hasten Hebrew Academy. We teach that when a student defines his identity as a Jew, it is axiomatic that he or she must practice kindness, believe in justice, and observe the Ten Commandments. We teach that to be a Jew is not merely an accident of birth; some religious baggage a person carries about. To be a Jew is to understand one's place in history, in society and in the world.

But what about me? How and when did I discover who I was? And why, as an adult, am I, as some would have it, obsessed with Jewish education? In facing these questions, I have concluded that my defining moments took place in those DP camps where I spent all of my teenage years. While millions were robbed of much more, I feel that Hitler robbed me of my childhood. As discussed in Chapter Five, some primitive education was available in the camps, but it was mediocre at best. I was denied the opportunity to develop my passions for writing, for music and most of all, for learning. What did develop, however, was a hunger, a lifelong unquenched thirst for knowledge.

When I arrived in the US at age 20, this thirst became all-consuming. I continually felt as though I had to catch up. I had to push a little harder, work a little longer, and be a bit more assertive than the other fellow because I got a late start. It was this mindset that drove me to support ways to insure that our children will not have to experience the same starvation of the soul that I endured as a young man long ago.

Looking back, I see now that I could easily have taken the road of bitterness as some opted to do. But, I thank G-d that this was not the path I chose back then. Today, when I witness the nourishment and nurturing that takes place everyday in the classrooms of the Academy, I feel as though this makes up for all those deprivations of the past. We are so fortunate to be able to freely imbue our children with a strong Jewish identity, not through hardship or through trauma, but as it should be done – naturally and joyfully and with love.

Much has been said in recent months about the impact upon American life brought on by the terrorist attacks of September 11, 2001. The vision of America living with the same sort of security constraints to which Israelis have sadly grown accustomed is indeed a disturbing one. It would represent a basic departure from the national life-style we have grown accustomed to. As recounted in the early chapters of this book, I immigrated to this country in 1951 and fell in love with it before I even arrived. The country I adored was carefree, fun loving, joyful, optimistic, innocent, and somewhat naïve. With the exception of its naïveté, I would hate to see American society lose these qualities at the hands of her enemies, whose one unifying ideology is hatred for the US, demonized as "The Great Satan," and for Israel, "The Small Satan." The ranks of those who hate us are populated with miserable, humorless, suicidal fanatics. It is the very existence of these brainwashed "Manchurian Candidates," – programmed killers with no minds of their own – who clearly threaten our security and our very way of life.

The type of indoctrination needed to create such fanatics requires training from an early age. Children must be "very carefully taught" to build up sufficient hatred that would drive them to such acts as adults. A current "Sesame Street"-type song being taught to children in the territories includes lyrics that translate to: "When I wander into Jerusalem I will become a suicide bomber."

This indoctrination process permeates all aspects of life in many sectors of the Arab and Muslim worlds. Hatred of America and our allies is dispensed with mother's milk and is evident in Palestinian textbooks and youth publications. What emerges from this early childhood training is a dedicated "soldier for Allah" willing to reap his heavenly reward for acts of extreme savagery.

As the US prosecutes its War on Terrorism, a condition of victory must include an inspection of textbooks and other teaching materials used in Arab and Muslim schools. Imagine if we were to learn that the German public education system was teaching Nazi racist dogma as part of their elementary school curriculum. What would our reaction be? Would we tolerate the specter of a nation dispensing an ideology to its youth that led to the ravages of the Second World War? For how long will we tolerate the continuing spread of equally vicious hatred among Muslim school children?

Incidentally, as much as the media would have us accept the image of Israel and the Palestinians as equally culpable for Middle East turmoil, there is no counterpart for this type of indoctrination in the Israeli school system. Jewish children are not taught to hate their Arab neighbors by their schoolteachers. In fact, just the opposite. An examination of standard Israeli schoolbooks shows a strong message of cooperation and tolerance. What a different world this would be if only Arab textbooks were written the same way.

I tend to think of myself, for lack of a better word, as an activist. And, of course, I've always been something of an entrepreneur. And, as mentioned earlier, I follow an Orthodox orientation when it comes to religion. So, if I wish to define myself using verbal shorthand, I would say I am, first and foremost, an Orthodox Jew, a political activist and an entrepreneur.

I recall addressing my fellow congregants during the *Kol Nidre* service several years ago at B'nai Torah synagogue. I announced that I had decided upon the words I wished to have inscribed upon my tombstone.

"I have selected a quote from *Pirkei Avot*, the Ethics of Our Fathers," I stated from the pulpit. "In chapter three, verses twelve and twenty-two, it reads: 'His deeds exceeded his wisdom.' In other words, I wish to be remembered as a practical man who believed that it's not only what you say but what you do that really matters. According to my understanding of Jewish concepts, study, learning and the acquisition of knowledge are very important, but these are not ends in themselves. They are the means to an end. What counts are tangible accomplishments. Results. Achievement. The Talmud teaches that 'Great is study because it leads to action. The Almighty requires not merely great thoughts, but also good deeds.'

In medieval times, the Jewish philosopher Yehuda Halevi compared Greek philosophy, which celebrates the contemplative life as the ideal, to a blossom that is lovely and full of potential but that has not yet born any fruit. We may regard Greek thought as attractive in its structural symmetry and logical form, but it is only a blossom that flowers for a moment and does not endure. Jewish thought, in contrast, requires fruit: tangible accomplishments in the real world and practical achievements in reforming the heart of man.

Judaism is not primarily a faith-based religion. It is a behavioral one. Judaism judges you, not by how much you know, or by the degree of devotion to your faith. Judaism judges you by your deeds. Do you keep kosher? Do you observe the Sabbath? Do you practice kindness and modesty? The Talmud warns against devoting one's life solely to intellectual pursuits at the expense of actual accomplishments. It is only through action that a person may hope to make a difference. The Talmud teaches that 'Wisdom that is not translated into deeds perishes with its possessor.' And this is why I wish to be remembered as someone whose deeds exceeded his wisdom."

The personal and political philosophies I have outlined in this book become increasingly important as I consider what sort of legacy my own life will establish. I have been fortunate in that I have come into close contact with more than my share of men and women who have played important roles on the stage of life. As I contemplate the historic impact of such luminaries as Menachem Begin and Ze'ev Jabotinsky, it humbles me and makes my own accomplishments seem quite trivial by comparison. Nevertheless, like all men, great and common, I wish for my life to have made a difference – if not on the stage of history, then at least within the confines of my own family and my community.

I believe that Mark and I would both have preferred if more of our children had opted to pursue careers in the family businesses, but I can honestly say that I'm genuinely proud of each one of them. I applaud their accomplishments and wish them only greater success in the future.

It was thoughts such as these, and perhaps the imminent close of the 20th century, that prompted me to draft a family mission statement in 1999 and to present it at a family gathering (the wedding of my grand-niece, Dina) in Israel that same year. I have included a transcript of the mission statement on the following pages exactly as it was presented to our assembled family members at that time. I feel it summarizes something of the legacy that I would like to leave behind for my family.

And now as the years pile one upon the next, the memories of little Lonka and my beloved Zayde come into ever-sharper focus. What would I say to them if I could reach back somehow? Should I say that, for some unfathomable reason, I was selected to live and they were not? What can the living say to the dead? Only that they are not forgotten. As long as I shall live, so will they.

And what may I ask of my children, grandchildren and generations yet unborn? Only that I be remembered. And that as long as they will live, so shall I.

And finally, I would ask that they remember and observe the words of the *Pirkei Avot:*

Eizehu ashir? Hasameach b'chelko.
Who is wealthy? He who is happy with his lot.

— Ethics of the Fathers
Chapter 4, Verse 1

Hasten Families' Business Mission Statement Meeting
Jerusalem, March 5, 1999

Remarks by Hart N. Hasten

My Dear Family,

A Great *Zechut* (Merit)
This meeting of the entire Hasten family is a great *Zechut*, particularly when the meeting is taking place in the city of Jerusalem, the eternal capital of Israel, on the occasion of Dina Hasten's wedding. This is very meaningful to me. It is more meaningful than you can possibly imagine. In fact, this to me is mind-boggling! It is surreal! The reason why I say this is because the odds of the Hasten family surviving World War II, the Shoah period, were close to zero.

The Right Decision
Had our father, Bernard Hasten *Zichrono Levracha*, on June 28, 1941, right after Hitler attacked the Soviet Union, made the decision *not* to take his family, that is my mother, my brother and myself, and leave the shtetl in Poland, as conventional wisdom at the time dictated, *we would not have survived*. We would have been wiped out with the rest of our large family who stayed behind. None of us would be here today. The Hasten name would have disappeared.

Deep Faith
I also believe that Divine Providence played a major role in Dad making the right decision. I strongly believe that our parents' deep faith in Hashem during those difficult years also helped us to survive. During those difficult war years in Kazakhstan, in the former Soviet Union, our parents gave up their own bread portions to us children. They must have suffered terribly

during those years. When we were ill, and that was a pretty regular occurrence, Mother and Dad not only nursed us, cared for us, and nurtured us, they also encouraged us never to lose hope. Again, that is why this gathering here in the holy city of Jerusalem means so much to me.

B'li ayin hara, the Hasten family has not only survived, but has grown. From a family of four, 58 years ago, we have multiplied by a factor of more than ten; we have grown from four to more than forty today. Yet our family still hasn't reached the number of souls of pre-World War II, or the pre-Holocaust period.

Great Achievements

The Hasten family not only survived, we thrived, and are proud of our accomplishments. We now claim many college graduates and Yeshiva graduates. We now have a doctor in the family, a lawyer, an accountant, a Rabbi, an engineer, bankers and businessmen. We started as *Yisraelim* and now we also have *Levi'im,* and in two more days we will have a *Cohen* in the family. We are, thank G-d, very blessed, and we are grateful to Hashem.

Morasha vs. Yerusha; Heritage vs. Inheritance

Now that my brother and I have reached the "golden years" of our lives, or to put it more bluntly, we have reached the age where we are closer to the end of our journey than to its beginning, we feel a need to convey to you certain legacies, ideals, beliefs and convictions that our parents conveyed to us. Our parents did not leave us a *Yerusha* – an inheritance, they did not leave us anything tangible. Neither did they have attorneys and accountants help them draft "family mission statements." However, our parents did leave us a wonderful *Morasha* – a heritage, intangible but very precious. Their legacy was their huge number of good deeds! They helped many people, and saved many lives during the difficult World War II years.

Our Humble New Beginnings

When Mom, Dad and I arrived in the United States we were, as the Yiddish expression goes, *Naki.* We were clean, empty – meaning we had no money, not a penny! In fact, after languishing for five years in Kazakhstan, and five years in DP camps in Austria, we were on the receiving end of charity.

In the DP Camps I used to stand in one line to receive CARE packages from the Joint Distribution Committee. In another line, I remember receiving sardines, powdered milk and powdered eggs. The HIAS, Hebrew Immigrant Aid Society, sponsored us and helped us to reach the shores of the United

States. The first few weeks in America we received assistance from the Jewish Welfare Federation of Minneapolis. The Family and Children's Service helped me find a job as a presser in a Jewish firm.

The Importance of Tzedaka

As soon as I started earning a paycheck, however, I stopped taking charity and started giving to charities. I remember my first donation to the Minneapolis Jewish Welfare Federation was $5. I also gave them my time, going door-to-door asking others to contribute to the JWF of Minneapolis.

Speaking of charity, I have always been fascinated by the custom of setting aside something for charity in Shul during the morning prayers. Specifically, during the *Pesukey Dezimra,* Verses of Praise, when we say *Vayevarech David*, we set aside money mentally, and later after the *Kedusha* we put the money into the *pushke* (charity box). Why this specific time? Because, as the verse says, "King David blessed Hashem in the presence of the entire congregation." Although King David had been denied divine permission to build the Holy Temple, he had assembled the necessary contributions and materials so that his son, Solomon, could be ready to build it. The Hasten family could learn a great deal from this.

We also learn that when King David prayed to G-d, he mentioned only our patriarch, Jacob, because Jacob was the first patriarch to make a vow to contribute tithes, or 10 percent, of his possessions. To quote from Genesis [28:22], *Vechol Asher Titen Li Asser Aassrenu Loch* (Whatever you will give me, I shall tithe to you). Reb Moishe Feinstein *z"l* urged Jews not only to give 10 percent of their possessions, but also 10 percent of their time. A very fine lesson for all of us. Giving *Tzedaka* is a great *Mitzvah*. I urge you to develop the habit of writing checks to worthy causes. And as I mentioned, although our parents could not contribute much financially, they did give of their time to worthy causes. Our dad used to help Rabbi Ginzberg by soliciting others to give to the *Shul*.

The Importance of Good Deeds

I recall the story of Mr. Kitsis, who was in his nineties and lived in a nursing home in St. Paul, Minnesota. Mr. Kitsis pledged $1,000 to Rabbi Ginzberg, which was a tremendous sum in 1951. Dad told me about the pledge, and I understood just from his body language that he wanted me to take Rabbi Ginzberg to St. Paul to find Mr. Kitsis. It was no easy task; I had never been to St. Paul before, but I drove Rabbi Ginzberg and found the Shalom Nursing Home, and sure enough Mr. Kitsis handed over a check of $1,000 to Rabbi

Ginzberg. Mr. Kitsis passed on a short time later. Had we not made the trip, the synagogue would not have benefited from this generous donation.

This is just one example of the wonderful legacy of our parents. As I mentioned before, they gave of themselves and they saved many lives during the War years.

Money and Its Consequences

Now I want to discuss with you the subject of money. You have heard the expression "the pursuit of money is the root of all evil." There is some truth in that. Money can be destructive. For instance, if money causes dissension among siblings, it is evil. If it leads to arguments, quarrels among relatives, it is evil. If it causes rivalry and animosity among friends, it is evil. But, if it draws people together to great and holy purposes, then money is not evil. If money is only a means, not an end in itself, then it is not evil. If you give money to worthy causes, then money is not evil. If you give money to build Jewish day schools, to promote Jewish Torah education, then it is certainly not evil.

A Heart-wrenching Story

I know the value of money. I learned it the hard way. Let me illustrate by telling you a heart-wrenching true story. The year was 1951 and we had been in America, in Minneapolis, Minnesota, no more than five or six months. Mother was taken ill. She was in great pain. I took her to see Dr. Goldman, our family physician. He examined mother and said she needed immediate hospitalization. He told me to take her to Mt. Sinai Hospital, the Jewish hospital in Minneapolis. When I brought Mother there I was told I would need a $100 deposit for her to be admitted. I did not have $100. I hadn't been in the country long enough to save $100. I was making 90 cents an hour at the time, so it wasn't easy to save $100. I pleaded with the admissions clerk, but to no avail. My pleading did not move her. They turned us away.

In desperation, I called Dr. Goldman. He suggested I take her to the city General Hospital, where no deposit was required. He also assured me that the doctors there were good, and that she would be receiving good care. I had no choice. I took mother to the General Hospital.

Mother Was Crying

In the evening when I came to visit her, she was crying and she showed me the black and blue marks on her body. It seemed that every intern examined her, and there were a lot of interns, and they weren't very gentle with her.

I decided I must get her out of the General Hospital and into Mt. Sinai. I must find a way to get $100. I called Dad at home, and he suggested that I go to Mr. Marvin Kohnen, our barber, also a refugee from Poland, and ask for a $100 loan.

In the meantime, while I was on the phone with Dad, the nurse put a red tag on the foot of Mother's bed. When I asked what the red tag was about, she informed me that Mother was to be operated on the first thing in the morning. When I asked why I, her son, was not notified, she said that, once I signed the admission form, they did not have to advise me on anything; this was General Hospital policy.

Now I was in a panic. It was already late at night, and I rushed to see our barber at his home. I described the situation to him, and without hesitation, he counted out one hundred $1 bills. I called the ambulance from his home and told them to meet me at the General Hospital. I told the nurse at the nurses' station that I was taking Mother to another hospital. She said she couldn't release Mother without the doctor's approval. I told the nurse to get out of my way. I also remember telling her that my mother was no guinea pig and their experiments on her were over.

It was almost midnight when I checked Mother into Mt. Sinai. As soon as she was comfortable in her bed, she said to me, in Yiddish: *"Ich fiel shoin besser"* – I already feel better. The next morning Mother's condition was vastly improved. The doctors examined her again. Her colitis attack had subsided and she would certainly not need an operation. A few weeks later I paid off the $100 loan and, as you know, Bubby Hannah lived to be 102 and was never operated upon in her life.

The Value of Money

Do I know the value of money? You bet your bottom dollar I know. We wouldn't have gathered here in Jerusalem if we didn't have any money. So money can be the root of all evil, but it can also be a life saver and a blessing.

You should know that my brother and I have never quarreled over money. We may have quarreled over many other things, but never over money!

Good Business Decision

The best business decision we ever made was when Mark and Anna Ruth joined Simona and me in Indianapolis and we decided to split the ownership of the nursing homes right down the middle, 50/50; that made us equal partners. We never regretted it, and together we worked very hard over many years to achieve what we have achieved.

I only hope and pray that you, the second generation, as well as future generations of Hastens, will develop the same kind of relationship with one another. Remember, never quarrel over money! Also, remember not to marry outside your faith because, if you do, we will disown you; it's in our wills. Another thing, if you ever decide to sue one another for any reason, you are out! This may sound harsh, but this is exactly how my brother and I feel about it. We will not compromise on these issues.

Godspeed

Now to conclude, we hope and pray that Hashem blesses you and watches over you, and that you will transmit to your children the same, or even better, legacies concerning money, concerning *Morasha, Yerusha and Tzedaka*. And that you learn to respect one another, to get along with one another, to love one another, and to live in harmony with one another.

Yevarechecha Hashem Veyishmerecha – May Hashem Bless You and Safeguard You. *Ken Yehi Ratzon* – So May it be the Will of G-d.

Thank you.

Glossary

ADL – see Anti-Defamation League

AIPAC – see American Israeli Public Affairs Committee

Aktion (German) – action, operation

Aliyah (Hebrew) – (lit., ascent) 1. immigration to Israel; 2. being called up for a Torah reading

Aliyah Bet (Hebrew) – illegal immigration to Palestine

Amcha (Hebrew) – (lit., your People), a simple Jew

American Israeli Public Affairs Committee – organization lobbying for Israel in the American Congress

Anti-Defamation League [of Bnai Brith] – American-Jewish organization fighting anti-Semitism

B'li ayin hara (Hebrew) – (lit., without an evil eye), expression used to forestall bad luck

B'nai Yisroel (Hebrew) – the Children of Israel

B'richa (Hebrew) – 1940s underground organization to promote illegal immigration to Palestine

Ba'alebatim (Hebrew) – lay leaders; heads of households

Balagan (Hebrew slang) – great disorder

Balfour Declaration – British promise of a Jewish Homeland in Palestine

Bar Kokhba, Simon – leader of Jewish revolt against the Romans in 135 BCE

Bar Mitzvah (Hebrew) – a Jewish boy's coming of age (13 years)

Baruch HaShem (Hebrew) – praise to G-d, thank G-d

Betar (Hebrew) – acronym for "Brith Trumpeldor," Revisionist youth movement

Birkat HaMazon (Hebrew) – (lit, blessings for the food), grace after meals

Bris [Milah] (Hebrew) – circumcision ceremony

Bubbie, Bubbe (Yiddish) – grandmother

Chabad (Hebrew acronym) – chassidic movement, also known as Lubavitch

Chassidism (adj. **chassidic**) (Hebrew derivative) – stream in religious Judaism

Cheder (Hebrew) – (lit. room), religious school

Chuppah (Hebrew) – wedding canopy

Chutzpah (Hebrew/Yiddish) – cheek, arrogance

Cohen [Cohanim] – Descendant[s] of Aharon, the High Priest, of the tribe of Levi. In Biblical times they served as Temple priests and as teachers of the people.

Conference of Presidents of Major American Jewish Organizations – umbrella body of heads of major American Jewish organizations

D'ror (Hebrew) – (lit., freedom), Socialist organization

D-Day – June 6, 1944, Allied invasion of Normandy

De goldene medinah (Yiddish) – (lit. the golden state), a Yiddish nickname for America

De kinder (Yiddish) – the children

Dead Sea Scrolls – 2,000-year-old Old Testament scrolls found in mid-20th century in the Qumran caves near the Dead Sea

Deutsch – German

Dir Yassin – Arab village destroyed in the Israeli War of Independence

Displaced persons – Holocaust survivors

DPS – see Displaced persons

Dvar Torah (Hebrew) – brief sermon on the week's Torah portion

Einsatzgruppen (German) – Operations Units which massacred Jewish populations

Emmes (Hebrew/Yiddish) – truth

Eretz Yisroel (Hebrew) – Land of Israel

Etzel (Hebrew acronym) – abbreviation for Irgun Tzvai Leumi (see Irgun)

Etzelnik – member of Etzel

Falashas – Ethiopian Jews (pejorative)

Ferdelach (Yiddish) – horses

Galut (Hebrew) – exile, diaspora

Gannof (Hebrew/Yiddish) – thief

Gezunter goy (Yiddish) – healthy gentile

Glasnost (Russian) – openness

Goyim (Hebrew/Yiddish) – Gentiles, non-Jewish nations

Greener (Yiddish) – greenhorn, pejorative term for new immigrant

Gulag (Russian) – prisoner camp

Hadar (Hebrew) – dignity, magnificence; here used to express Jewish pride

Hagganah – (lit., defense), Jewish para-military defense organization in Mandate Palestine

Halacha (Hebrew) – Jewish law

Hashomer Hatzair (Hebrew) – (lit. the young watchman), leftist Zionist youth movement

Hatikva (Hebrew) – (lit., The Hope), Israeli national anthem; name of impoverished Tel Aviv neighborhood

Havlagah (Hebrew) – self-restraint

Hazzan (Hebrew) – cantor

Hebrew Immigrant Aid Society – US Jewish organization extending help to refugees

Herut (Hebrew) – (lit., freedom). right-wing political party in Israel

HIAS – see Hebrew Immigrant Aid Society

Histadrut (Hebrew) – Israel's trade union umbrella organization

IDF – Israel Defense Forces

International Refugee Organization – an arm of the United States dealing with refugees

Intifada (Arabic) – Palestinian uprising against Israel

Irgun Tzvai Leumi (Hebrew) – (lit., national military organization), Jewish underground organization in Mandate Palestine

IRO – see International Refugee Organization

Israel Bonds Organization – organization issuing investment securities for the benefit of the State of Israel

JCRC – Jewish Community Relations Council, defense and advocacy organization in many US communities

JDC – see Joint Distribution Committee

Joint Distribution Committee – US Jewish organization providing assistance to needy Jews world-wide, arm of the Jewish Agency (Sochnut)

Judea, Judah – Biblical kingdom, now area contested by Arabs and Jews

Judenrat (German) – Jewish council appointed by the Nazis to administer ghettoes internally

Judenrein (German) – cleansed of Jews

Kaddish (Hebrew) – mourners' prayer, partly in the Aramaic language

Kaiser (German) – emperor

Kapo (German) – Jewish concentration camp inmate appointed to police other inmates

Kashrut – the law of ritually permitted foods

Kedusha (Hebrew) – (lit., holiness), prayer recited during the repetition of the Shemoneh Esrei

Kel Male Rachamim (Hebrew) – (lit., G-d full of mercy), prayer for the dead

Ken Yehi Ratzon (Hebrew) – So may it be the Will of G-d

Kibbutz (Hebrew) – communal settlement

Kiddush (Hebrew) – benediction made over wine on the Sabbath

Kinder (Yiddish) – children

Kippa (Hebrew) – skullcap

Kishkes (Yiddish) – guts, intestines

Klezmer (Yiddish) – style of Jewish folk music

Knesset (Hebrew) – Israeli parliament

Kol Nidre (Hebrew) – prayer that opens the evening service on Yom Kippur

Kolchoz (Russian) – collective farm

Kosher (Hebrew/Yiddish) – ritually permitted (food)

Krechtz (Yiddish) – moan

Kultur (German) – culture

L'arche – French newspaper

Landsmen (Yiddish) – people from one's country of origin

Lehi (Hebrew acronym) – Jewish underground organization in Mandate Palestine

Levi['im] – Descendant[s] of Moses, of the tribe of Levi. In Biblical times they served as assistants to the Temple priests and as teachers of the people

Likud – right-wing political party in Israel

Luach (Hebrew) – calendar

Lubavitch – see Chabad

Maccabees – Jewish revolutionaries in 168 BCE that successfully fought the Syrian-Greek King Antiochus

Maccabiah Games – "Jewish Olympics," held quadrennially in Israel

Macher (Yiddish) – community activist, big shot

Machetonem (Hebrew/Yiddish) – parents of a daughter-in-law or son-in-law

Mapai (Hebrew) – one time Israeli labor party

Mapainik – member of Mapai

Masada – site near Dead Sea of Herod's fortress; in 73 AD, after a two-year siege by the Romans, its defenders committed mass suicide

Mashiach (Hebrew) – Messiah

Matzayvah (Hebrew) – tombstone; stone memorial

Matzoh (Hebrew) – unleavened bread

Maven (Hebrew/Yiddish) – expert

Mazel Tov (Hebrew) – (lit., good luck), congratulations

Medi-Cal – California state-subsidized medical insurance for elderly

Menahel (Hebrew) – manager, principal

Metzudat Ze'ev (Hebrew) – (lit., Ze'ev's citadel), Likud party headquarters

Mikvah, mikveh (Hebrew) – ritual bath

Mincha (Hebrew) – Jewish afternoon prayer

Minyan (Hebrew) – prayer quorum of ten Jews

Misnahgged (pl. misnaggdim) (Hebrew) – those opposing Chassidism

Mitzvah (Hebrew) – good deed, Torah commandment

Morasha (Hebrew) – heritage

Naftali – one of the twelve tribes of Israel

Natchalnik (Russian) – manager

National Council of Synagogue Youth – youth division of OU

NCSY – see National Council of Synagogue Youth

Neder (Hebrew) – vow

Neshamot [sing: Neshama] (Hebrew) – souls

NKVD – Soviet secret police (abbreviation)

Oblast (Russian) – district

Operation Enduring Freedom – US war against Taliban and al-Qaida in Afghanistan in 2001

Operation Moses – operation to rescue Ethiopian Jews

Operation Peace for Galilee – incursion by Israeli forces into Lebanon in 1982

ORT – Obschestvo Remeslenovo I zemledelcheskovo (Russian) – Society for Trades and Agricultural Labor

Orthodox Union – body representing Orthodox congregations in the US and Canada; known also for its provision of kashruth certification

OU – see Orthodox Union (of Jewish Congregations of America)

PLO – Palestine Liberation Organization

Parnosa (Yiddish/Hebrew) – livelihood

Parsha (Hebrew) – weekly Torah portion

Pecklach (Yiddish) – hand luggage

Perestroika (Russian) – economic restructuring

Perreneh (Russian, Polish) – comforter, blanket

Phalangists – Lebanese Christian group

Pidyon Shevuyim (Hebrew) – ransoming of captives

Pikuach Nefesh (Hebrew) – (lit., protection of a soul), permission to violate Jewish law to save a life

Pirkei Avot (Hebrew) – Ethics of our Fathers; studied on Sabbath afternoons from Passover through Rosh Hashana

Protekzia (Russian, Hebrew) – Special dispensation, protection from the authorities, influence, pull, connections

Psukey Dezimra (Hebrew) – verses of praise said during morning prayers

Rak Kach (Hebrew) – (lit., only thus), Irgun slogan

Rebbe (Yiddish) – spiritual leader, teacher

Reconstructionism – a stream in religious Judaism based upon the teachings of Rabbi Mordechai Kaplan

Reich (German) – (lit., empire), the Nazi regime (1933–1945) was called the Third Reich

Reidlach (Yiddish) – (lit., wheels), used to describe a circle of men having a discussion

Rosh HaShana (Hebrew) – Jewish New Year

Sabra and Shatillah – refugee camps in Lebanon, sites of massacres during Operation Peace for Gaililee

Samaria – one-time capital of kingdom of Israel, now area contested by Arabs and Jews

Sandek, sandak (Hebrew) – godfather, one who holds the baby during the Bris Milah (circumcision ceremony).

Schnorrer (Yiddish) – (lit., beggar), fund-raiser

Schnorring (Yiddish) – begging for a handout, fund-raising

Seder (Hebrew) – (lit., order), festive meal on the first two nights of Passover at which the story of the exodus from Egypt is re-told

Shabbos (Hebrew/Yiddish) – Sabbath

She'eirit HaPleitah (Hebrew) – (lit., remnant of the survivors), Holocaust survivors

Shemoneh Esrei (Hebrew) – Jewish prayer containing 18 benedictions, said thrice daily

Shiddach, Shidduch (Hebrew) – match between boy and girl

Shiksa (Yiddish) – non-Jewish girl or woman

Shir Ha-Shirim (Hebrew) – Song of Songs

Shiva (Hebrew) – (lit., seven), seven-day period of mourning

Shlepp (Yiddish) – drag, carry

Shoah (Hebrew) – Holocaust

Shochet (Hebrew) – ritual slaughterer

Shreib (Yiddish) – to write

Shtarker Yid (Yiddish) – strong Jew

Shtei Gedot LaYarden (Hebrew) – (lit., both sides of the Jordan), Revisionist and Betar motto

Shtetl (Yiddish) – little town

Shtreimel, Streimel (Yiddish) – circular fur hat worn by Chassidim

Siddur (Hebrew) – (lit., arrangement), Hebrew prayer book

Simcha (Hebrew) – joy, joyous occasion

Sinai (Hebrew) – mountain on which Moses received the Torah; also the desert surrounding it

Sochnut (Hebrew) – [Jewish] Agency

Spekulatzia (Russian) – speculation, commerce for profit

Stern Group – see Lehi

T'chiah (Hebrew) – (lit., revival), one-time Israeli right-wing political party

T'noyim (Yiddish, Hebrew) – an engagement contract

Tachlis (Hebrew/Yiddish) – (lit., purpose), down-to-earth

Talmid Chacham (Hebrew) – (lit., wise student), one well versed in Jewish learning

Talmud (Hebrew) – compendium of Jewish Oral Law

Tanakh (Hebrew) – Hebrew Bible, the 24 books of the Torah, Prophets and Scriptures

Tel-Hai – settlement in northern Israel in whose defense Joseph Trumpeldor fell in 1920

Tel-Hai Fund – fund established to pay off debts of Irgun pension fund

Torah (Hebrew) – Five Books of Moses; Pentateuch

Torah Umesorah (Hebrew) – (lit., Torah and Tradition,) National Society of Jewish Day Schools

Tovarish (Russian) – comrade

Traif (Hebrew/Yiddish) – ritually forbidden (food)

Tzadaykes, tzadekes (Hebrew/Yiddish) – righteous woman

Tzadik (Hebrew) – righteous man

Tze'enah Urenah (Hebrew) – Jewish study book about the weekly Torah portion written in Yiddish, employed mostly by women

Tzedakah (Hebrew) – (lit., righteousness), charity contribution

Tzitzit (Hebrew) – four-cornered fringed garment, or the fringes themselves

U'netaneh Tokef (Hebrew) – prayer recited during Jewish High Holidays

UJA – see United Jewish Appeal

UJF – United Jewish Federation

Umglick (Yiddish) – misfortune

United Jewish Appeal – fund-raising organization benefiting Jewish social service agencies in US and Israel

UNRRA – United Nations Relief and Rehabilitation Administration

VE Day – May 8, 1945, end of World War II in Europe

West Bank – Judea and Samaria, areas lying west of the Jordan river

White Paper – British position paper restricting Jewish immigration to Palestine

Ya'ar Yerushalayim (Hebrew) – Jerusalem Forest

Yahrzeit (Yiddish) – memorial day for deceased relative

Yarmulke (Yiddish) – skullcap

Yediot Aharonot – Israeli newspaper

Yerusha (Hebrew) – inheritance
Yiddishkeit (Yiddish) – Jewishness
Yidn (Yiddish) – Jews
Yisrael[im] (Hebrew) – Jew[s] not of the priestly tribe
Yom Kippur (Hebrew) – Day of Atonement, holiest day on Jewish calendar
Zatyerucha (Russian) – thin gruel
Zayde (Yiddish) – grandfather
Zechut (Hebrew) – privilege, good fortune
Zionism – movement of return to Zion
Zjid, Zjiduha (Russian) – Jew [derogatory]

Index